ドラゴン騎士団.16
DRAGON KNIGHTS 16

押上美猫

Mineko Ohkami

Dragon Knights

Written and Illustrated by
Mineko Ohkami

Volume 16

HAMBURG // LONDON // LOS ANGELES // TOKYO

Dragon Knights Vol. 16
Created by Mineko Ohkami

Translation - Yuki N. Johnson
English Adaptation - Stephanie Sheh
Associate Editor - Tim Beedle
Retouch and Lettering - Junemoon Studios
Production Artist - Sophia Hong
Cover Design - Anna Kernbaum

Editor - Paul Morrissey
Digital Imaging Manager - Chris Buford
Pre-Press Manager - Antonio DePietro
Production Managers - Jennifer Miller and Mutsumi Miyazaki
Art Director - Matt Alford
Managing Editor - Jill Freshney
VP of Production - Ron Klamert
President and C.O.O. - John Parker
Publisher and C.E.O. - Stuart Levy

A  Manga

TOKYOPOP Inc.
5900 Wilshire Blvd. Suite 2000
Los Angeles, CA 90036

E-mail: info@TOKYOPOP.com
Come visit us online at www.TOKYOPOP.com

ISBN: 1-59182-444-3

First TOKYOPOP printing: October 2004
10 9 8 7 6 5 4 3 2 1
Printed in the USA

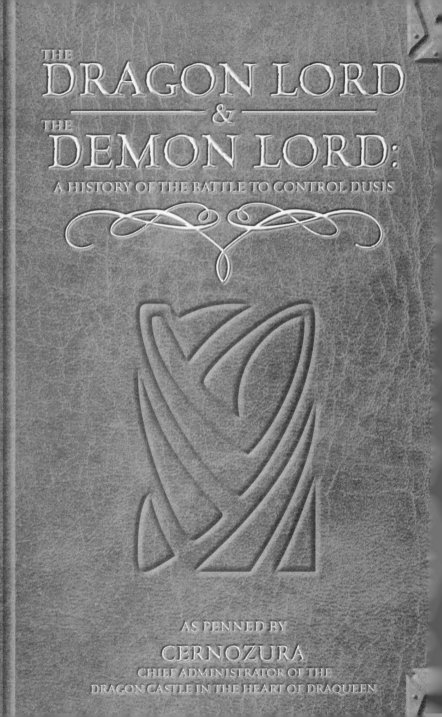

THE DRAGON LORD
&
THE DEMON LORD:
A HISTORY OF THE BATTLE TO CONTROL DUSIS

AS PENNED BY

CERNOZURA
CHIEF ADMINISTRATOR OF THE
DRAGON CASTLE IN THE HEART OF DRAQUEEN

The Reeper of the Tome

My name is Cernozura and I am the chief administrator for the Dragon Castle, Draqueen, in the heart of Dragoon, the Dragon Kingdom. Within these pages I will attempt to chronicle the events of yesteryear in the hopes that it will in turn offer some future understanding of the chaos that currently befalls us. I feel it's imperative that I record a comprehensive history of the events that have led to this dark hour, for I fear that none will remain to tell the tale. My only hope is that this tome may survive so that future generations will know of the valiance of the Dragon Tribe.

Rise of the Demon Lord

Our worst fears have come to pass. The Demon Lord Nadil has been resurrected and he has stolen from the bosom of our care the fortuneteller Cesia, who harbors an incredible magic that we have only just begun to witness. In the service of a villain as pernicious as Nadil, Cesia, whether against her will or willingly giving in to the seductive charm of the dreaded Demon Lord, may prove to be the most dangerous threat we've faced.

Three Rnights, Two Missions, One Nation United in Fear

The Dragon Rnights have been dispatched to Rainaldia, the kingdom of the Demon Lord, charged with rescuing Cesia from the wretched grip of Nadil. While their countrymen wait in terror, besieged by countless followers of the Demon Lord, our brave warriors have themselves been besieged by challenges grave enough to threaten their very existence. At last, one has proven too difficult to overcome, effectively cleaving our small band in two. Upon encountering his beloved Tintlet wandering the forests of Rainaldia, Rune soon made a horrific discovery. Intending to trap the Dragon Rnight of Water and steal the power of Varawoo from within him, the demon Lim Raana ravaged the faerie leader, robbing her of her spirit and memories. The body found by the Dragon Rnights was nothing more than a hollow shell, and while the demon remained in possession of Tintlet's memory, her spirit had been lost.

Rune's battle with the wicked Lim Raana proved short, with Lim Raana fleeing the sword of the Dragon Knight of Water before the good blade met with her neck. Unable to leave his beloved to such a cruel fate, Rune steadfastly vowed to rescue her. Still possessing Tintlet's body, the noble elf promised to reunite with his two compatriots after finding her spirit and stealing her memory back from Lim Raana.

A Chance Encounter

On a quest to retrieve three powerful treasures for Lord Lykouleon, the thief Ritchel and her faerie companion Ringleys, after successfully obtaining the prizes, have also found themselves traversing Rainaldia. Having previously endeavored to make haste back to Draqueen, the pair now find themselves unexpectedly journeying towards that which they once fled—Nadil's castle. Their reason is, to say the least, a remarkable one. Fortuitously running across Zoma, Cesia's dear friend and companion, who himself is undertaking a separate mission to save Cesia, the trio now travel together, determined to assist each other in attaining their goals. Even more miraculously, Zoma possesses the spirit of Tintlet, having discovered it while bridging the ether between the Dragon Realm and Demon Realm. Oh, were it but in my power to send quick word to our Knight of Water, I would do so in the greatest haste, so that he could rejoin with his companions in their fateful and glorious mission. But it is not, so I do wait with all of Draqueen for news of Rune and the rest of our heroic emissaries.

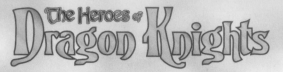

The Heroes of Dragon Knights

Lord Lykouleon

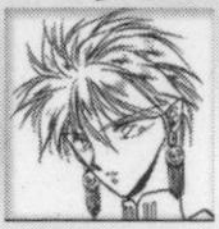

The beloved Dragon Lord, Lykouleon is the sovereign ruler of Dragoon. The resources of the Dragon Clan and the might of the Dragon Army are at his command.

Lady Raseleane

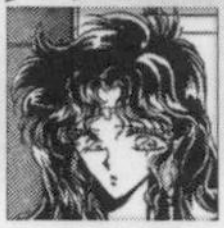

Lykouleon's queen, the Lady Raseleane was rendered barren by the Demon Lord and unable to provide Lykouleon with an heir.

Dragon Officers

Harnessing the power of the five Dragon Balls, the Dragon Officers should number five strong, but after the Demon Army's assault on Draqueen, only two officers remain.

Ruwalk

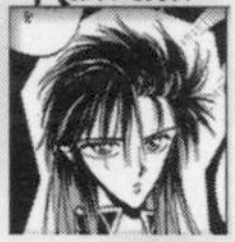

The Yellow Dragon Officer and Secretary of State.

Tetheus

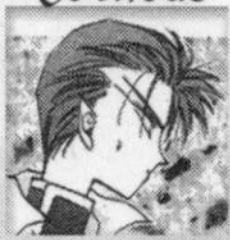

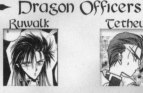

The Black Dragon Officer and Secretary of Security.

Cernozura

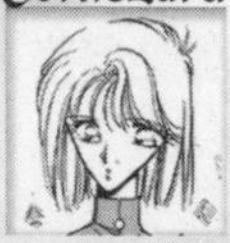

The Dragon Castle Administrator, Cernozura is also a self-appointed castle historian.

Dragon Knights

Rath

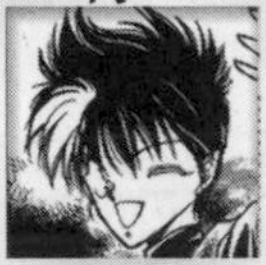

The Dragon Knight of Fire, Rath is part Yokai and lives for killing demons.

Thatz

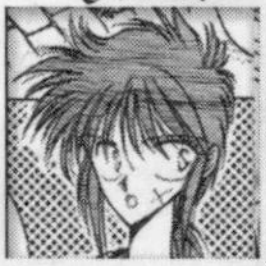

The Dragon Knight of Earth, the human Thatz was once a thief, and his love for gold hasn't abated.

Rune

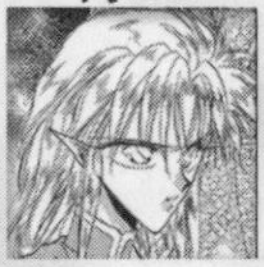

The Dragon Knight of Water, Rune is an elf and has abilities the other two Dragon Knights lack.

Other Allies

Cesia

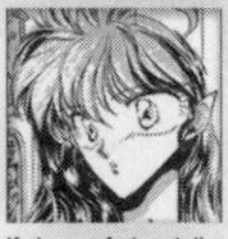

A half-demon fortuneteller with the ability to enhance the power of those in close proximity to her.

Zoma

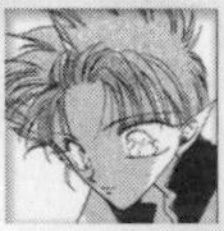

Cesia's demon friend and companion.

Tintlet

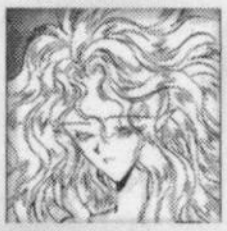

A faerie who has sacrificed much for her beloved Rune and her dying race.

Kitchel

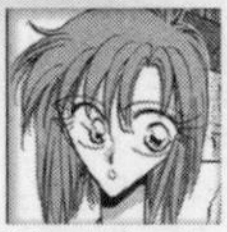

Another thief loyal to Lykouleon, Kitchel possesses the powerful Three Treasures and is trying to get them to Draqueen.

Ringleys

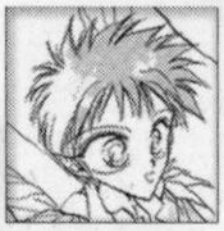

A faerie who was rescued from a demon and now accompanies Kitchel.

Delte

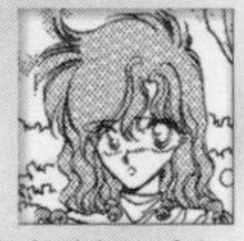

Lykouleon's human fortuneteller.

Star Princess

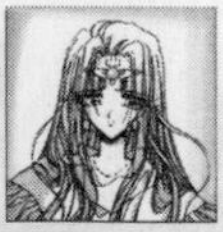

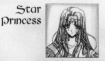

Not much is known about this powerful princess, but she has assisted Rath on several occasions.

Grinfish

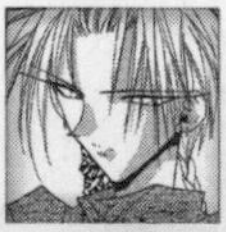

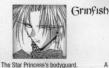

The Star Princess's bodyguard. Both the Princess and Grinfish seem to be friendly to Lykouleon's cause.

Nohiro

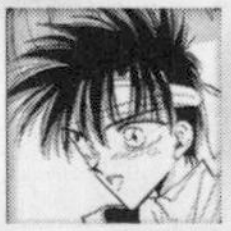

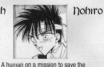

A human on a mission to save the dying faerie race. Has assisted Rune in the past.

The Villians of Dragon Knights

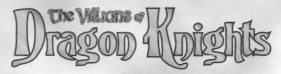

Nadil

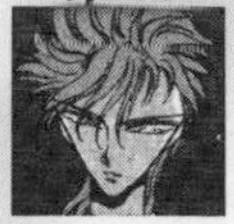

The evil and justly feared Demon Lord. Nadil had been slain by the Dragon Lord, but his body was recently retrieved and resurrected by his loyal army. Now he once again presides over the Demon Realm, hungry for revenge.

Demon Officers

Shydeman

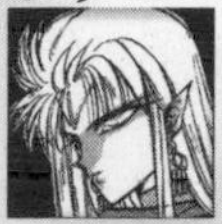

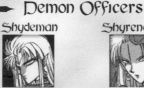

One of Nadil's generals, Shydeman led the successful attack on Draqueen that brought back the Demon Lord.

Shyrendora

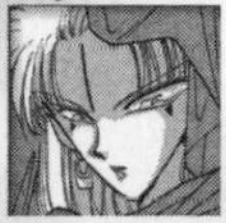

Another general, Shyrendora is sister to Shydeman and also to Tetheus, who fights against her as one of the Dragon Officers.

Fedelta

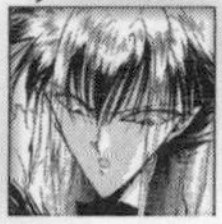

Answering directly to Shydeman, Fedelta has become one of the most vicious officers in the Demon Army.

Lady Medicinea

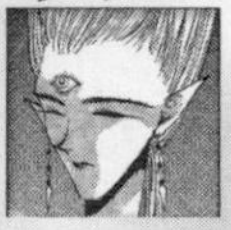

Another officer in Nadil's army, Medicinea has an ongoing rivalry with Fedelta.

Other Enemies

Bierrez

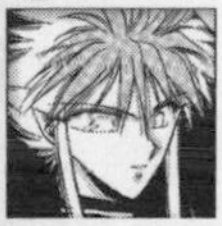

The infamous rogue demon, Bierrez's loyalties lie not with the Demon Lord, but with himself.

Saabel

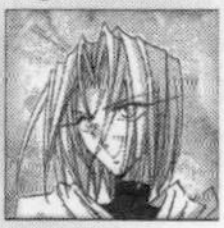

The so-called "Collector of Corpses," Saabel possesses the ability to reanimate the dead into puppets he controls.

Lim Kaana

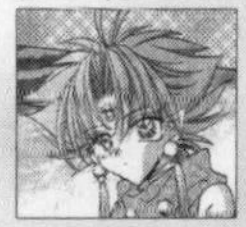

A feisty little demon charged with stealing Varawoo's power from Rune.

Perhaps the most unpredictable of Lykouleon's enemies is the Renkin Wizard. Residing on the lost continent of Arinas, Kharl is unbelievably powerful and longs to rule both the Dragon and Demon Realms. Thus far, Kharl has focused on defeating Lykouleon, but it's only a matter of time until he sets his sights on Nadil as well.

Kharl

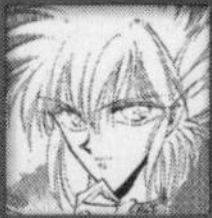

The Renkin Wizard, Kharl is an alchemist capable of creating demons. He has "fathered" legions of them, including Rath.

Garfakcy

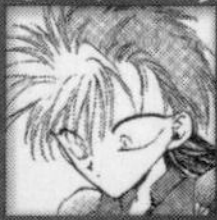

Kharl's human assistant, Garfakcy is sneaky and insidious. He wishes to become a demon, a desire Kharl has repeatedly dismissed.

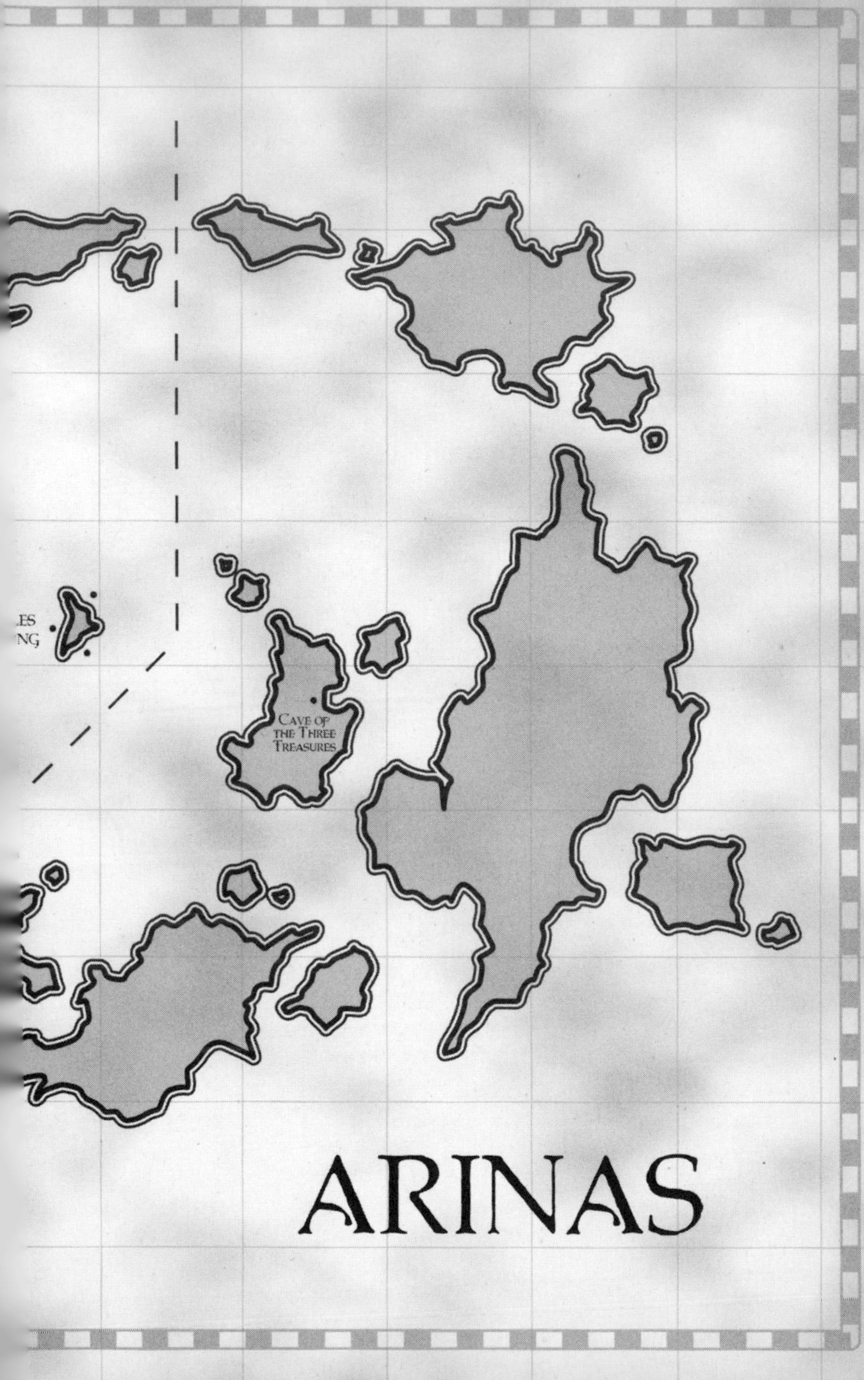

LES
NG
CAVE OF THE THREE TREASURES
CAVE OF THE THREE TREASURES
ARINAS

DUSIS

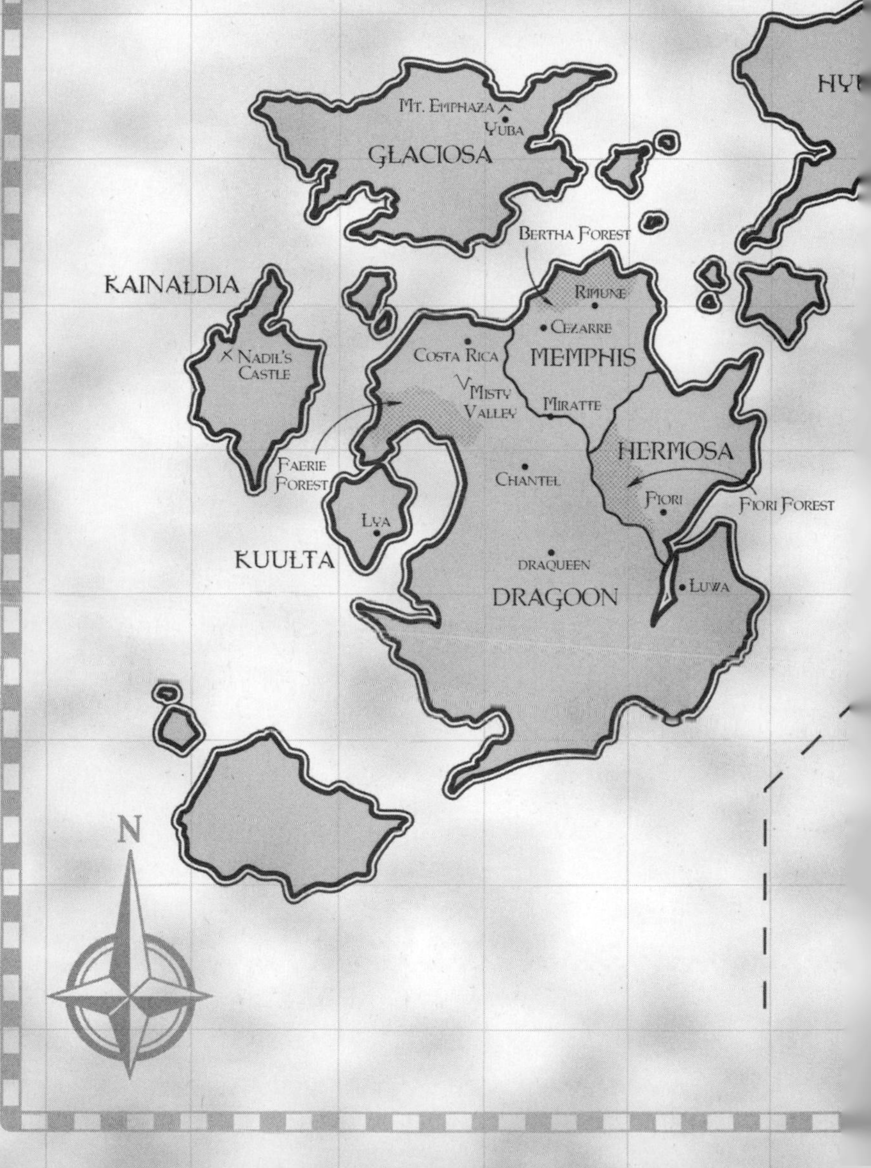
Mt. Emphaza
Yuba
Glaciosa
Bertha Forest
Kainaldia
Rimune
Cezarre
Nadil's Castle
Costa Rica
Memphis
Misty Valley
Miratte
Hermosa
Faerie Forest
Chantel
Fiori
Fiori Forest
Lya
Kuulta
draqueen
Luwa
Dragoon
N
Hy

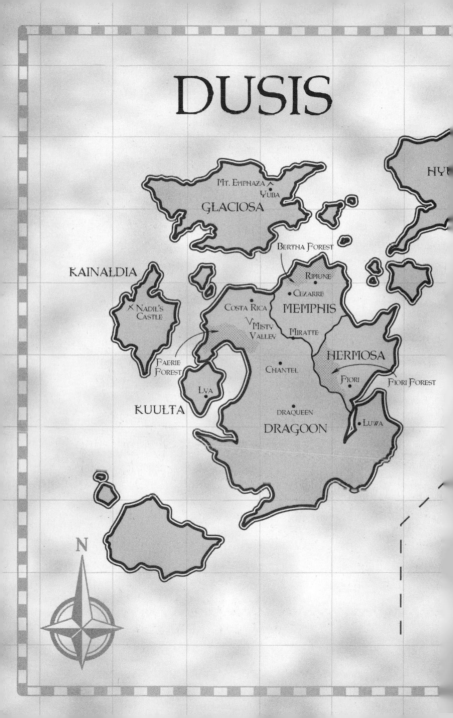

CONTENTS

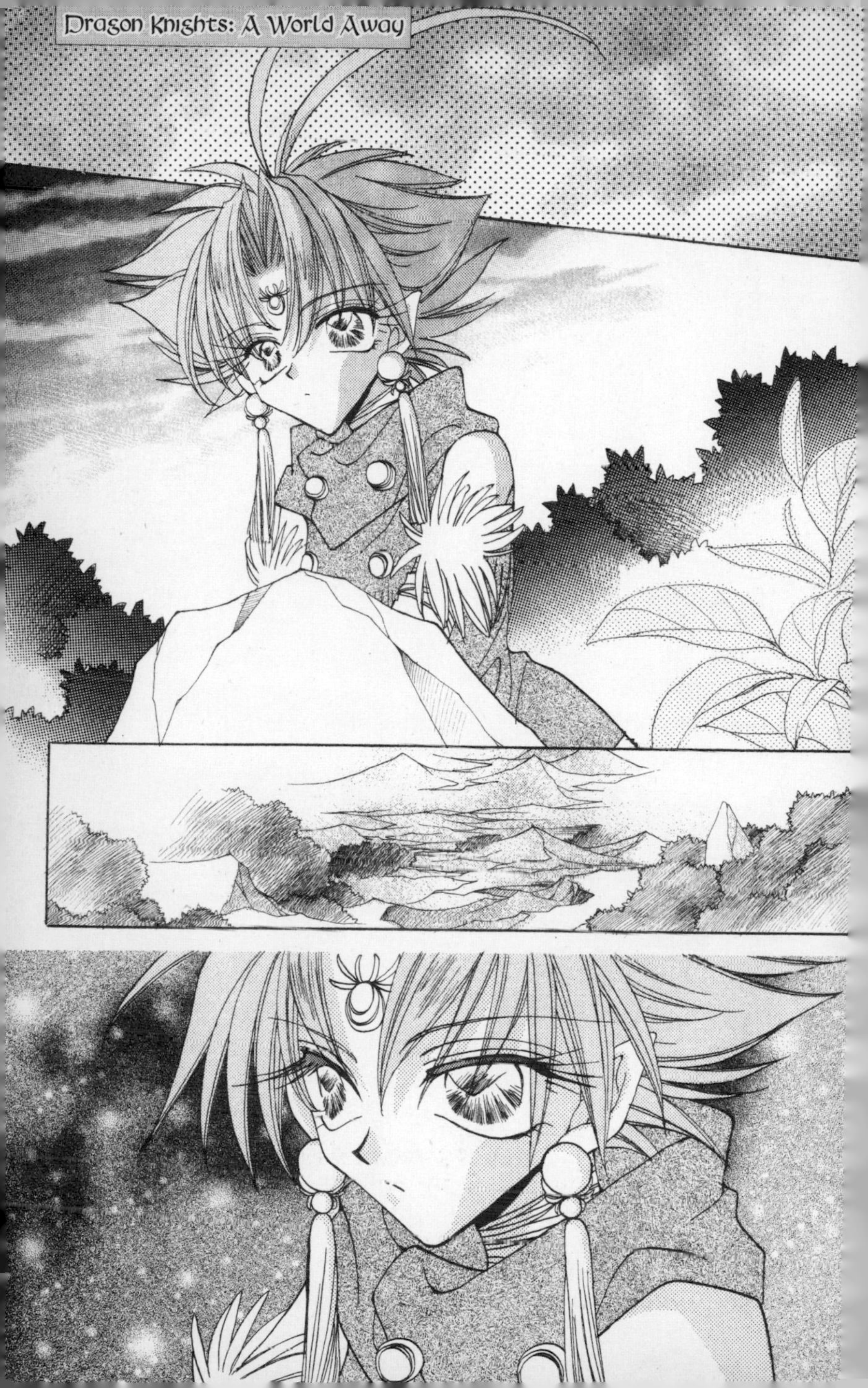

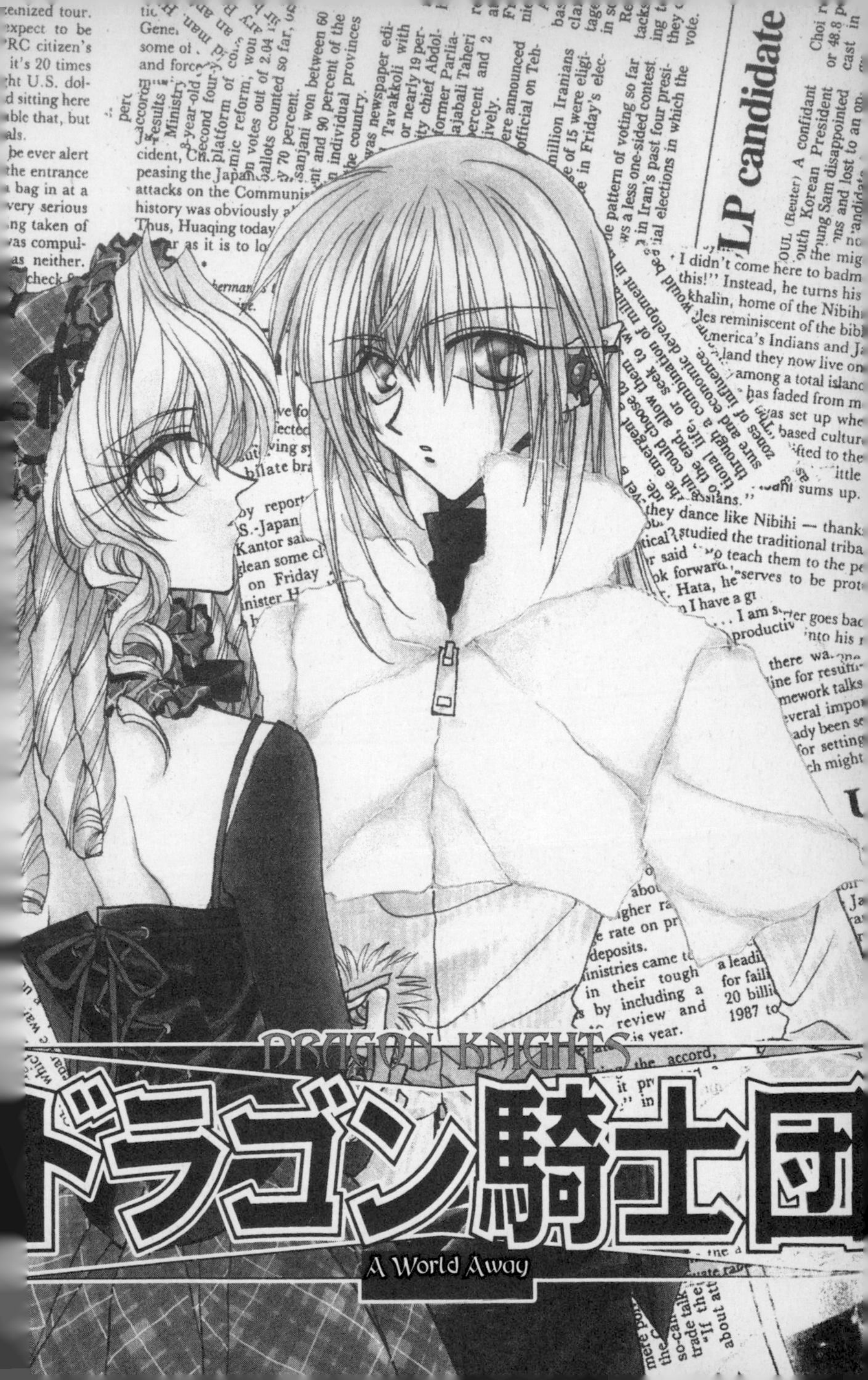
DRAGON KNIGHTS
ドラゴン騎士団
A World Away

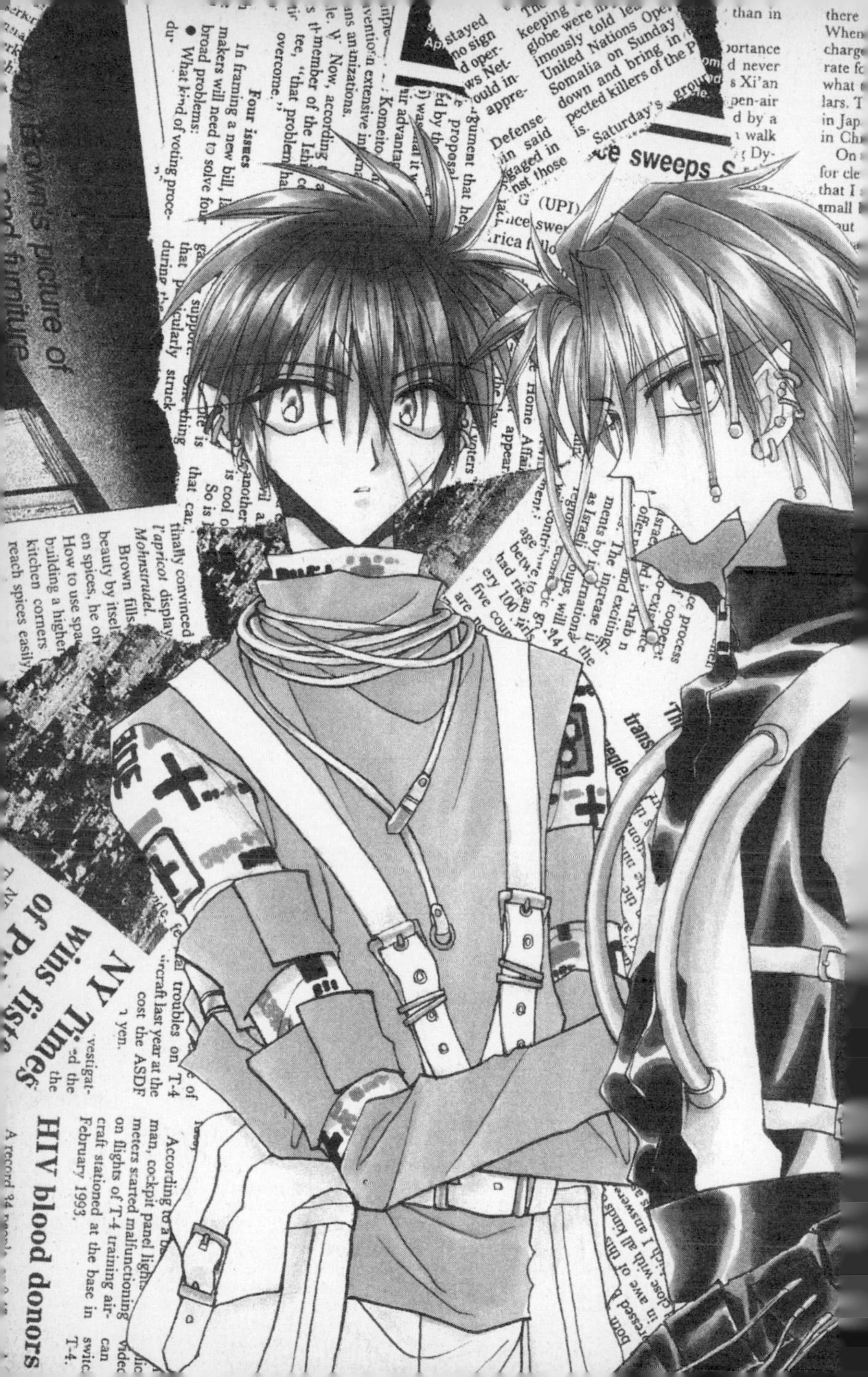
Four issues
NY Times
HIV blood donors

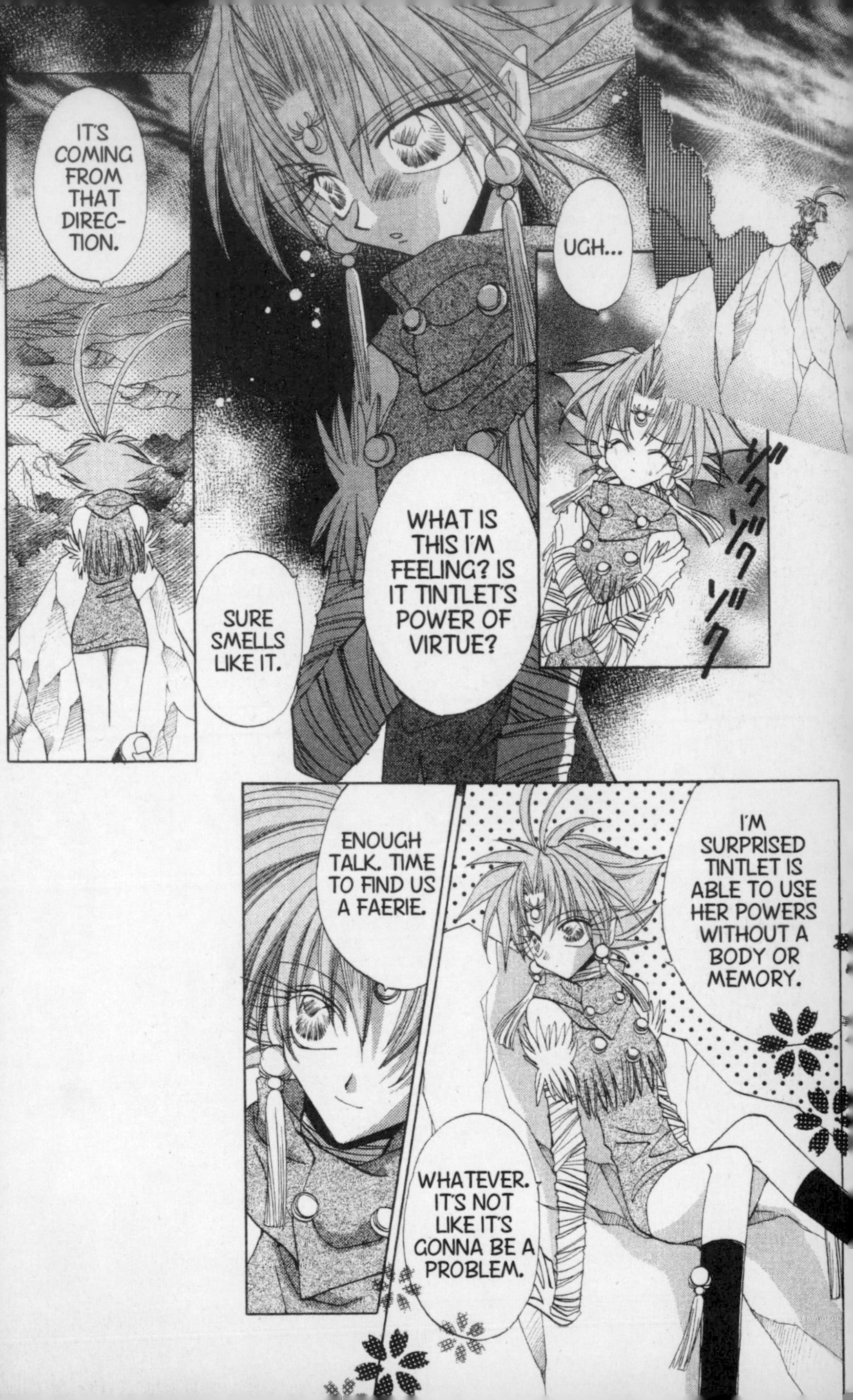
UGH...
WHAT IS THIS I'M FEELING? IS IT TINTLET'S POWER OF VIRTUE?
SURE SMELLS LIKE IT.
IT'S COMING FROM THAT DIRECTION.
I'M SURPRISED TINTLET IS ABLE TO USE HER POWERS WITHOUT A BODY OR MEMORY.
WHATEVER. IT'S NOT LIKE IT'S GONNA BE A PROBLEM.
ENOUGH TALK. TIME TO FIND US A FAERIE.

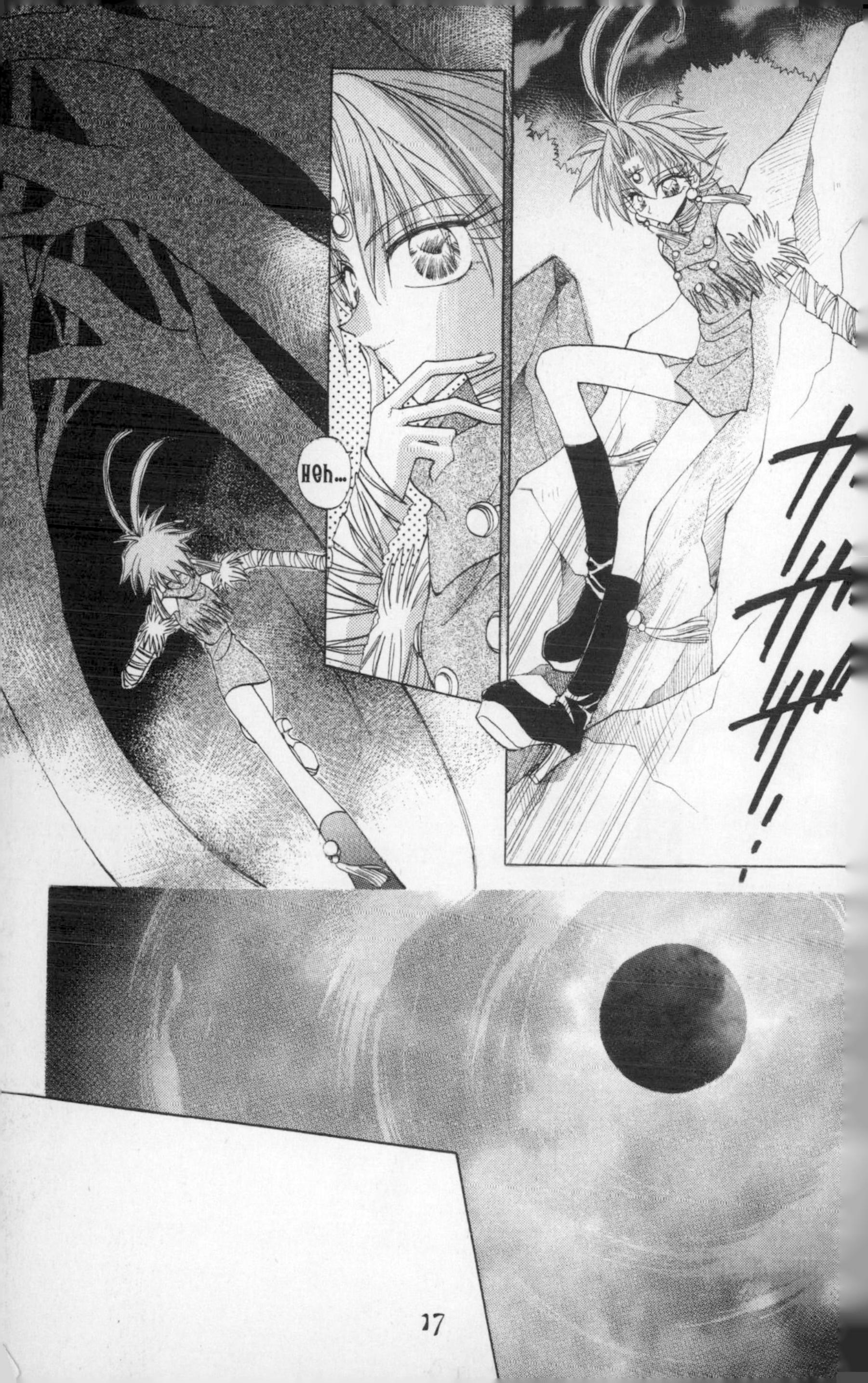
Heh...

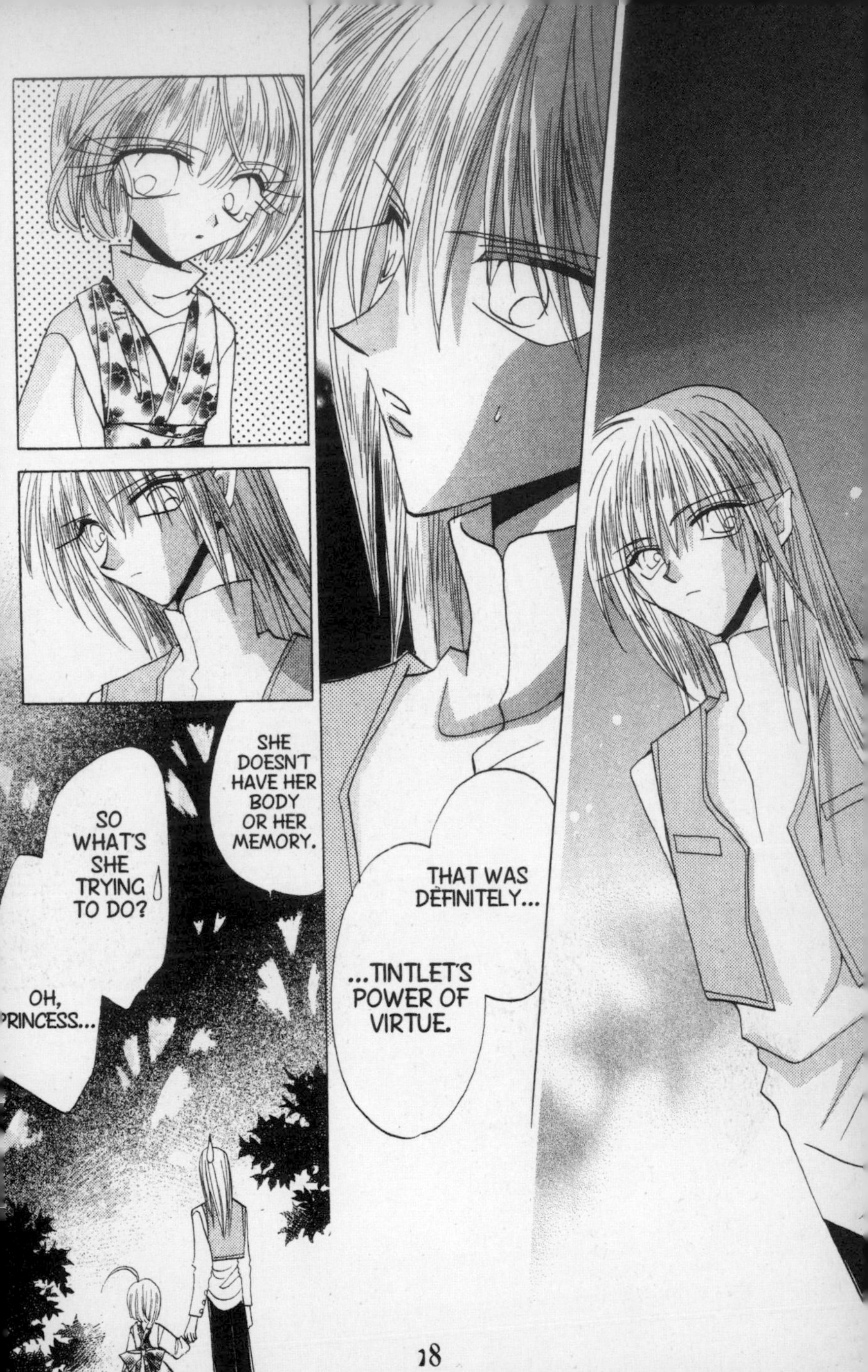
THAT WAS DEFINITELY...
...TINTLET'S POWER OF VIRTUE.
SHE DOESN'T HAVE HER BODY OR HER MEMORY.
SO WHAT'S SHE TRYING TO DO?
OH, PRINCESS...

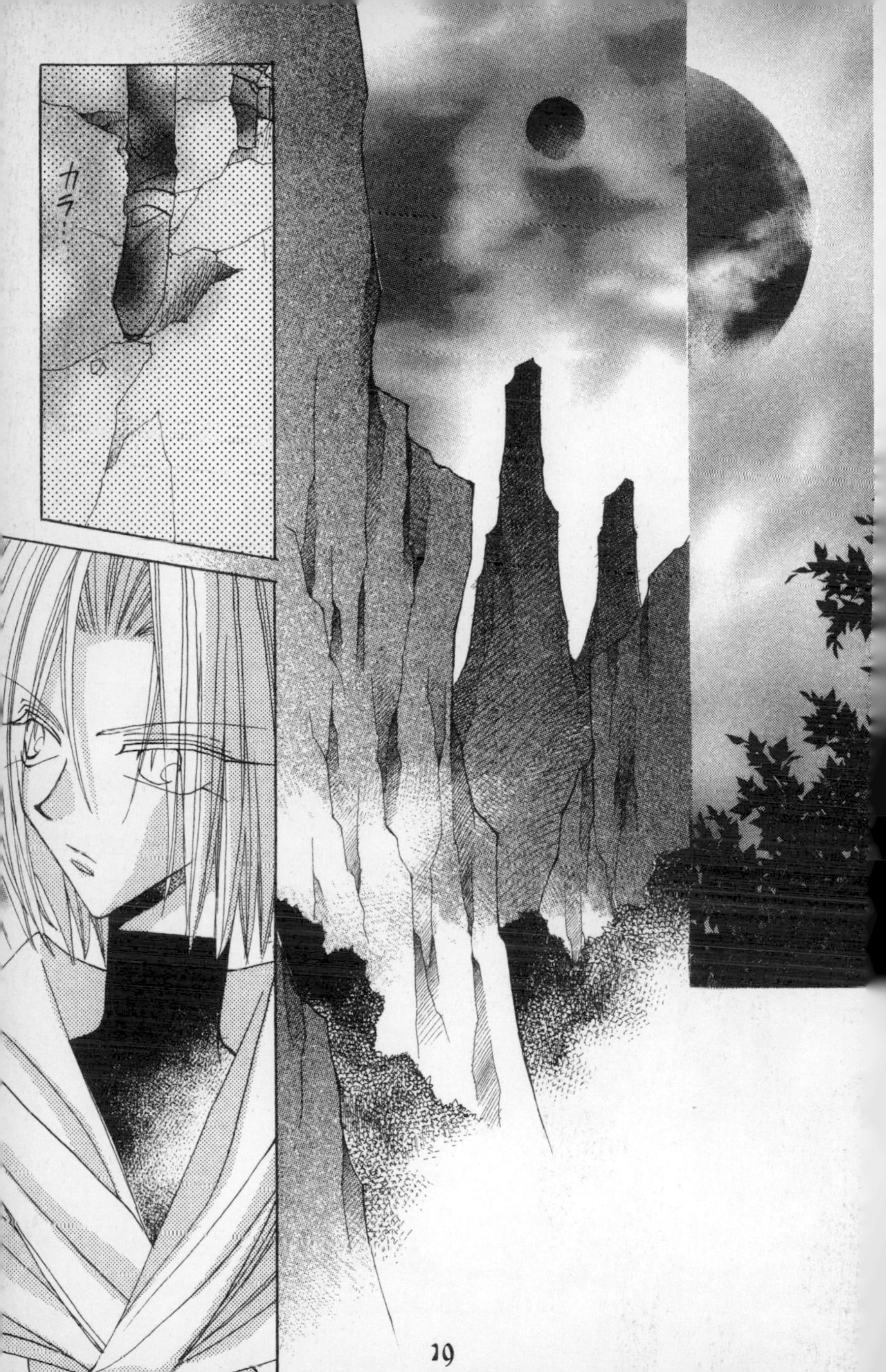
カラ…

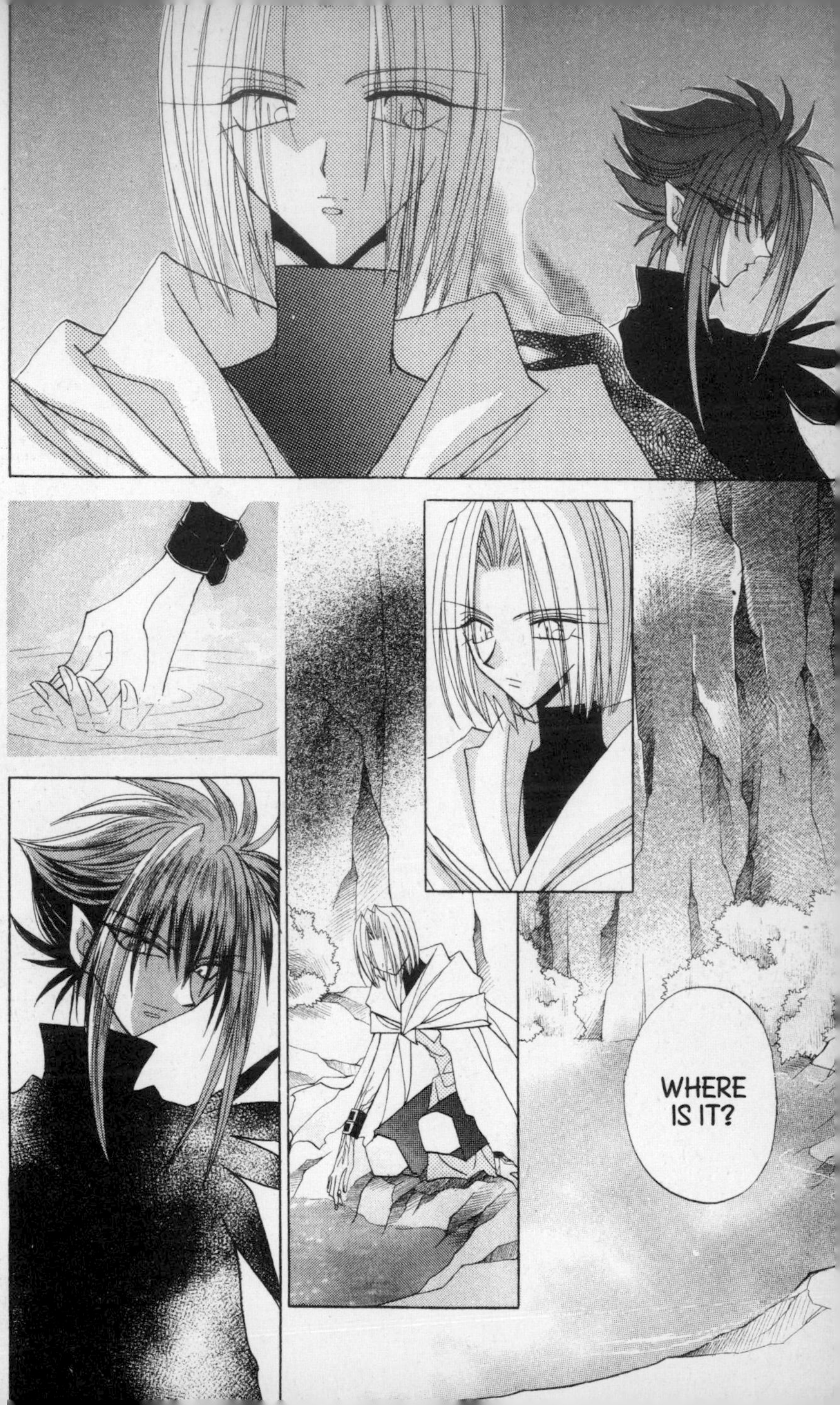
WHERE IS IT?

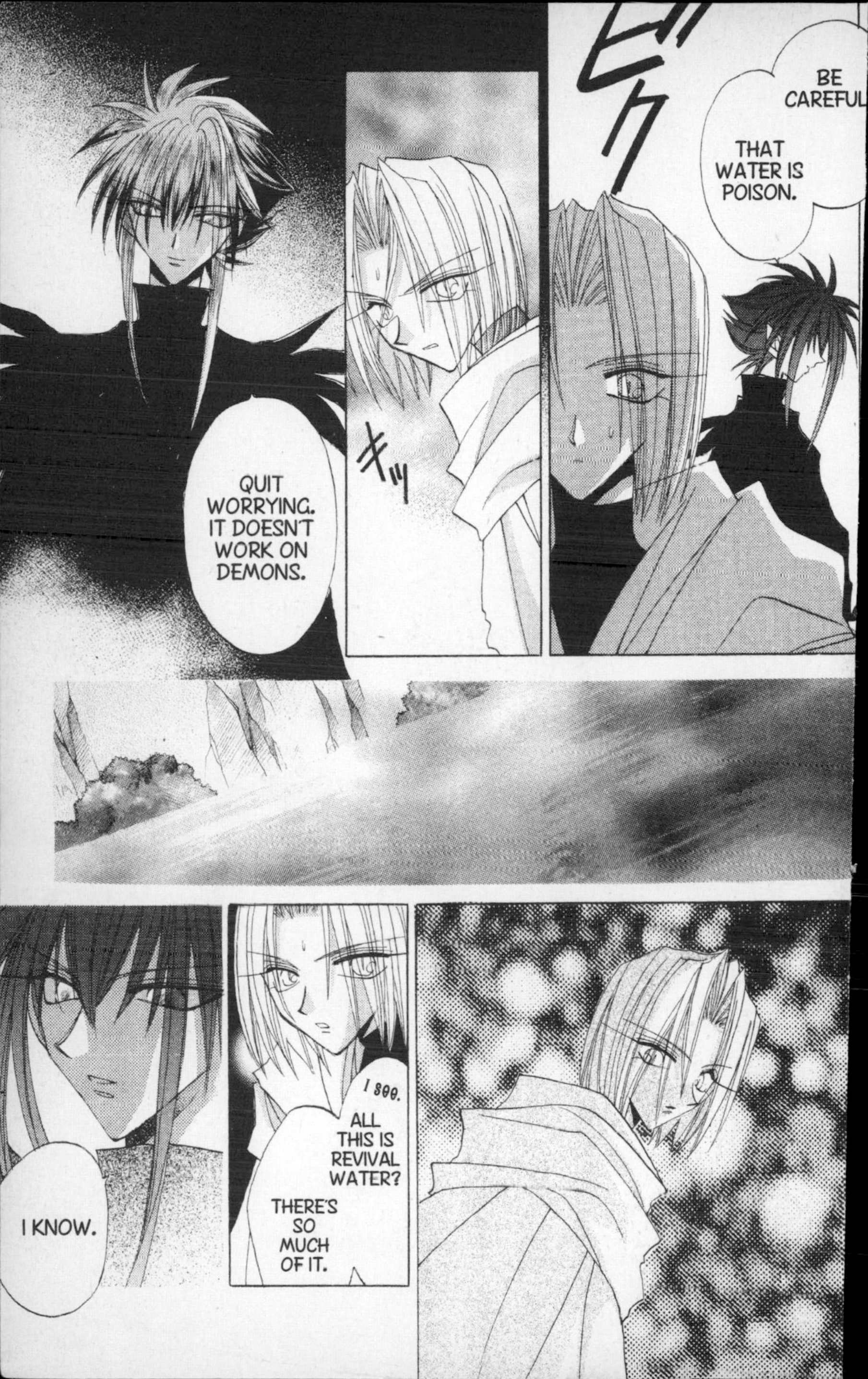
ビク
BE CAREFUL
THAT WATER IS POISON.
キッ
QUIT WORRYING. IT DOESN'T WORK ON DEMONS.
I see.
ALL THIS IS REVIVAL WATER?
THERE'S SO MUCH OF IT.
I KNOW.

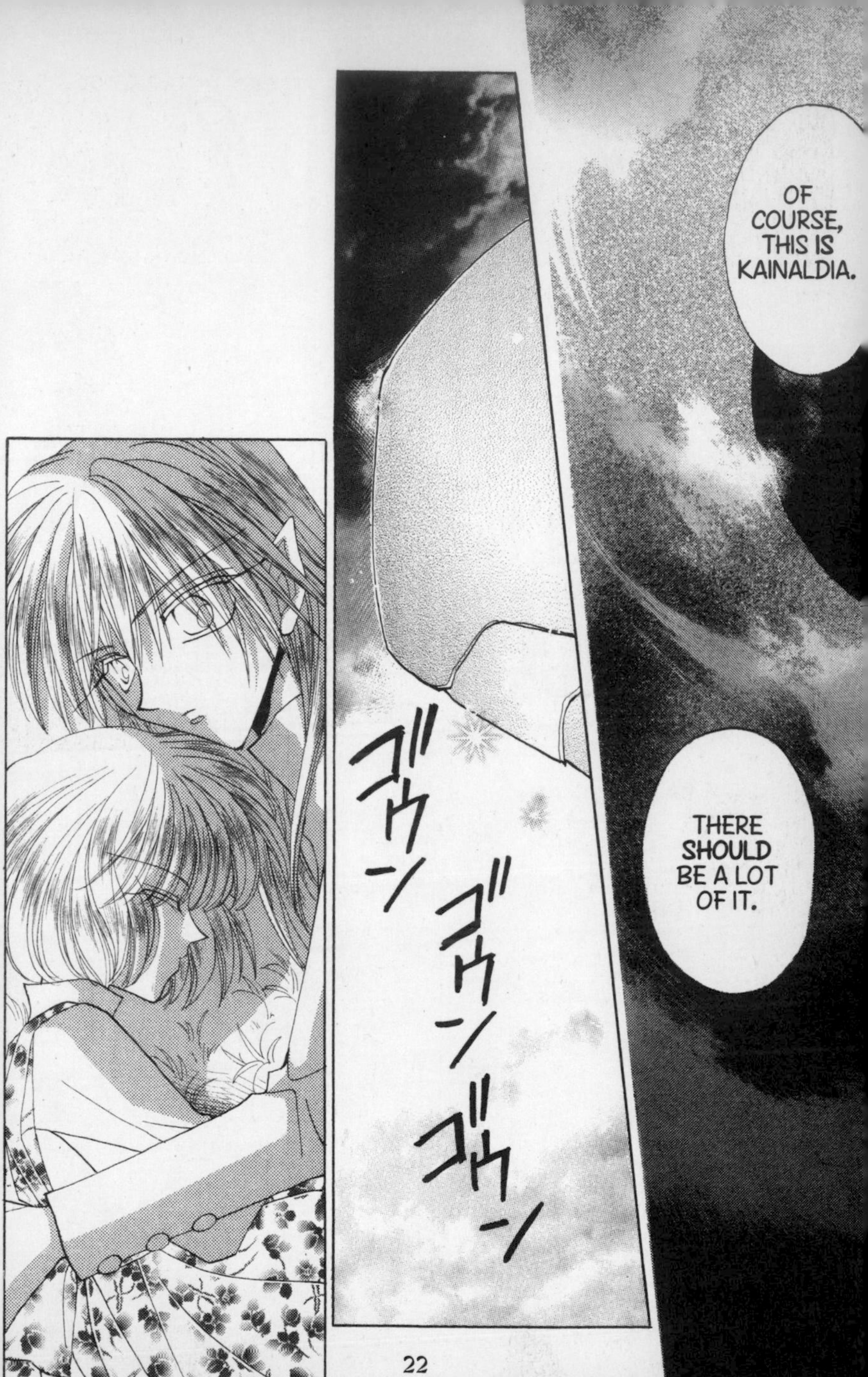
OF COURSE, THIS IS KAINALDIA.
THERE SHOULD BE A LOT OF IT.
ゴウン
ゴウン
ゴウーン

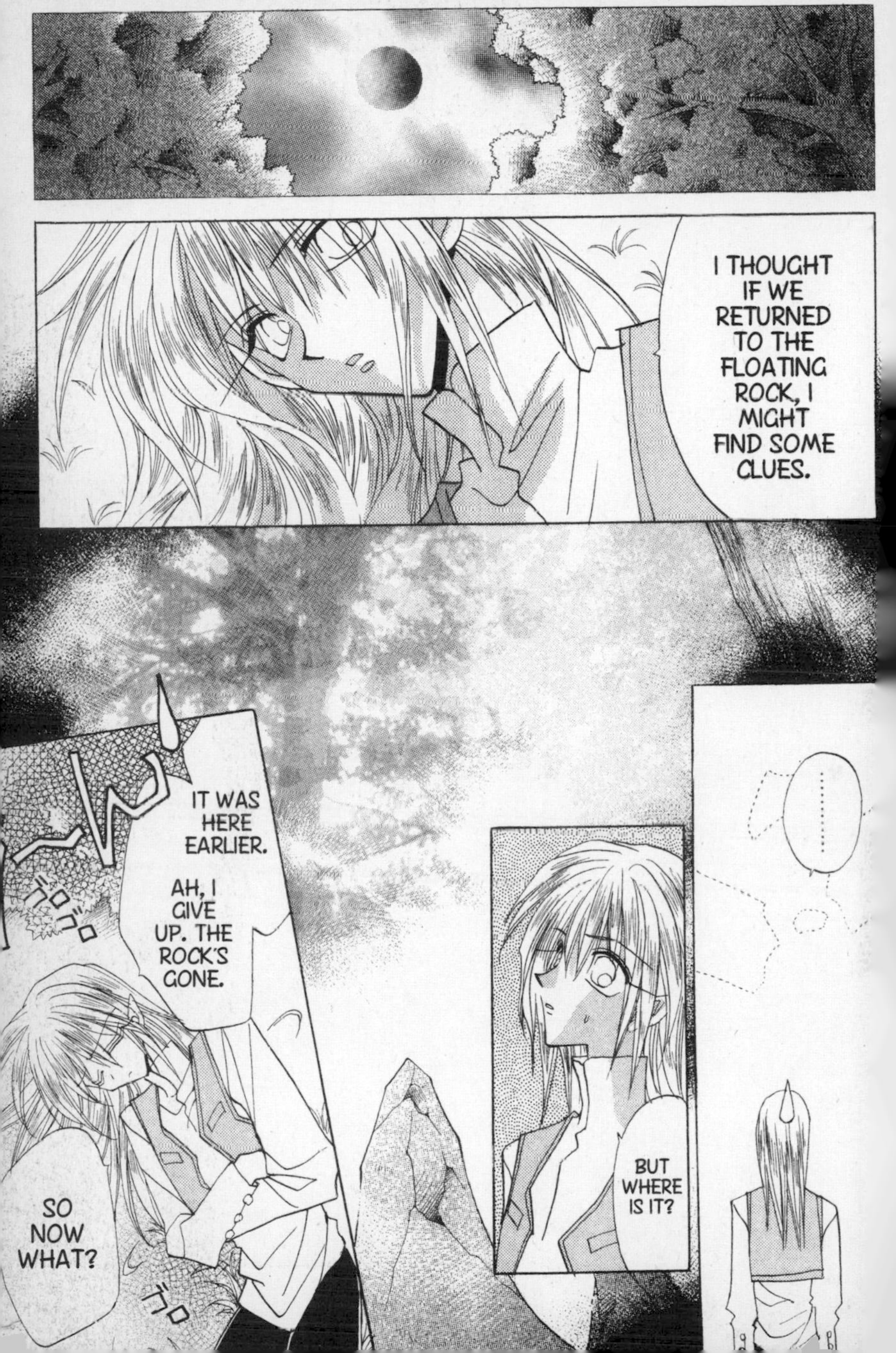
I THOUGHT IF WE RETURNED TO THE FLOATING ROCK, I MIGHT FIND SOME CLUES.
BUT WHERE IS IT?
IT WAS HERE EARLIER.
AH, I GIVE UP. THE ROCK'S GONE.
SO NOW WHAT?

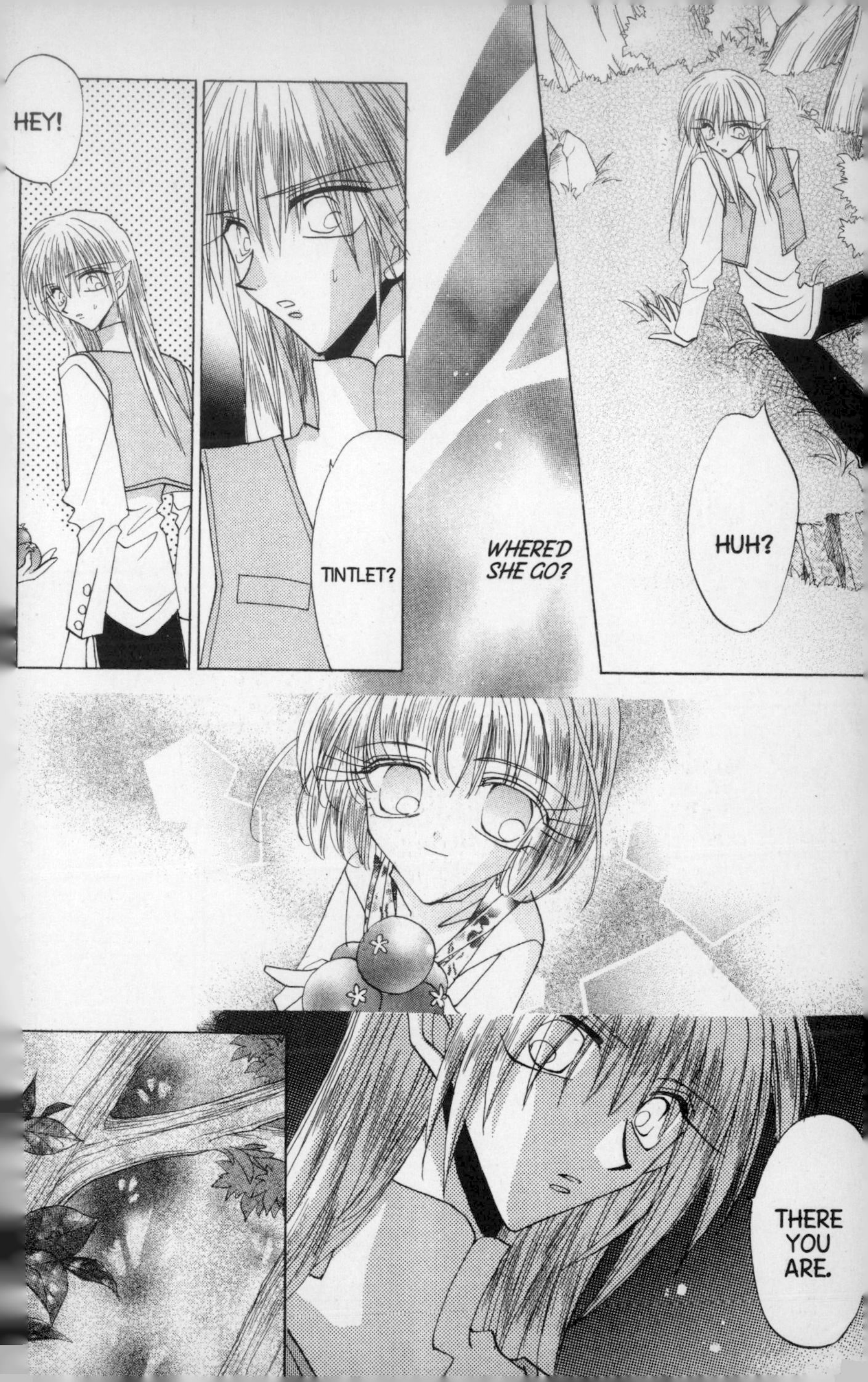
HUH?
WHERE'D SHE GO?
TINTLET?
HEY!
THERE YOU ARE.

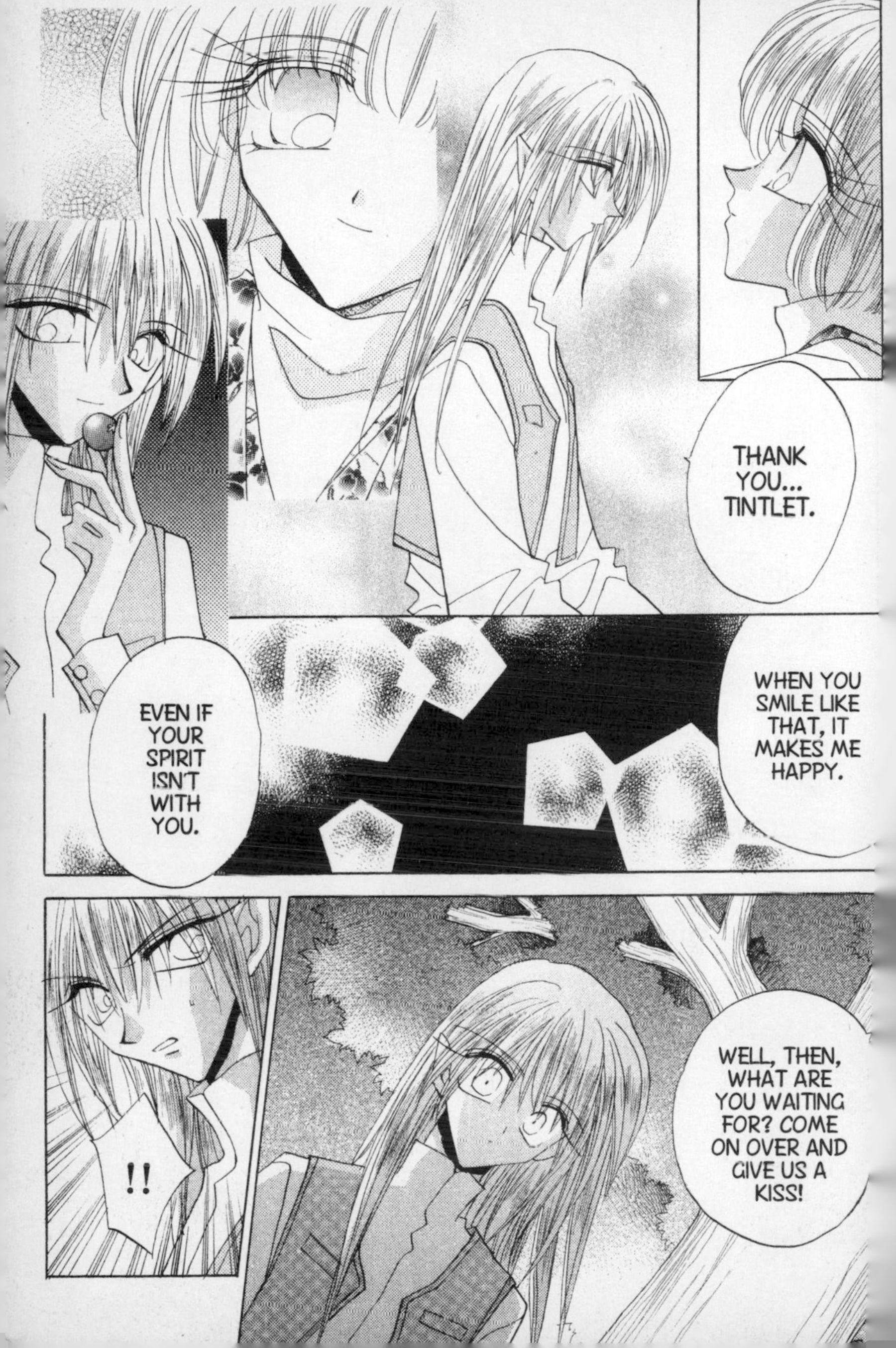
THANK YOU... TINTLET.
WHEN YOU SMILE LIKE THAT, IT MAKES ME HAPPY.
EVEN IF YOUR SPIRIT ISN'T WITH YOU.
WELL, THEN, WHAT ARE YOU WAITING FOR? COME ON OVER AND GIVE US A KISS!
!!

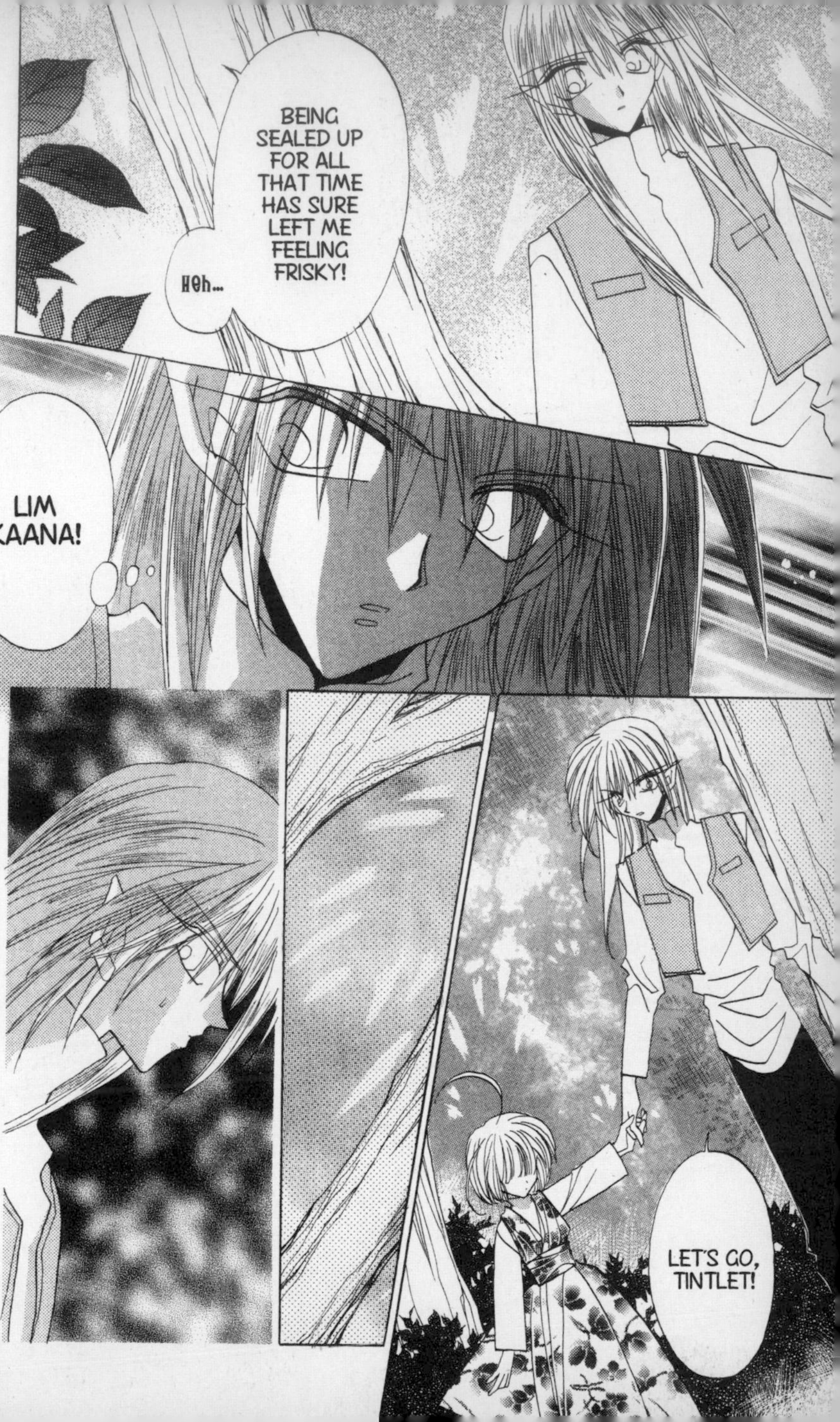
BEING SEALED UP FOR ALL THAT TIME HAS SURE LEFT ME FEELING FRISKY!
Heh...
LIM KAANA!
LET'S GO, TINTLET!

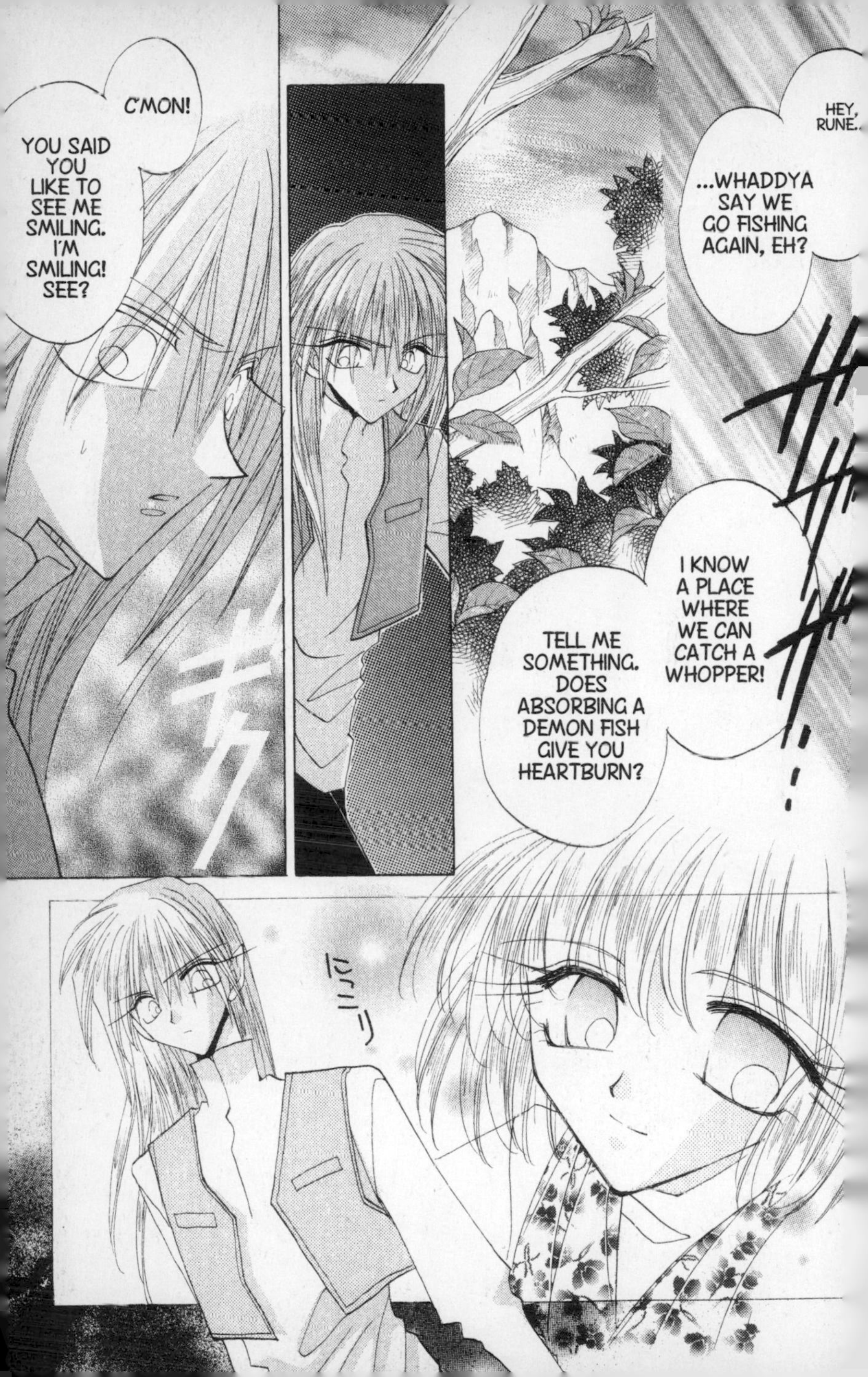
HEY, RUNE...
...WHADDYA SAY WE GO FISHING AGAIN, EH?
I KNOW A PLACE WHERE WE CAN CATCH A WHOPPER!
TELL ME SOMETHING. DOES ABSORBING A DEMON FISH GIVE YOU HEARTBURN?
C'MON!
YOU SAID YOU LIKE TO SEE ME SMILING. I'M SMILING! SEE?

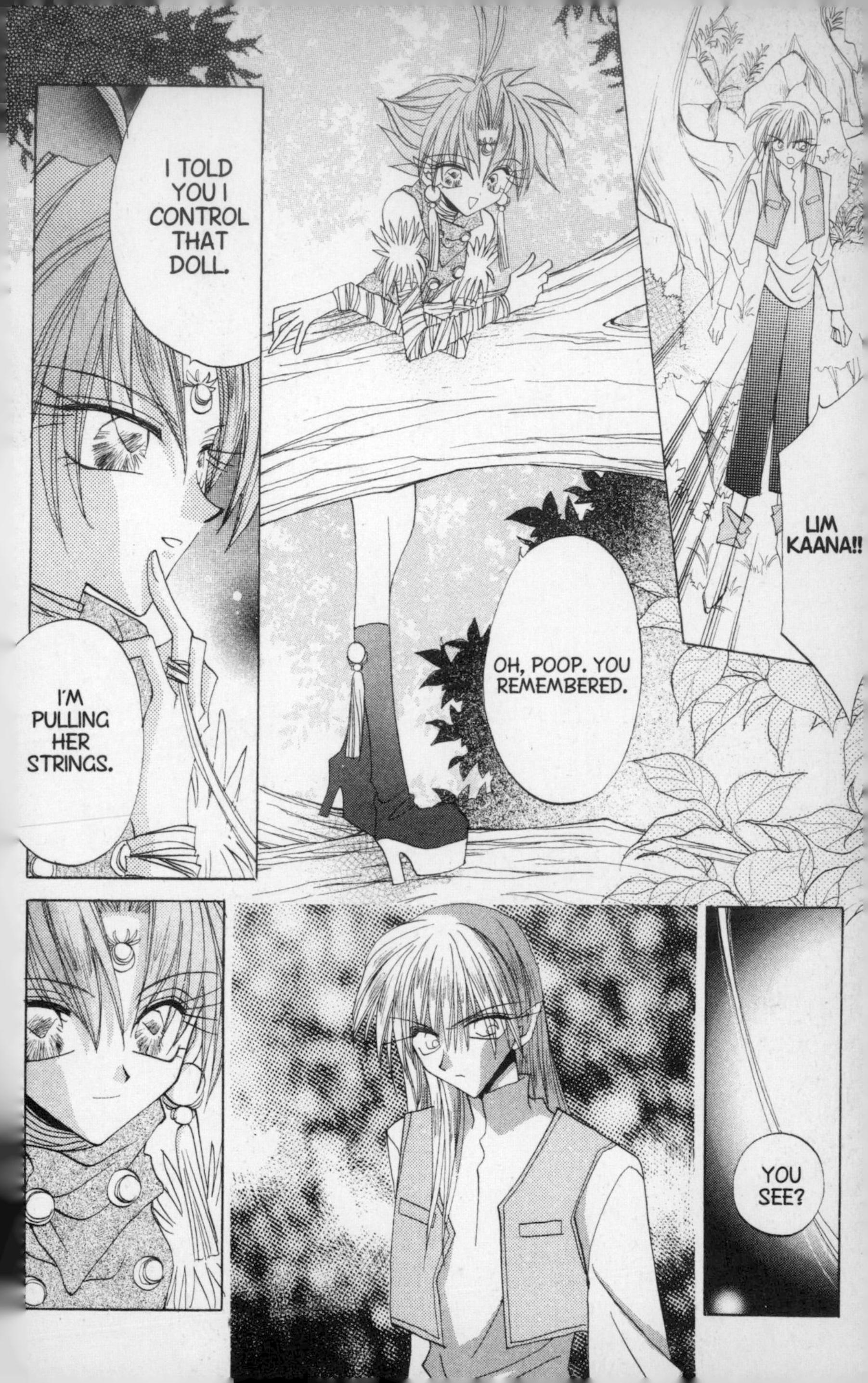
LIM KAANA!!
OH, POOP. YOU REMEMBERED.
I TOLD YOU I CONTROL THAT DOLL.
I'M PULLING HER STRINGS.
YOU SEE?

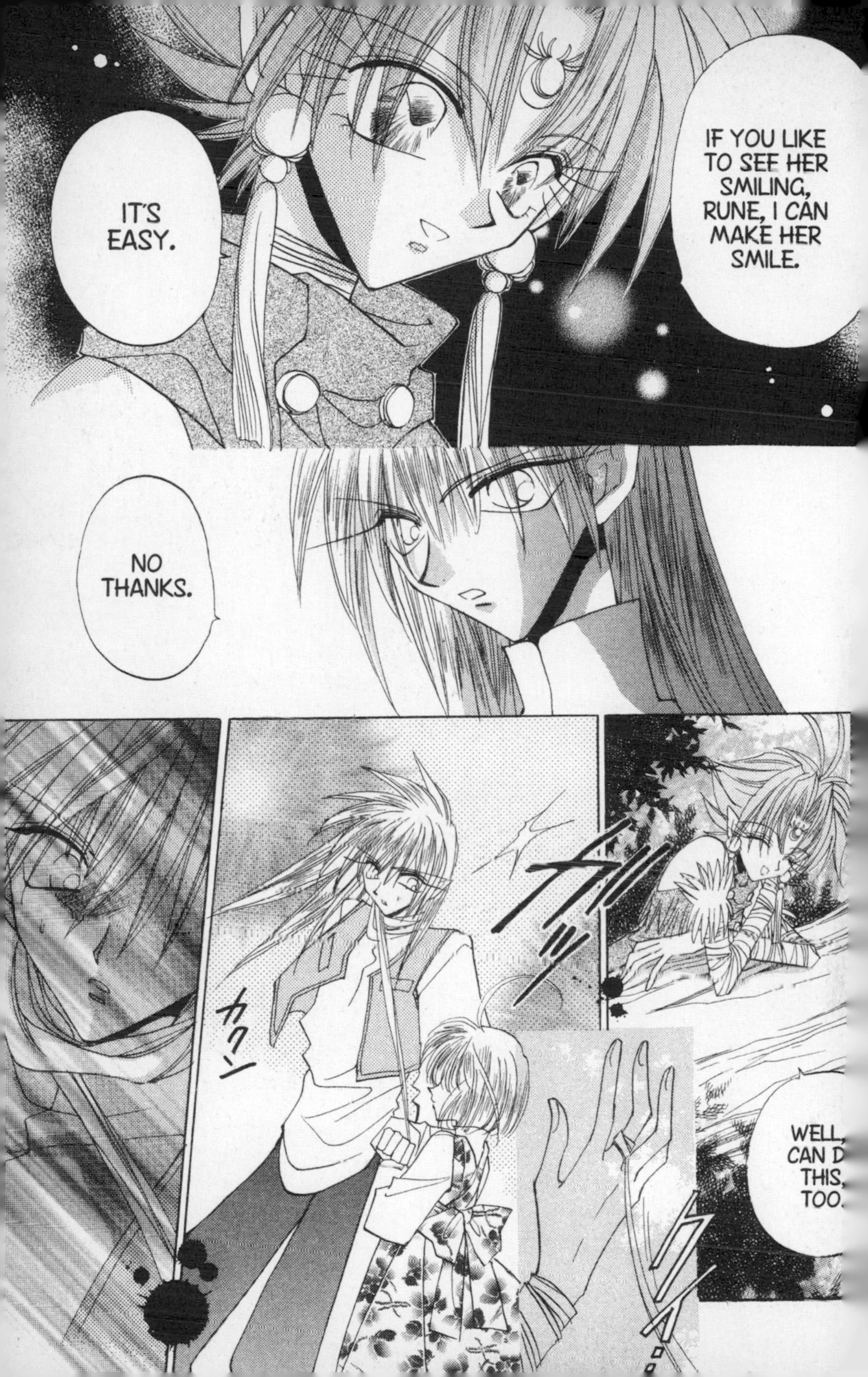
IF YOU LIKE TO SEE HER SMILING, RUNE, I CAN MAKE HER SMILE.
IT'S EASY.
NO THANKS.
WELL, CAN D THIS, TOO.

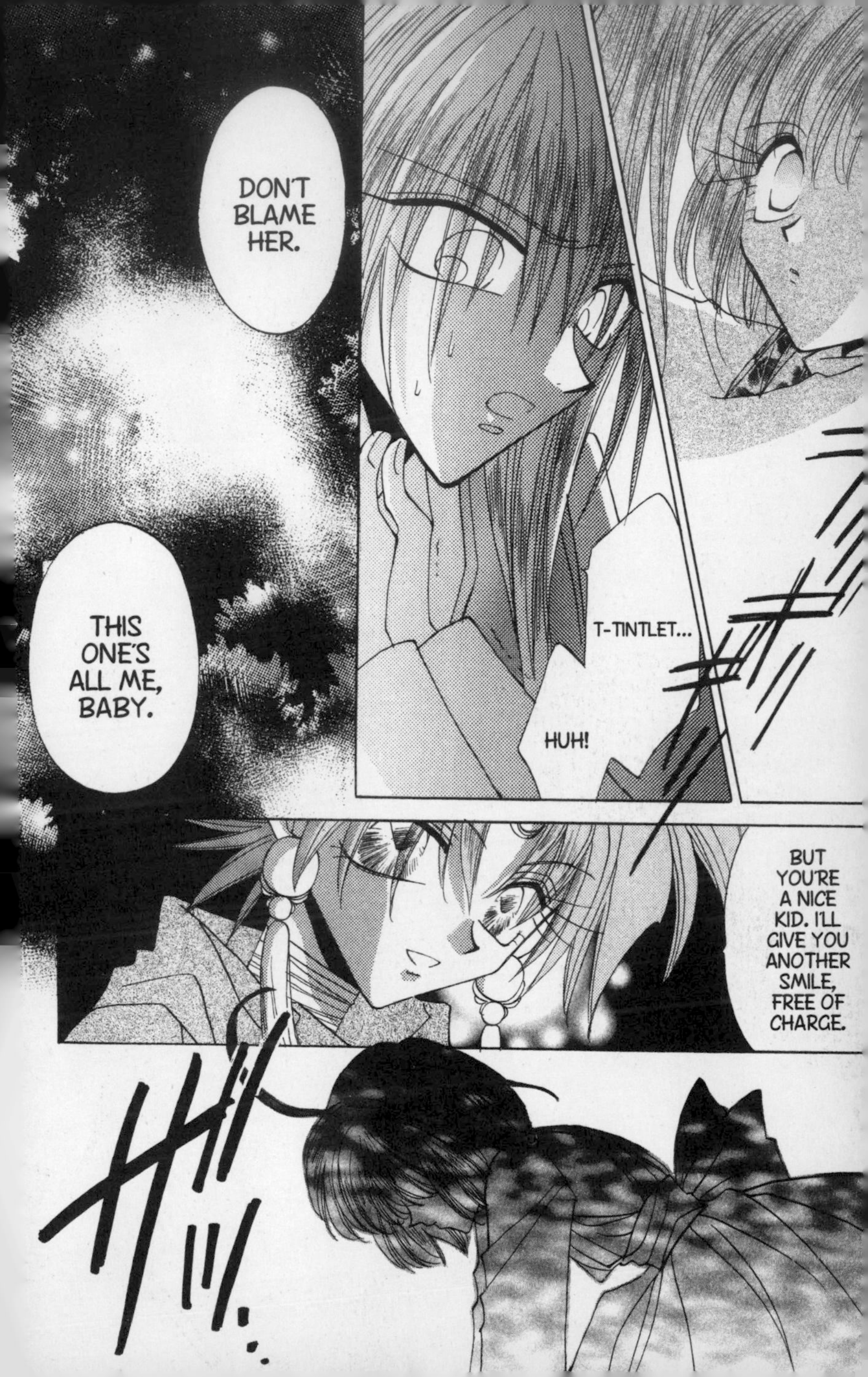
T-TINTLET...
HUH!
DON'T BLAME HER.
THIS ONE'S ALL ME, BABY.
BUT YOU'RE A NICE KID. I'LL GIVE YOU ANOTHER SMILE, FREE OF CHARGE.

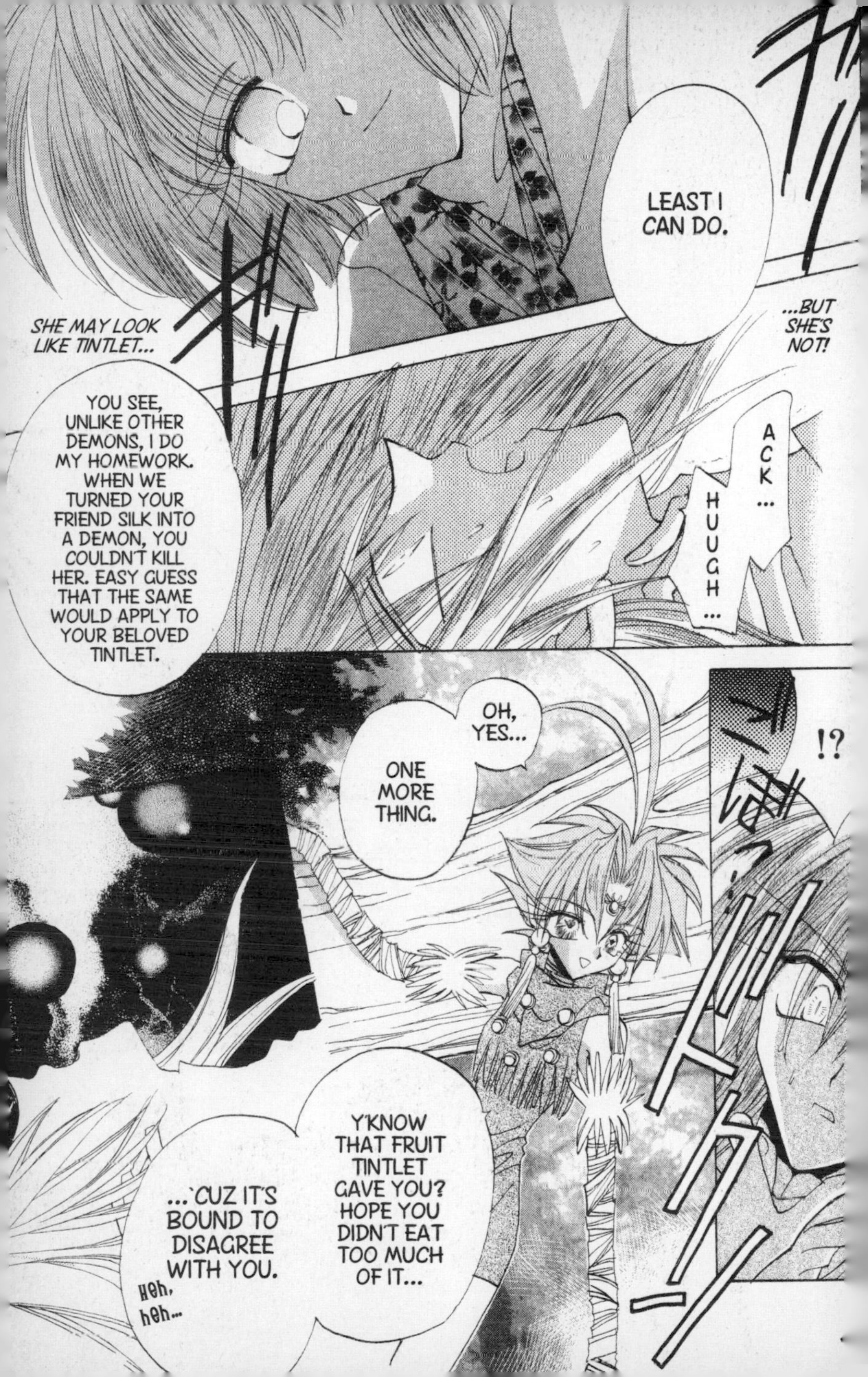
LEAST I CAN DO.
SHE MAY LOOK LIKE TINTLET...
...BUT SHE'S NOT!
ACK...
HUUGH...
YOU SEE, UNLIKE OTHER DEMONS, I DO MY HOMEWORK. WHEN WE TURNED YOUR FRIEND SILK INTO A DEMON, YOU COULDN'T KILL HER. EASY GUESS THAT THE SAME WOULD APPLY TO YOUR BELOVED TINTLET.
!?
OH, YES...
ONE MORE THING.
Y'KNOW THAT FRUIT TINTLET GAVE YOU? HOPE YOU DIDN'T EAT TOO MUCH OF IT...
...'CUZ IT'S BOUND TO DISAGREE WITH YOU.
Heh, heh...

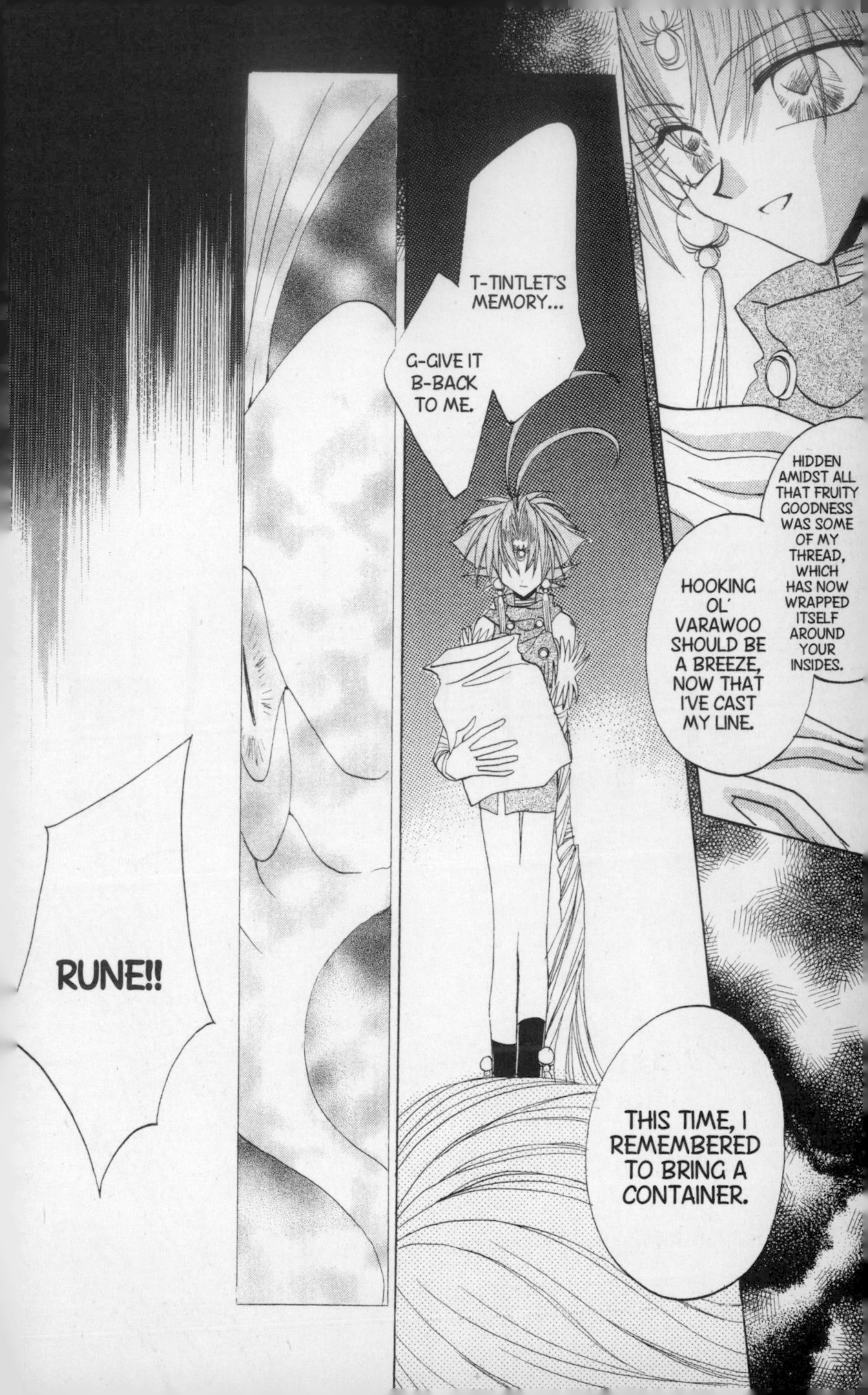
HIDDEN AMIDST ALL THAT FRUITY GOODNESS WAS SOME OF MY THREAD, WHICH HAS NOW WRAPPED ITSELF AROUND YOUR INSIDES.
HOOKING OL' VARAWOO SHOULD BE A BREEZE, NOW THAT I'VE CAST MY LINE.
THIS TIME, I REMEMBERED TO BRING A CONTAINER.
T-TINTLET'S MEMORY...
G-GIVE IT B-BACK TO ME.
RUNE!!

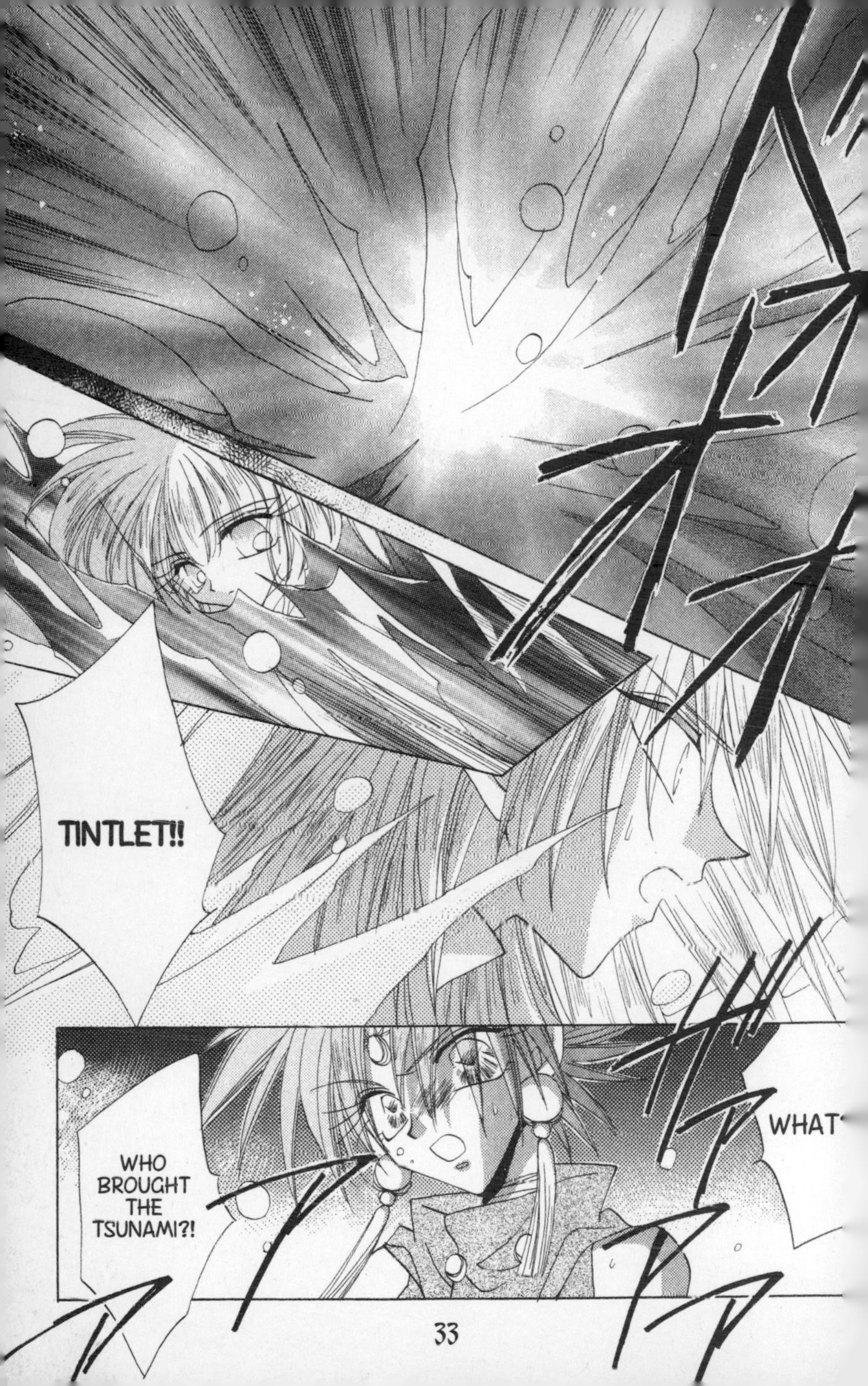
TINTLET!!
WHAT
WHO BROUGHT THE TSUNAMI?!

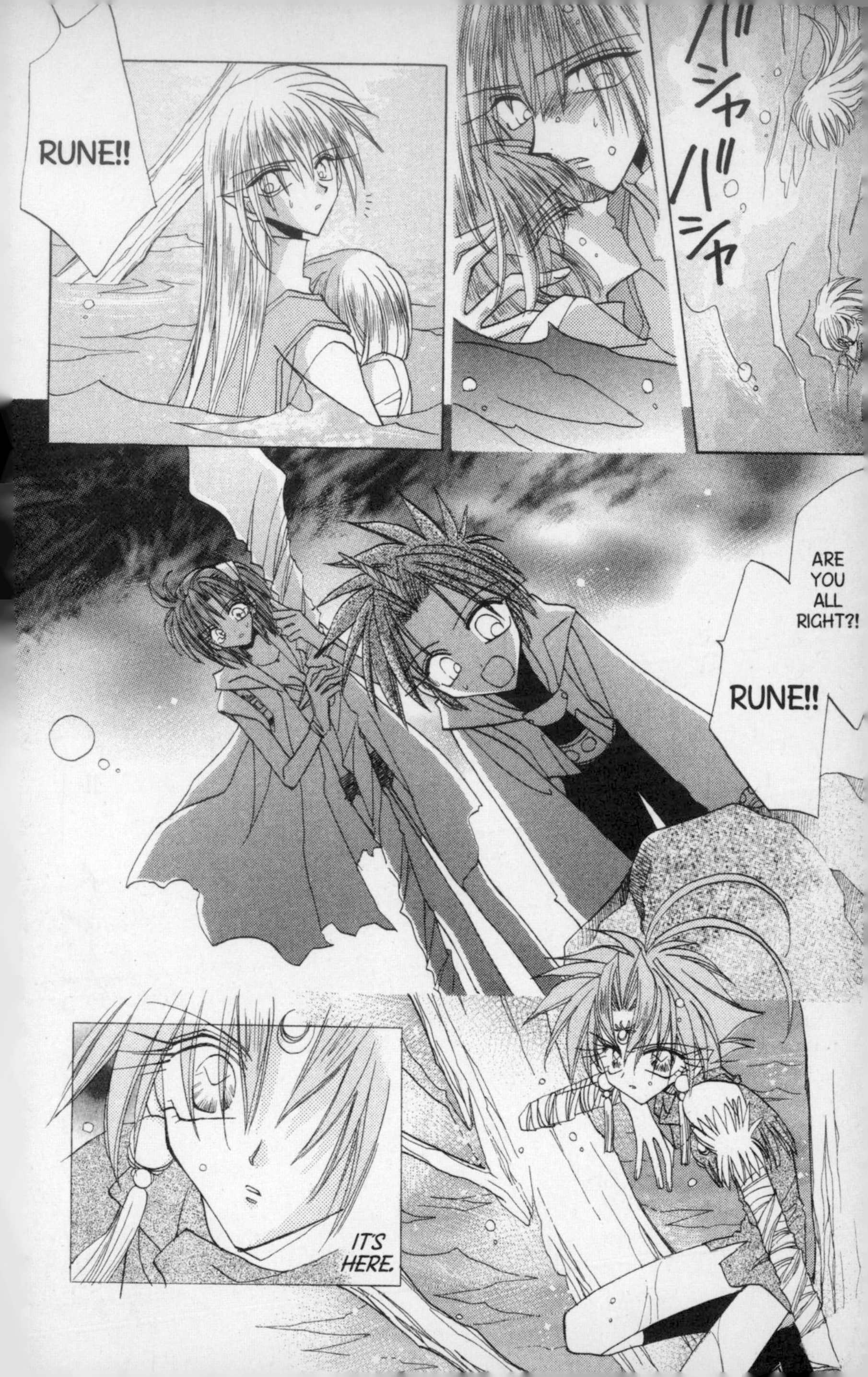
バシャバシャ
RUNE!!
ARE YOU ALL RIGHT?!
RUNE!!
IT'S HERE.

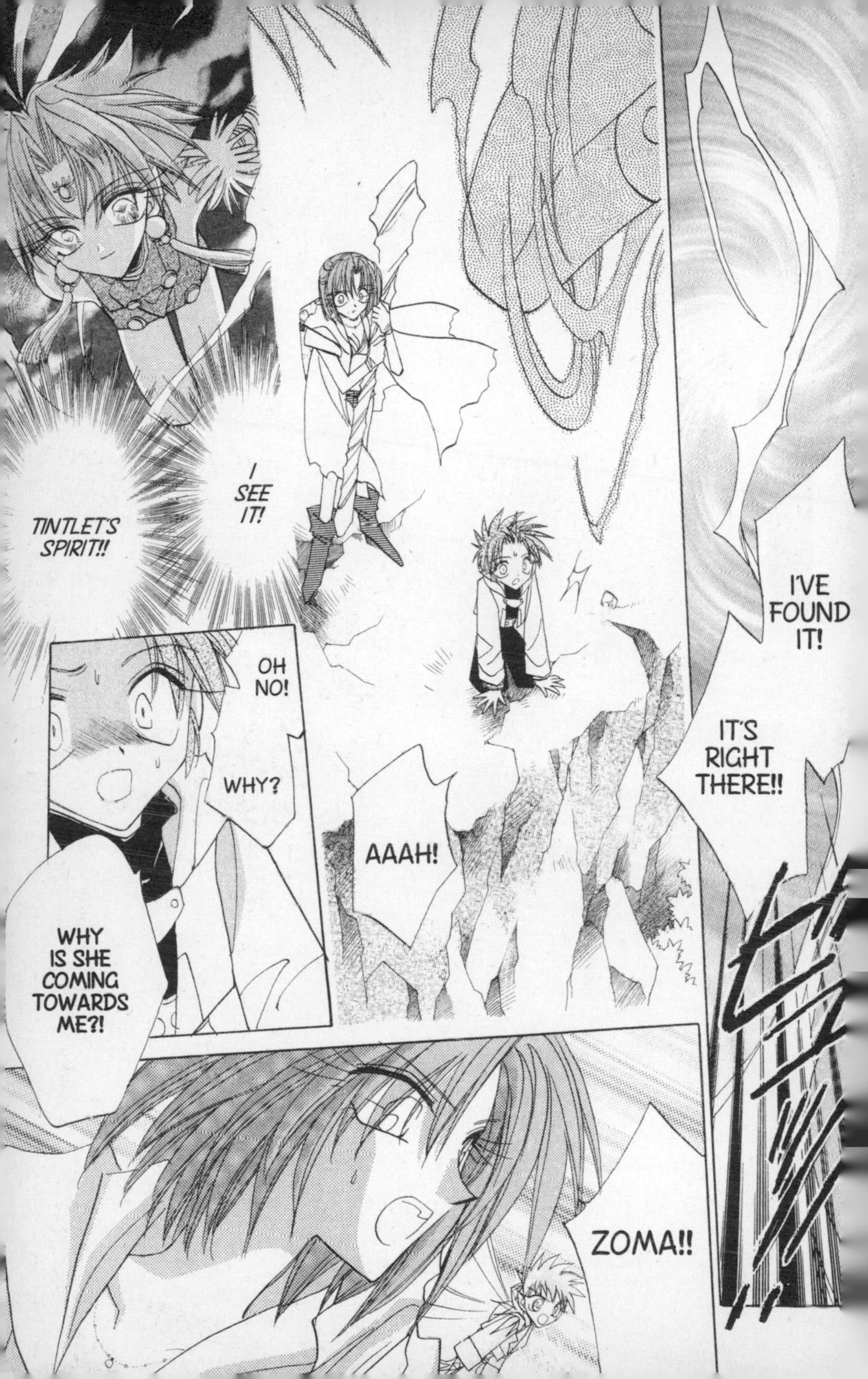
I'VE FOUND IT!
IT'S RIGHT THERE!!
I SEE IT!
TINTLET'S SPIRIT!!
AAAH!
OH NO!
WHY?
WHY IS SHE COMING TOWARDS ME?!
ZOMA!!

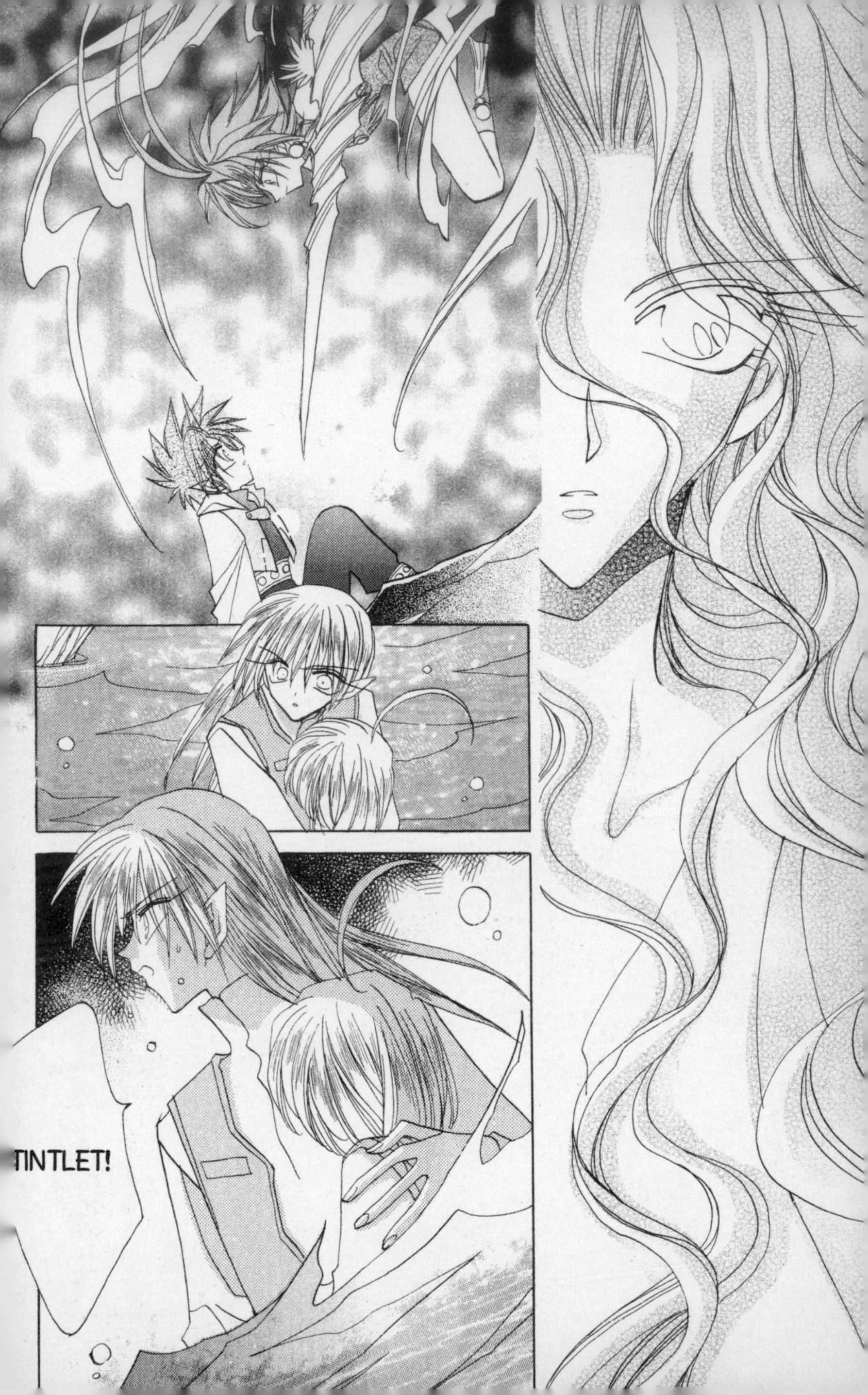
TINTLET!

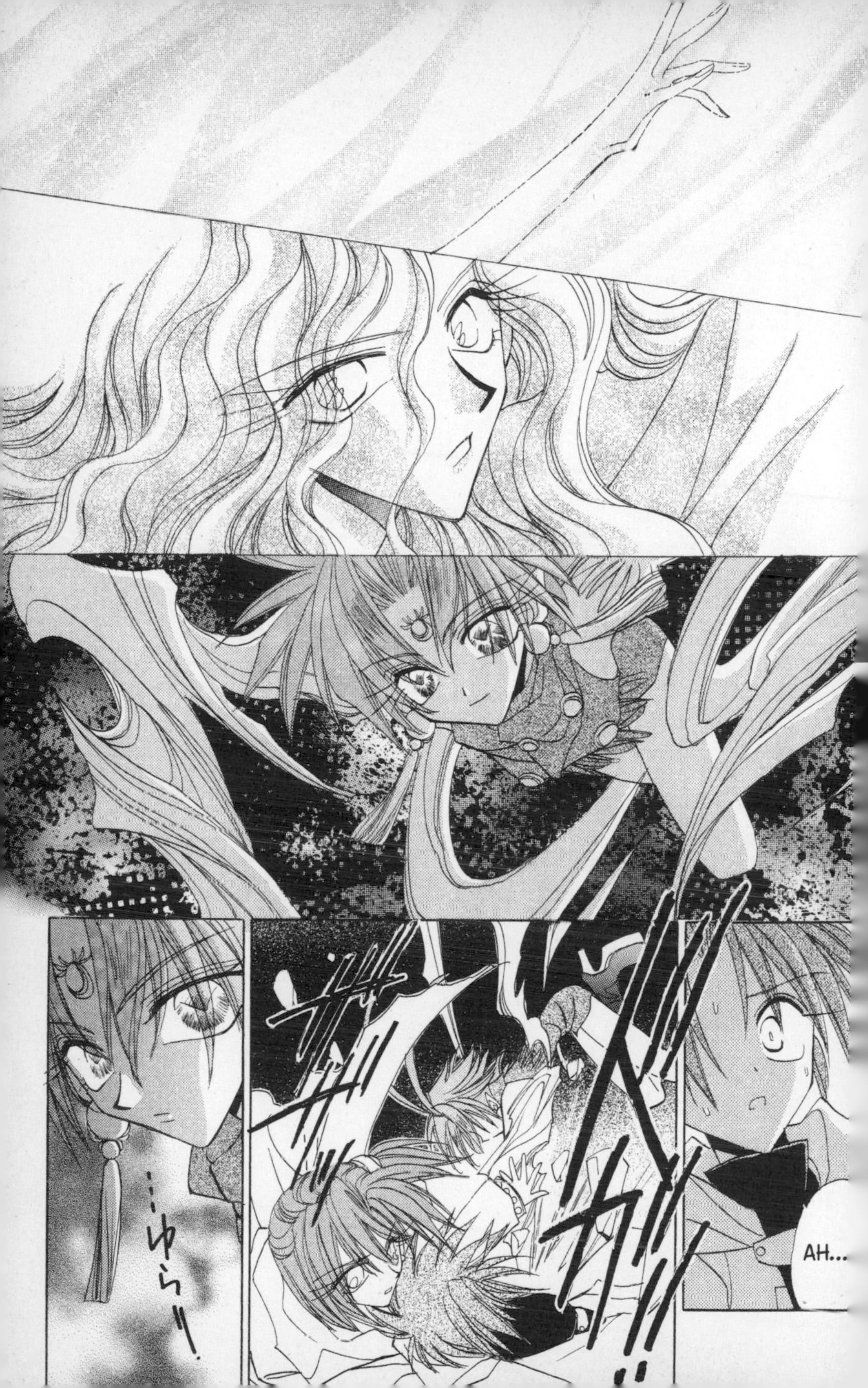
AH...
…ゆらり!

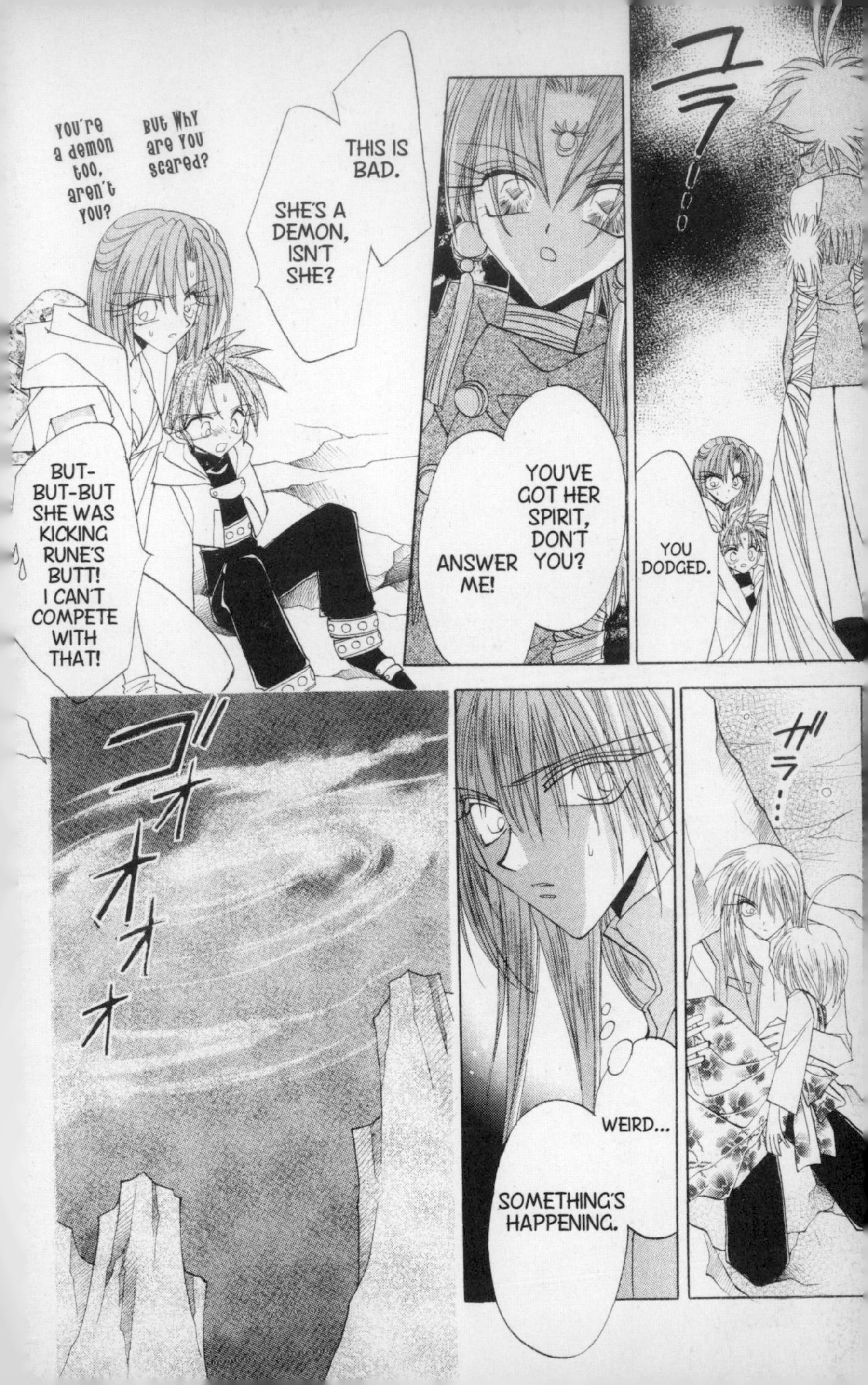
ユラ…
YOU DODGED.
YOU'VE GOT HER SPIRIT, DON'T YOU?
ANSWER ME!
THIS IS BAD.
SHE'S A DEMON, ISN'T SHE?
But Why are You scared?
You're a demon too, aren't You?
BUT-BUT-BUT SHE WAS KICKING RUNE'S BUTT! I CAN'T COMPETE WITH THAT!
ガラ・・・
WEIRD...
SOMETHING'S HAPPENING.
ゴオオオオ

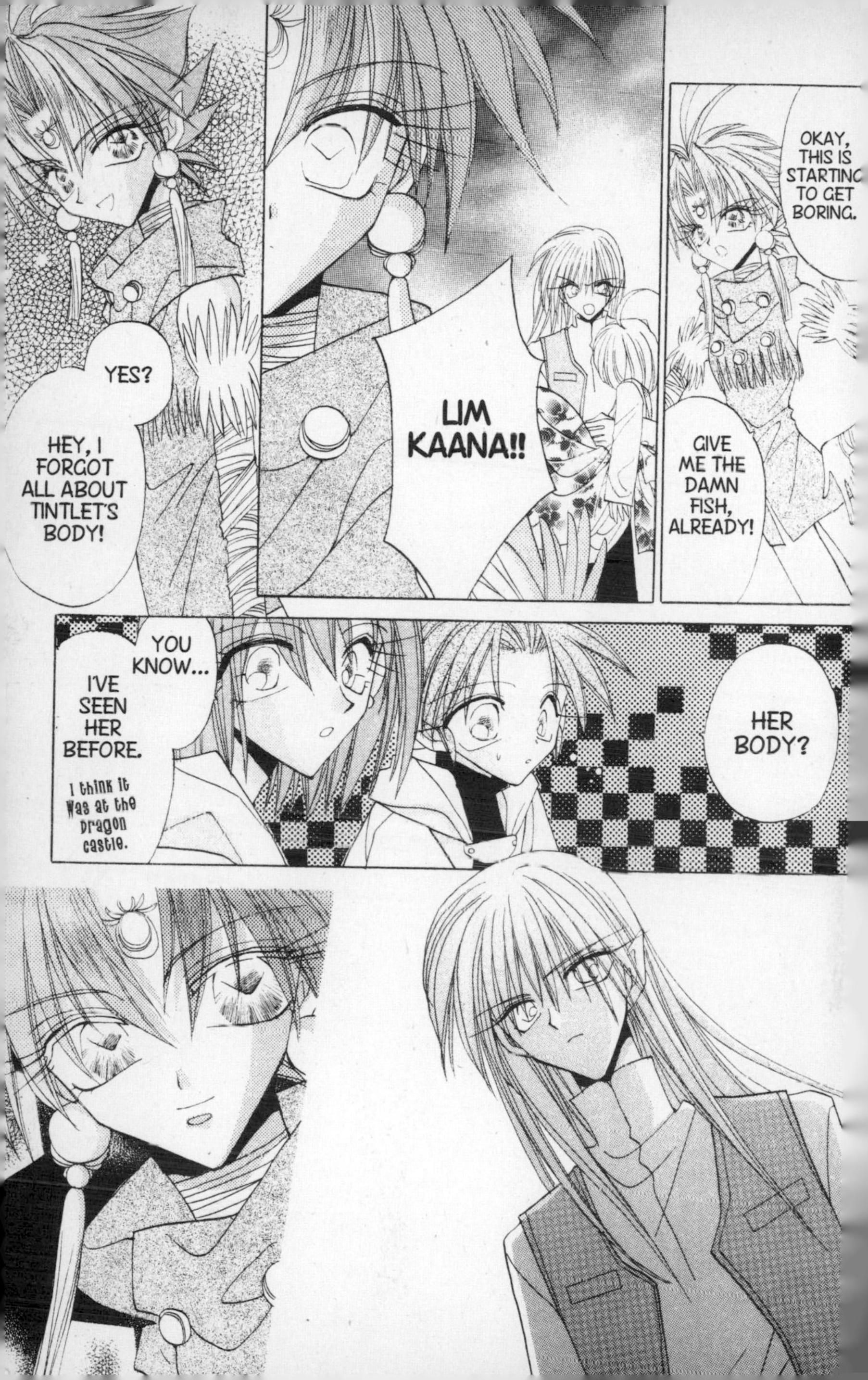
OKAY, THIS IS STARTING TO GET BORING.
GIVE ME THE DAMN FISH, ALREADY!
LIM KAANA!!
YES?
HEY, I FORGOT ALL ABOUT TINTLET'S BODY!
HER BODY?
YOU KNOW...
I'VE SEEN HER BEFORE.
I think it was at the dragon castle.

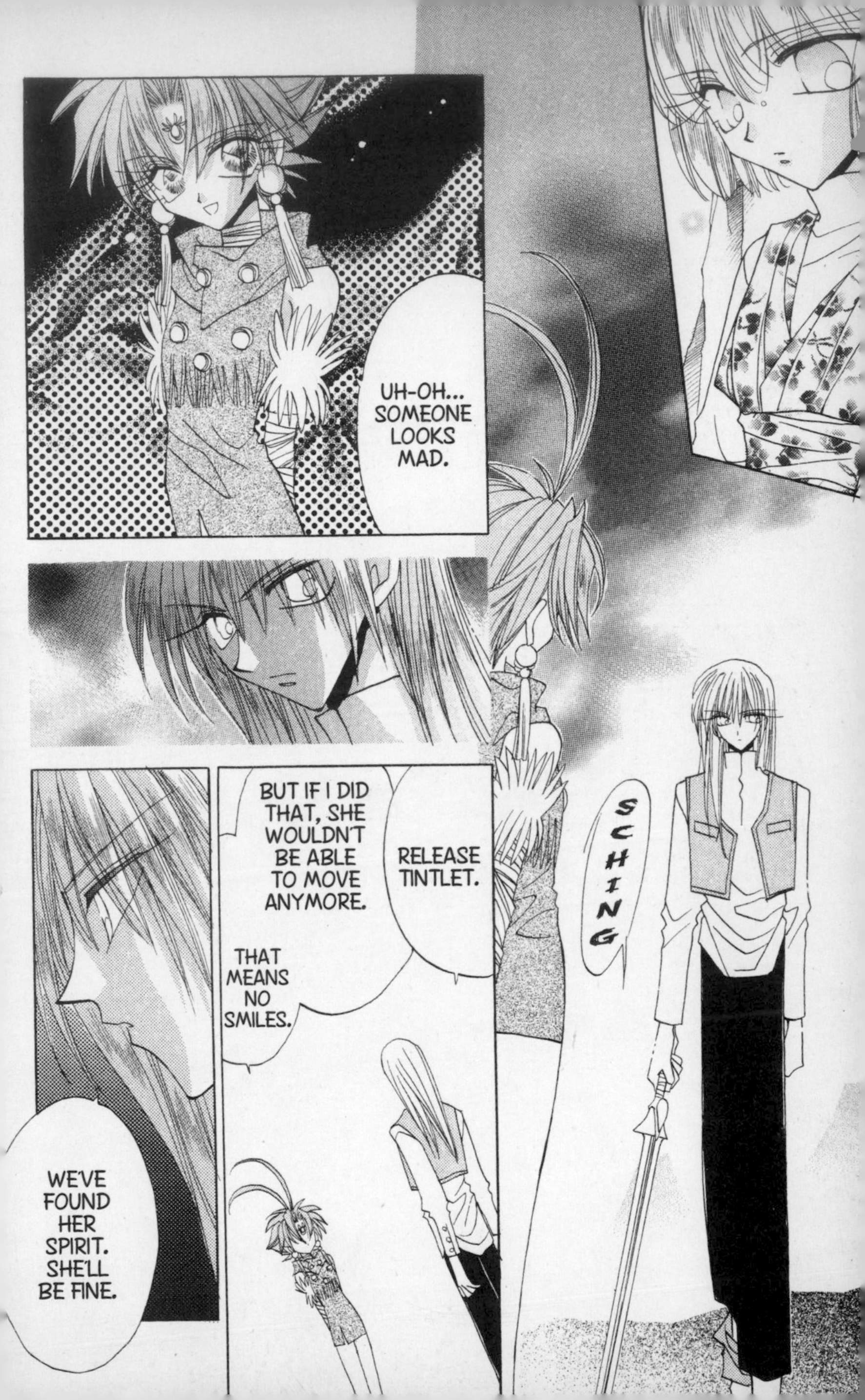
UH-OH... SOMEONE LOOKS MAD.
SCHING
RELEASE TINTLET.
BUT IF I DID THAT, SHE WOULDN'T BE ABLE TO MOVE ANYMORE.
THAT MEANS NO SMILES.
WE'VE FOUND HER SPIRIT. SHE'LL BE FINE.

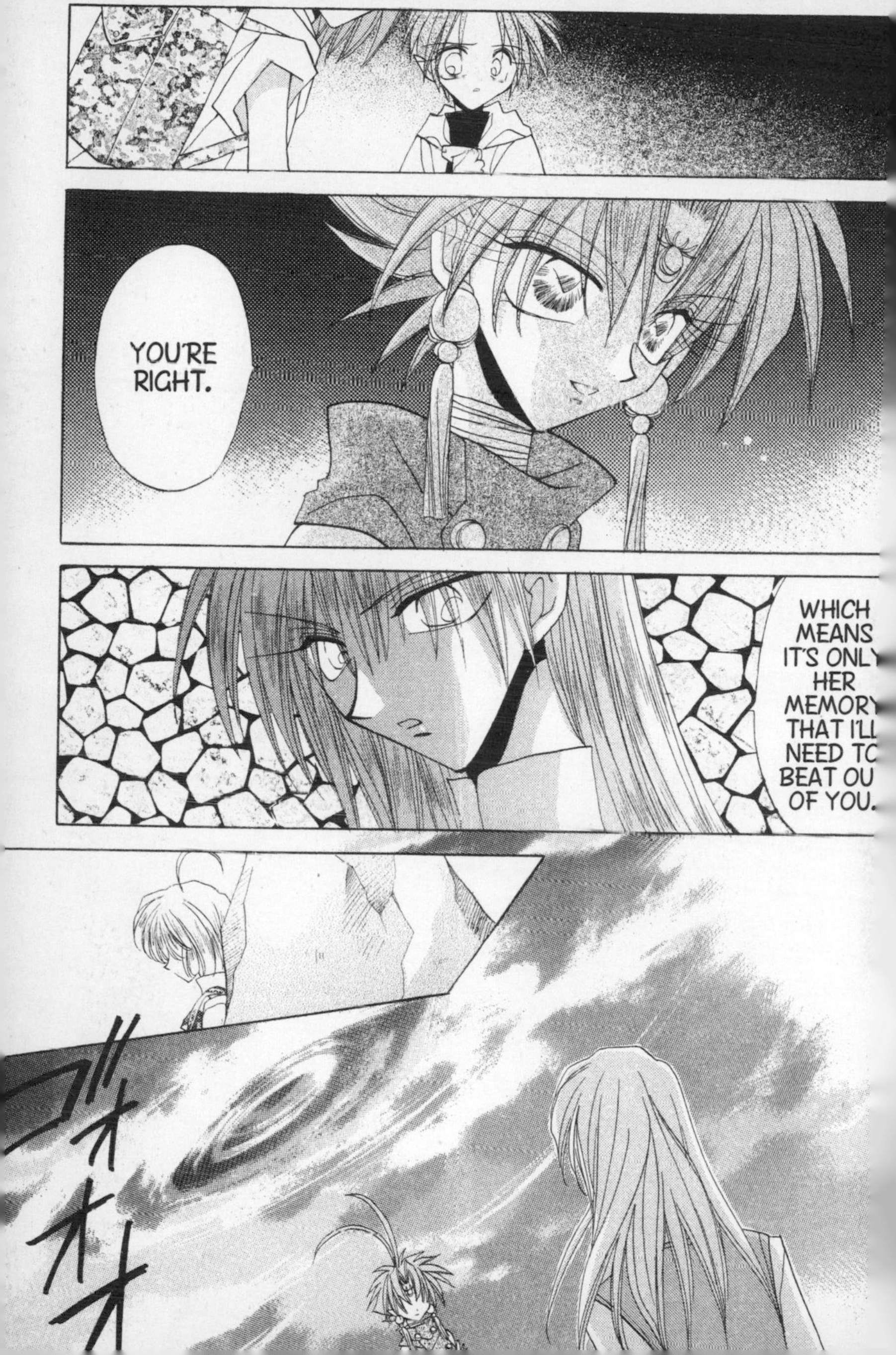
YOU'RE RIGHT.
WHICH MEANS IT'S ONLY HER MEMORY THAT I'LL NEED TO BEAT OUT OF YOU.
ゴォォォ

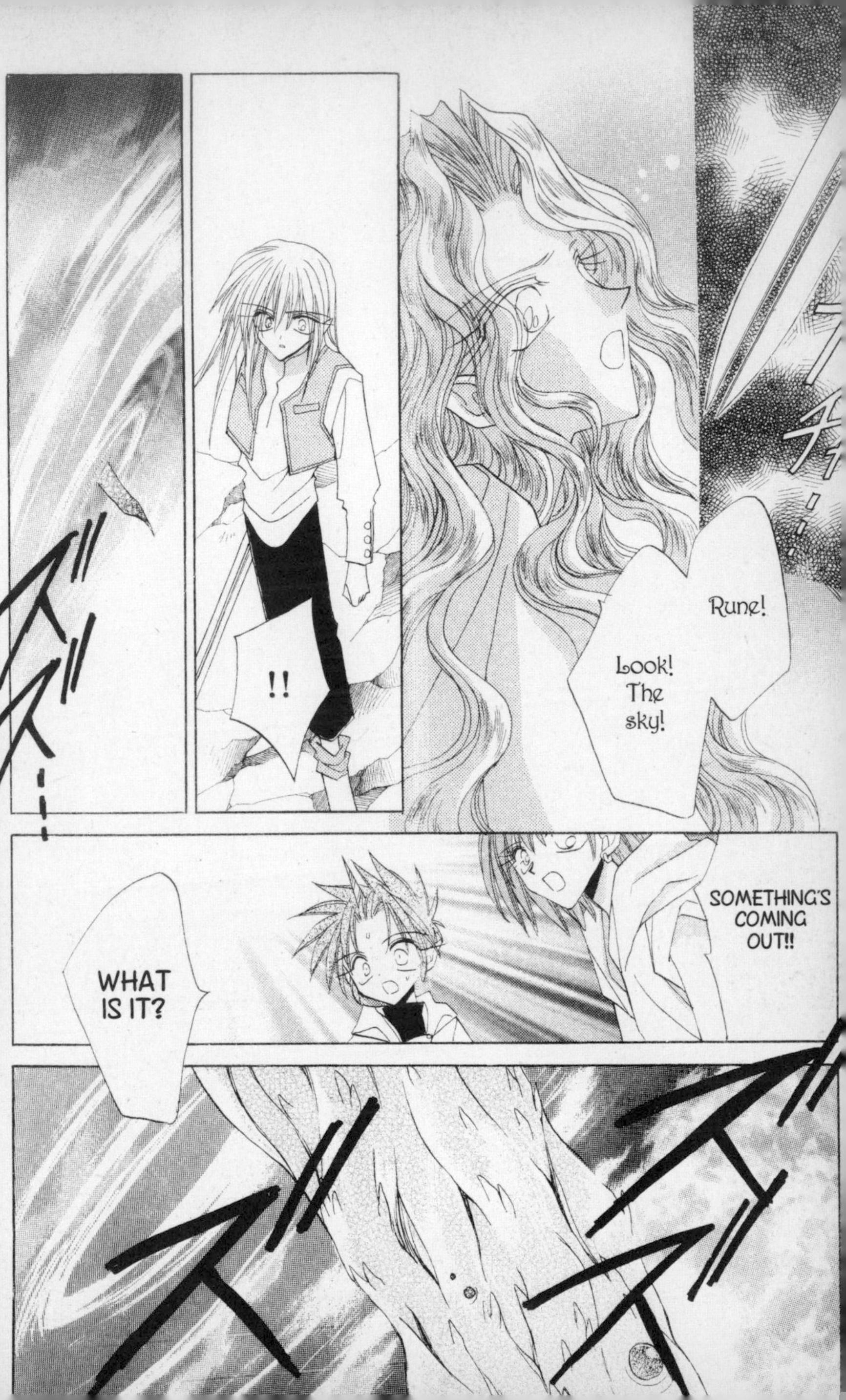

Rune!
Look! The sky!
!!
SOMETHING'S COMING OUT!!
WHAT IS IT?

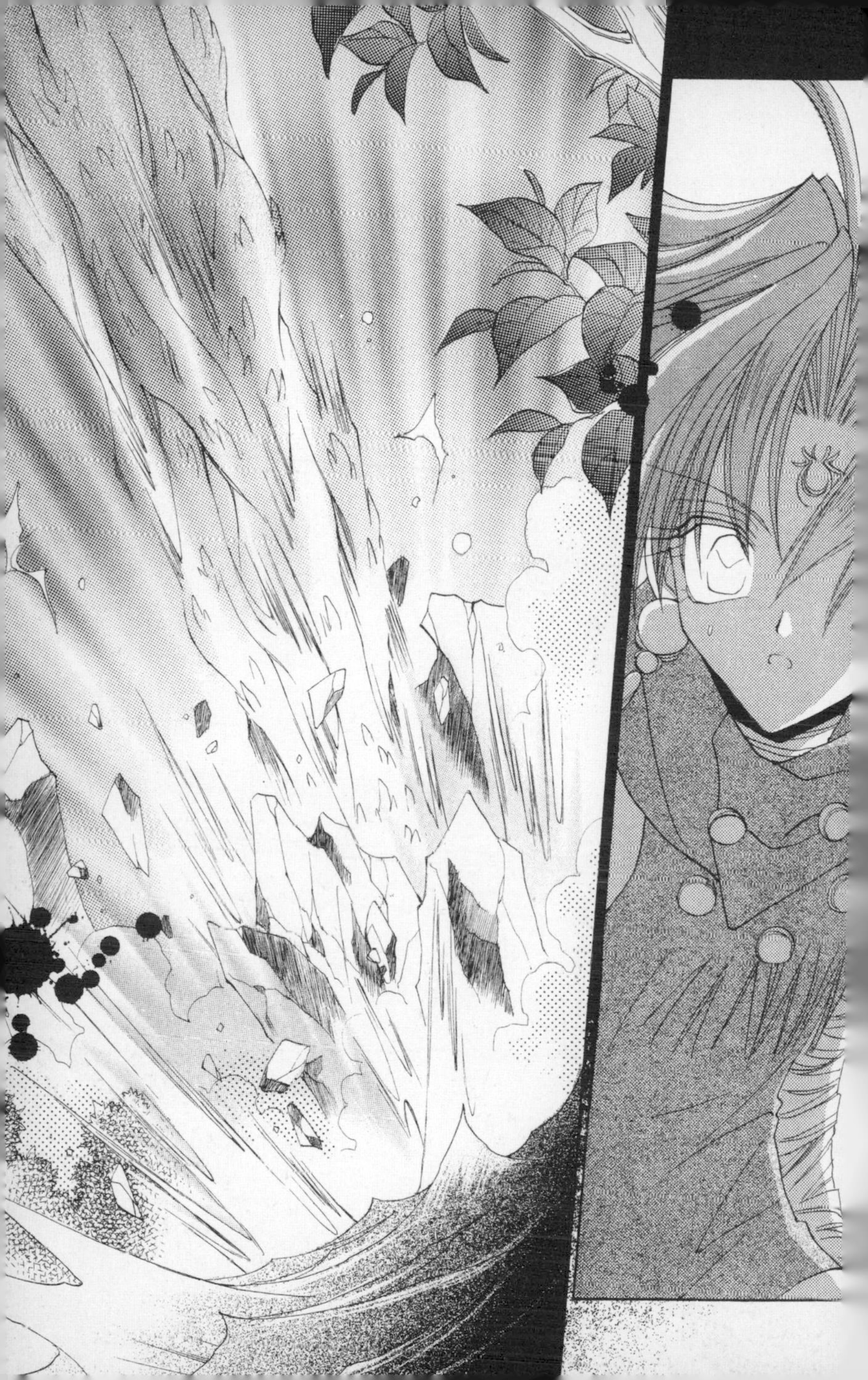

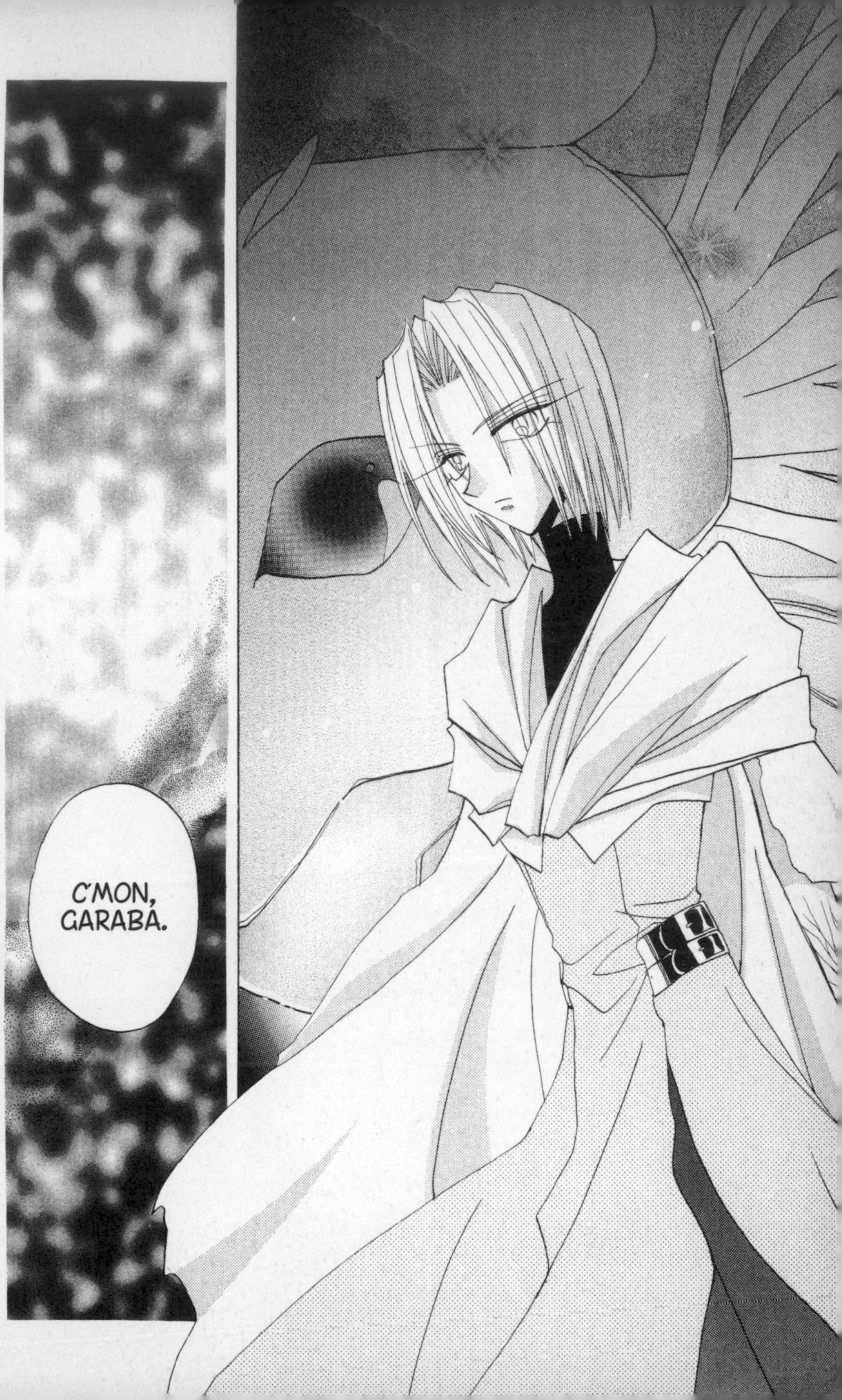
C'MON, GARABA.

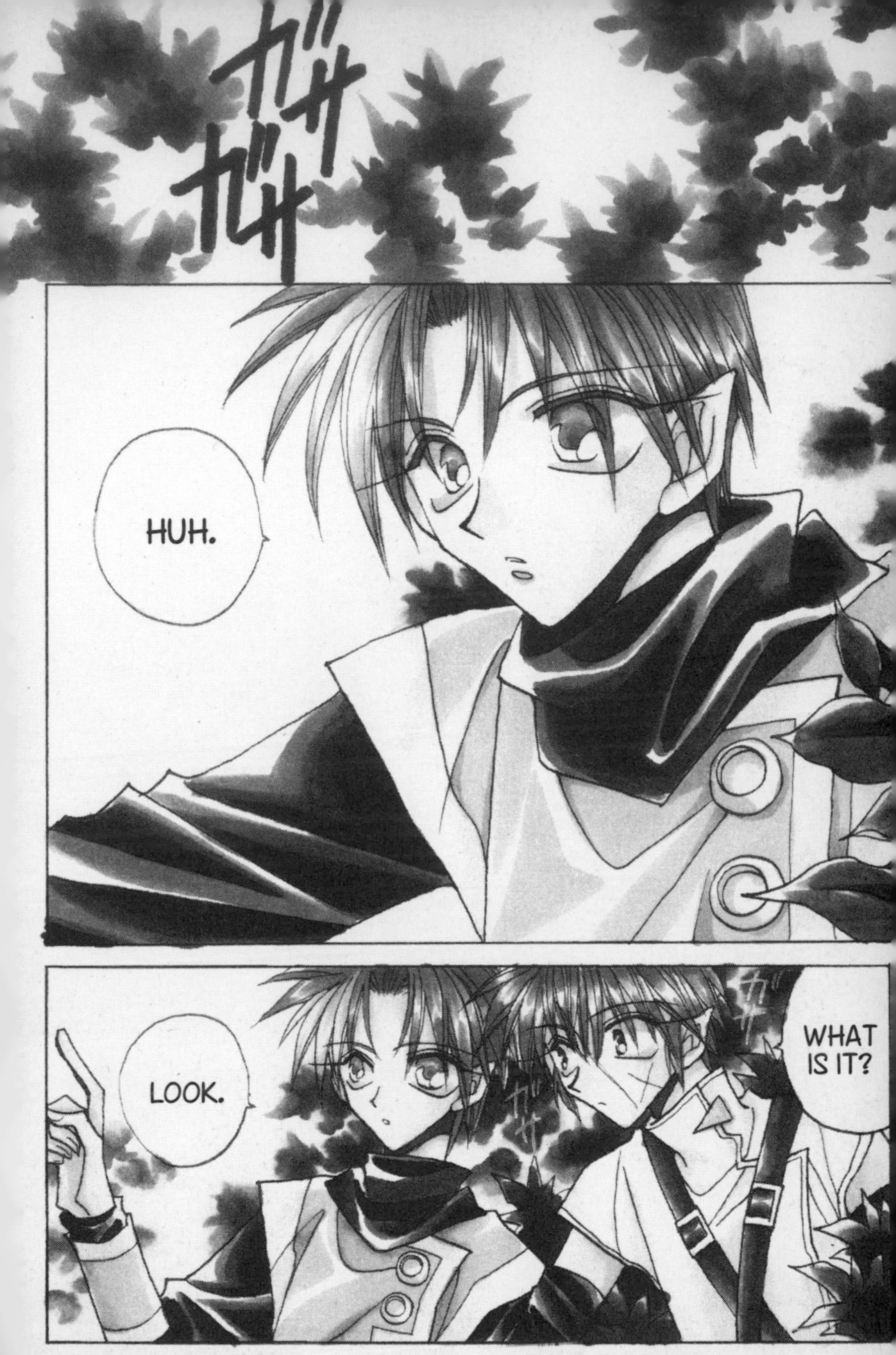
ガサ ガサ
HUH.
WHAT IS IT?
LOOK.

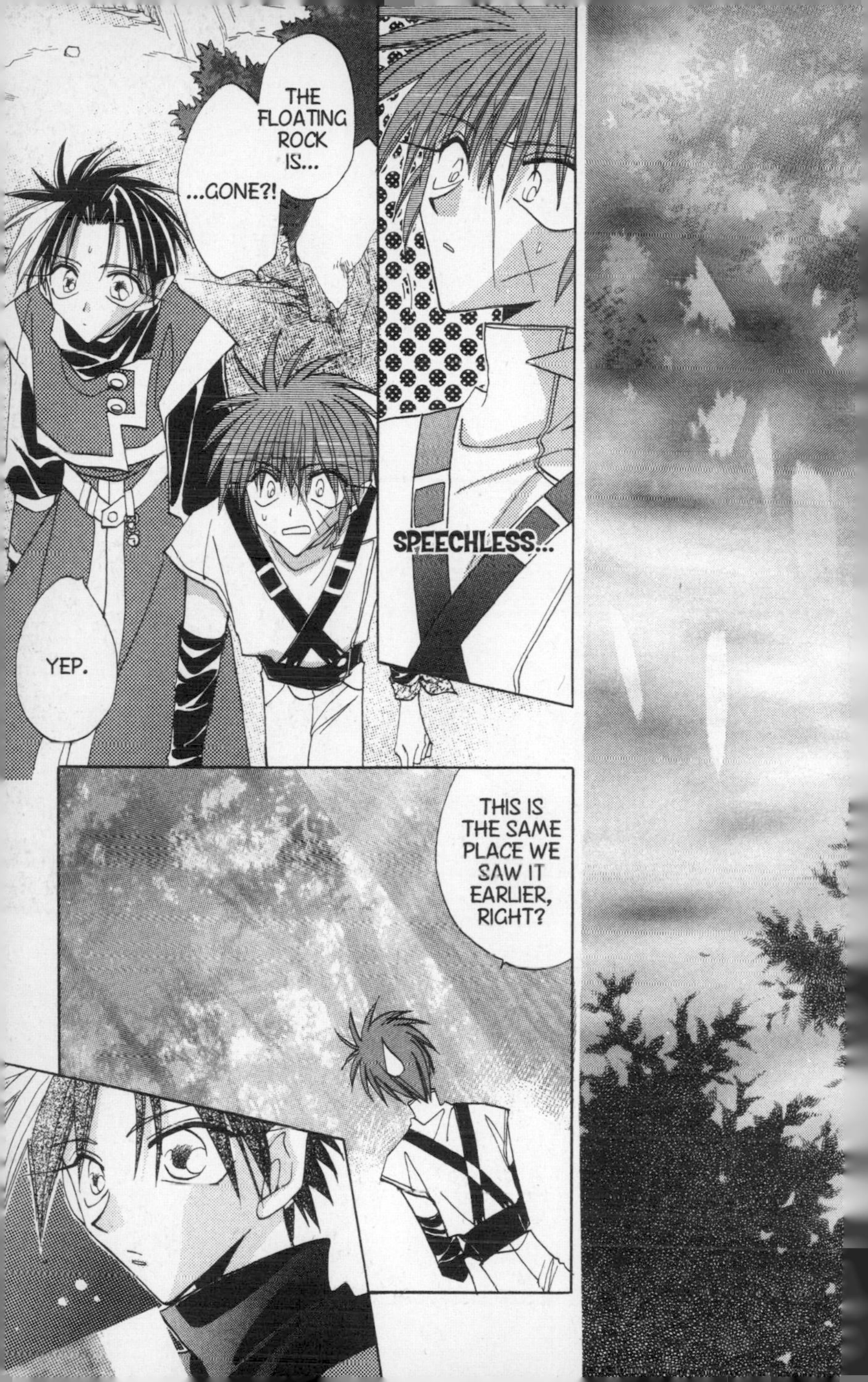
SPEECHLESS...
THE FLOATING ROCK IS...
...GONE?!
YEP.
THIS IS THE SAME PLACE WE SAW IT EARLIER, RIGHT?

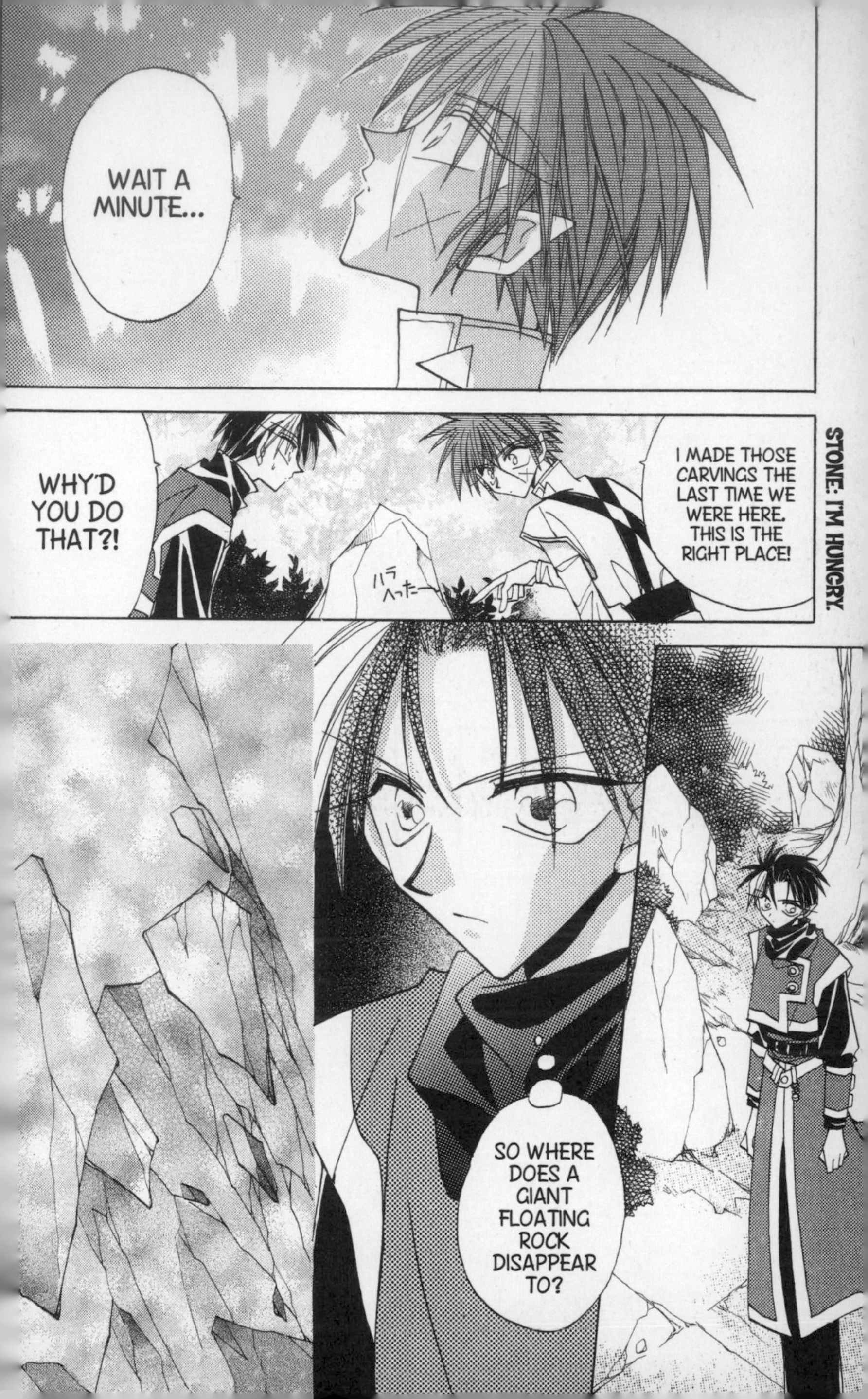
WAIT A MINUTE...
I MADE THOSE CARVINGS THE LAST TIME WE WERE HERE. THIS IS THE RIGHT PLACE!
ハラへったー
STONE: I'M HUNGRY.
WHY'D YOU DO THAT?!
SO WHERE DOES A GIANT FLOATING ROCK DISAPPEAR TO?

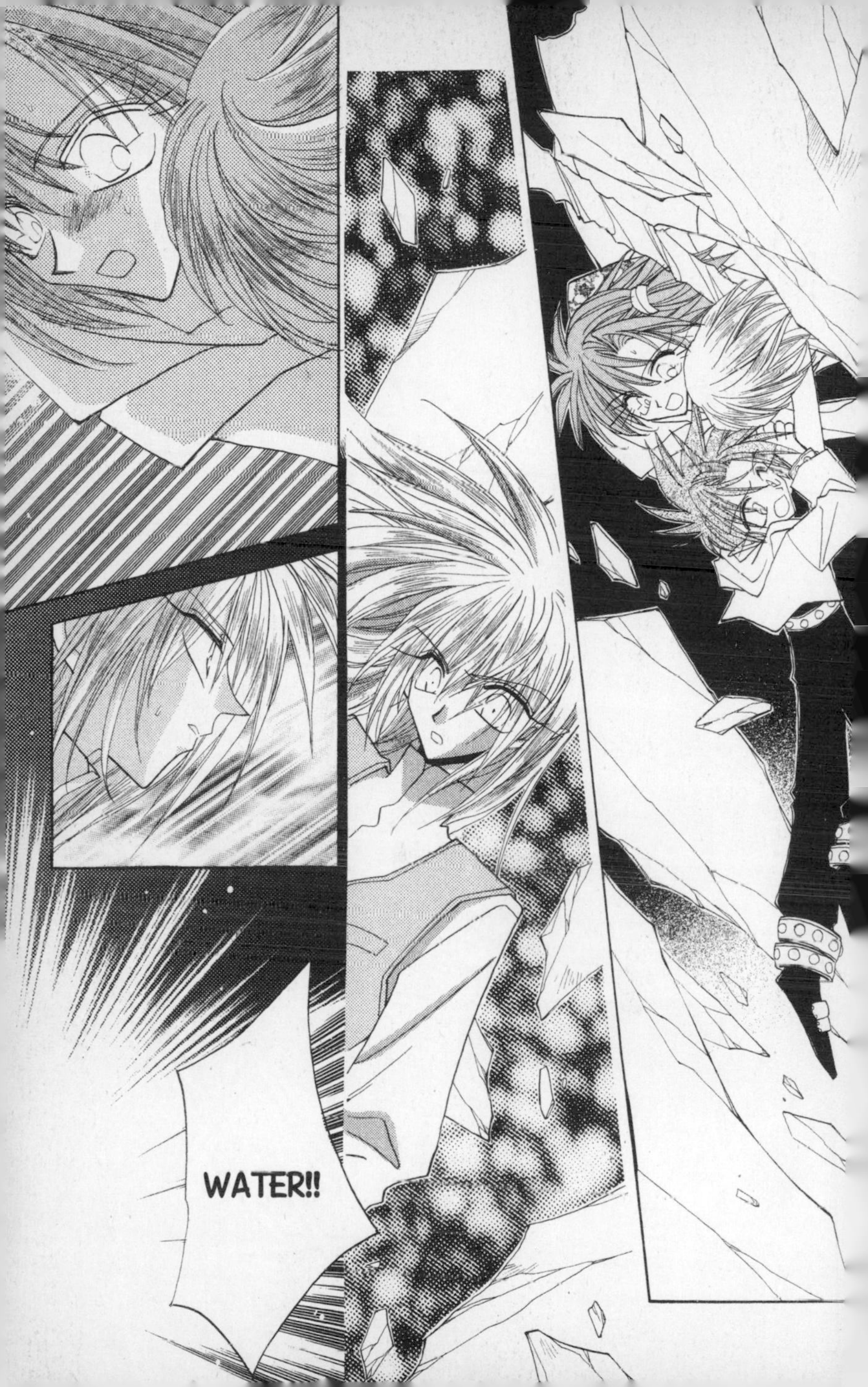
WATER!!

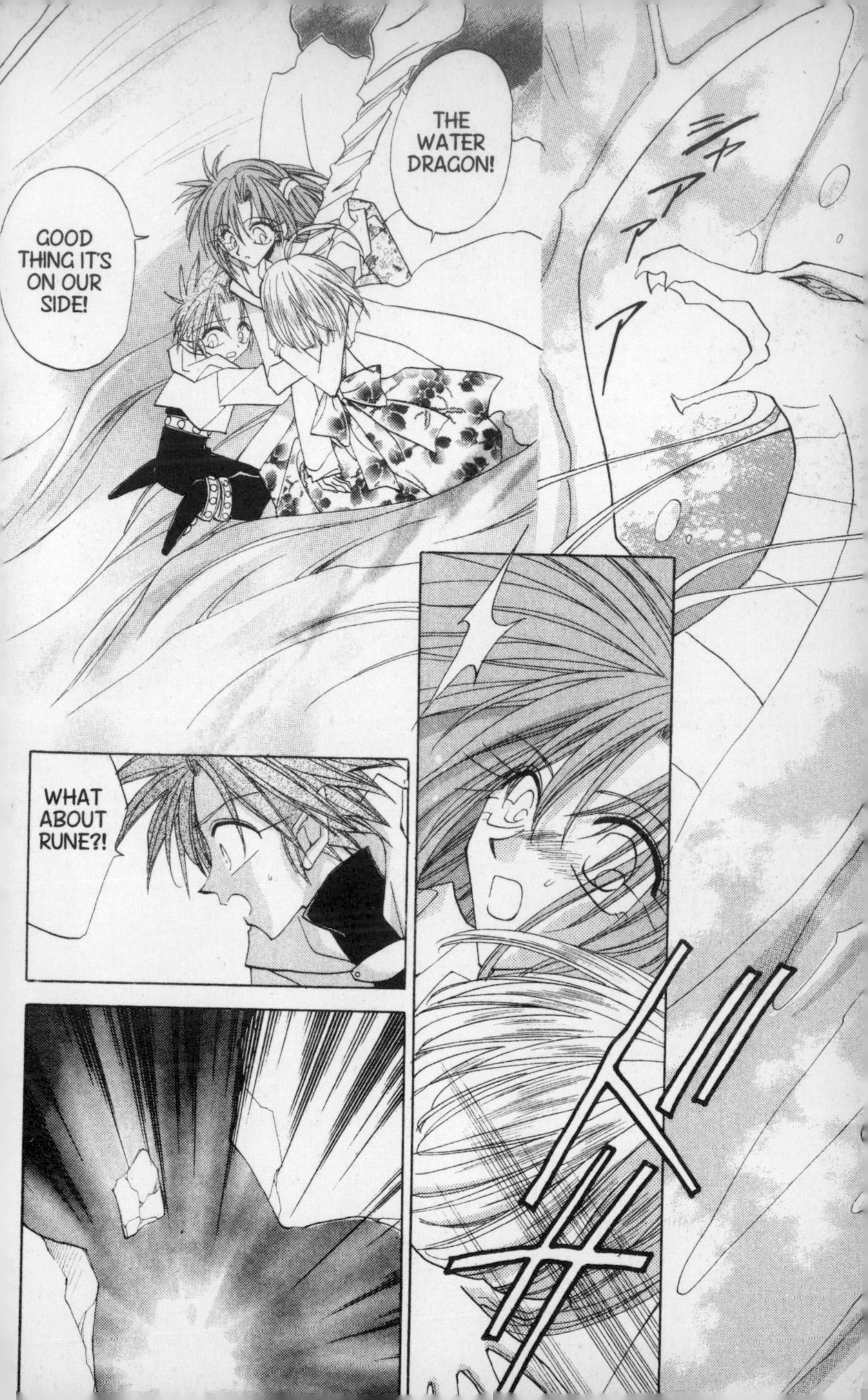
THE WATER DRAGON!
GOOD THING IT'S ON OUR SIDE!
シャアアア
WHAT ABOUT RUNE?!

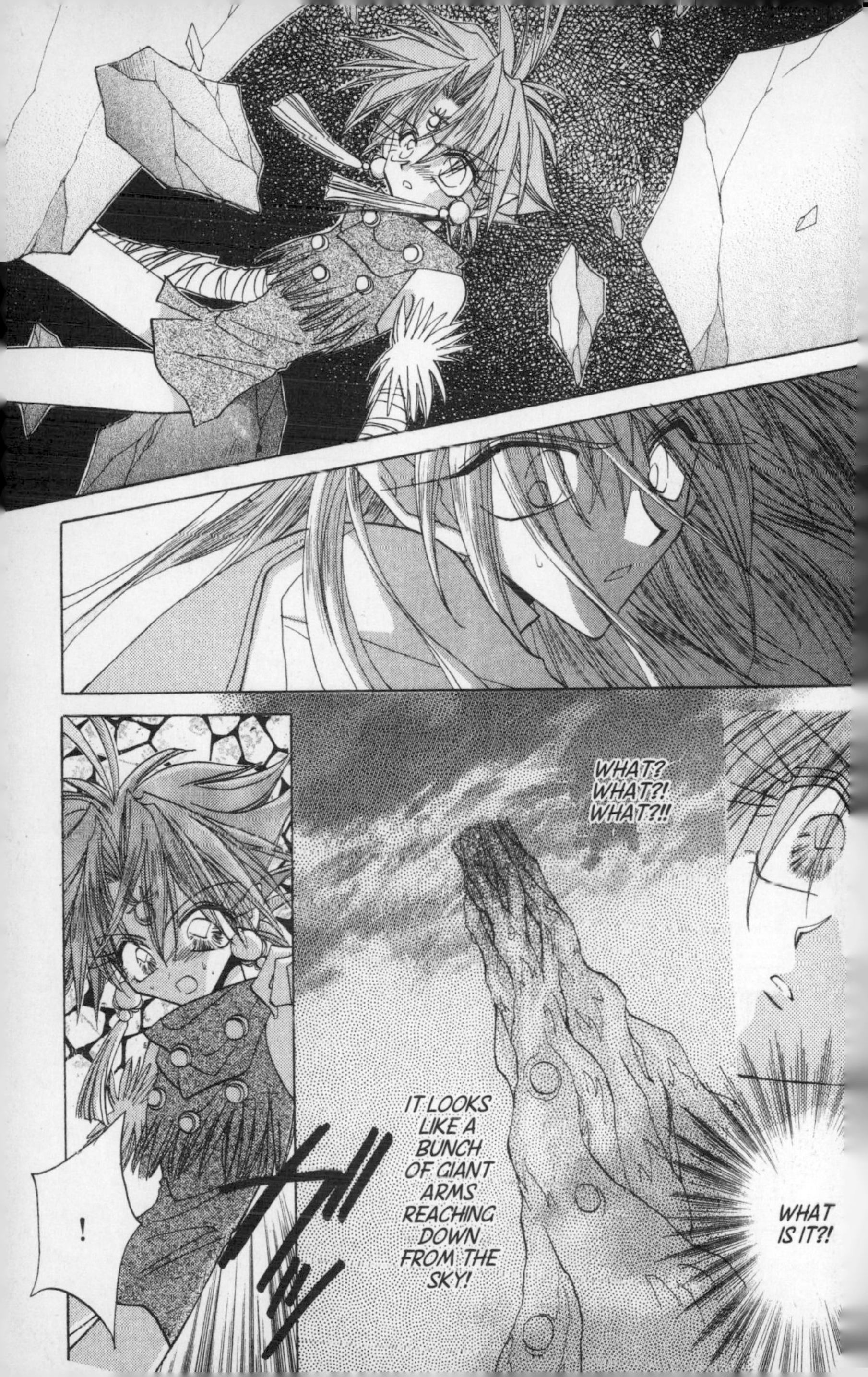
WHAT IS IT?!
WHAT? WHAT?! WHAT?!!
IT LOOKS LIKE A BUNCH OF GIANT ARMS REACHING DOWN FROM THE SKY!
!

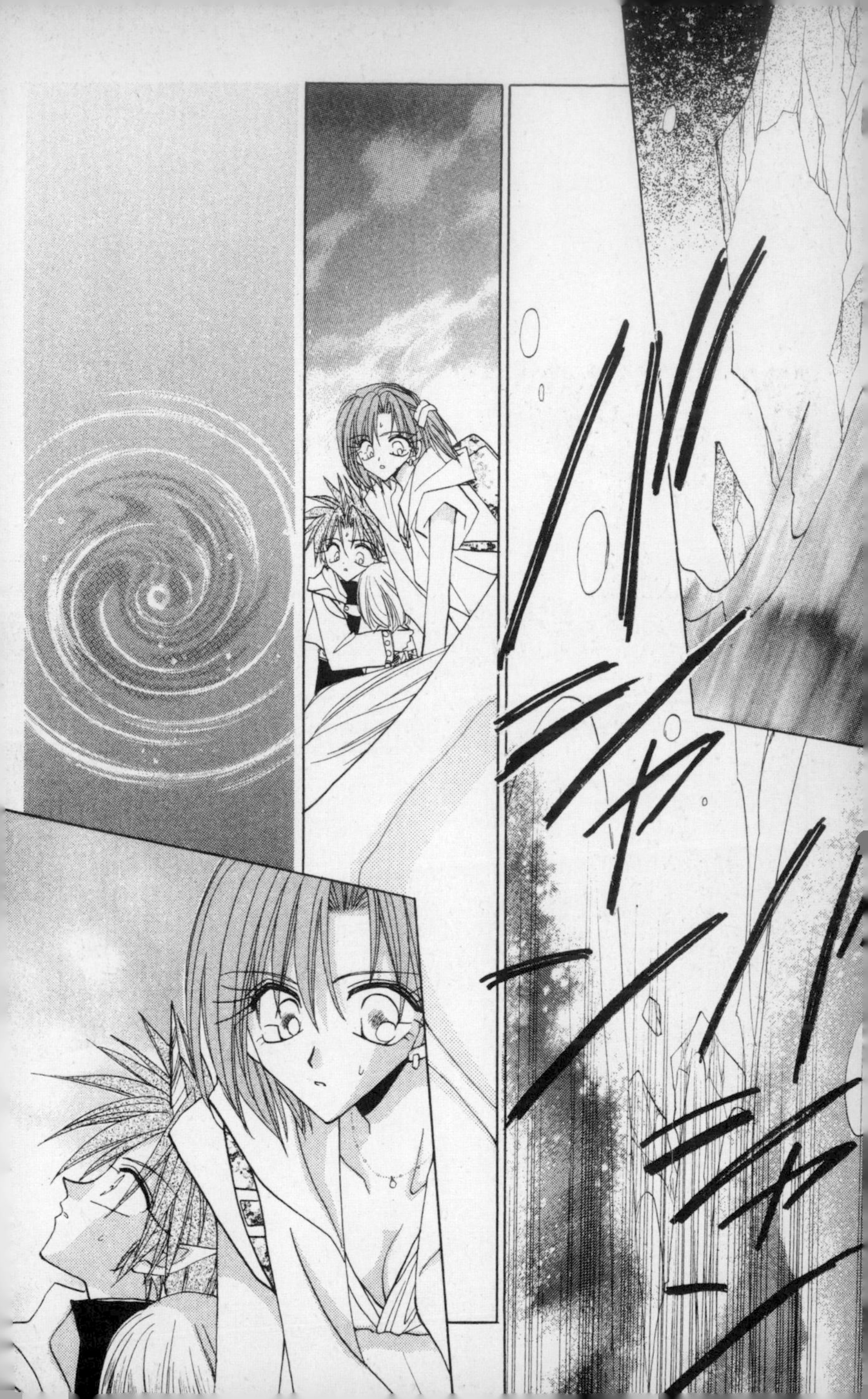

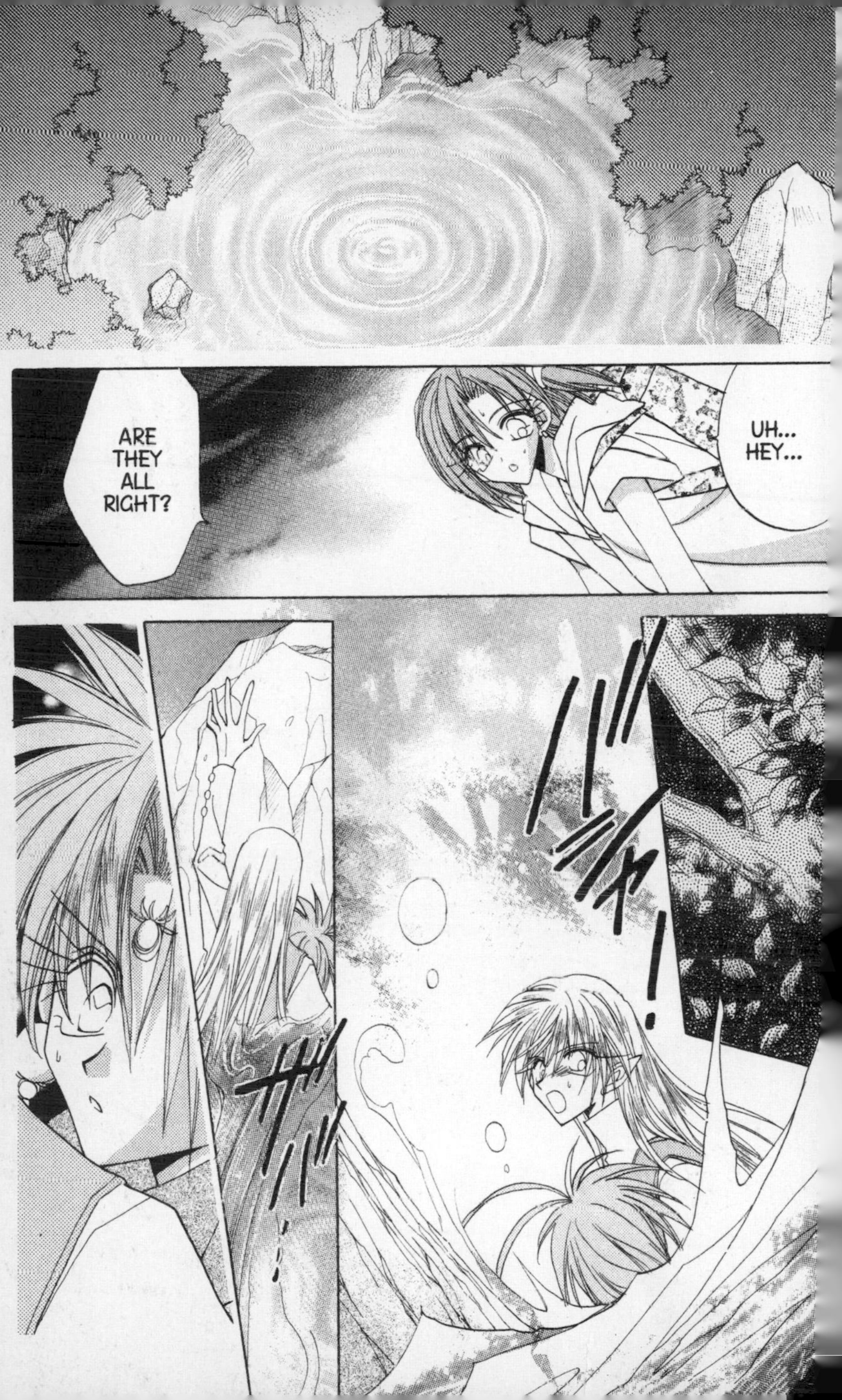
UH... HEY...
ARE THEY ALL RIGHT?

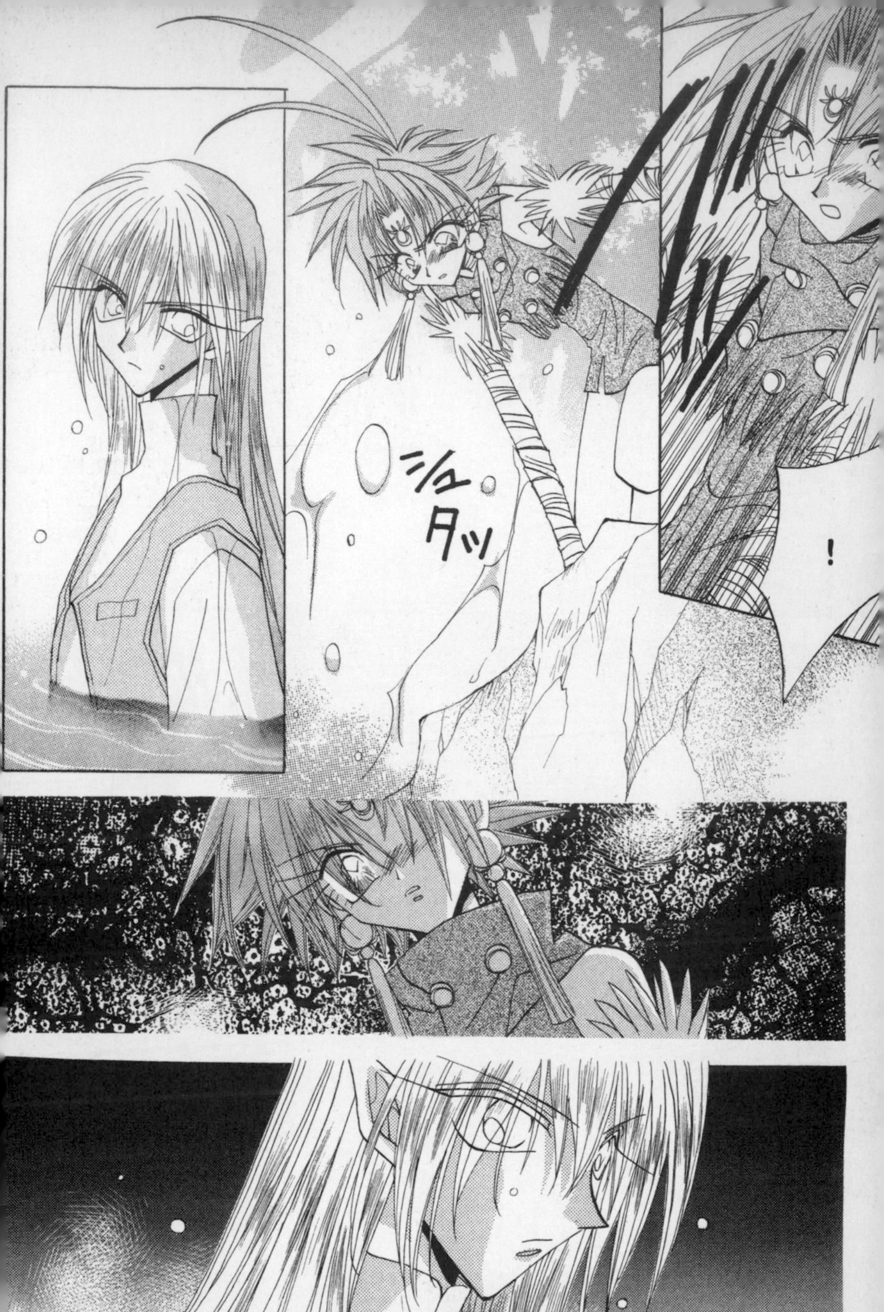
!
シュタッ

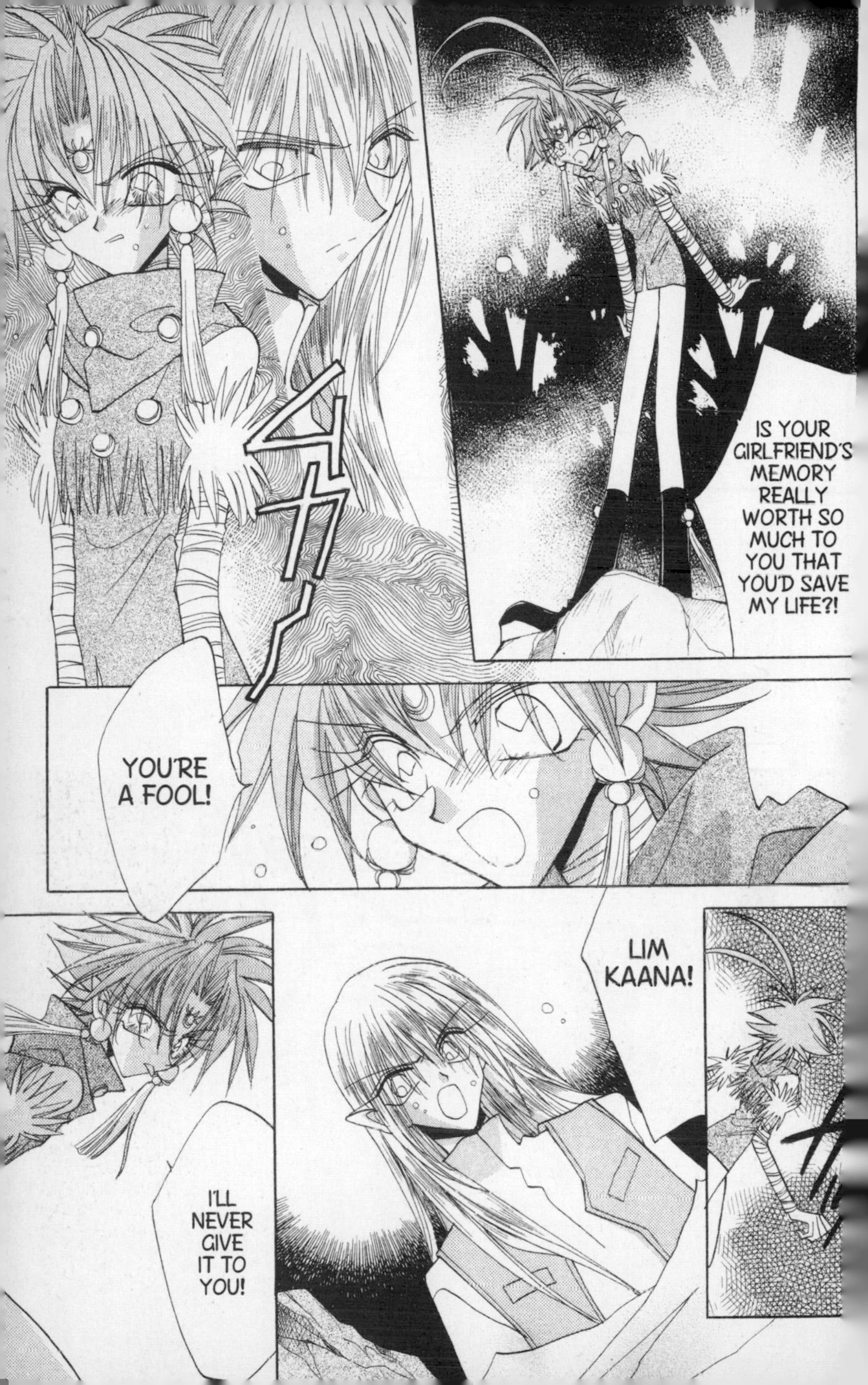
IS YOUR GIRLFRIEND'S MEMORY REALLY WORTH SO MUCH TO YOU THAT YOU'D SAVE MY LIFE?!
YOU'RE A FOOL!
LIM KAANA!
I'LL NEVER GIVE IT TO YOU!

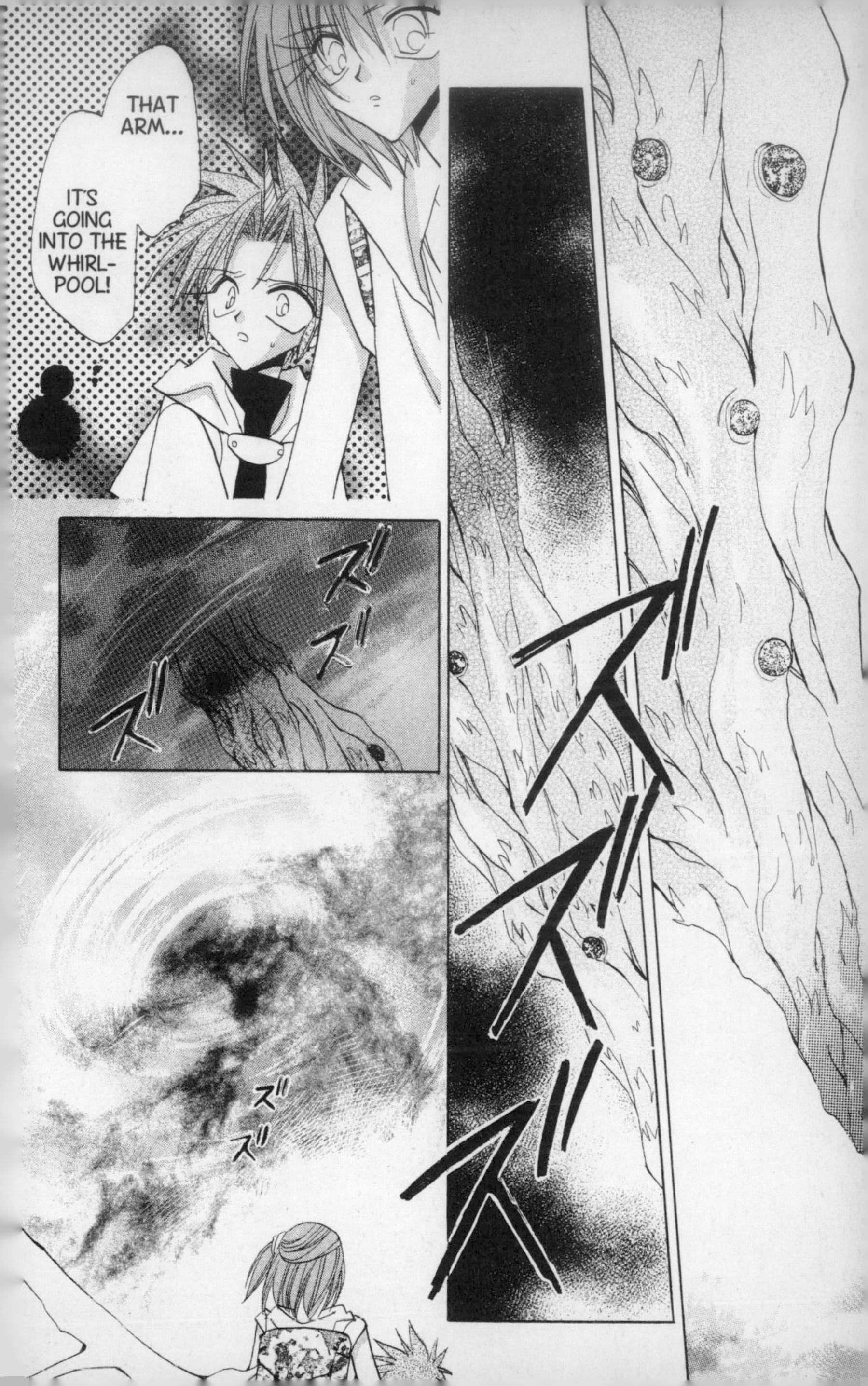
THAT ARM...
IT'S GOING INTO THE WHIRLPOOL!

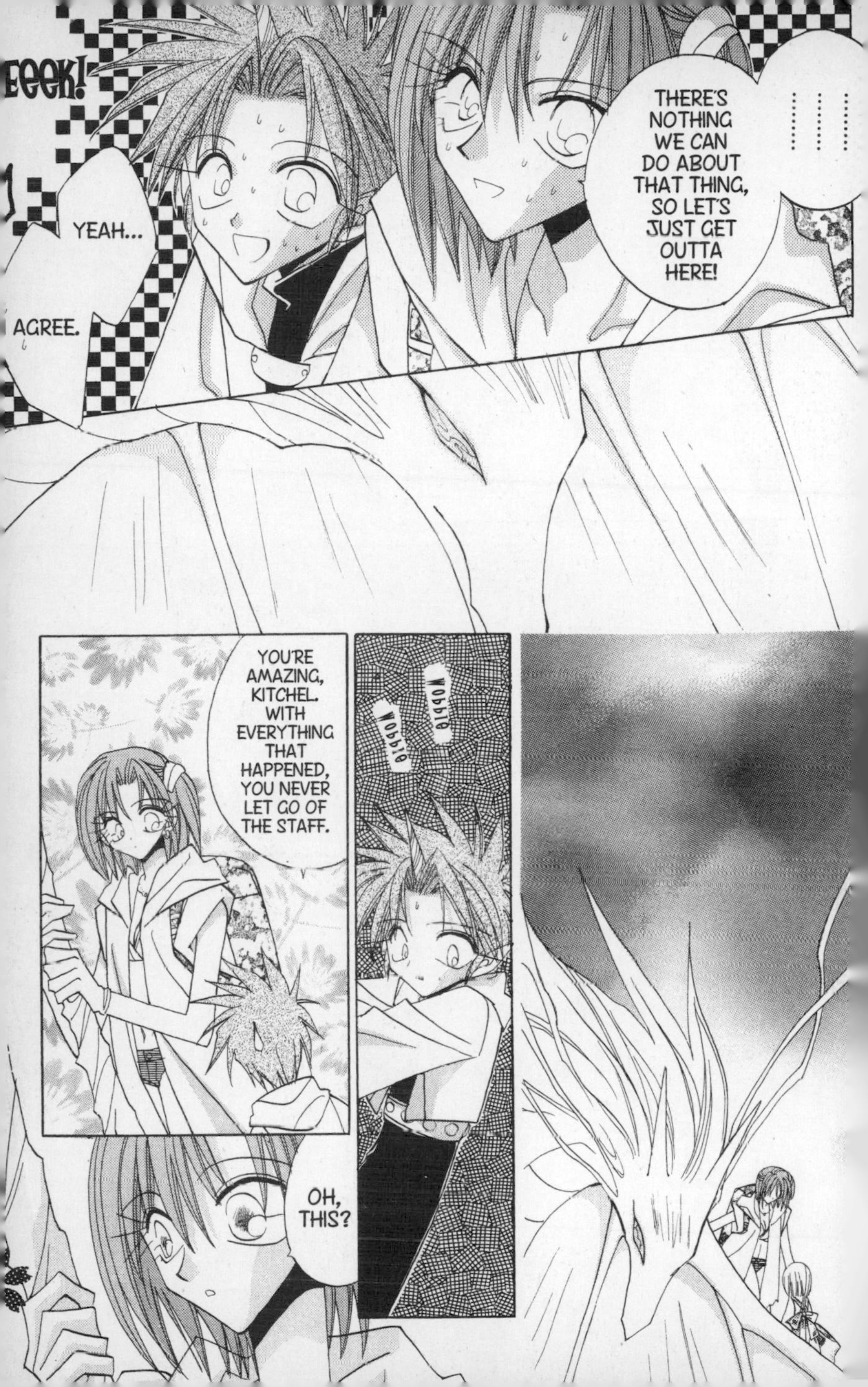
......
THERE'S NOTHING WE CAN DO ABOUT THAT THING, SO LET'S JUST GET OUTTA HERE!
EEEK!
YEAH...
AGREE.
Wobble
Wobble
YOU'RE AMAZING, KITCHEL. WITH EVERYTHING THAT HAPPENED, YOU NEVER LET GO OF THE STAFF.
OH, THIS?

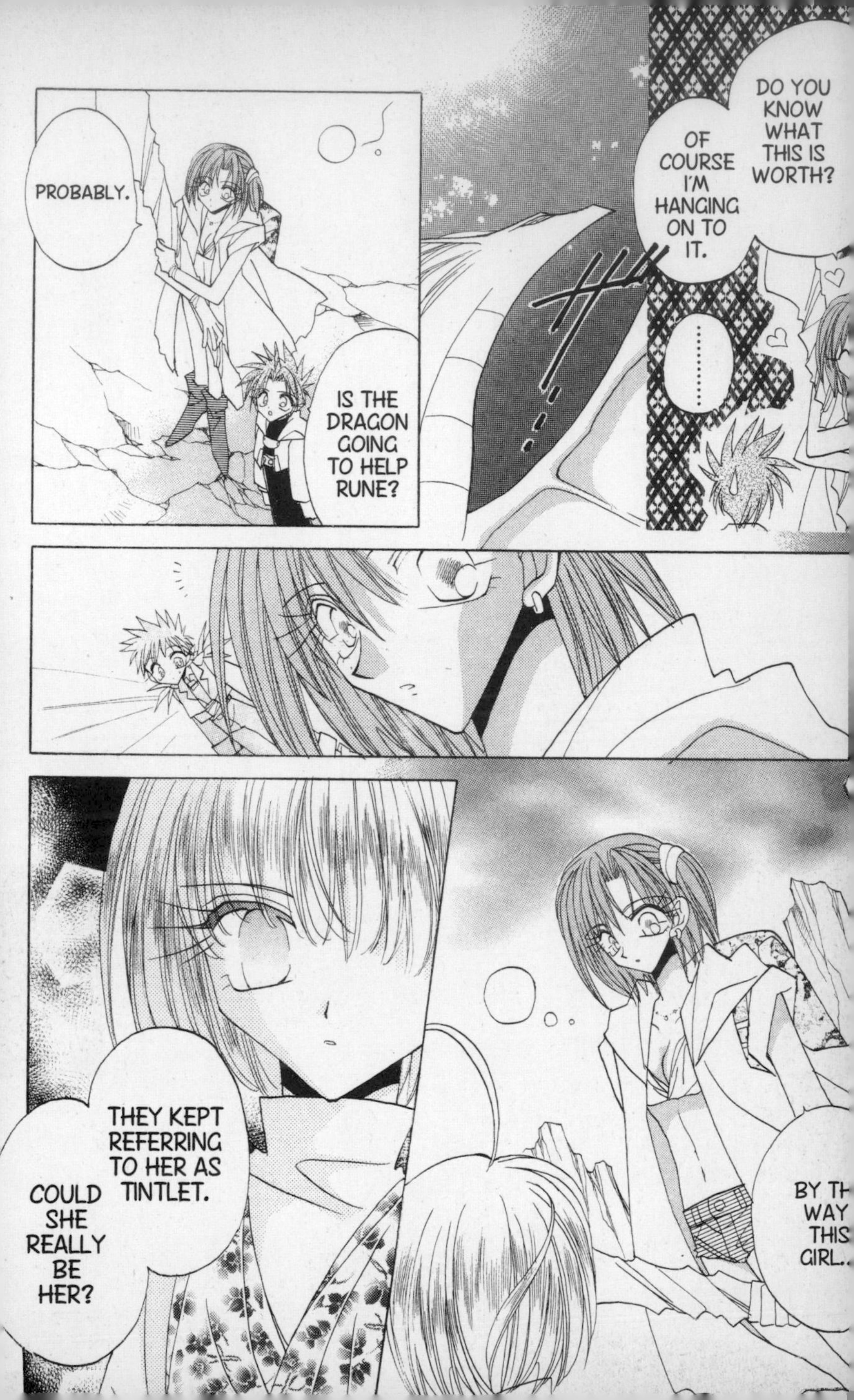
DO YOU KNOW WHAT THIS IS WORTH?
OF COURSE I'M HANGING ON TO IT.
......
IS THE DRAGON GOING TO HELP RUNE?
PROBABLY.
BY TH WAY THIS GIRL...
THEY KEPT REFERRING TO HER AS TINTLET.
COULD SHE REALLY BE HER?

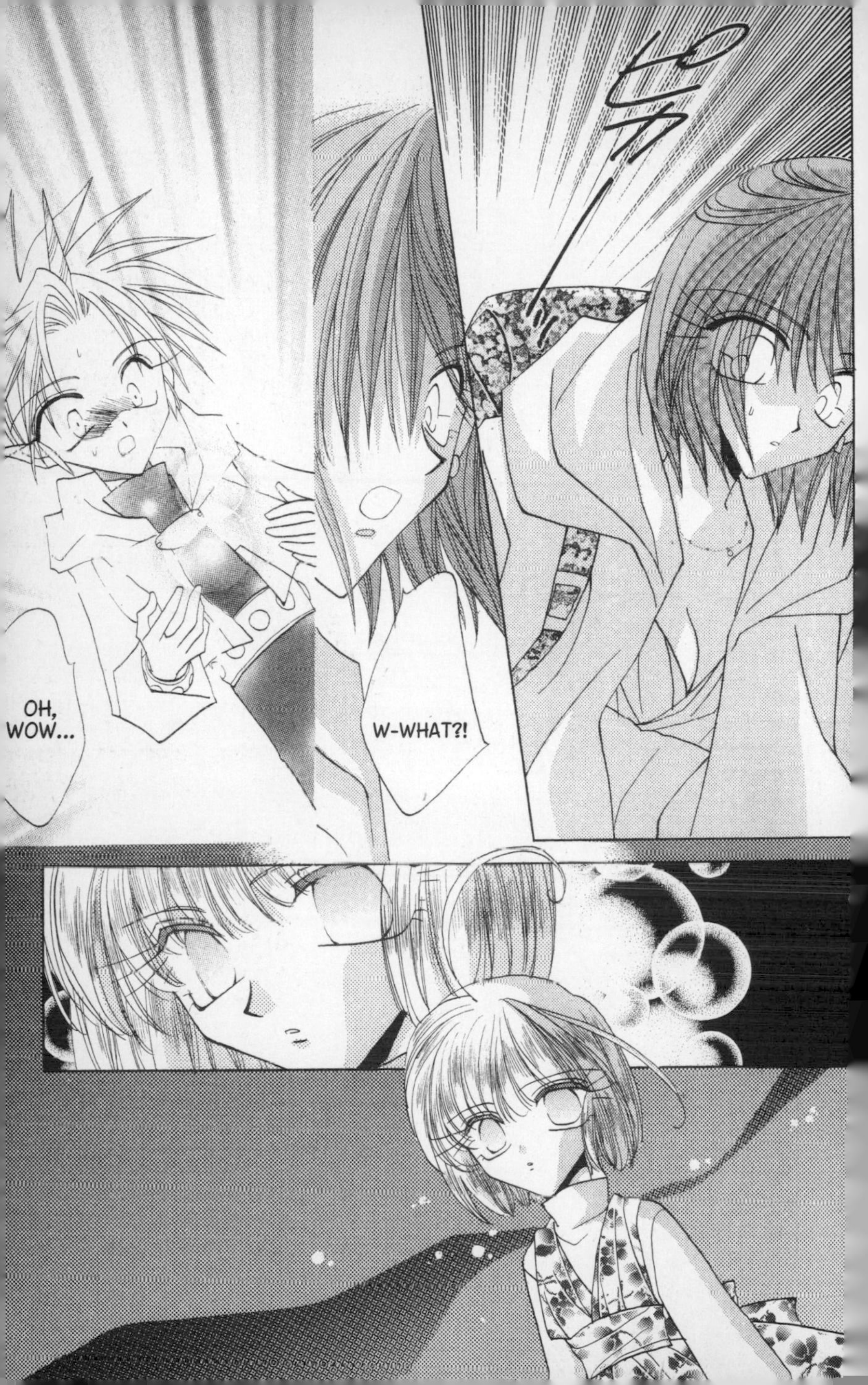
ピカー
W-WHAT?!
OH, WOW...

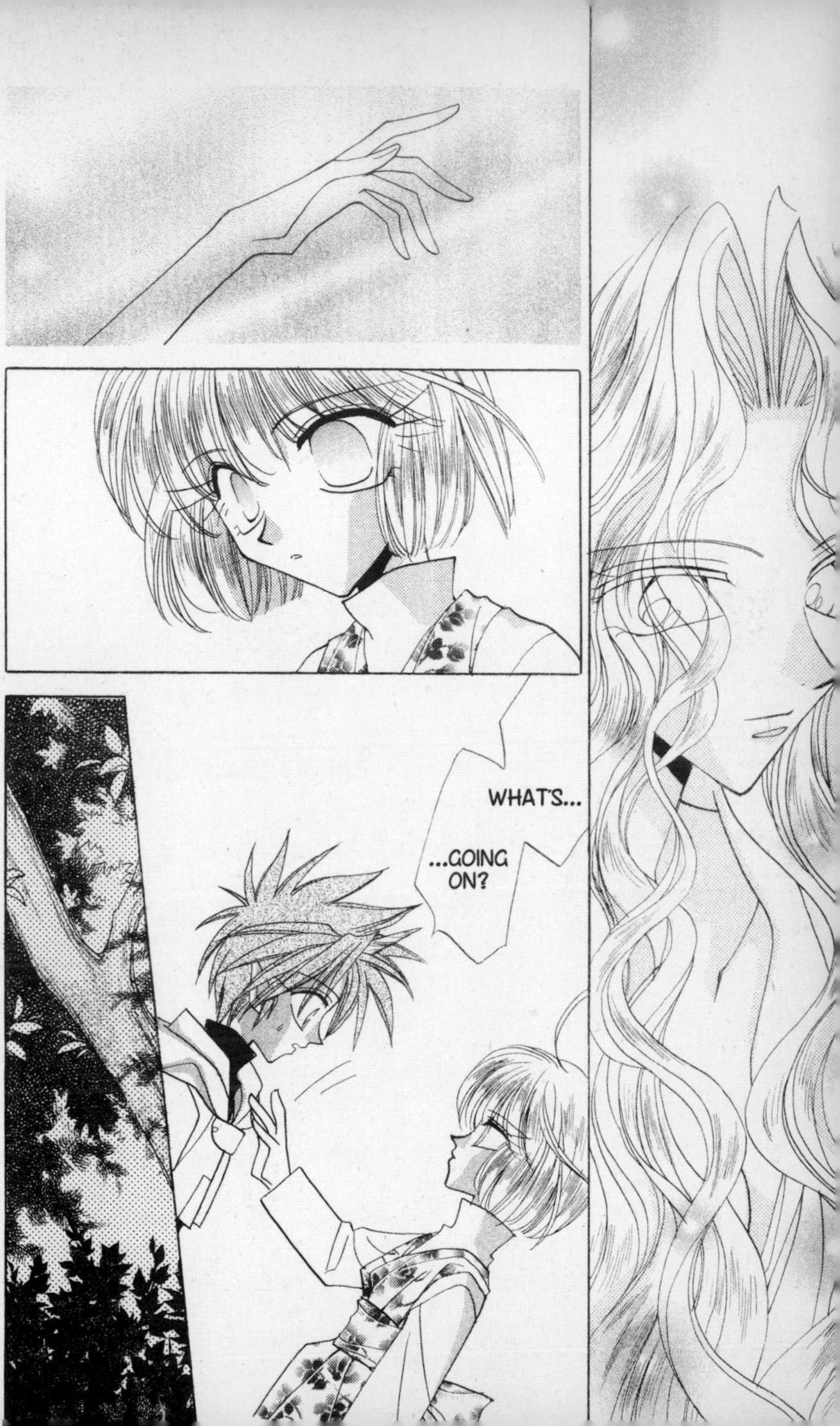
WHAT'S...
...GOING ON?

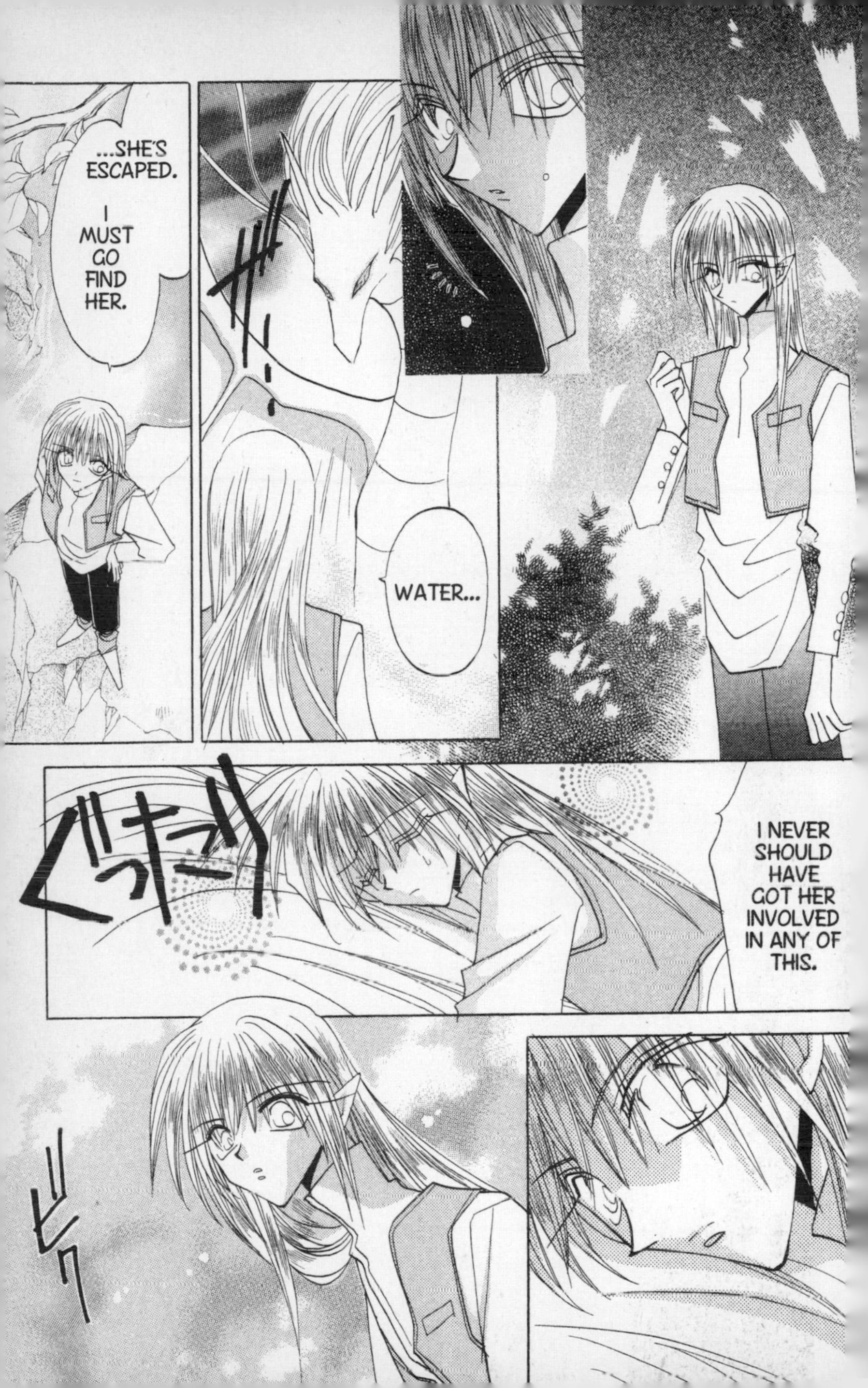
WATER...
...SHE'S ESCAPED.
I MUST GO FIND HER.
I NEVER SHOULD HAVE GOT HER INVOLVED IN ANY OF THIS.

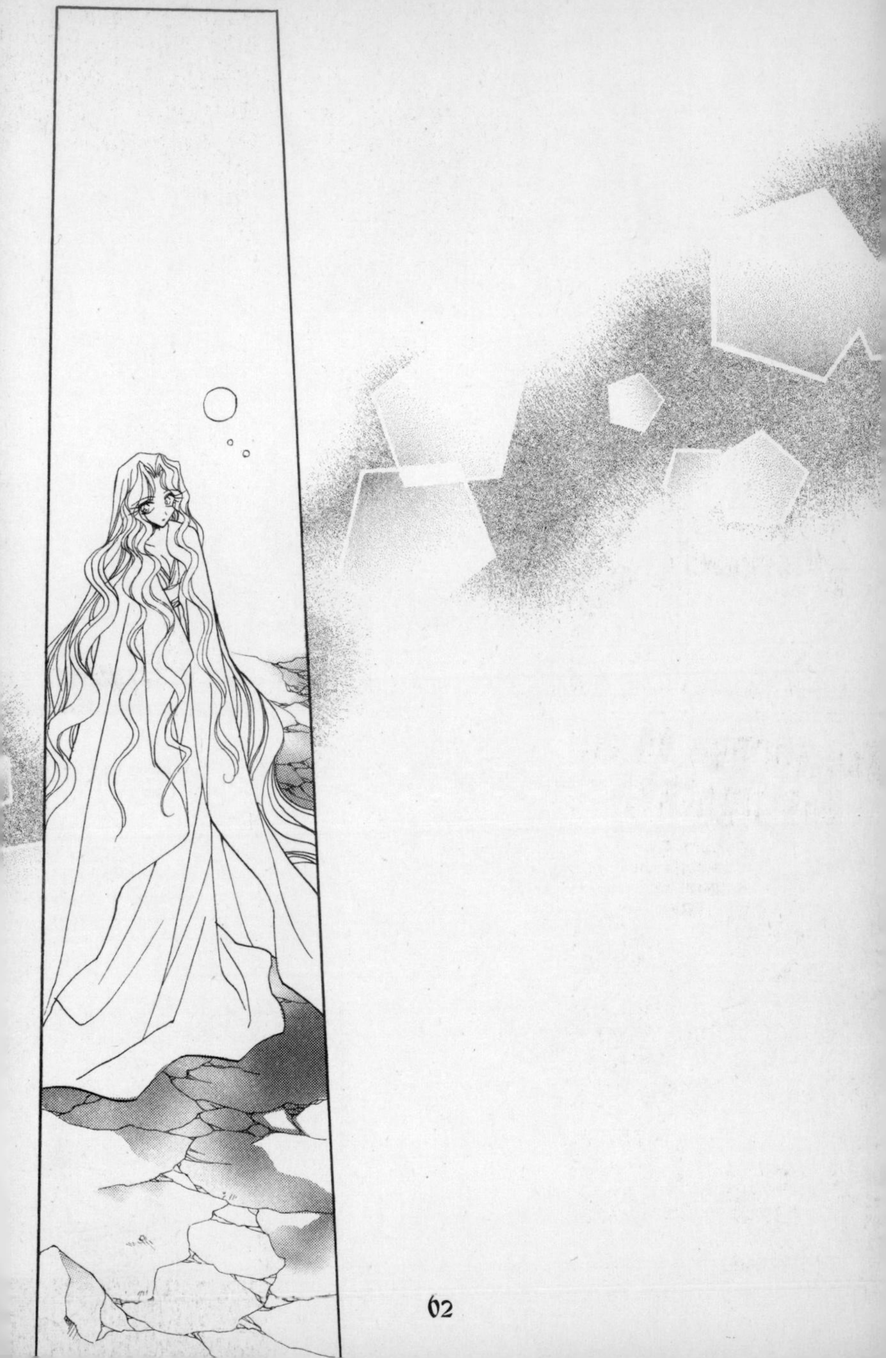

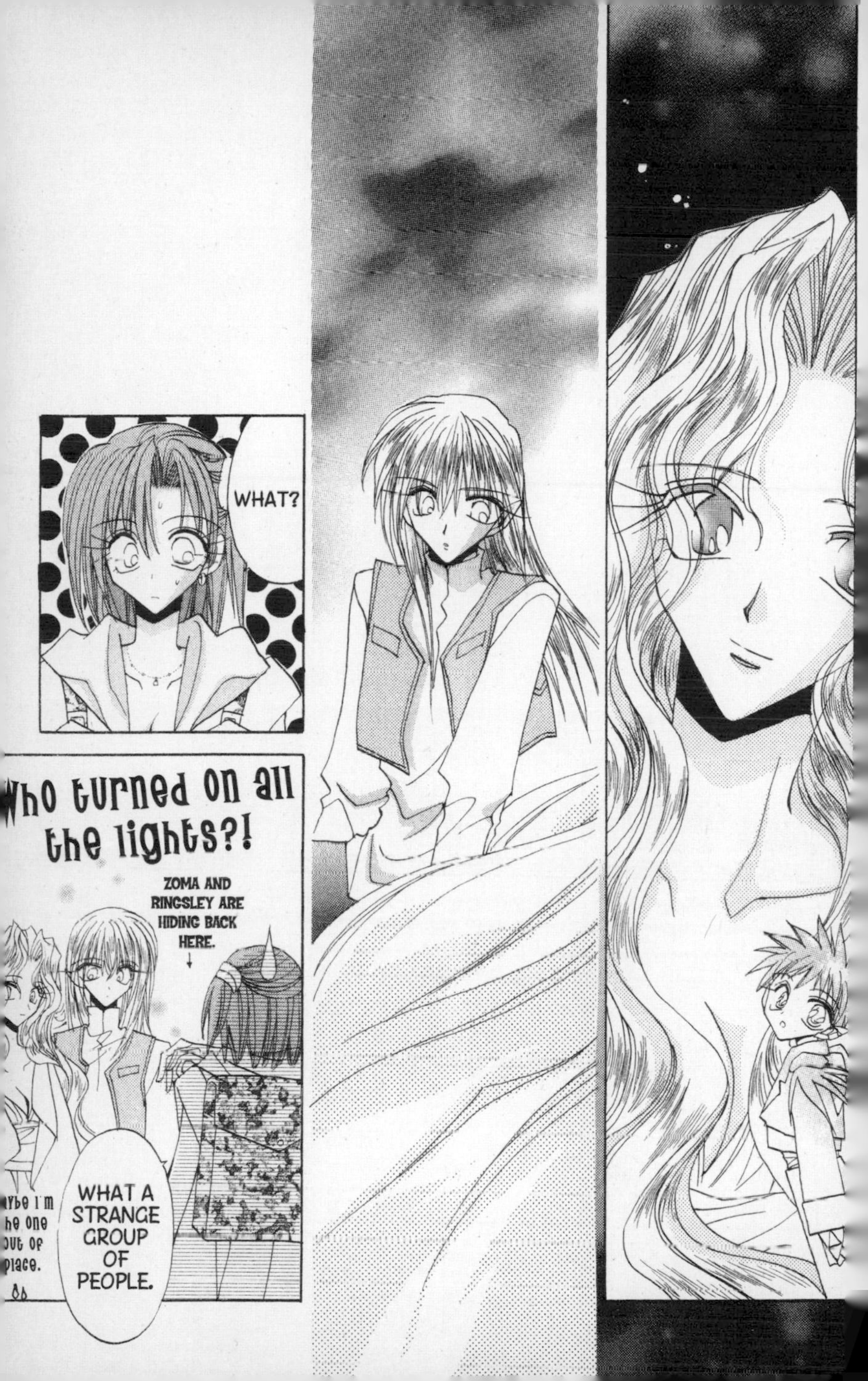
WHAT?
Who turned on all the lights?!
ZOMA AND RINGSLEY ARE HIDING BACK HERE.
WHAT A STRANGE GROUP OF PEOPLE.
aybe I'm he one out of place.

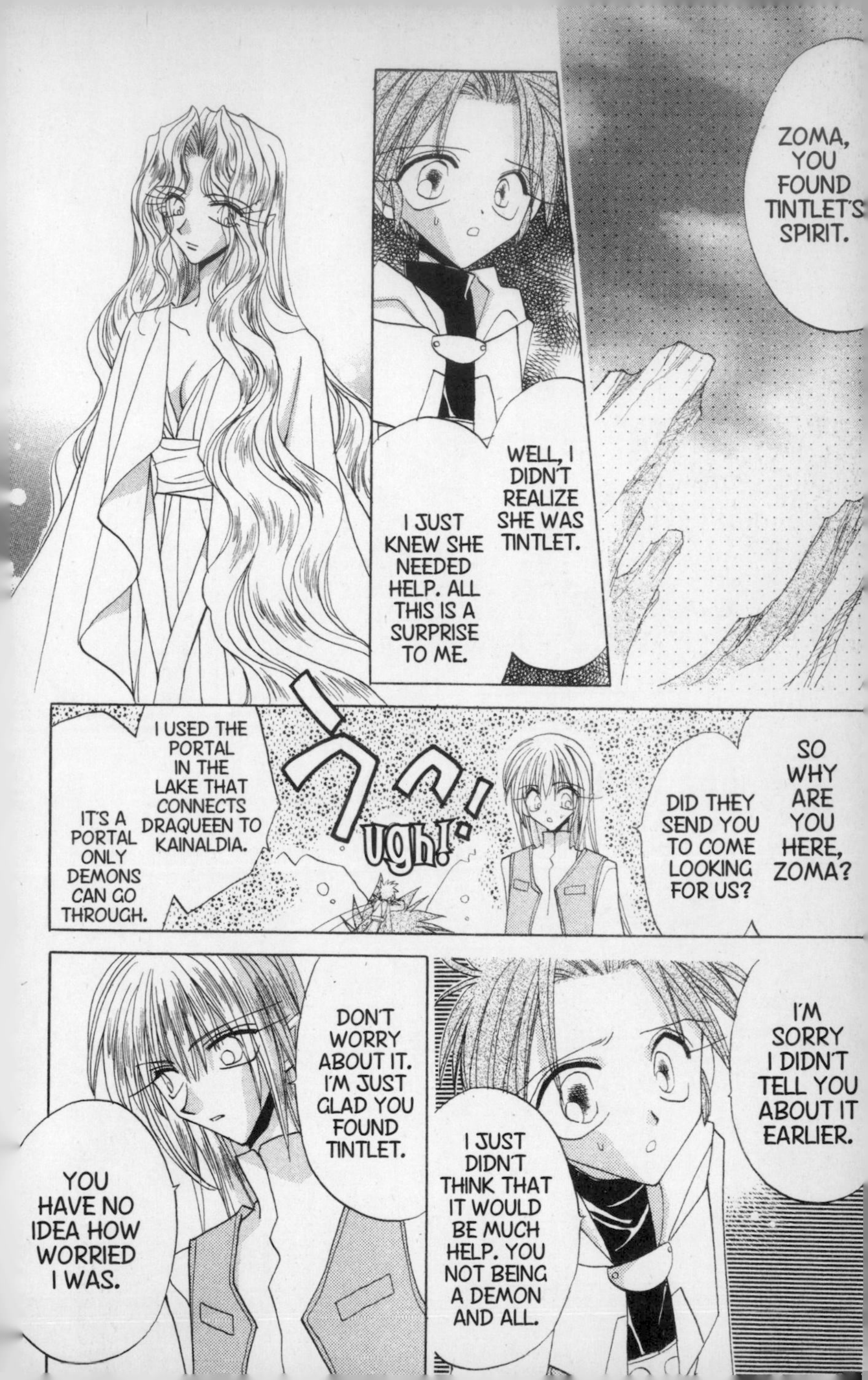
ZOMA, YOU FOUND TINTLET'S SPIRIT.
WELL, I DIDN'T REALIZE SHE WAS TINTLET.
I JUST KNEW SHE NEEDED HELP. ALL THIS IS A SURPRISE TO ME.
SO WHY ARE YOU HERE, ZOMA?
DID THEY SEND YOU TO COME LOOKING FOR US?
UGH!
I USED THE PORTAL IN THE LAKE THAT CONNECTS DRAQUEEN TO KAINALDIA.
IT'S A PORTAL ONLY DEMONS CAN GO THROUGH.
I'M SORRY I DIDN'T TELL YOU ABOUT IT EARLIER.
I JUST DIDN'T THINK THAT IT WOULD BE MUCH HELP. YOU NOT BEING A DEMON AND ALL.
DON'T WORRY ABOUT IT. I'M JUST GLAD YOU FOUND TINTLET.
YOU HAVE NO IDEA HOW WORRIED I WAS.

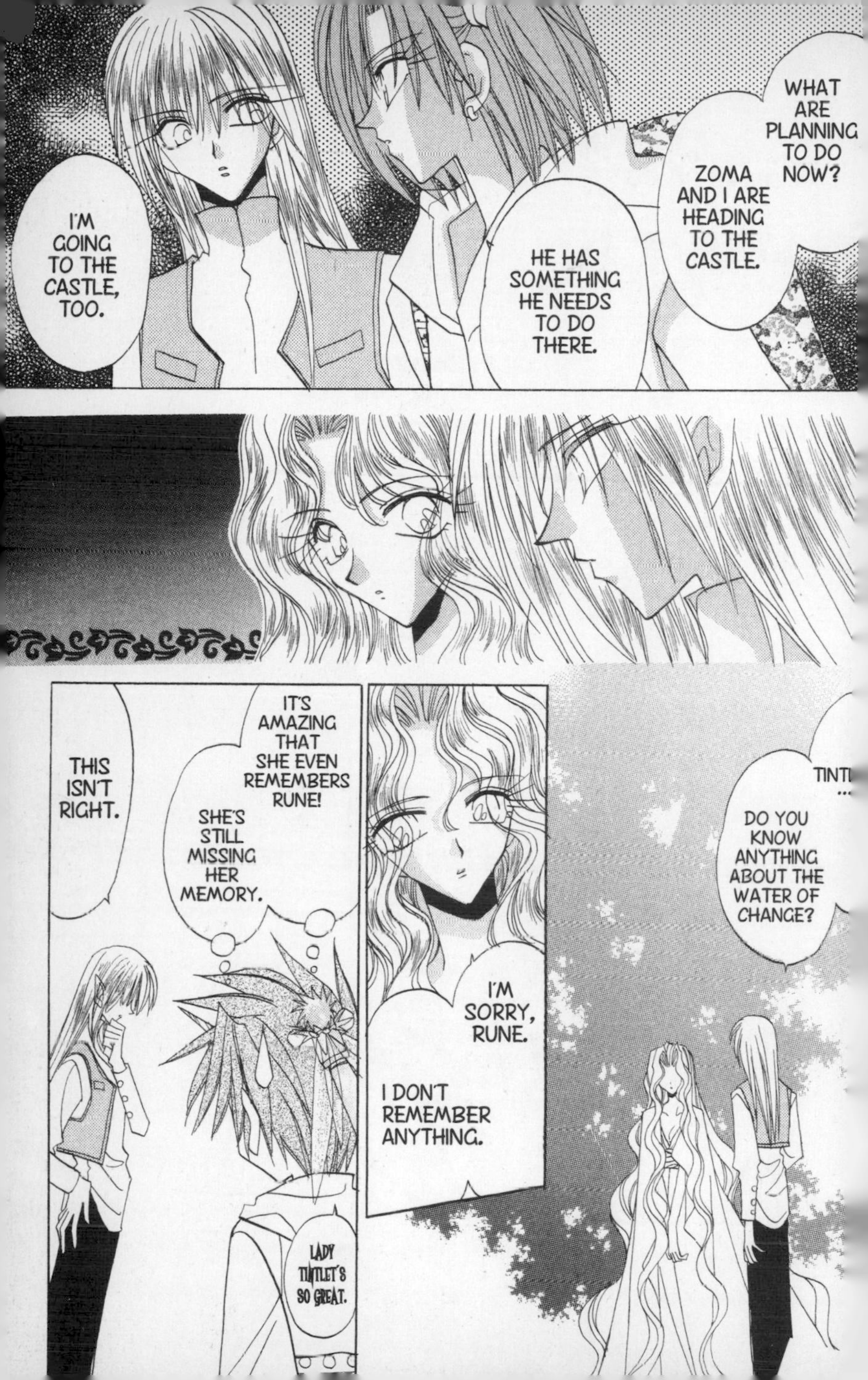
WHAT ARE PLANNING TO DO NOW?
ZOMA AND I ARE HEADING TO THE CASTLE.
HE HAS SOMETHING HE NEEDS TO DO THERE.
I'M GOING TO THE CASTLE, TOO.
TINTL...
DO YOU KNOW ANYTHING ABOUT THE WATER OF CHANGE?
I'M SORRY, RUNE.
I DON'T REMEMBER ANYTHING.
IT'S AMAZING THAT SHE EVEN REMEMBERS RUNE!
SHE'S STILL MISSING HER MEMORY.
THIS ISN'T RIGHT.
LADY TINTLET'S SO GREAT.

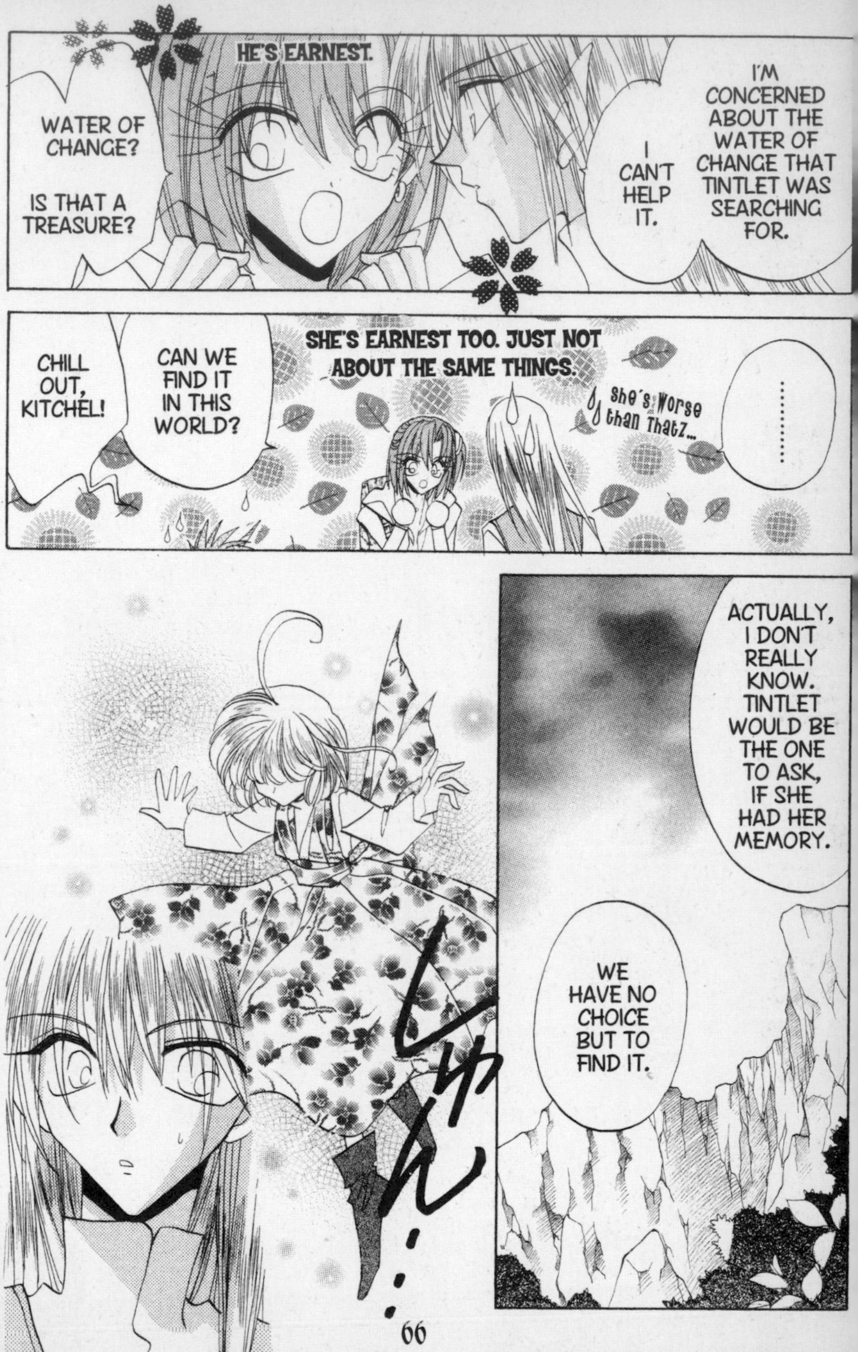
I'M CONCERNED ABOUT THE WATER OF CHANGE THAT TINTLET WAS SEARCHING FOR.
I CAN'T HELP IT.
HE'S EARNEST.
WATER OF CHANGE?
IS THAT A TREASURE?
......
She's worse than Thatz...
SHE'S EARNEST TOO. JUST NOT ABOUT THE SAME THINGS.
CAN WE FIND IT IN THIS WORLD?
CHILL OUT, KITCHEL!
ACTUALLY, I DON'T REALLY KNOW. TINTLET WOULD BE THE ONE TO ASK, IF SHE HAD HER MEMORY.
WE HAVE NO CHOICE BUT TO FIND IT.
しゅん...

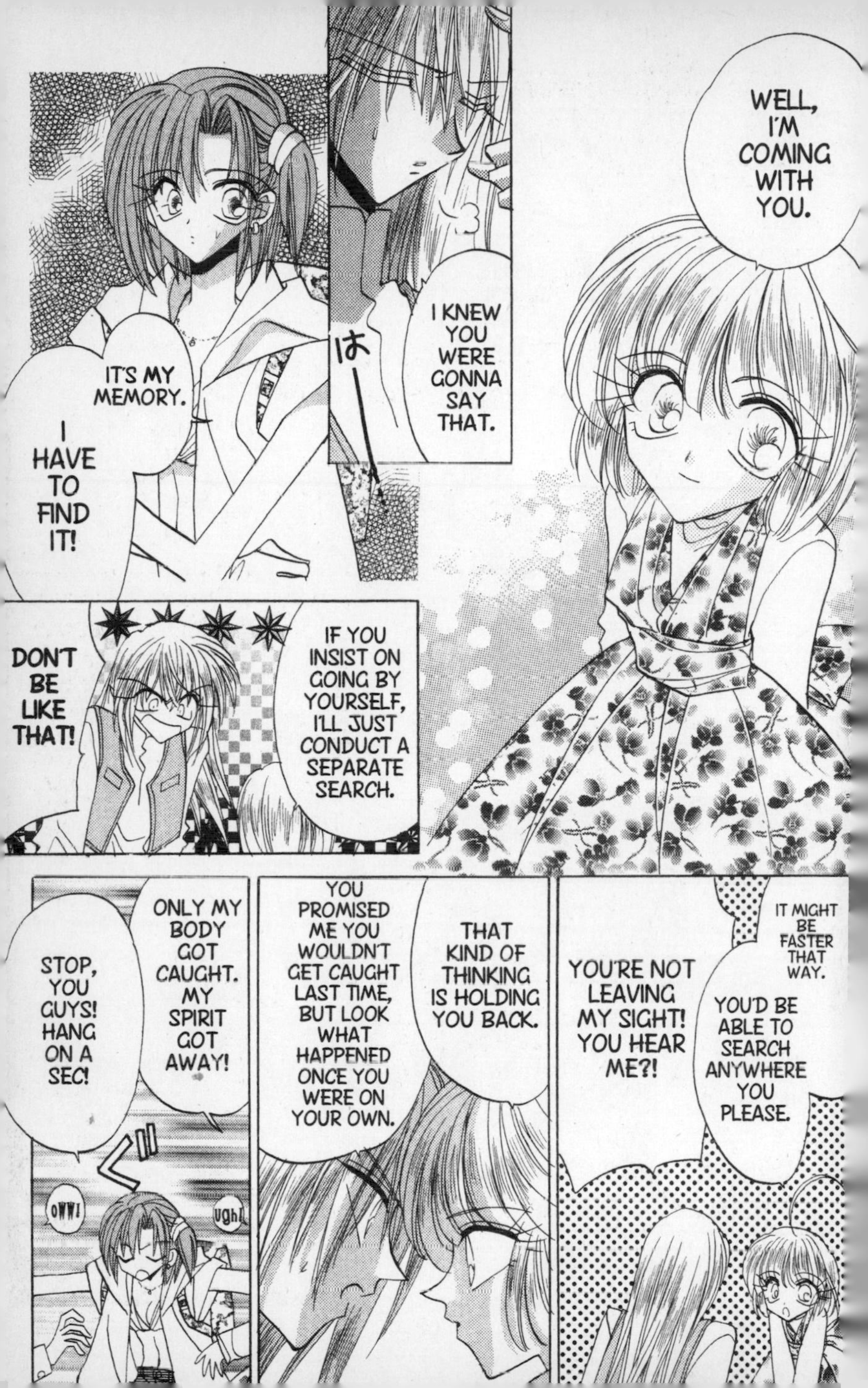
WELL, I'M COMING WITH YOU.
I KNEW YOU WERE GONNA SAY THAT.
は
IT'S MY MEMORY.
I HAVE TO FIND IT!
IF YOU INSIST ON GOING BY YOURSELF, I'LL JUST CONDUCT A SEPARATE SEARCH.
DON'T BE LIKE THAT!
IT MIGHT BE FASTER THAT WAY.
YOU'D BE ABLE TO SEARCH ANYWHERE YOU PLEASE.
YOU'RE NOT LEAVING MY SIGHT! YOU HEAR ME?!
THAT KIND OF THINKING IS HOLDING YOU BACK.
YOU PROMISED ME YOU WOULDN'T GET CAUGHT LAST TIME, BUT LOOK WHAT HAPPENED ONCE YOU WERE ON YOUR OWN.
ONLY MY BODY GOT CAUGHT. MY SPIRIT GOT AWAY!
STOP, YOU GUYS! HANG ON A SEC!
ugh!
OWW!

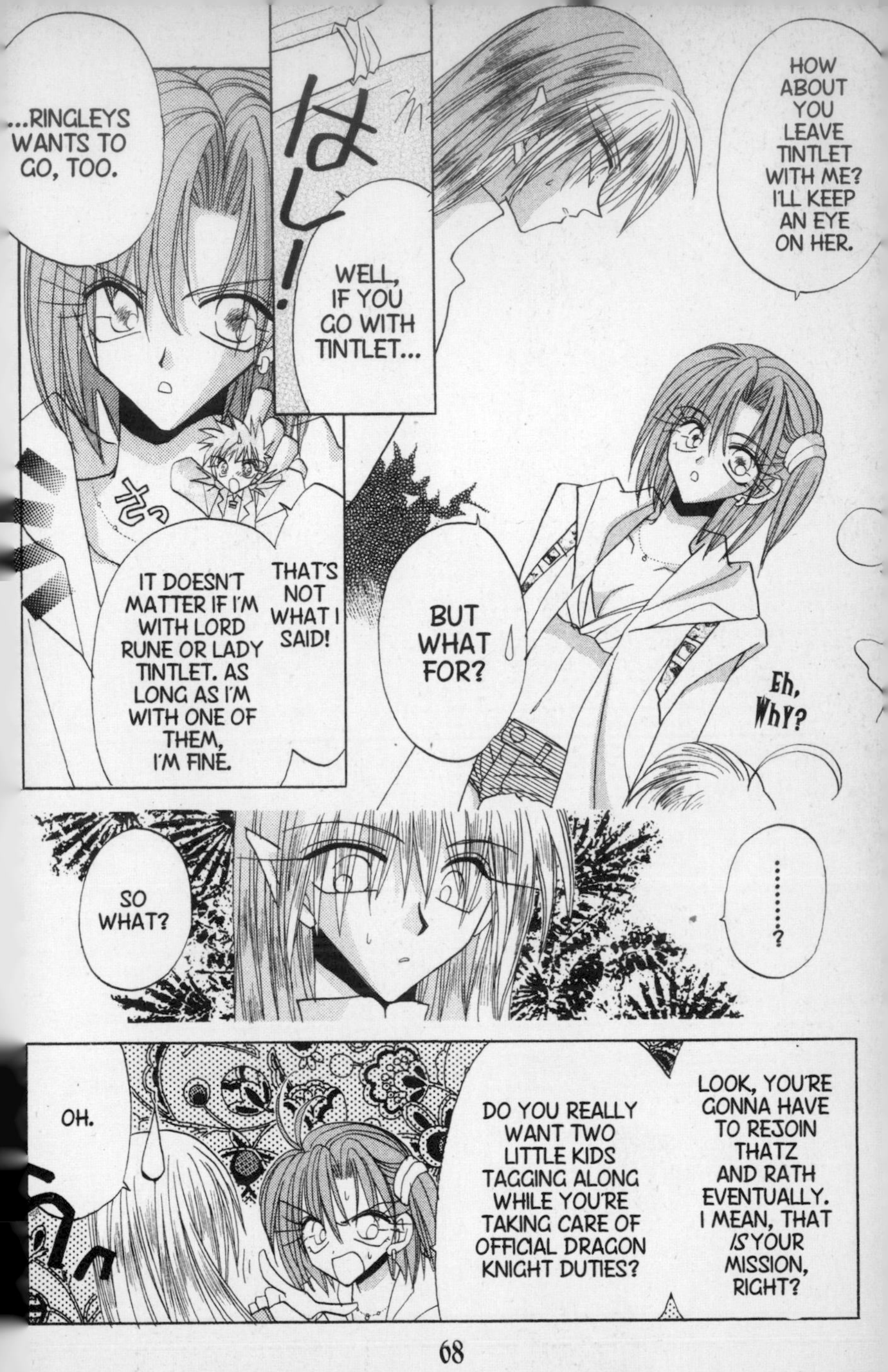
HOW ABOUT YOU LEAVE TINTLET WITH ME? I'LL KEEP AN EYE ON HER.
はし!
WELL, IF YOU GO WITH TINTLET...
...RINGLEYS WANTS TO GO, TOO.
Eh, Why?
BUT WHAT FOR?
THAT'S NOT WHAT I SAID!
さっ
IT DOESN'T MATTER IF I'M WITH LORD RUNE OR LADY TINTLET. AS LONG AS I'M WITH ONE OF THEM, I'M FINE.
......?
SO WHAT?
LOOK, YOU'RE GONNA HAVE TO REJOIN THATZ AND RATH EVENTUALLY. I MEAN, THAT *IS* YOUR MISSION, RIGHT?
DO YOU REALLY WANT TWO LITTLE KIDS TAGGING ALONG WHILE YOU'RE TAKING CARE OF OFFICIAL DRAGON KNIGHT DUTIES?
OH.

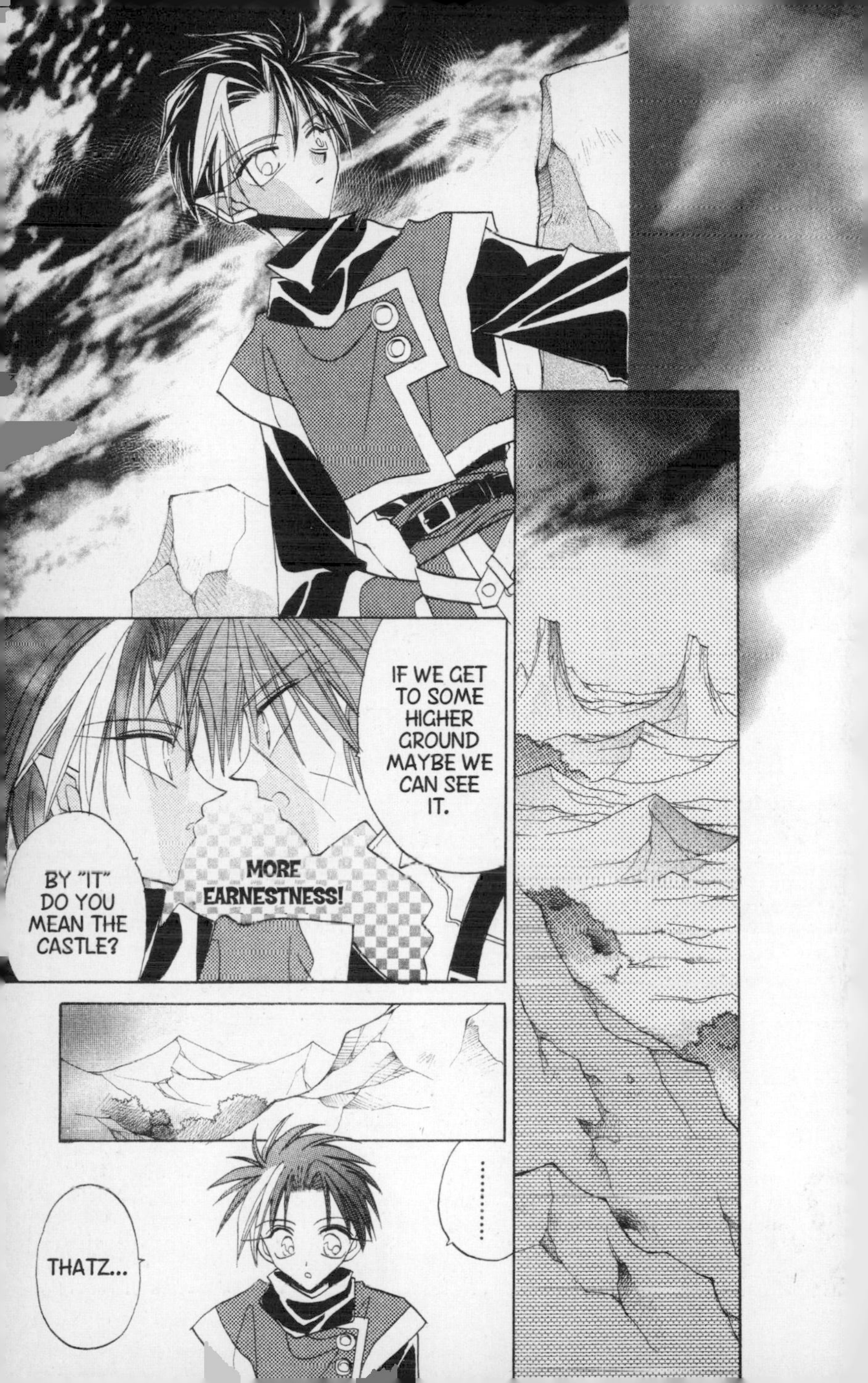
IF WE GET TO SOME HIGHER GROUND MAYBE WE CAN SEE IT.
MORE EARNESTNESS!
BY "IT" DO YOU MEAN THE CASTLE?
....
THATZ...

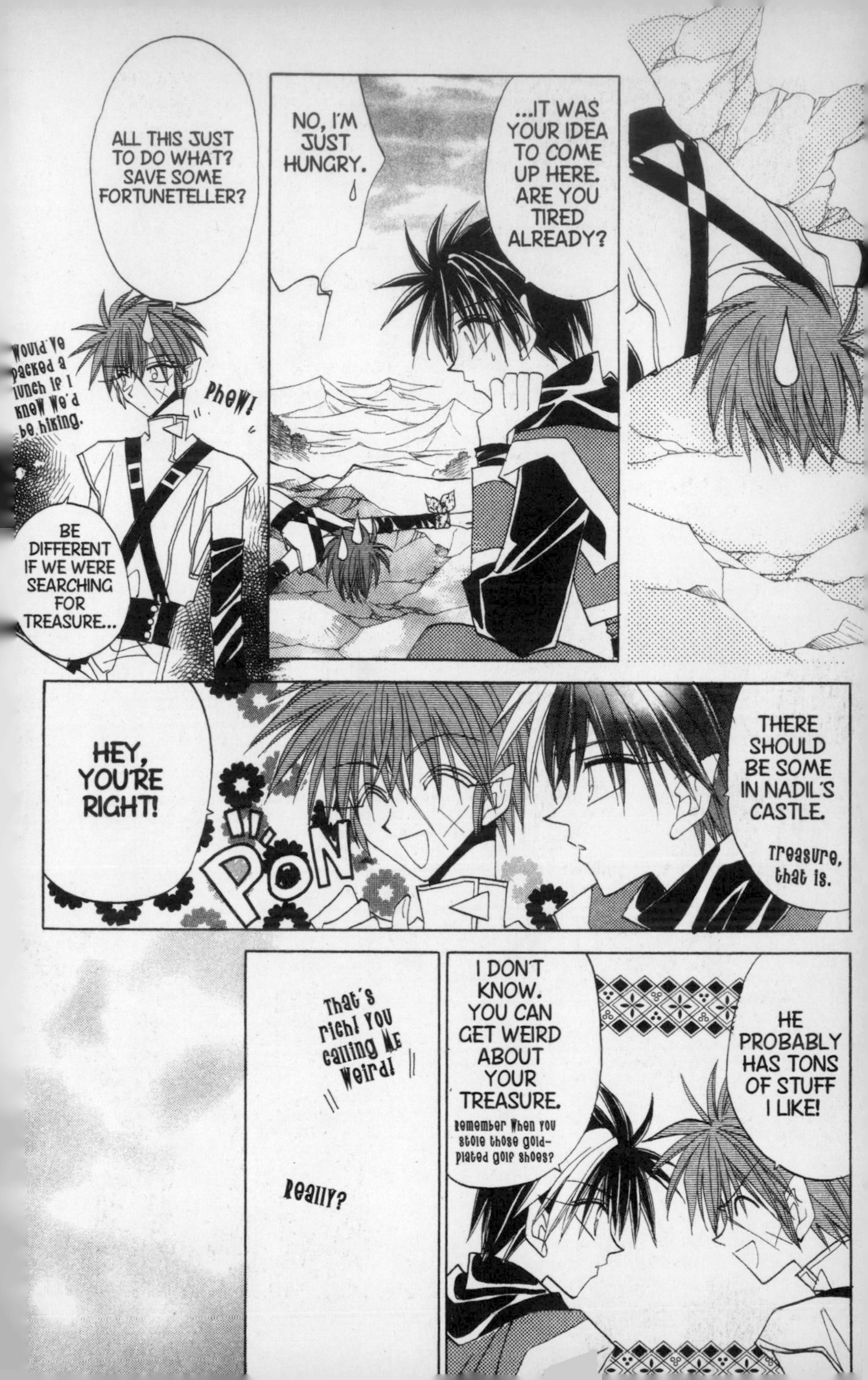
...IT WAS YOUR IDEA TO COME UP HERE. ARE YOU TIRED ALREADY?
NO, I'M JUST HUNGRY.
ALL THIS JUST TO DO WHAT? SAVE SOME FORTUNETELLER?
PHEW!
Would've packed a lunch if I knew we'd be hiking.
BE DIFFERENT IF WE WERE SEARCHING FOR TREASURE...
THERE SHOULD BE SOME IN NADIL'S CASTLE.
Treasure, that is.
HEY, YOU'RE RIGHT!
PON
HE PROBABLY HAS TONS OF STUFF I LIKE!
I DON'T KNOW. YOU CAN GET WEIRD ABOUT YOUR TREASURE.
Remember when you stole those gold-plated golf shoes?
That's rich! You calling me weird!
Really?

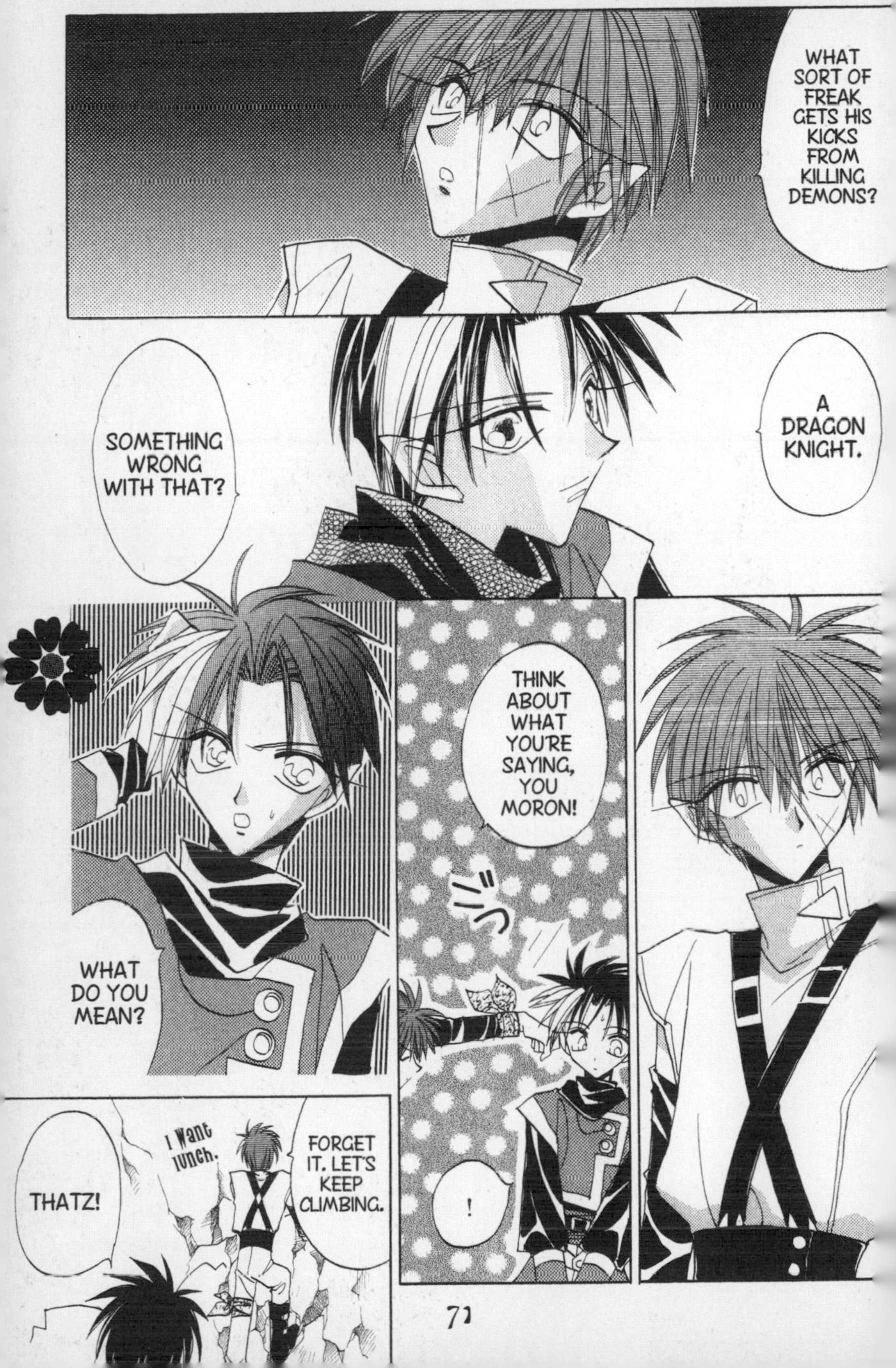
WHAT SORT OF FREAK GETS HIS KICKS FROM KILLING DEMONS?
A DRAGON KNIGHT.
SOMETHING WRONG WITH THAT?
THINK ABOUT WHAT YOU'RE SAYING, YOU MORON!
ゴッ
!
WHAT DO YOU MEAN?
FORGET IT. LET'S KEEP CLIMBING.
I want lunch.
THATZ!

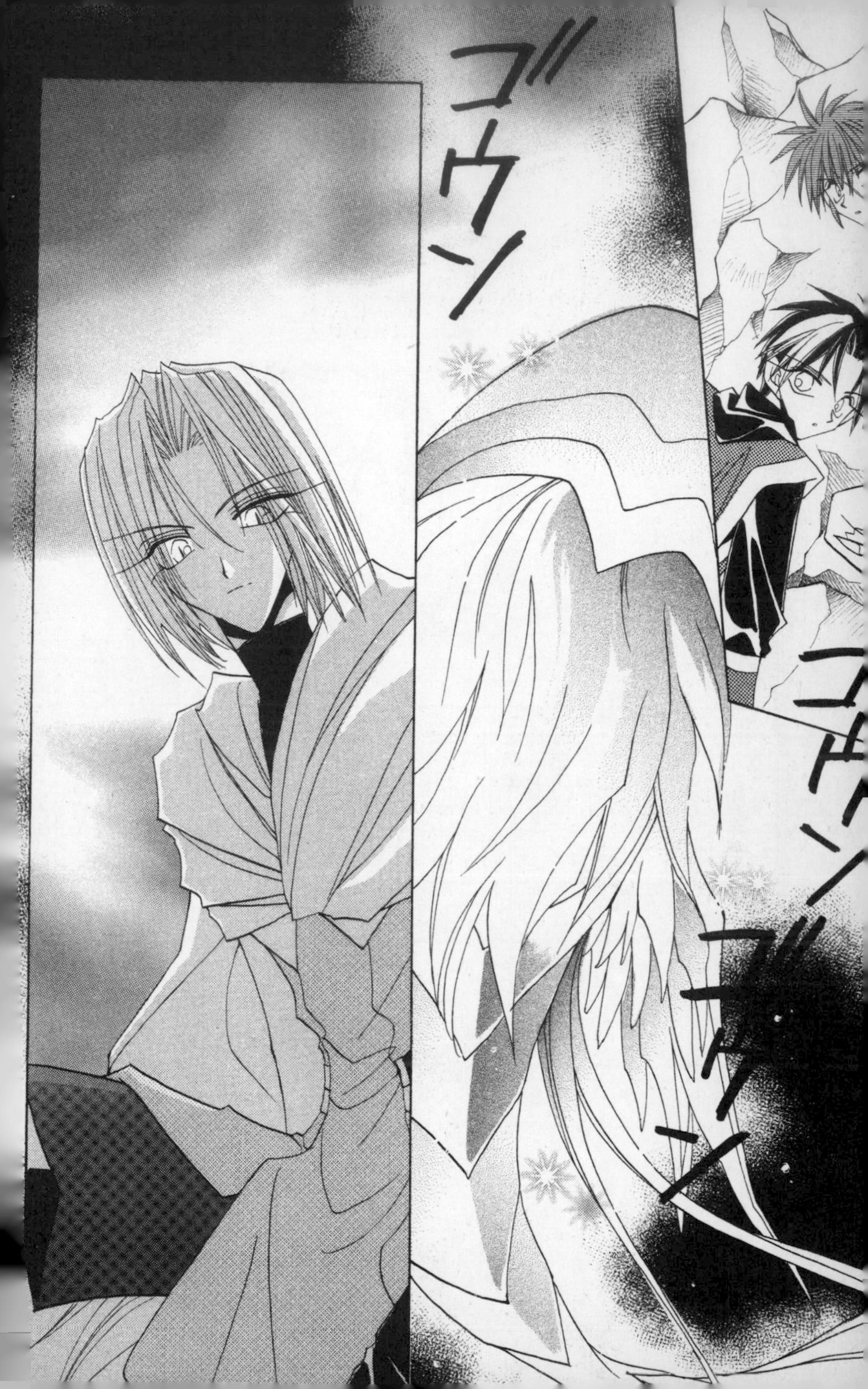
ゴウン

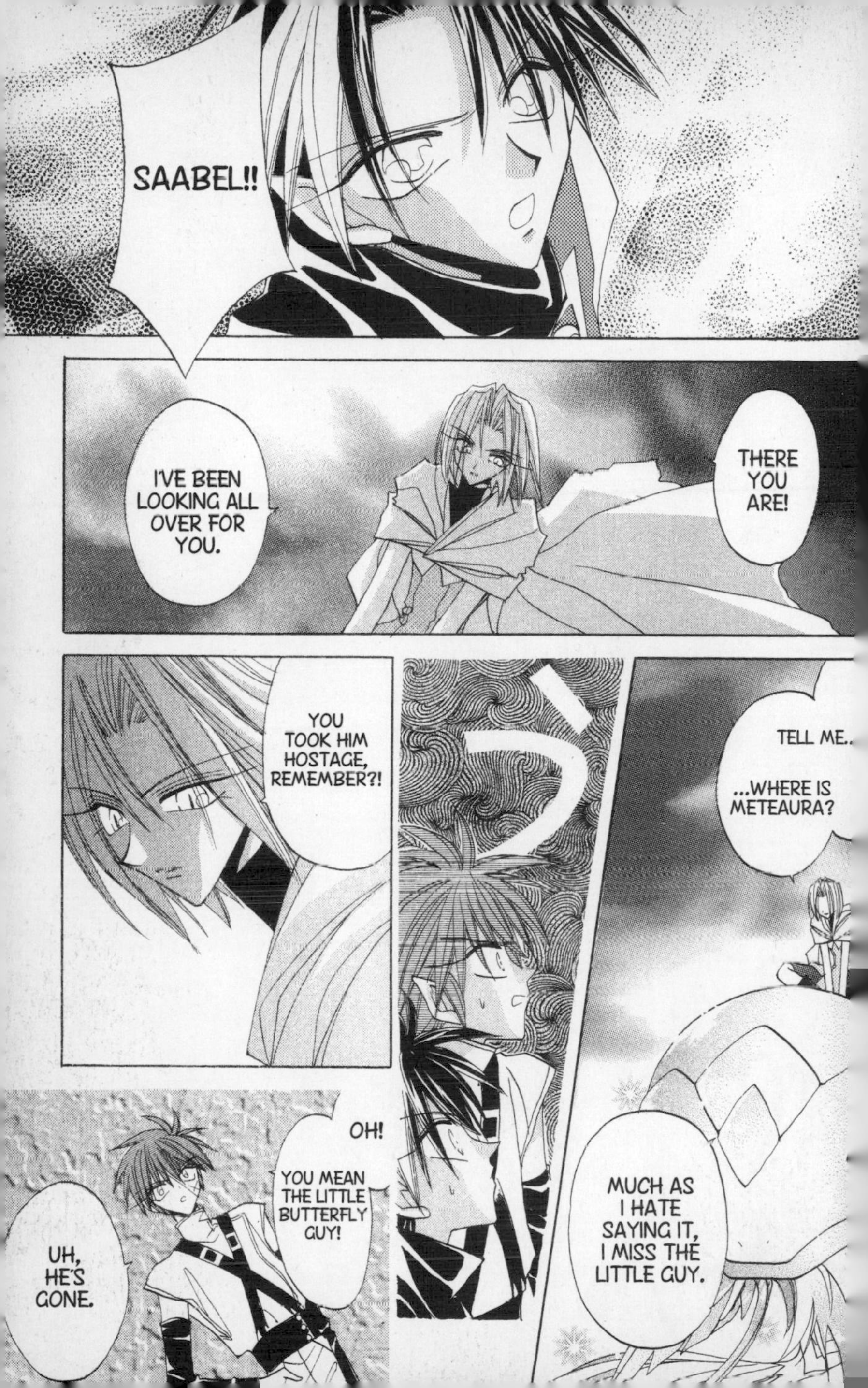
SAABEL!!
THERE YOU ARE!
I'VE BEEN LOOKING ALL OVER FOR YOU.
TELL ME...
...WHERE IS METEAURA?
YOU TOOK HIM HOSTAGE, REMEMBER?!
MUCH AS I HATE SAYING IT, I MISS THE LITTLE GUY.
OH!
YOU MEAN THE LITTLE BUTTERFLY GUY!
UH, HE'S GONE.

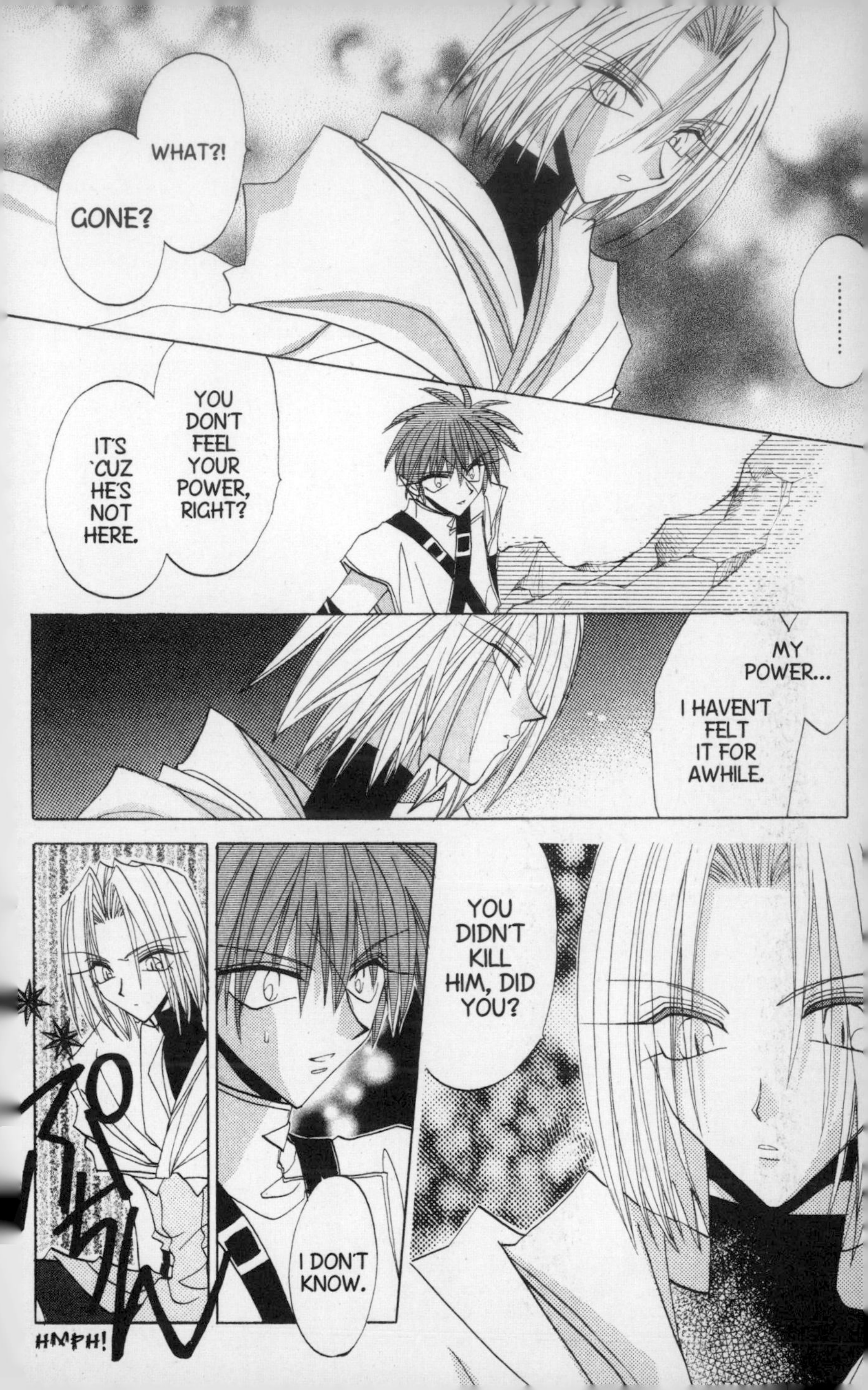
......
WHAT?! GONE?
YOU DON'T FEEL YOUR POWER, RIGHT?
IT'S 'CUZ HE'S NOT HERE.
MY POWER...
I HAVEN'T FELT IT FOR AWHILE.
YOU DIDN'T KILL HIM, DID YOU?
I DON'T KNOW.
HMPH!

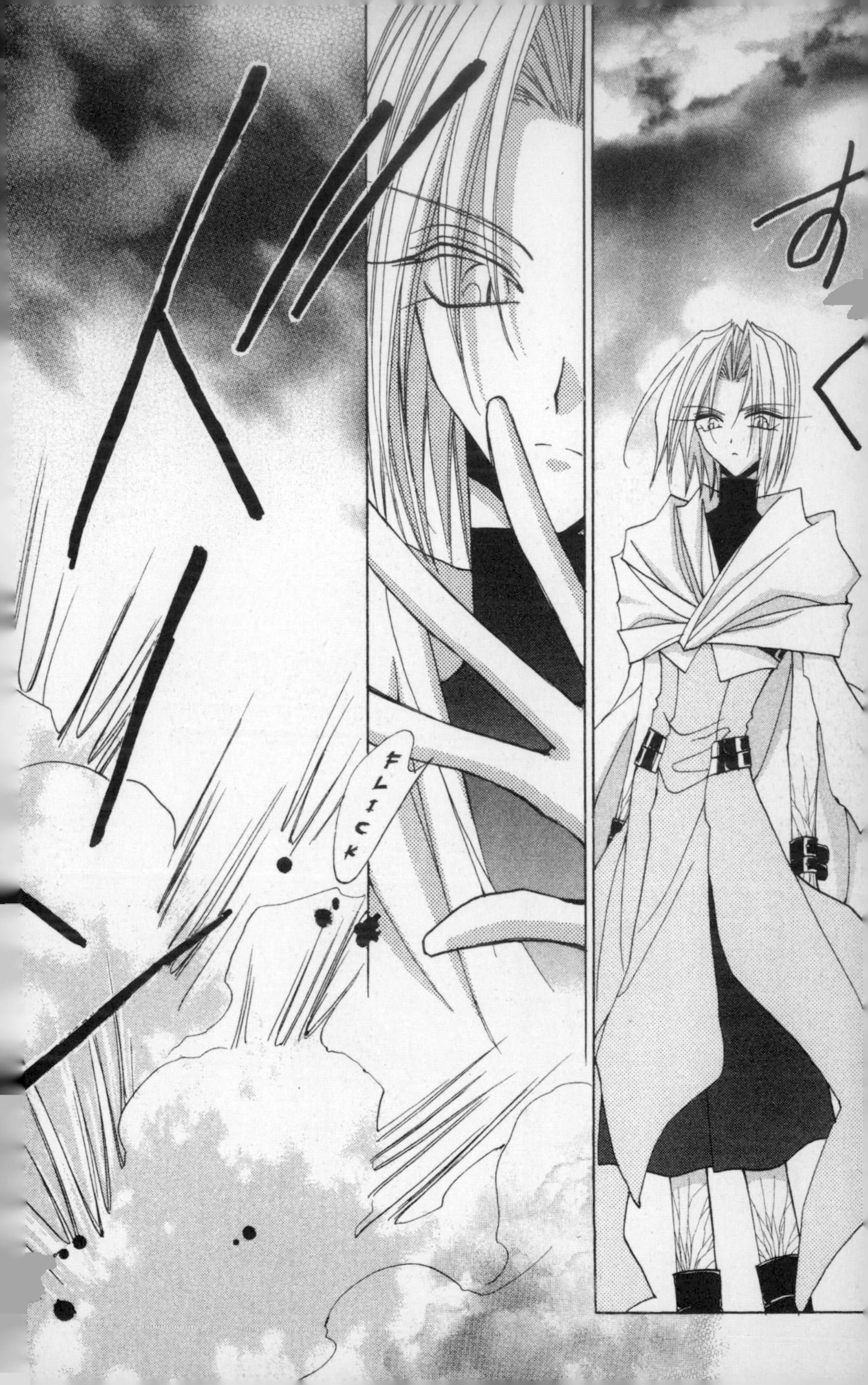
すく
FLICK

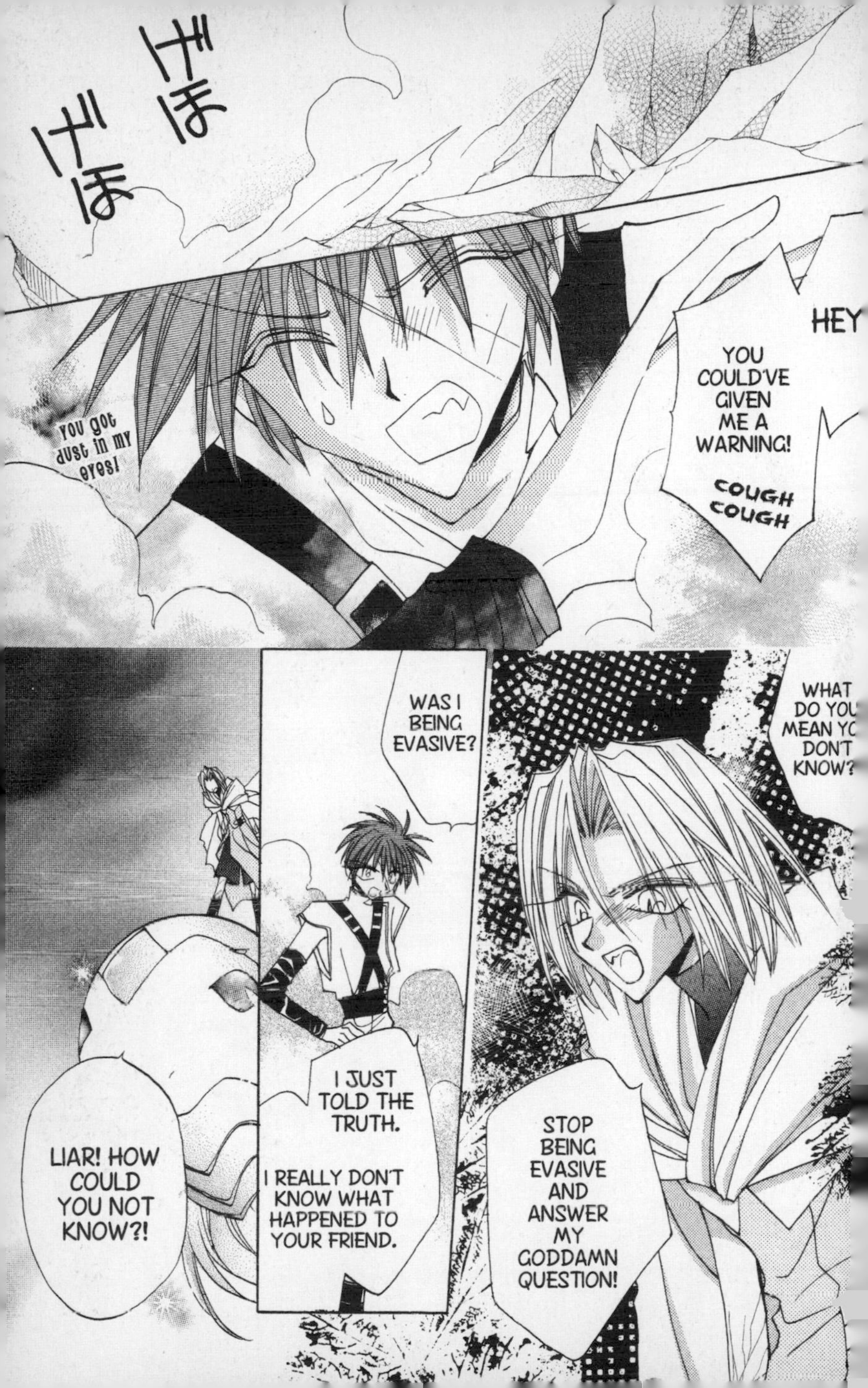
げほ げほ
HEY
YOU COULD'VE GIVEN ME A WARNING!
COUGH COUGH
You got dust in my eyes!
WHAT DO YOU MEAN YO DON'T KNOW?
STOP BEING EVASIVE AND ANSWER MY GODDAMN QUESTION!
WAS I BEING EVASIVE?
I JUST TOLD THE TRUTH.
I REALLY DON'T KNOW WHAT HAPPENED TO YOUR FRIEND.
LIAR! HOW COULD YOU NOT KNOW?!

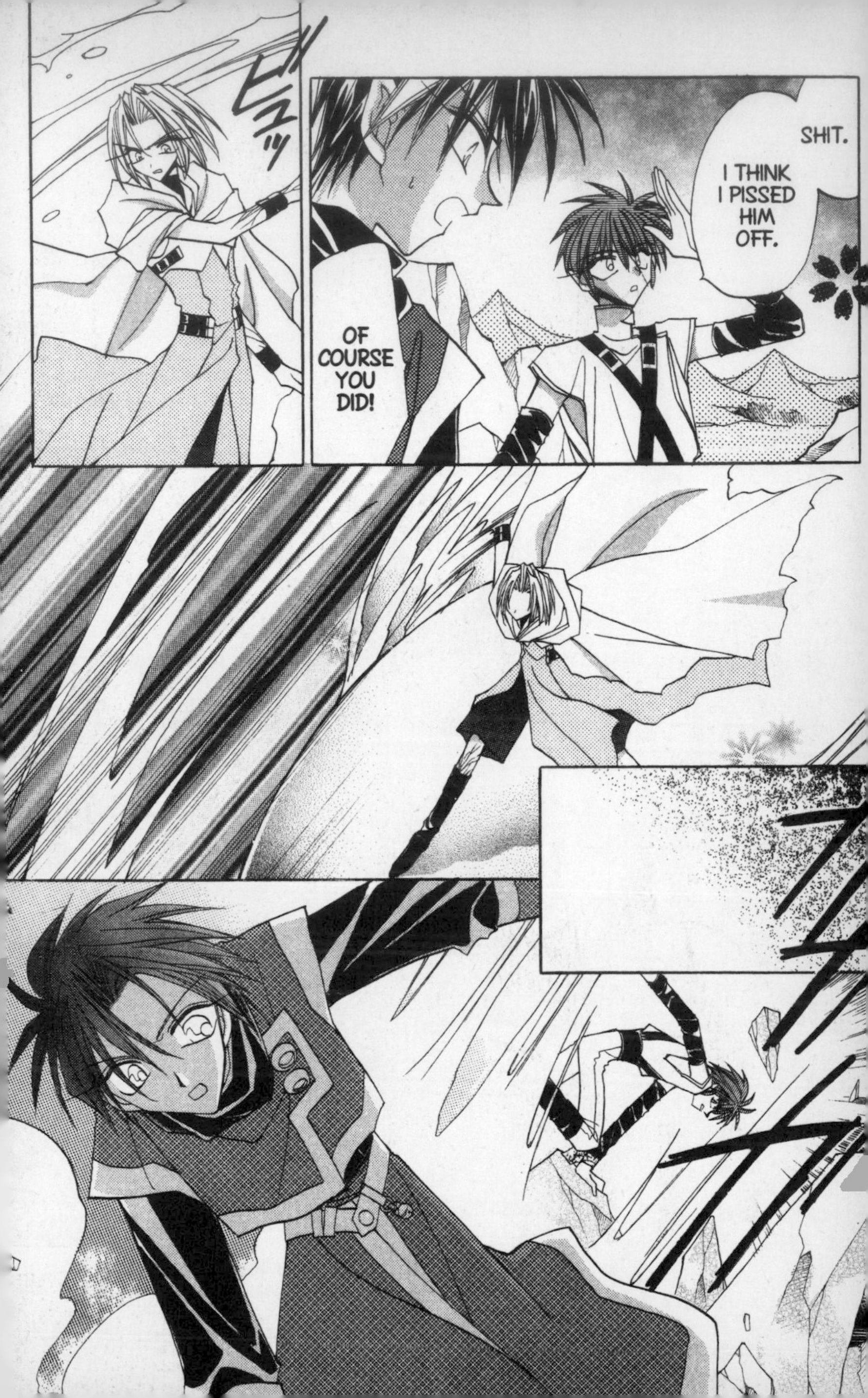
SHIT.
I THINK I PISSED HIM OFF.
OF COURSE YOU DID!
ビュッ

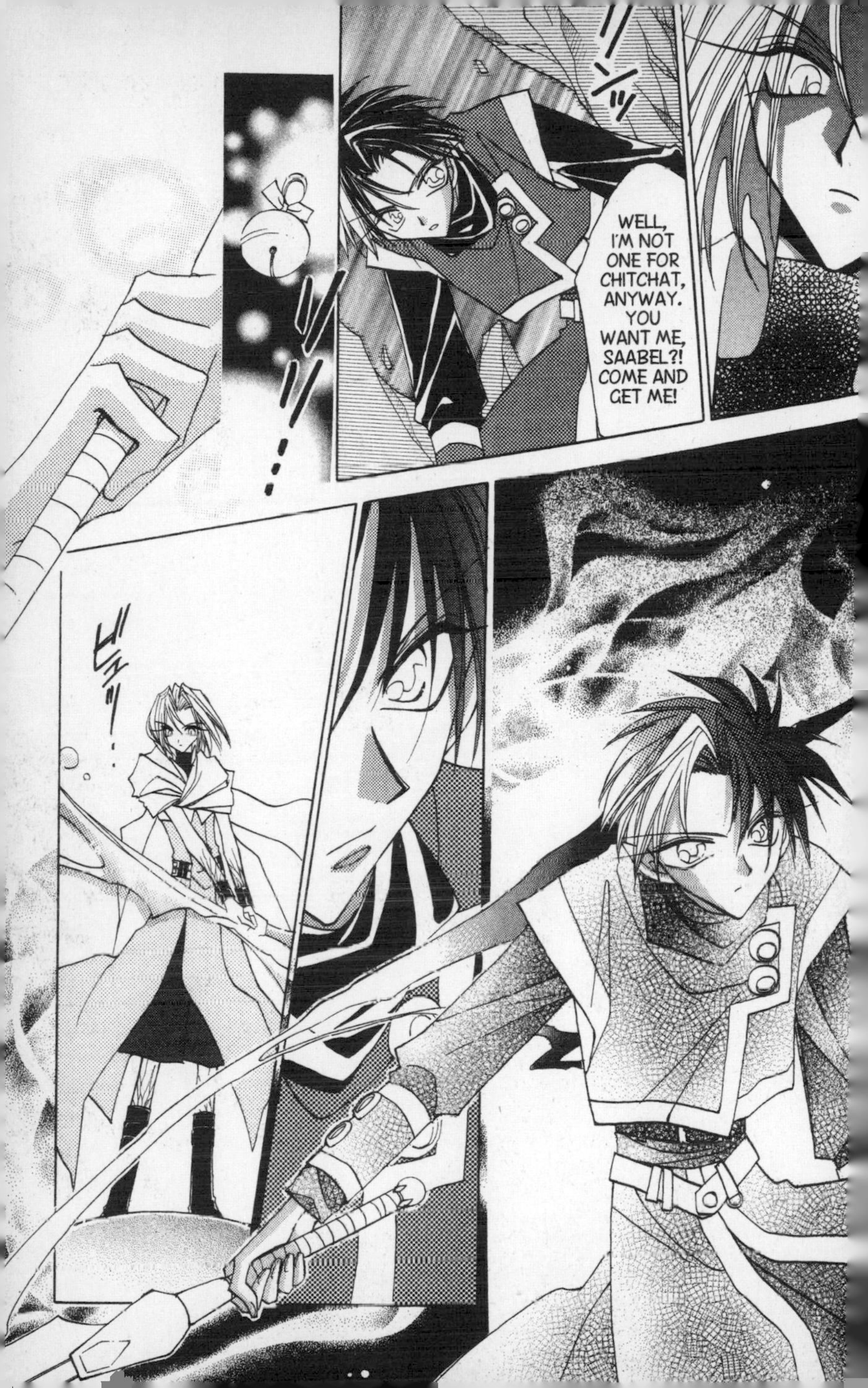
WELL, I'M NOT ONE FOR CHITCHAT, ANYWAY. YOU WANT ME, SAABEL?! COME AND GET ME!

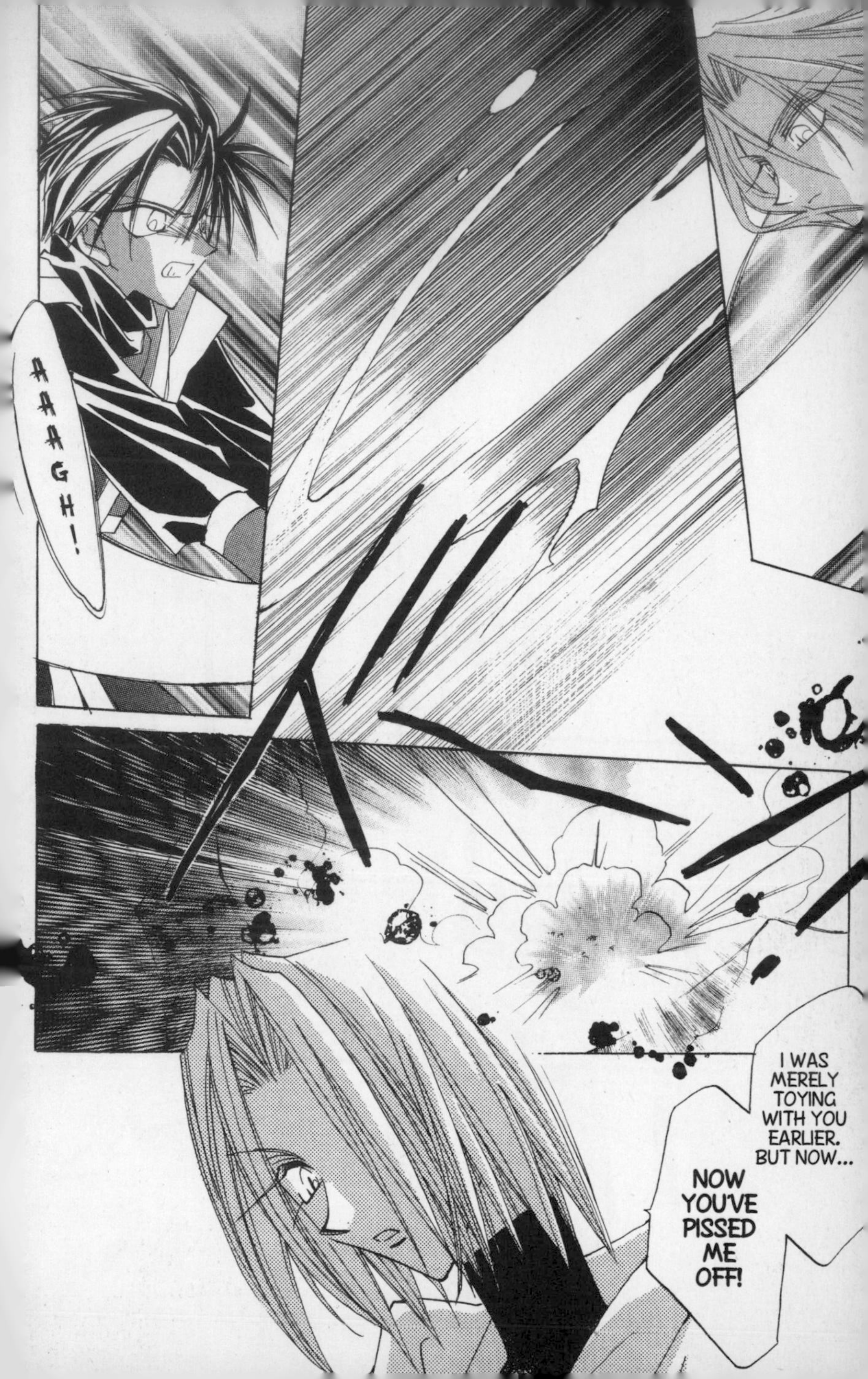
AAAAGH!
I WAS MERELY TOYING WITH YOU EARLIER. BUT NOW...
NOW YOU'VE PISSED ME OFF!

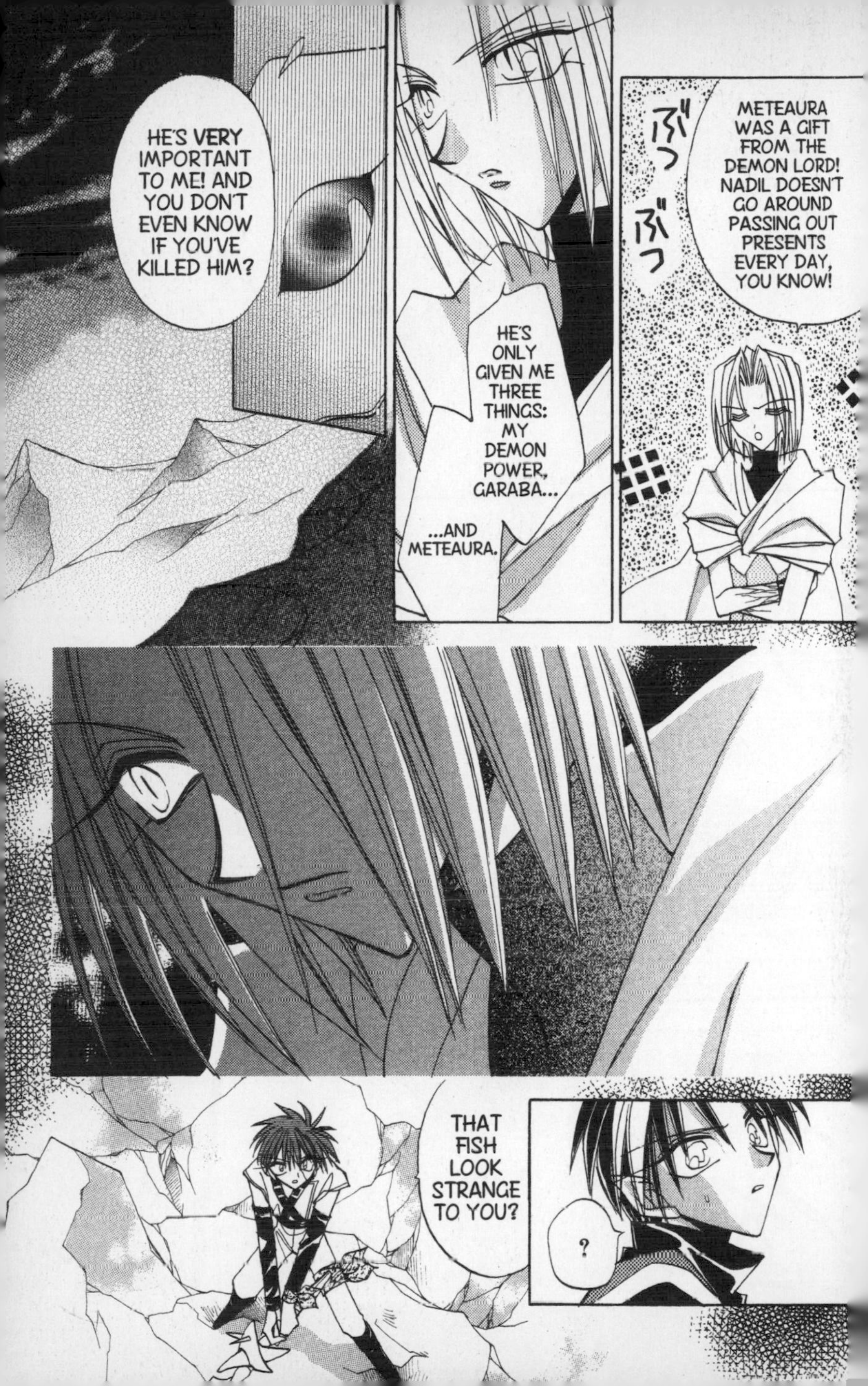
ぶつぶつ
METEAURA WAS A GIFT FROM THE DEMON LORD! NADIL DOESN'T GO AROUND PASSING OUT PRESENTS EVERY DAY, YOU KNOW!
HE'S ONLY GIVEN ME THREE THINGS: MY DEMON POWER, GARABA...
...AND METEAURA.
HE'S VERY IMPORTANT TO ME! AND YOU DON'T EVEN KNOW IF YOU'VE KILLED HIM?
?
THAT FISH LOOK STRANGE TO YOU?

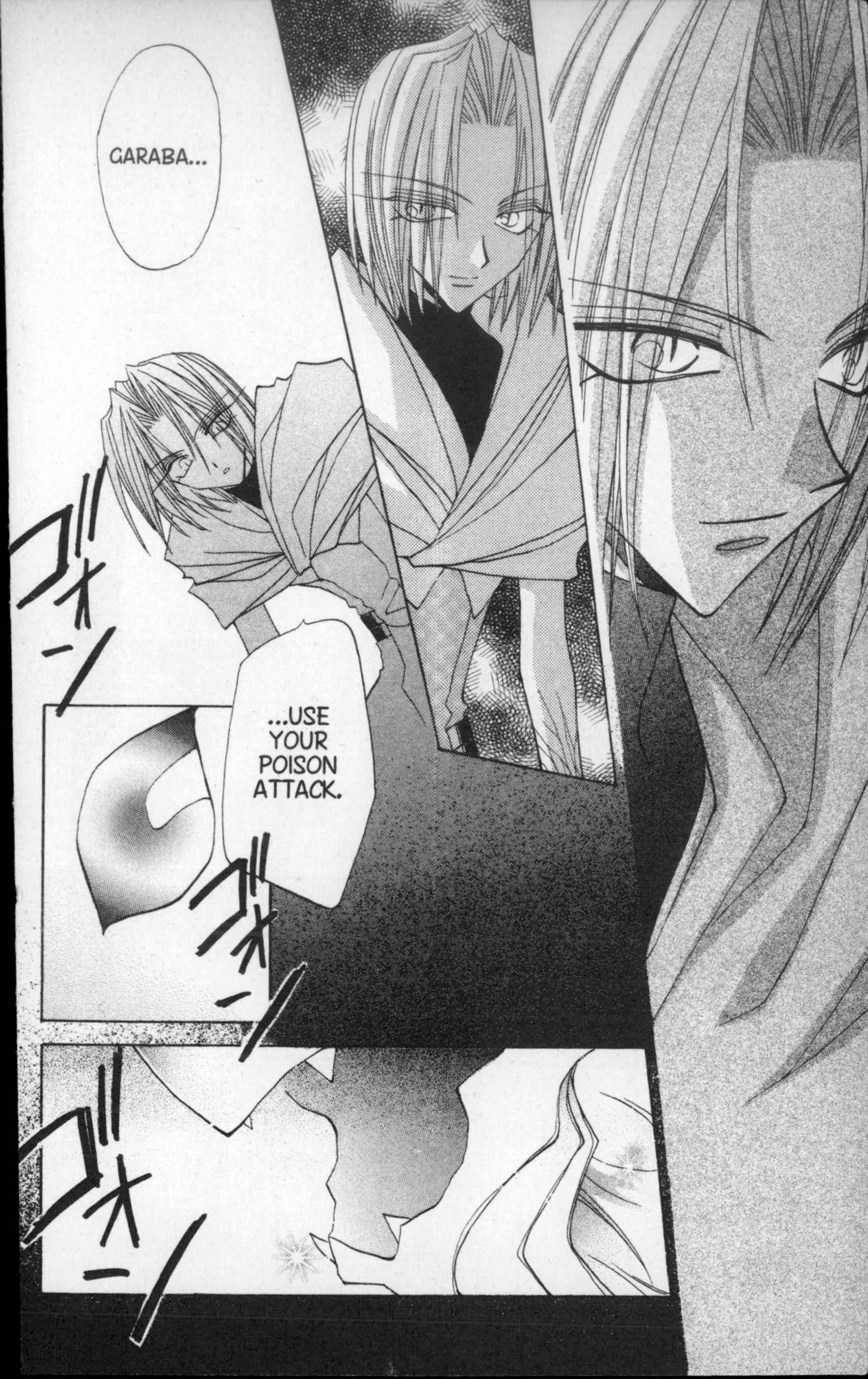
GARABA...
...USE YOUR POISON ATTACK.

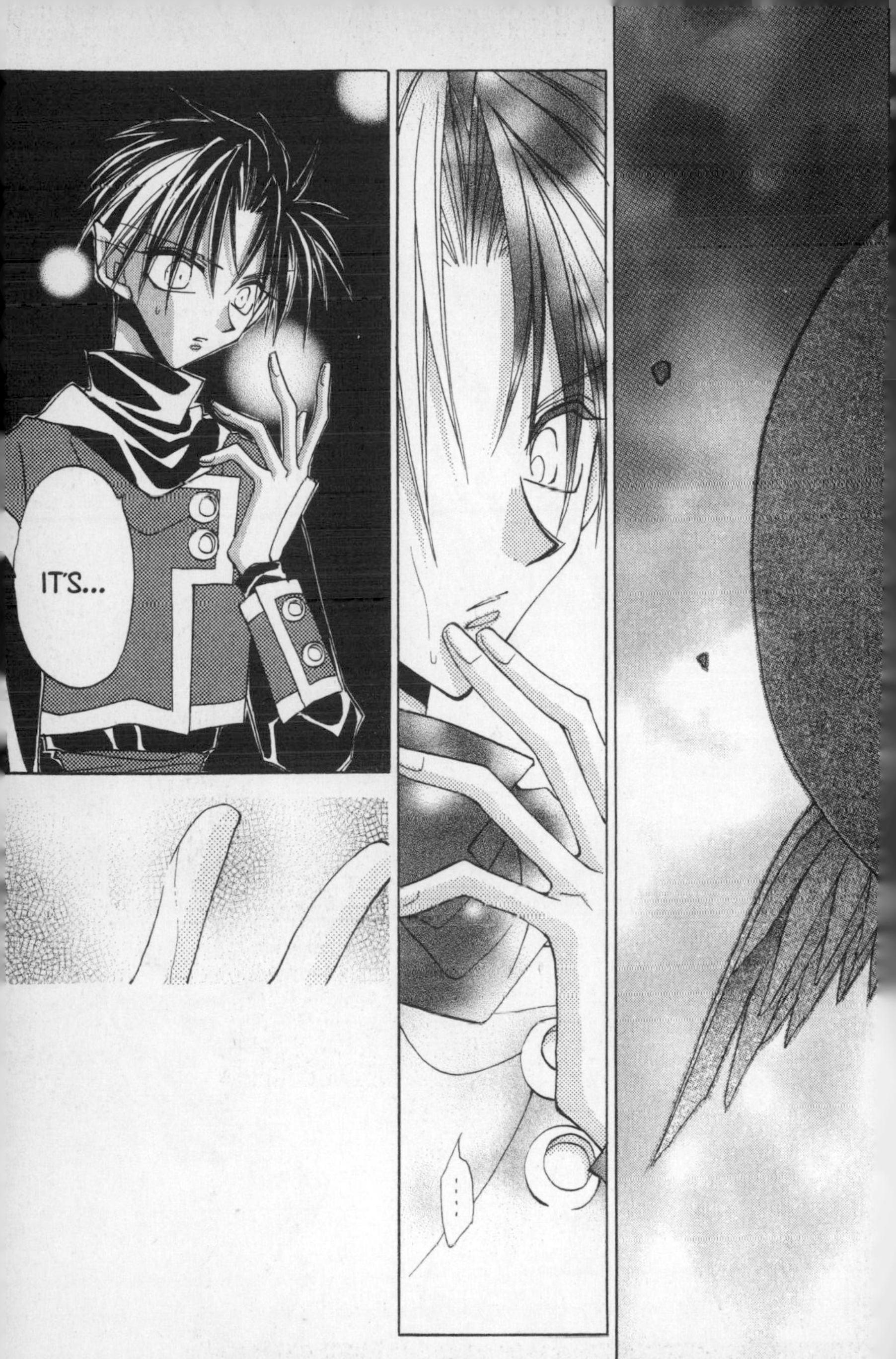
...
IT'S...

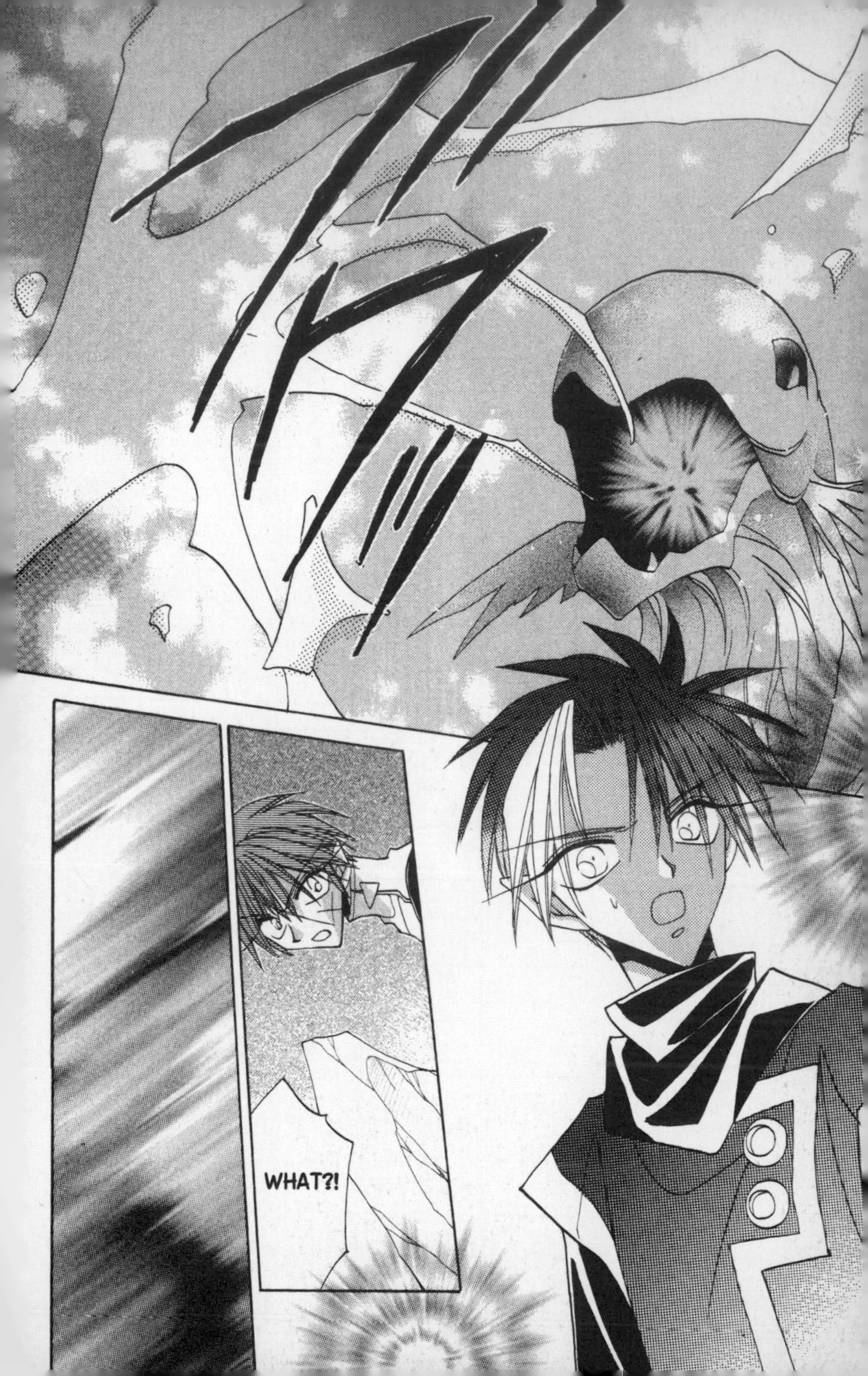
WHAT?!

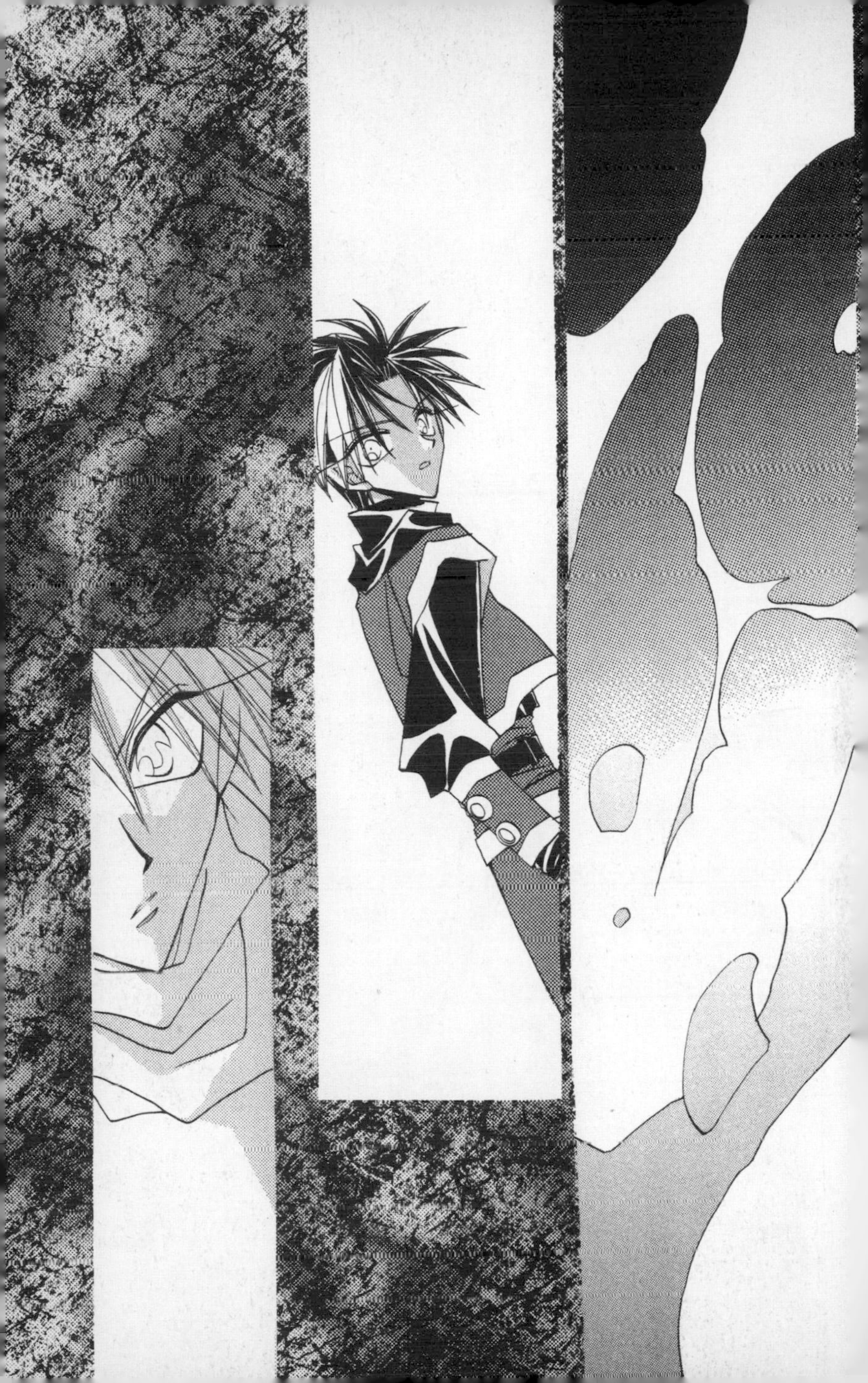

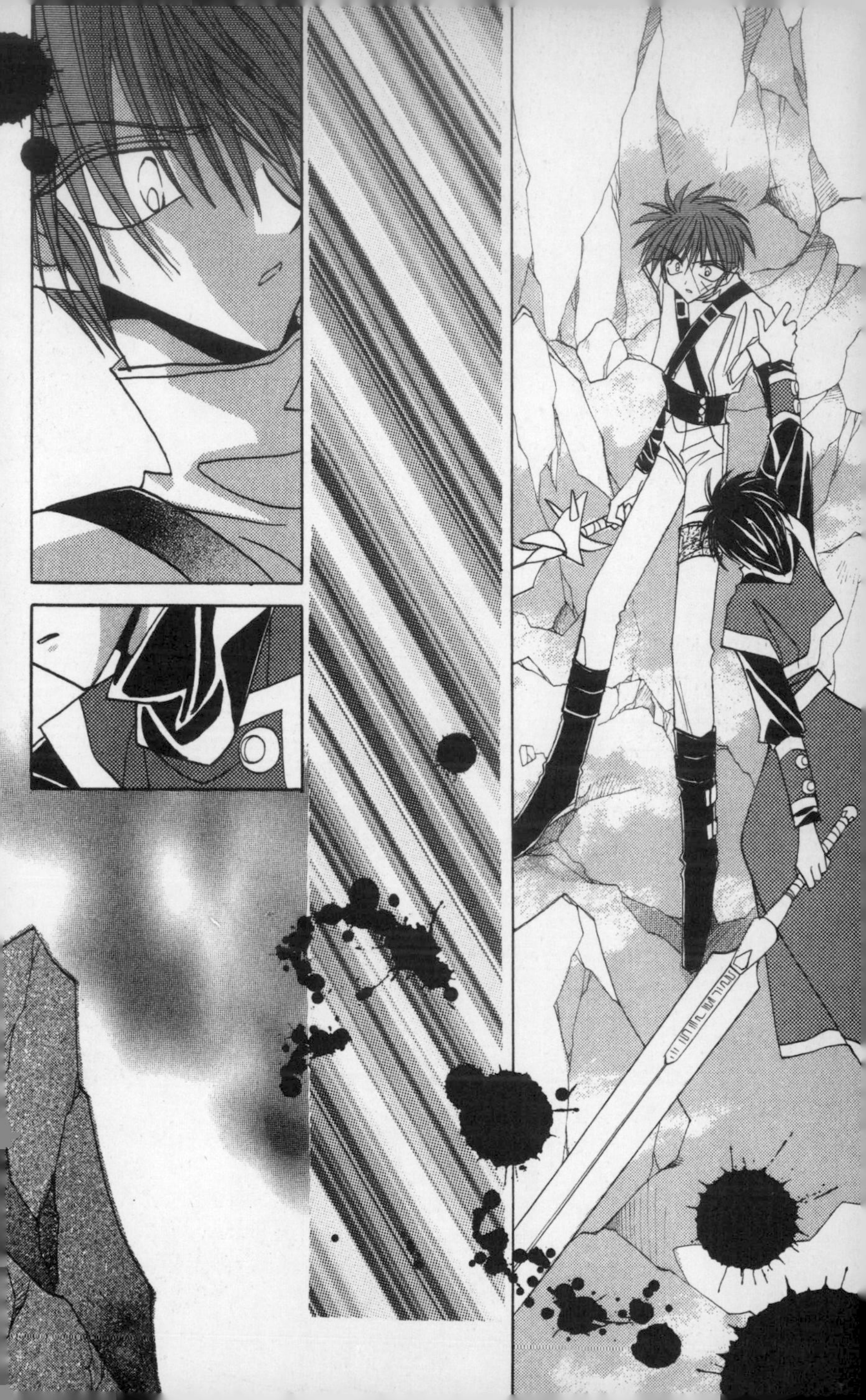

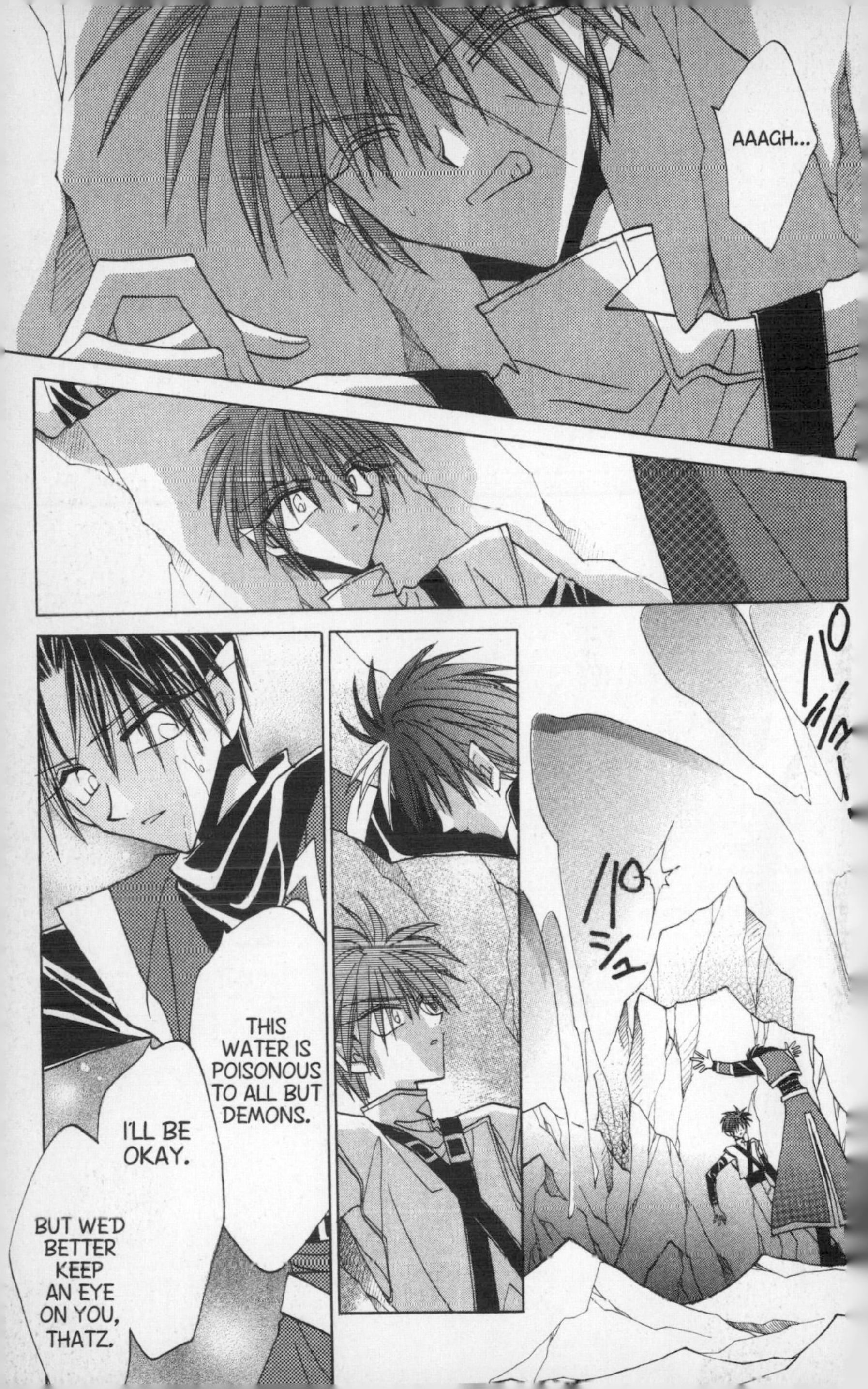
AAAGH...
THIS WATER IS POISONOUS TO ALL BUT DEMONS.
I'LL BE OKAY.
BUT WE'D BETTER KEEP AN EYE ON YOU, THATZ.

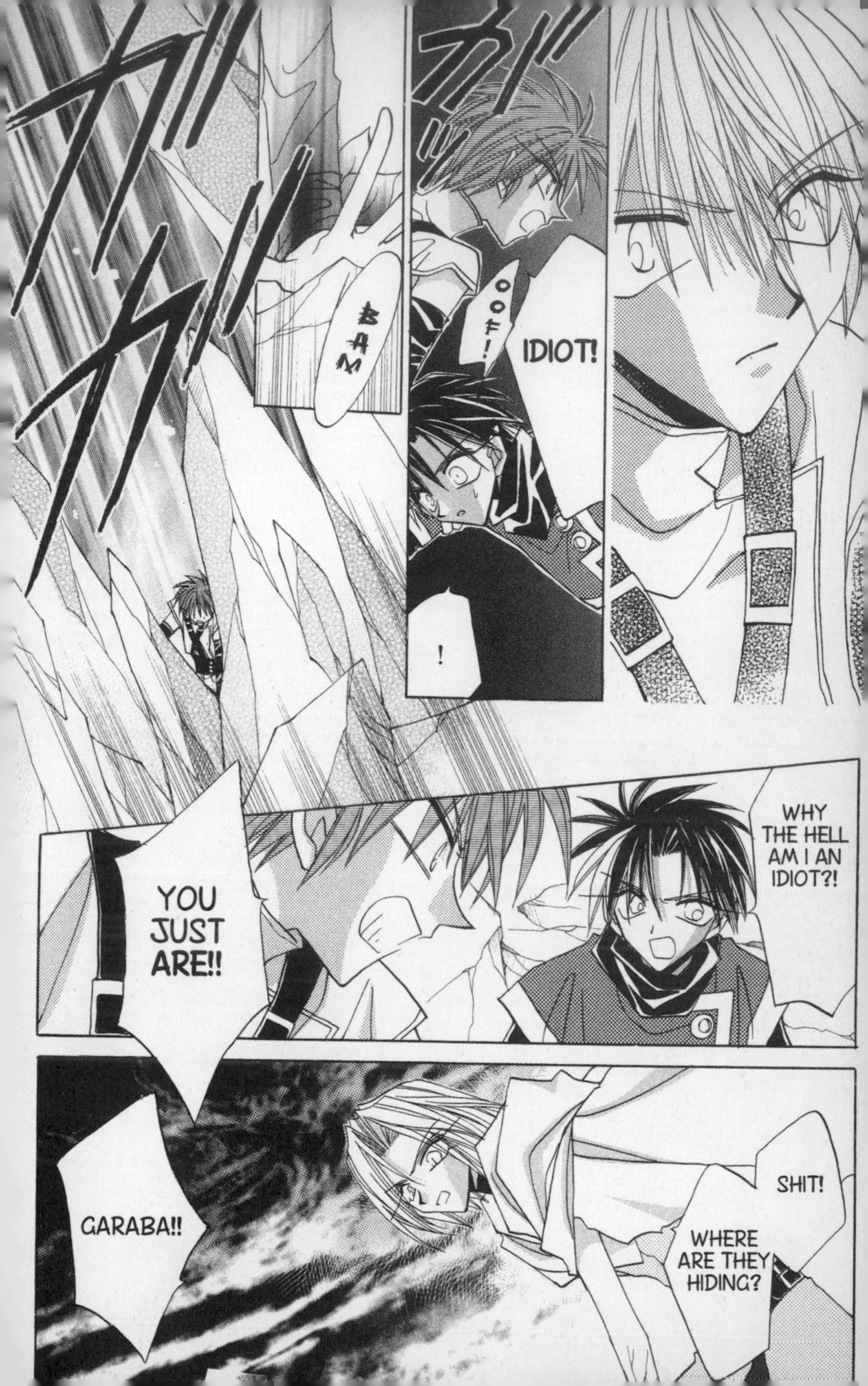
IDIOT!
OOF!
!
BAM
WHY THE HELL AM I AN IDIOT?!
YOU JUST ARE!!
SHIT!
WHERE ARE THEY HIDING?
GARABA!!

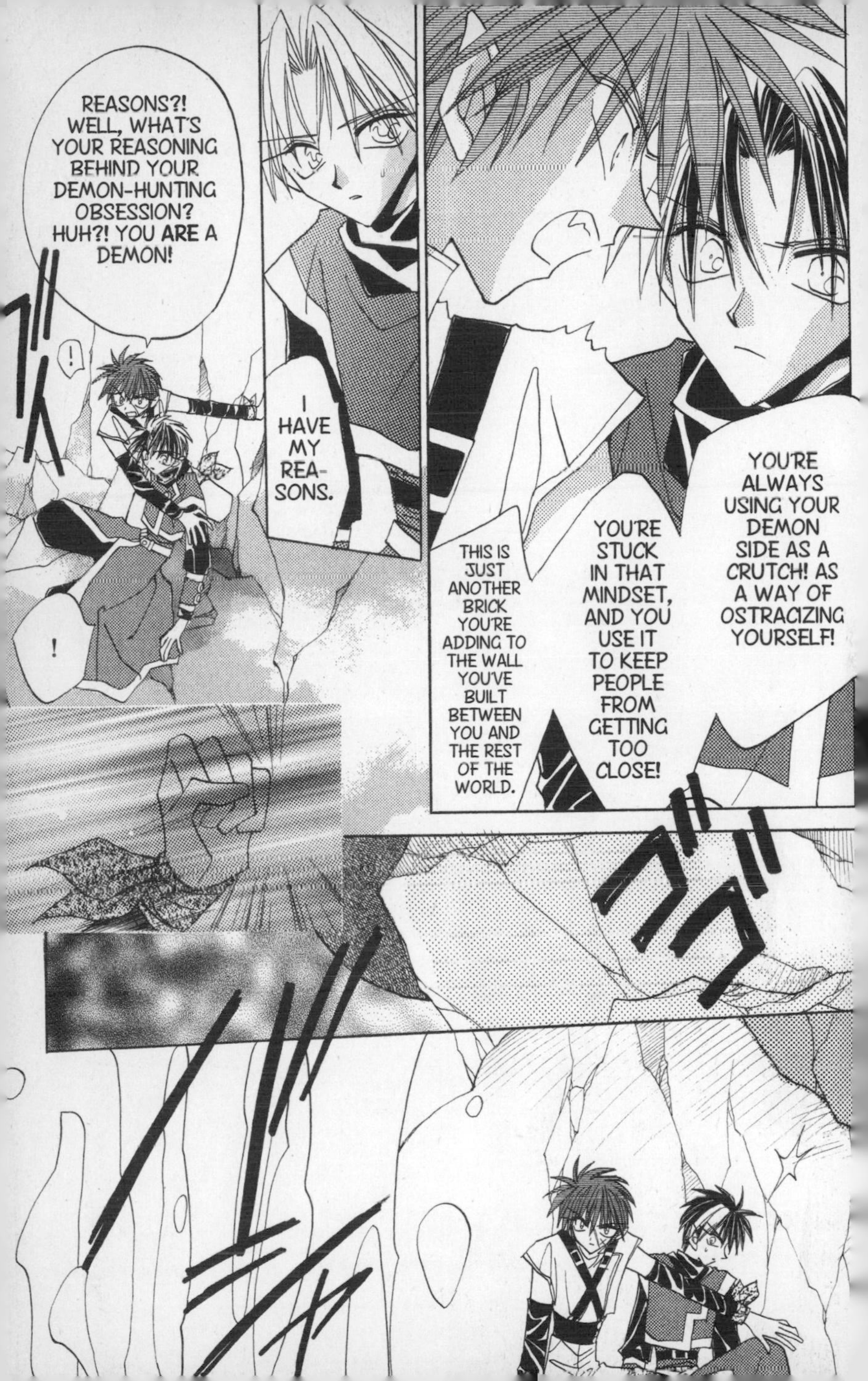
YOU'RE ALWAYS USING YOUR DEMON SIDE AS A CRUTCH! AS A WAY OF OSTRACIZING YOURSELF!
YOU'RE STUCK IN THAT MINDSET, AND YOU USE IT TO KEEP PEOPLE FROM GETTING TOO CLOSE!
THIS IS JUST ANOTHER BRICK YOU'RE ADDING TO THE WALL YOU'VE BUILT BETWEEN YOU AND THE REST OF THE WORLD.
I HAVE MY REA-SONS.
REASONS?! WELL, WHAT'S YOUR REASONING BEHIND YOUR DEMON-HUNTING OBSESSION? HUH?! YOU ARE A DEMON!
!
!

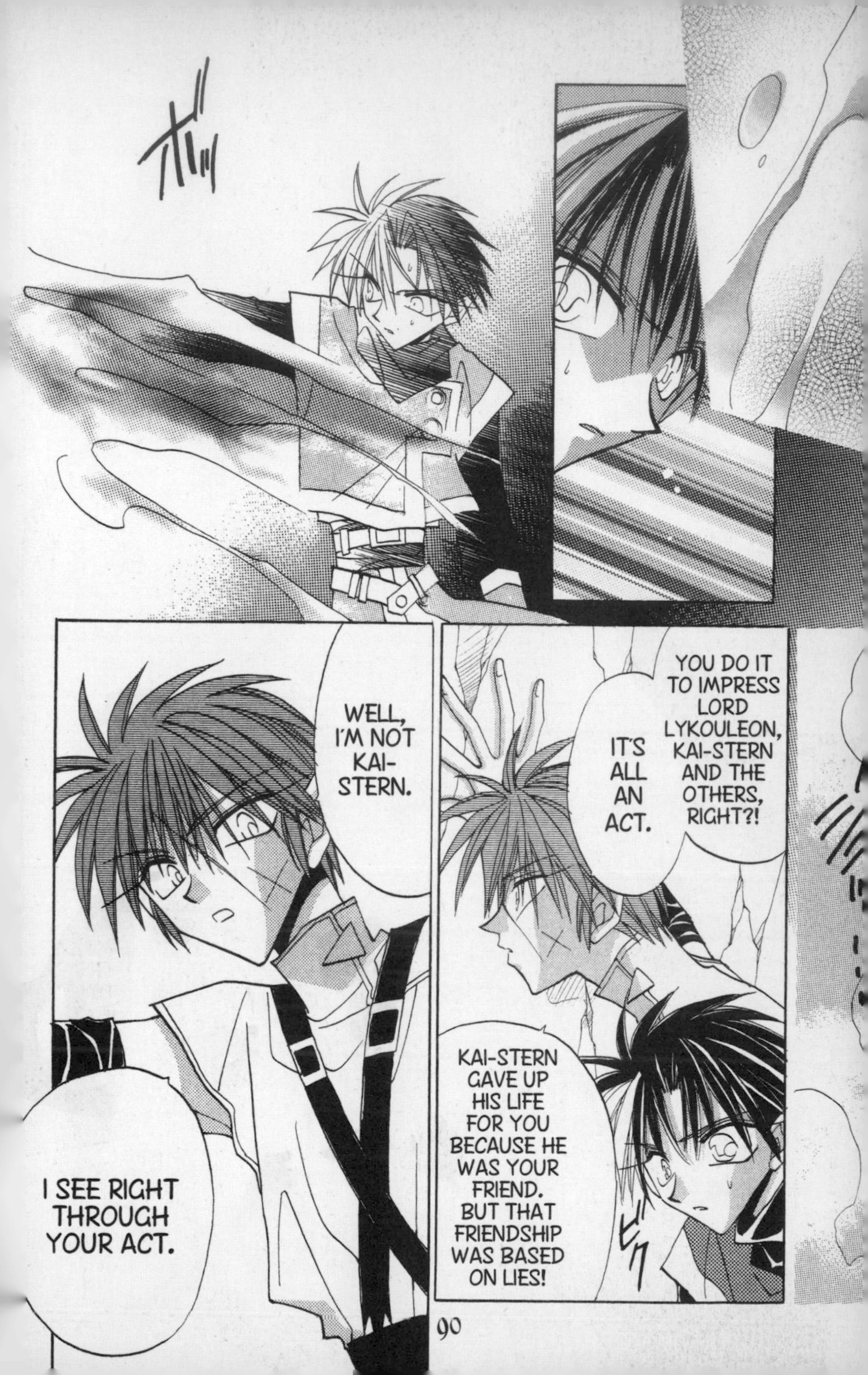
YOU DO IT TO IMPRESS LORD LYKOULEON, KAI-STERN AND THE OTHERS, RIGHT?!
IT'S ALL AN ACT.
KAI-STERN GAVE UP HIS LIFE FOR YOU BECAUSE HE WAS YOUR FRIEND. BUT THAT FRIENDSHIP WAS BASED ON LIES!
WELL, I'M NOT KAI-STERN.
I SEE RIGHT THROUGH YOUR ACT.

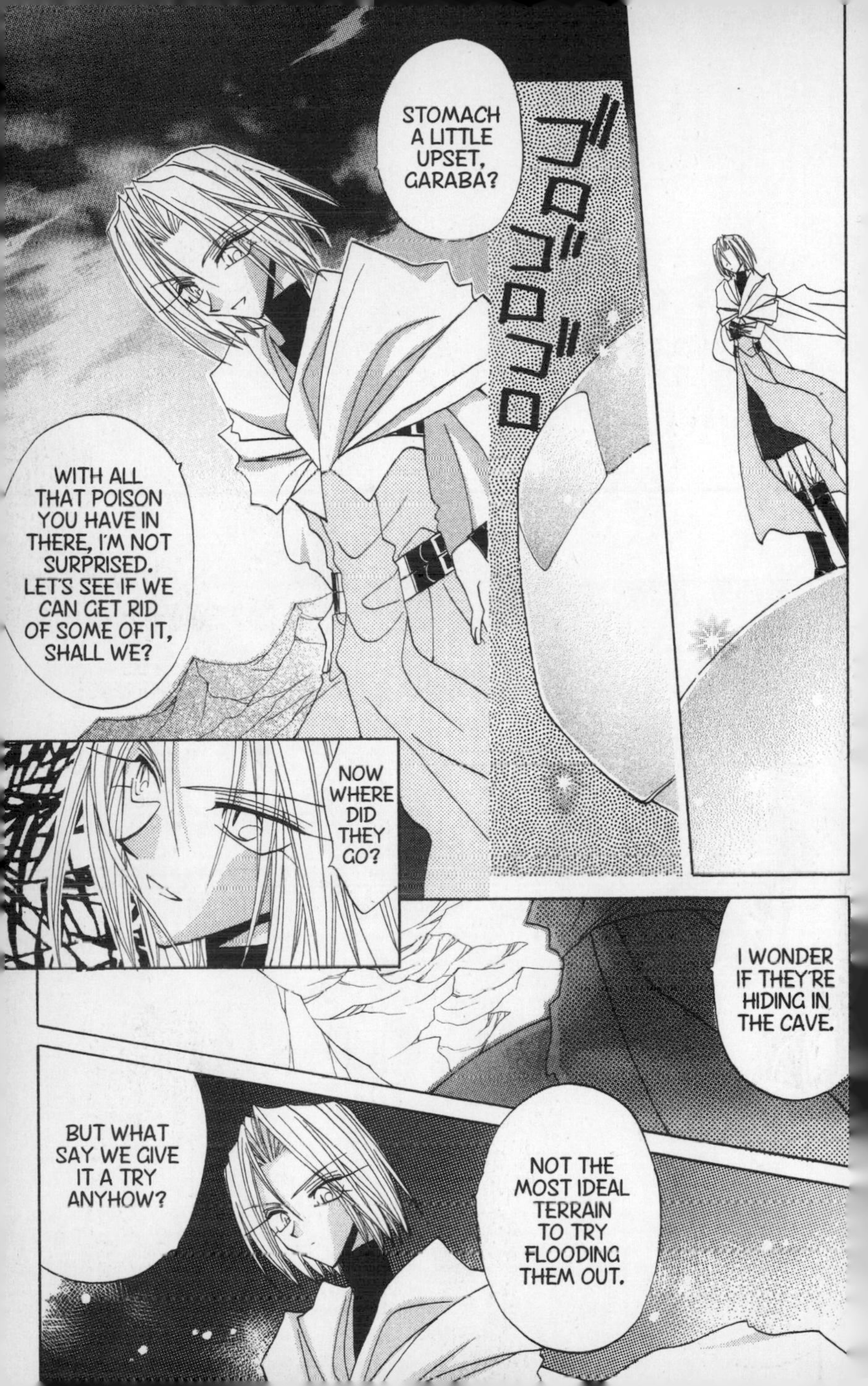
STOMACH A LITTLE UPSET, GARABA?
ゴロゴロゴロ
WITH ALL THAT POISON YOU HAVE IN THERE, I'M NOT SURPRISED. LET'S SEE IF WE CAN GET RID OF SOME OF IT, SHALL WE?
NOW WHERE DID THEY GO?
I WONDER IF THEY'RE HIDING IN THE CAVE.
NOT THE MOST IDEAL TERRAIN TO TRY FLOODING THEM OUT.
BUT WHAT SAY WE GIVE IT A TRY ANYHOW?

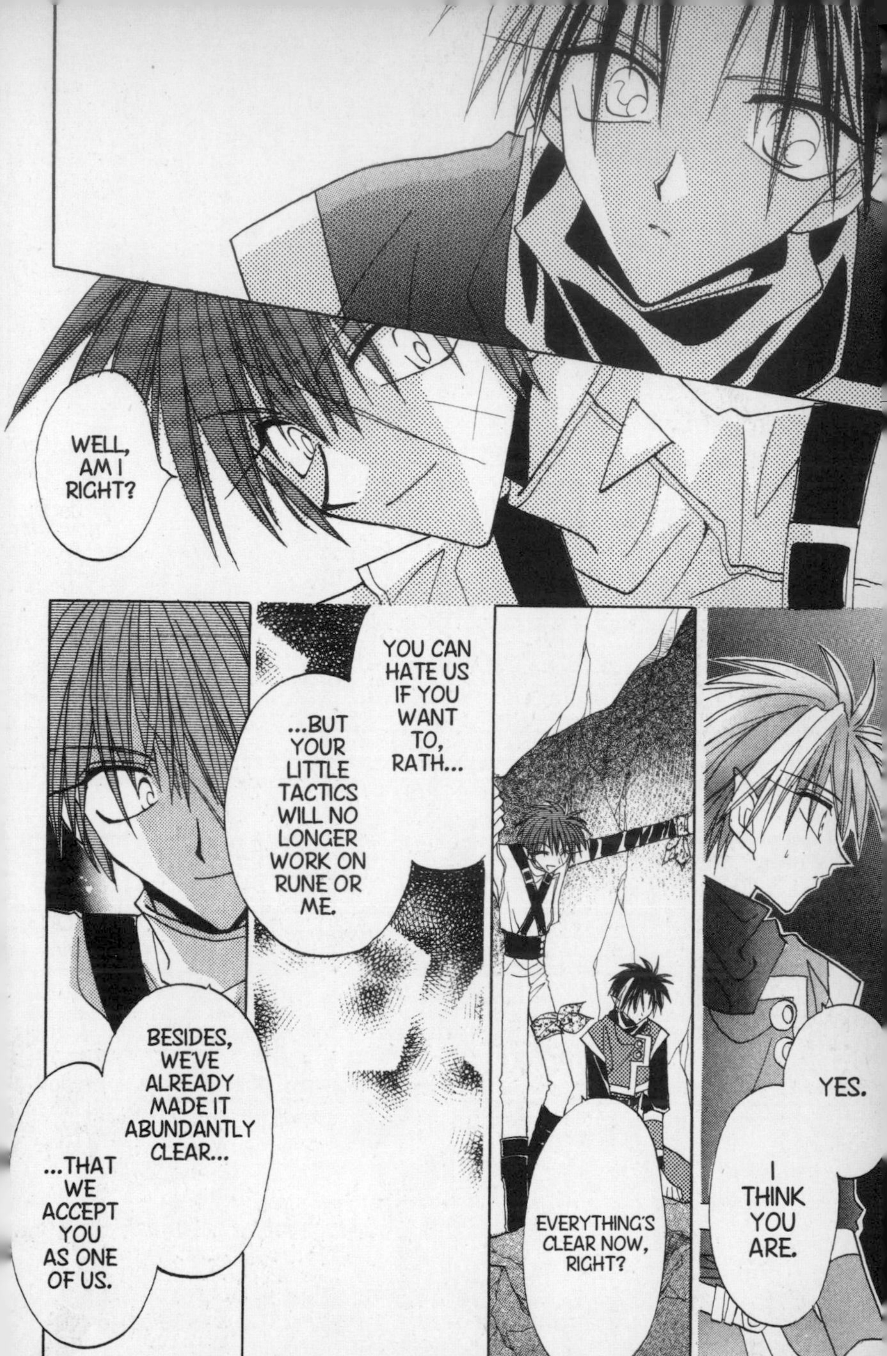
WELL, AM I RIGHT?
YES.
I THINK YOU ARE.
EVERYTHING'S CLEAR NOW, RIGHT?
YOU CAN HATE US IF YOU WANT TO, RATH...
...BUT YOUR LITTLE TACTICS WILL NO LONGER WORK ON RUNE OR ME.
BESIDES, WE'VE ALREADY MADE IT ABUNDANTLY CLEAR...
...THAT WE ACCEPT YOU AS ONE OF US.

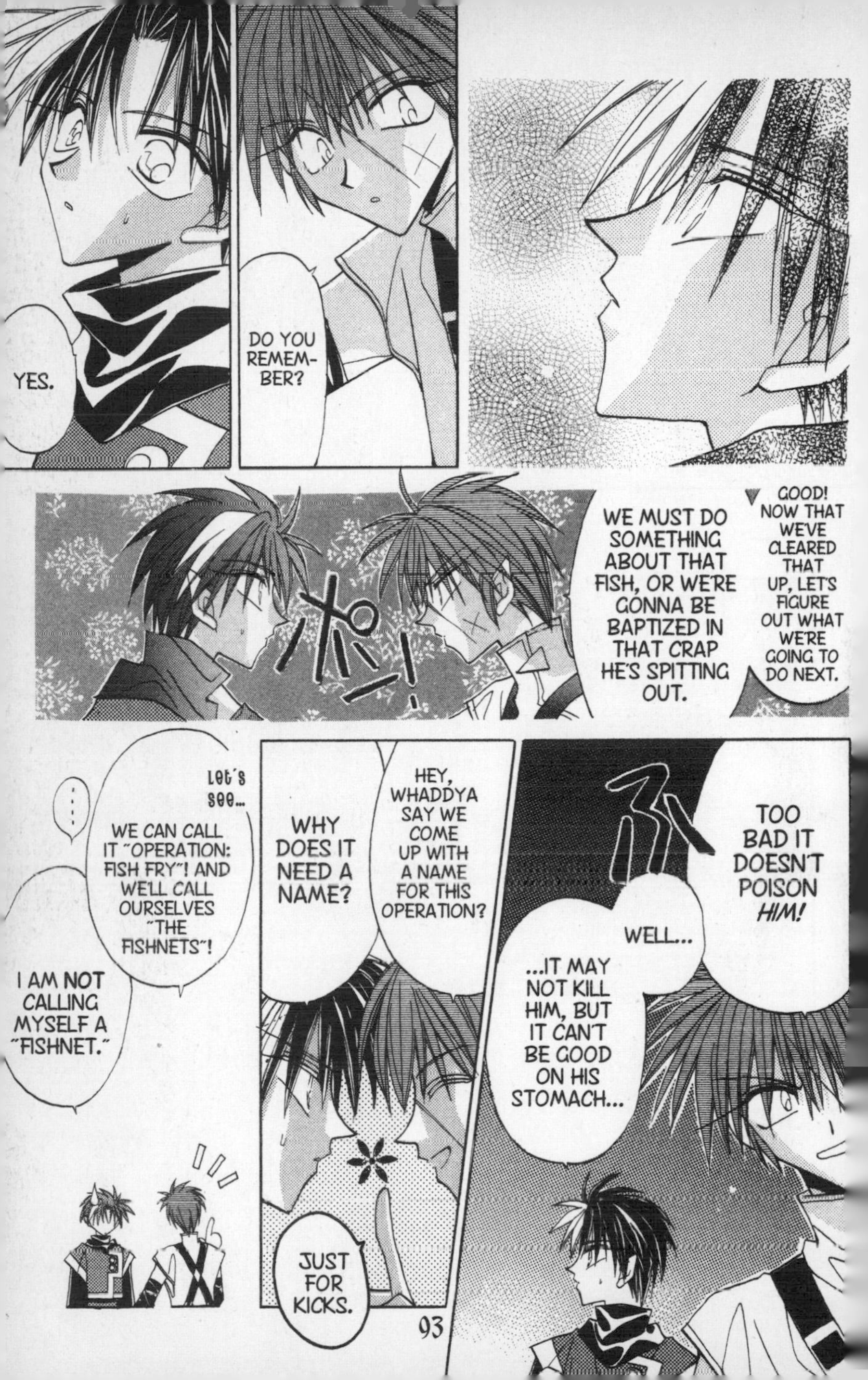
DO YOU REMEMBER?
YES.
GOOD! NOW THAT WE'VE CLEARED THAT UP, LET'S FIGURE OUT WHAT WE'RE GOING TO DO NEXT.
WE MUST DO SOMETHING ABOUT THAT FISH, OR WE'RE GONNA BE BAPTIZED IN THAT CRAP HE'S SPITTING OUT.
TOO BAD IT DOESN'T POISON *HIM!*
WELL...
...IT MAY NOT KILL HIM, BUT IT CAN'T BE GOOD ON HIS STOMACH...
HEY, WHADDYA SAY WE COME UP WITH A NAME FOR THIS OPERATION?
WHY DOES IT NEED A NAME?
JUST FOR KICKS.
Let's see...
WE CAN CALL IT "OPERATION: FISH FRY"! AND WE'LL CALL OURSELVES "THE FISHNETS"!
...
I AM NOT CALLING MYSELF A "FISHNET."

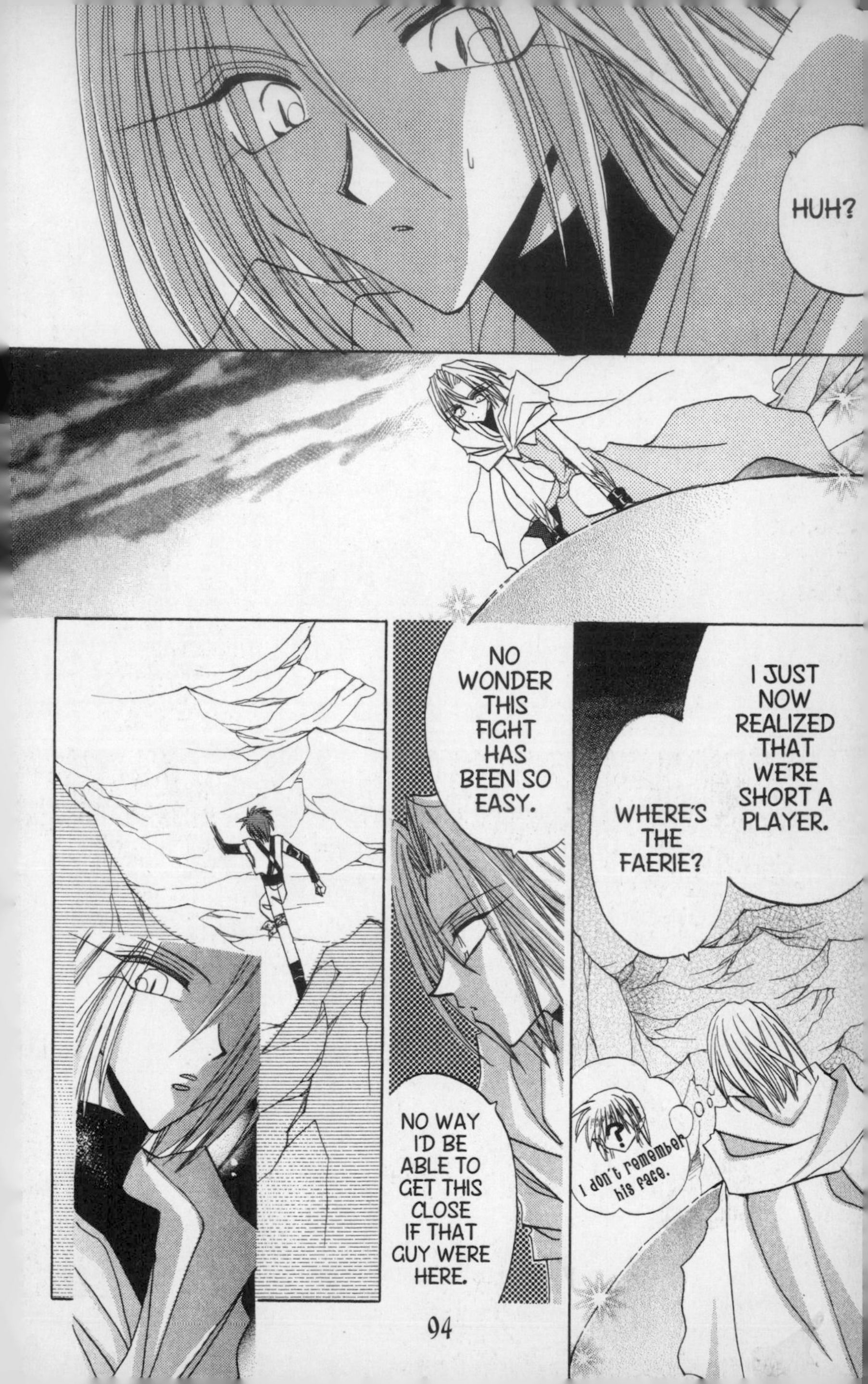
HUH?
I JUST NOW REALIZED THAT WE'RE SHORT A PLAYER.
WHERE'S THE FAERIE?
I don't remember his face.
NO WONDER THIS FIGHT HAS BEEN SO EASY.
NO WAY I'D BE ABLE TO GET THIS CLOSE IF THAT GUY WERE HERE.

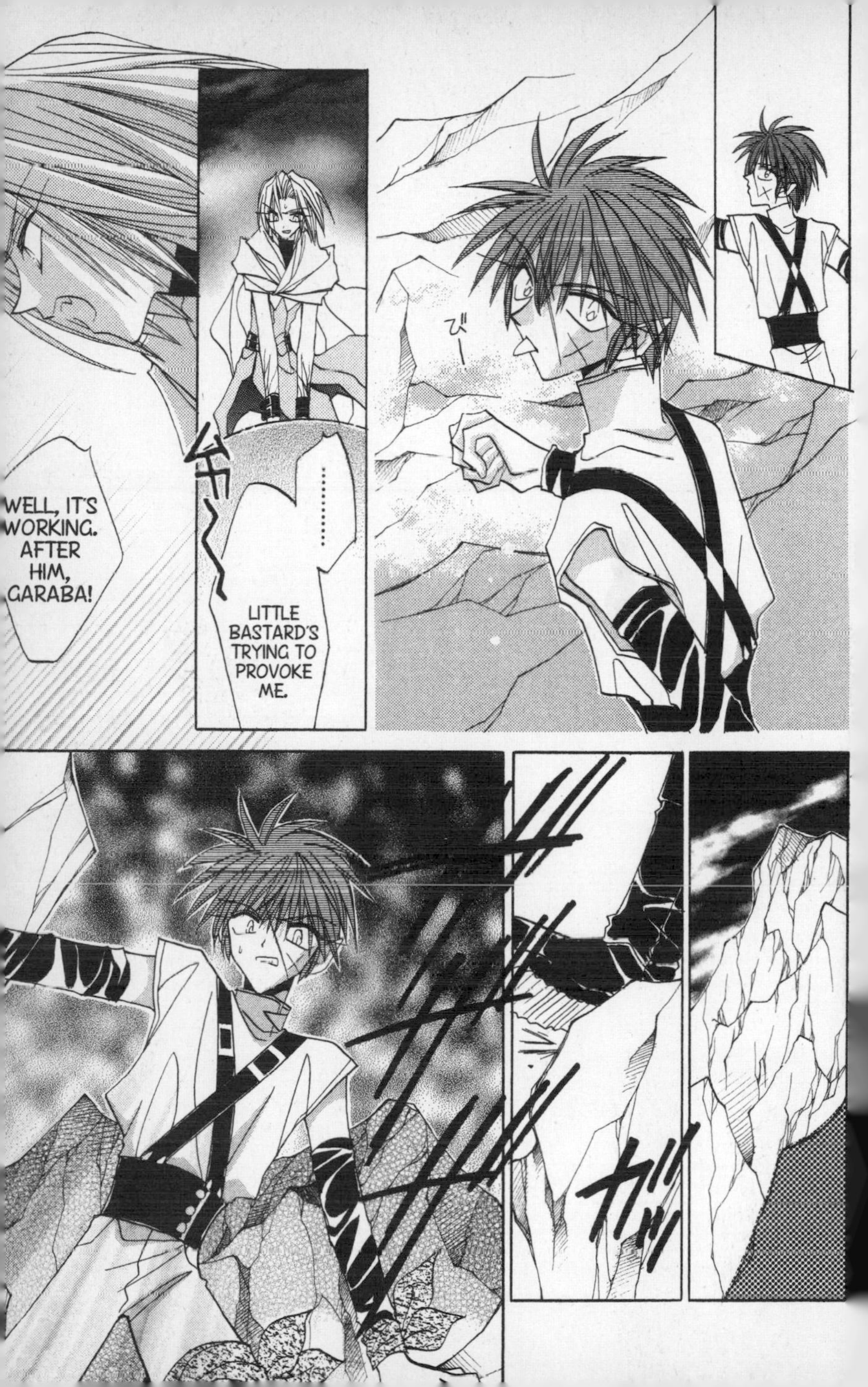
びー
ムキ〜
......
LITTLE BASTARD'S TRYING TO PROVOKE ME.
WELL, IT'S WORKING. AFTER HIM, GARABA!
ガッ

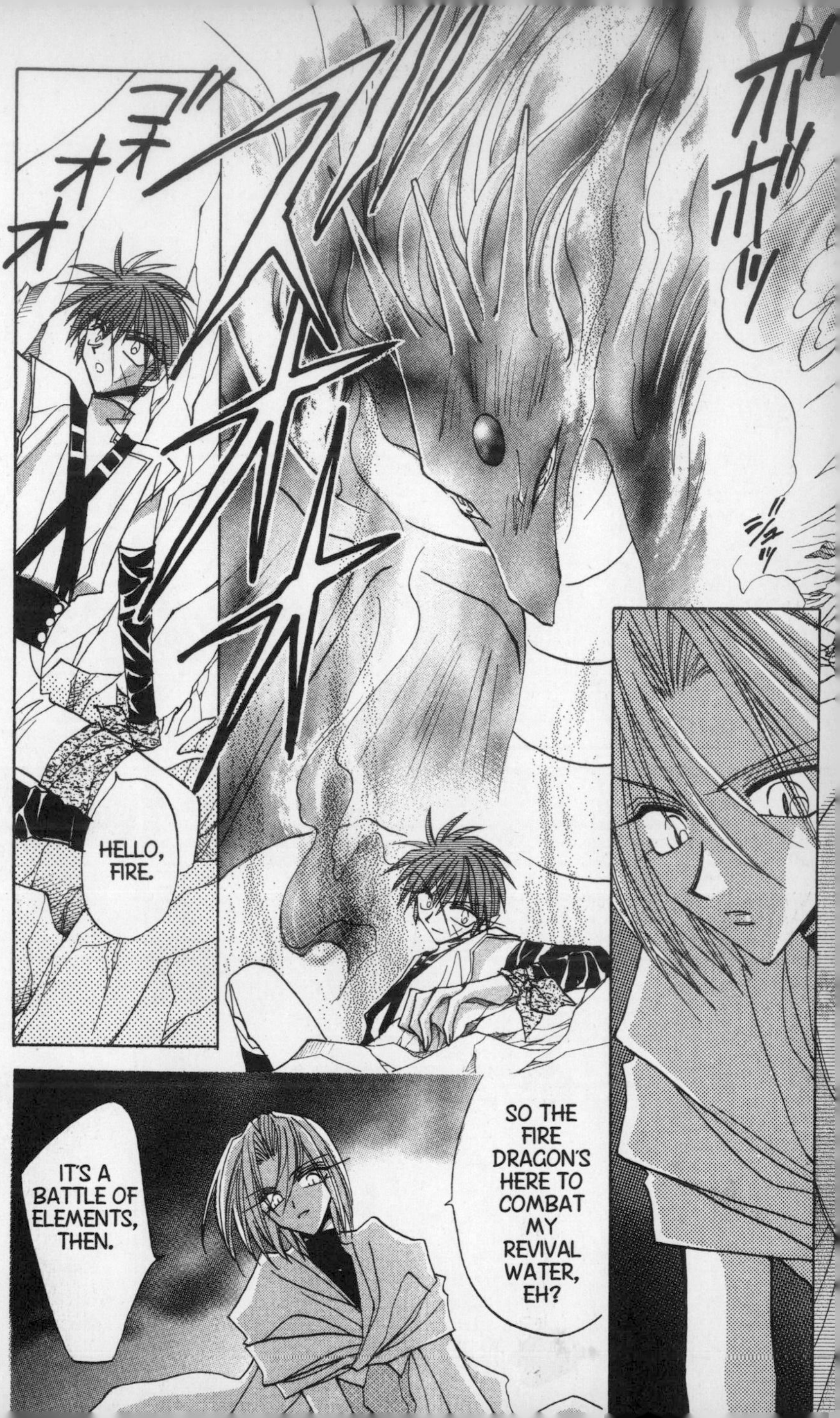
ボボッ
ジュッ
ゴオオオオ
HELLO, FIRE.
SO THE FIRE DRAGON'S HERE TO COMBAT MY REVIVAL WATER, EH?
IT'S A BATTLE OF ELEMENTS, THEN.

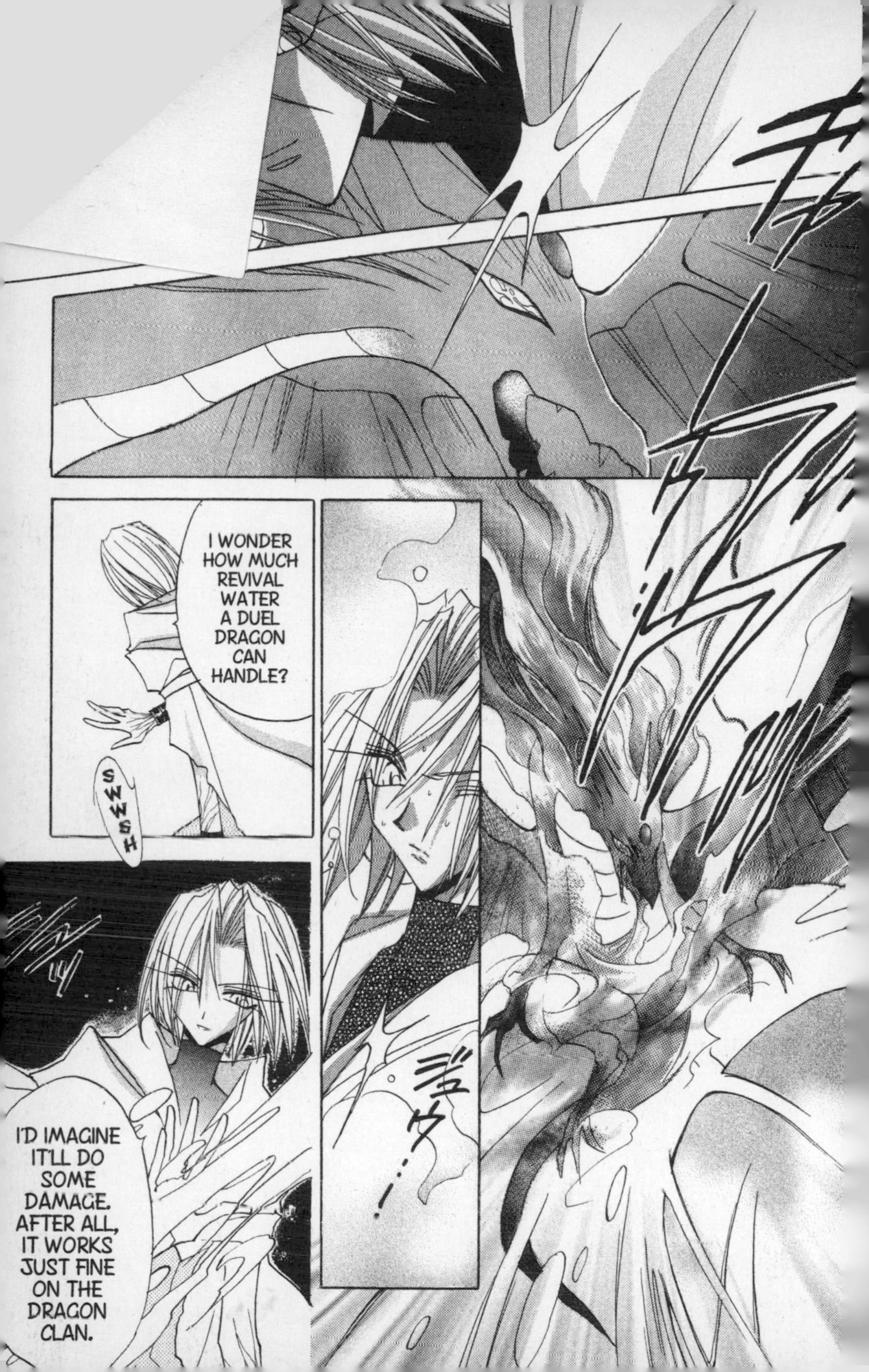
ジュウ…!
I WONDER HOW MUCH REVIVAL WATER A DUEL DRAGON CAN HANDLE?
SWWSH
I'D IMAGINE IT'LL DO SOME DAMAGE. AFTER ALL, IT WORKS JUST FINE ON THE DRAGON CLAN.

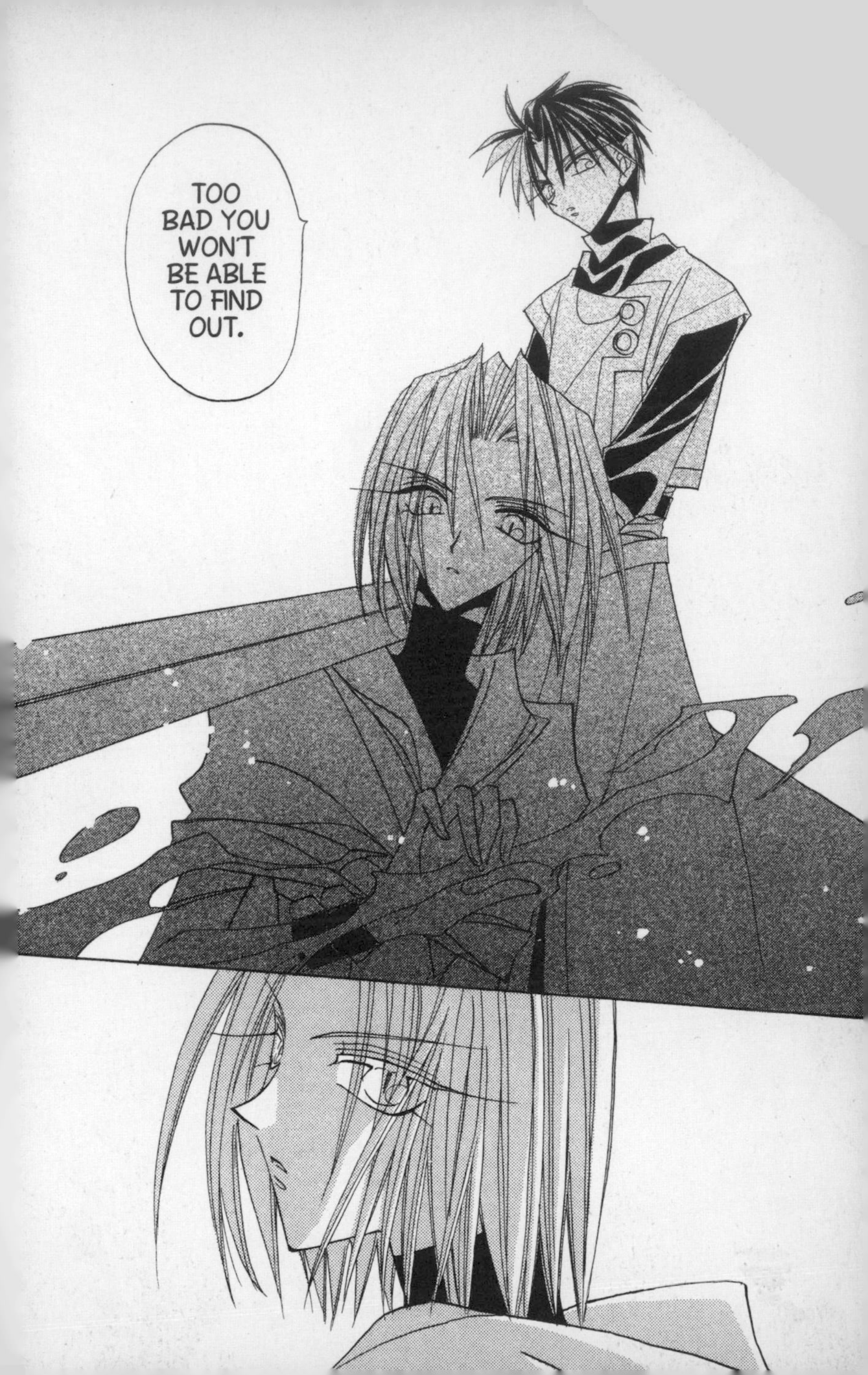
TOO BAD YOU WON'T BE ABLE TO FIND OUT.

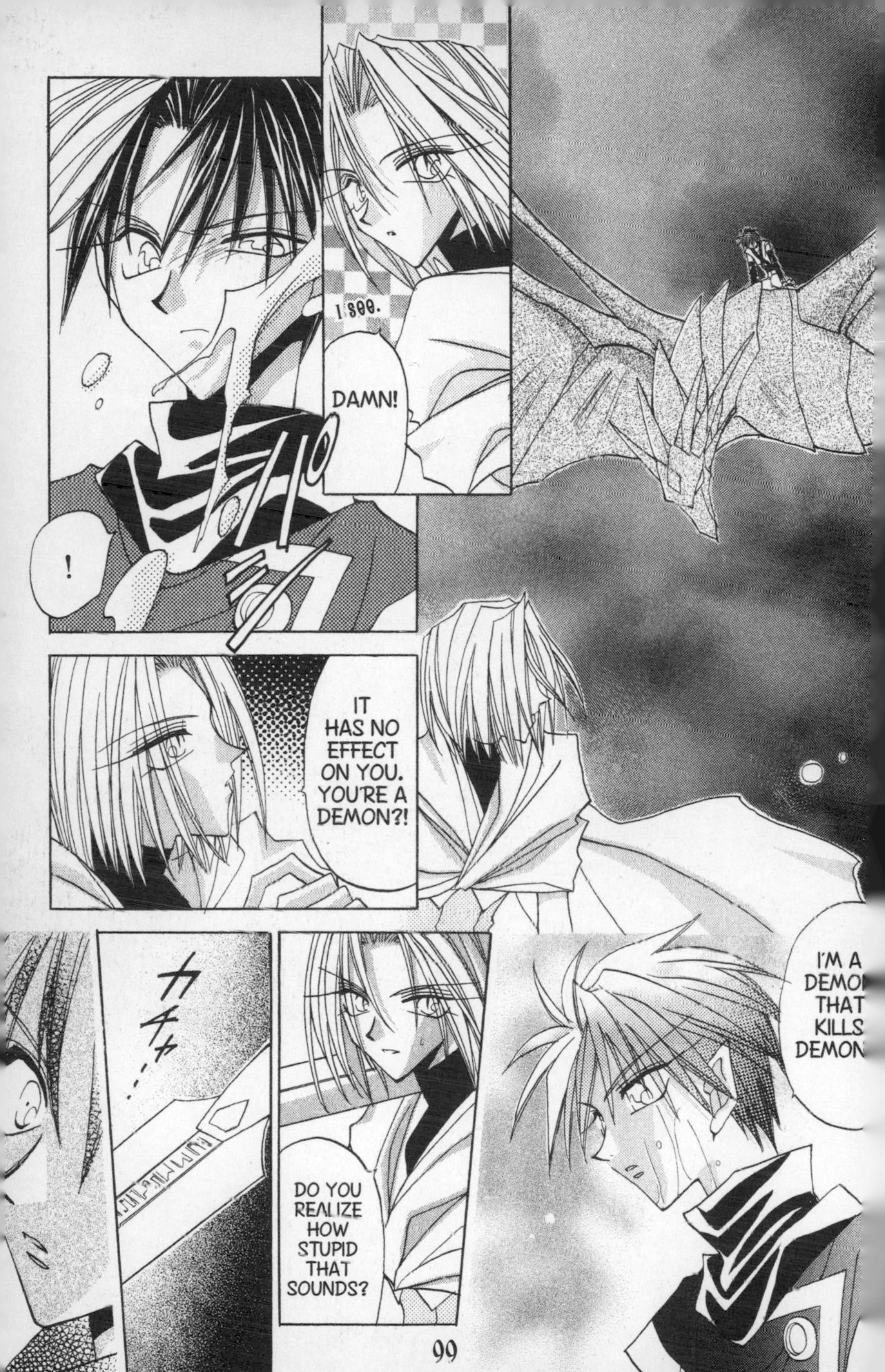
I see.
DAMN!
!
IT HAS NO EFFECT ON YOU. YOU'RE A DEMON?!
I'M A DEMO THAT KILLS DEMON
DO YOU REALIZE HOW STUPID THAT SOUNDS?
カチャ…

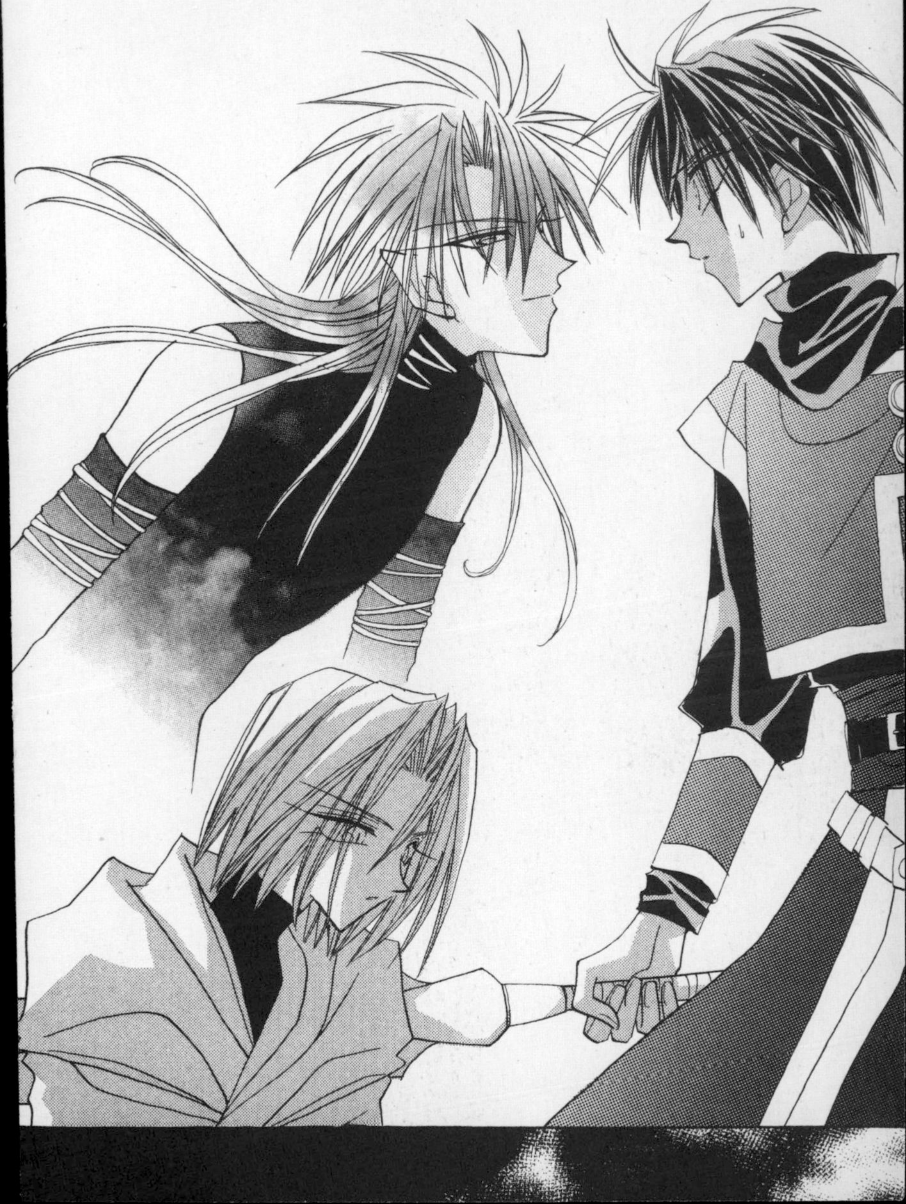

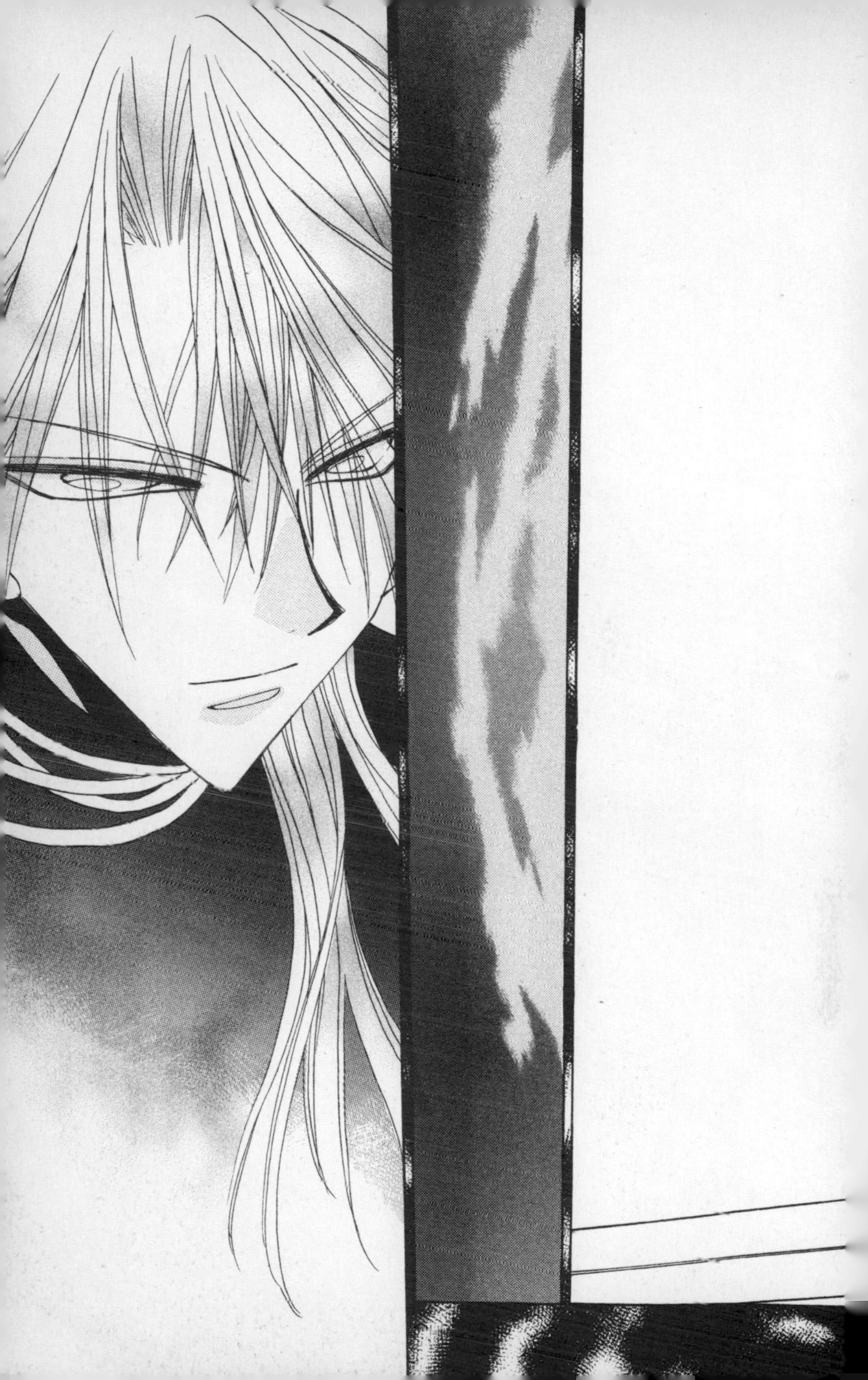

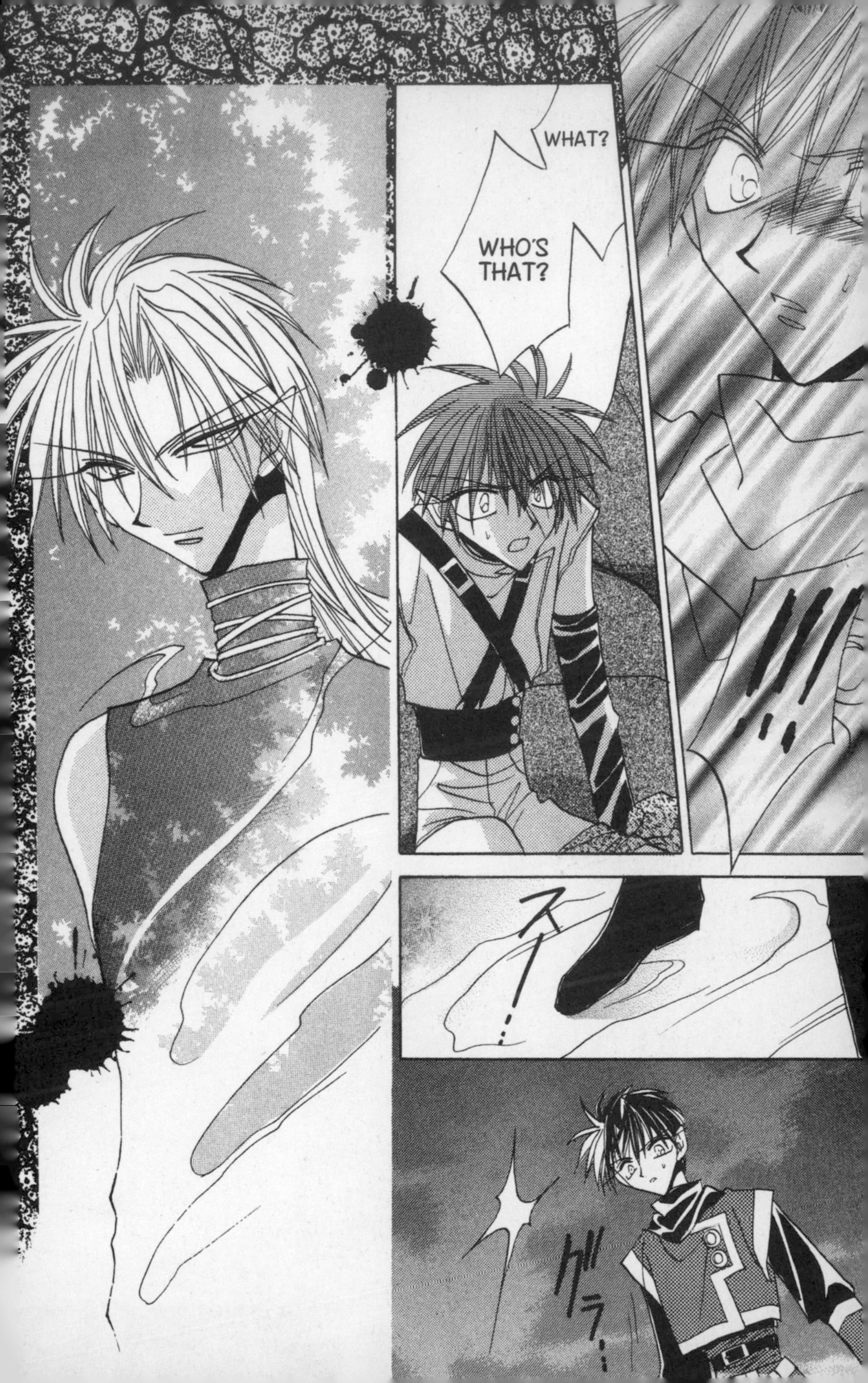
WHAT?
WHO'S THAT?

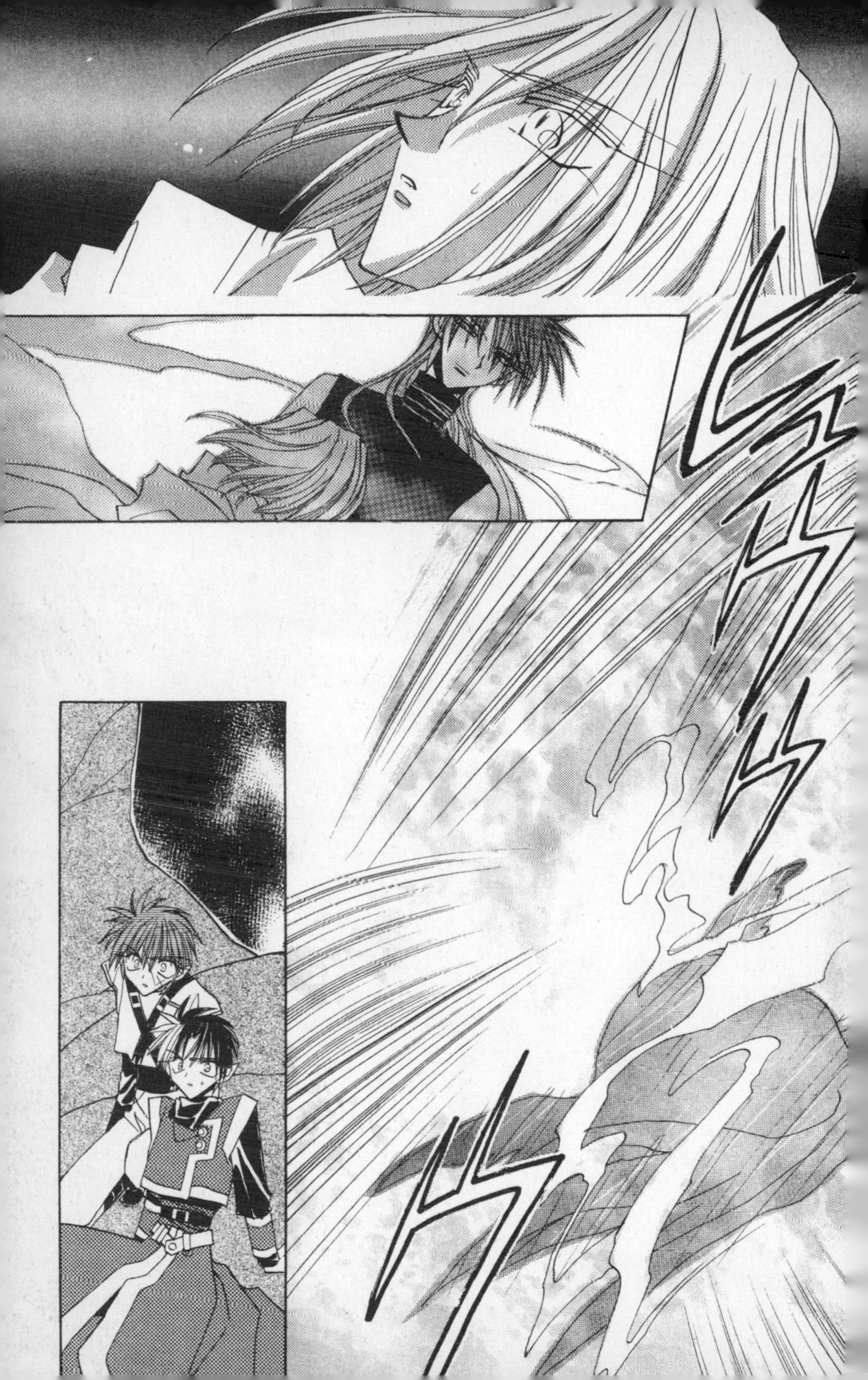

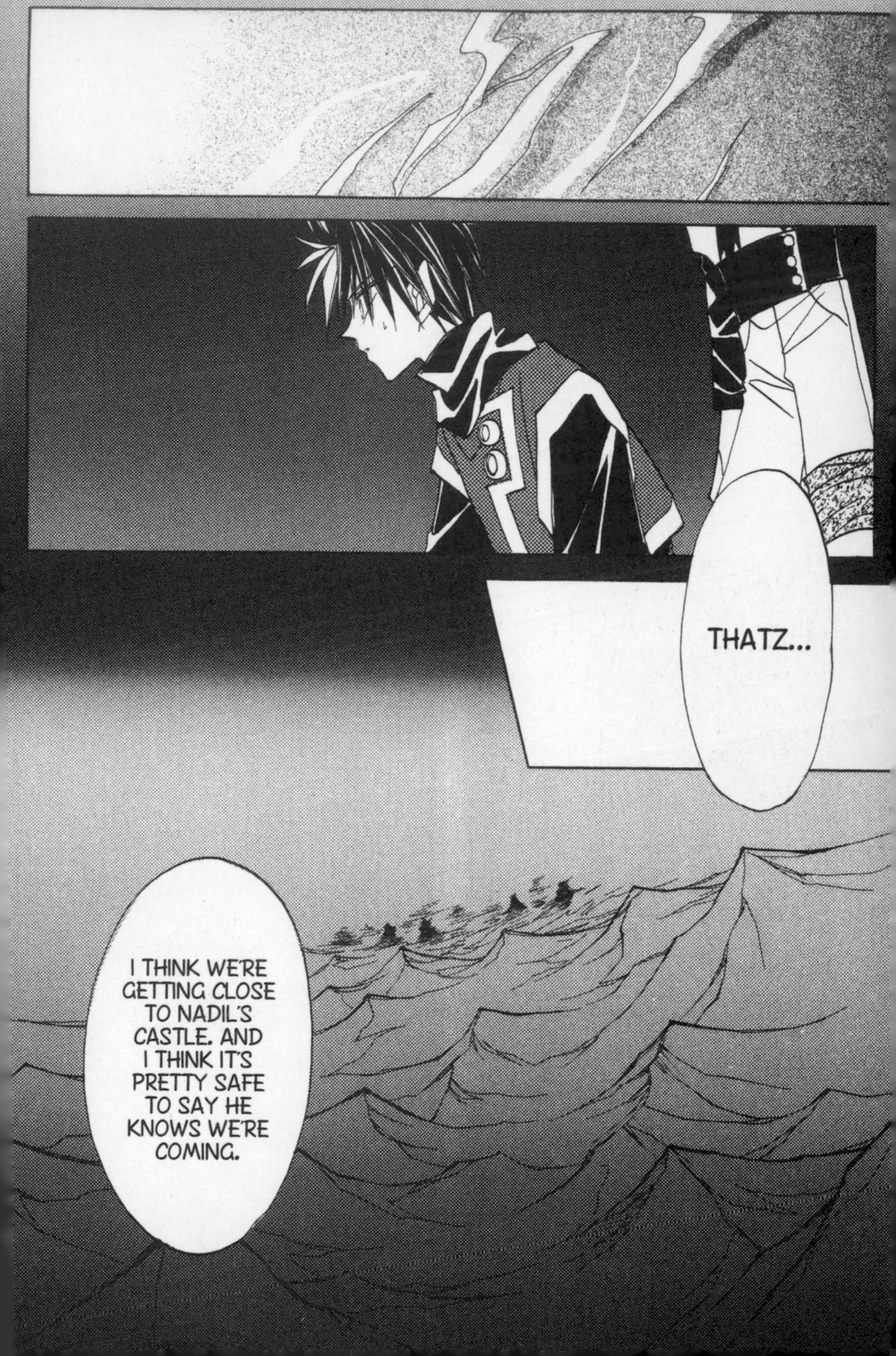
THATZ...
I THINK WE'RE GETTING CLOSE TO NADIL'S CASTLE. AND I THINK IT'S PRETTY SAFE TO SAY HE KNOWS WE'RE COMING.

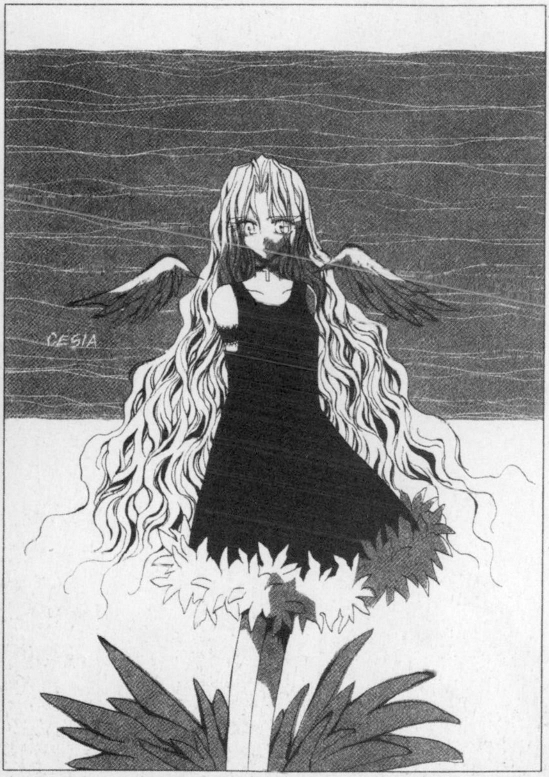
CESIA

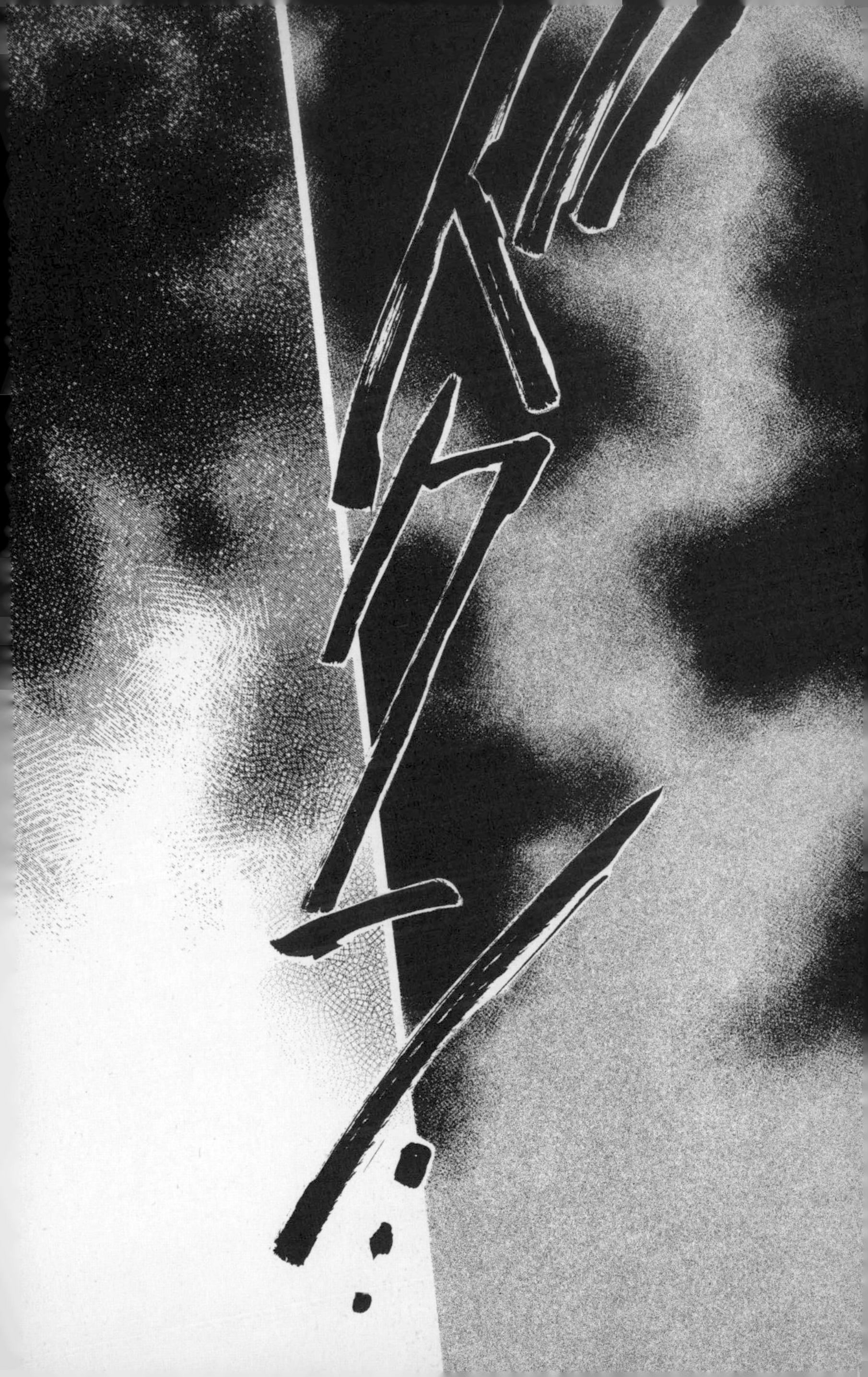

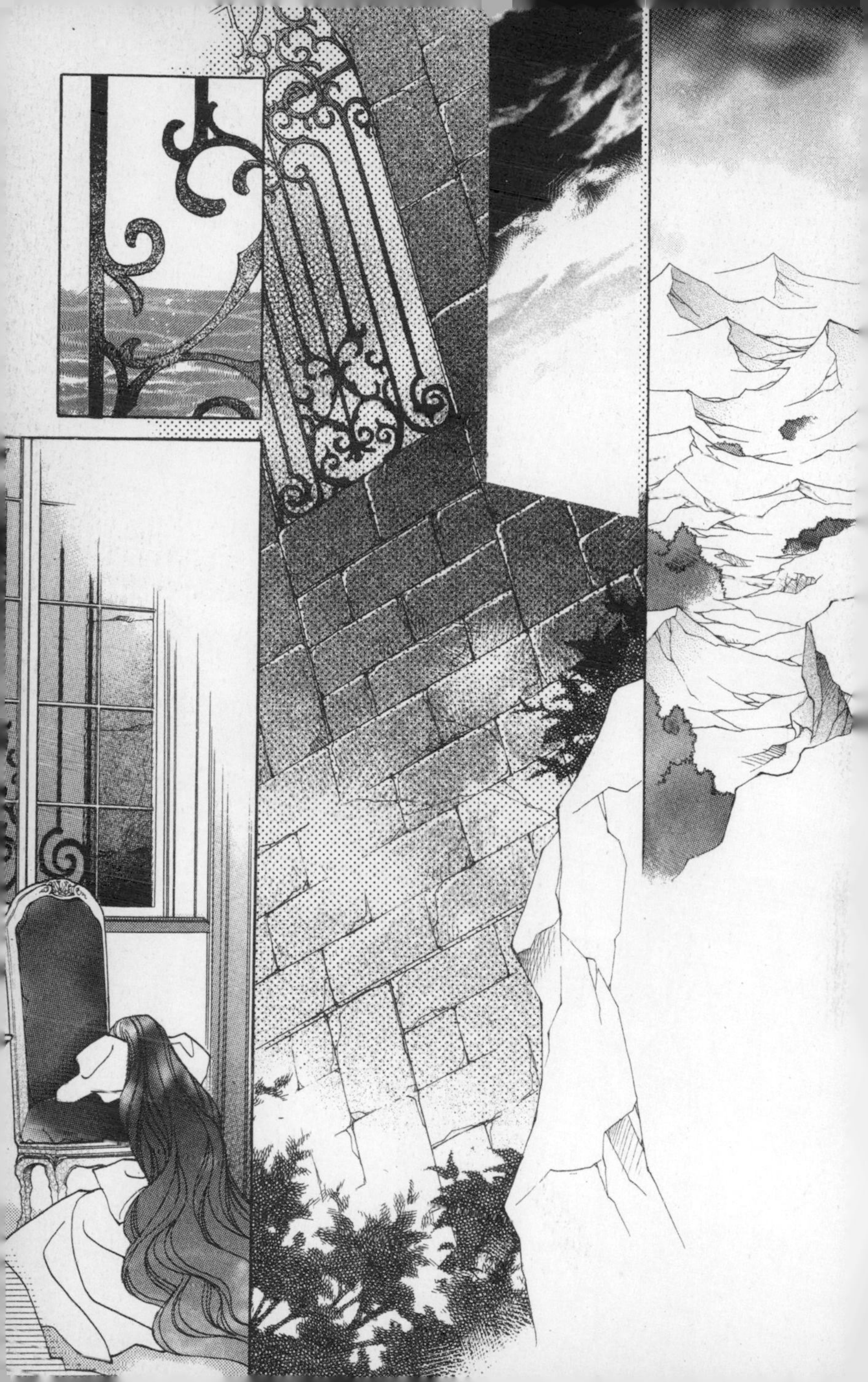

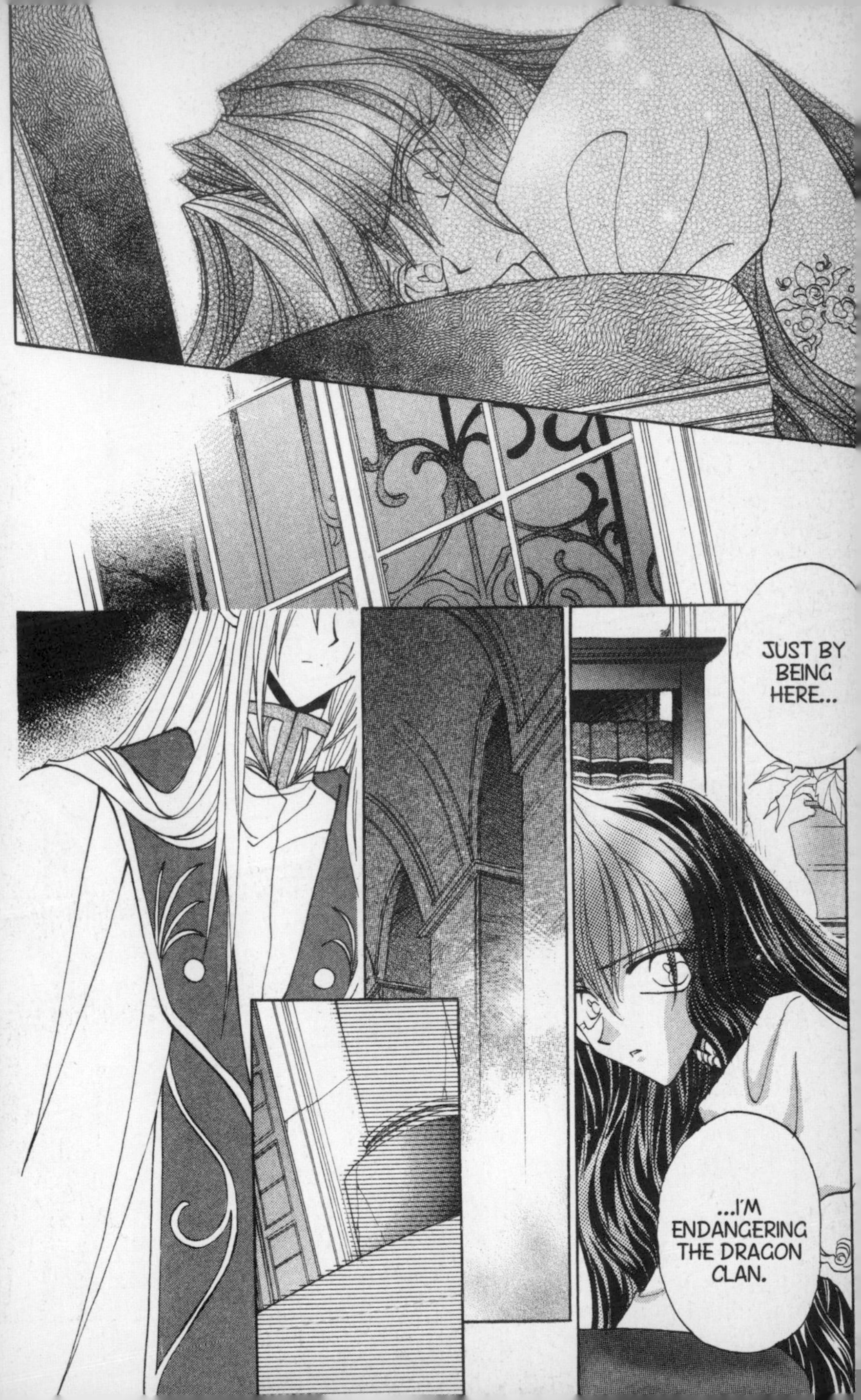
JUST BY BEING HERE...
...I'M ENDANGERING THE DRAGON CLAN.

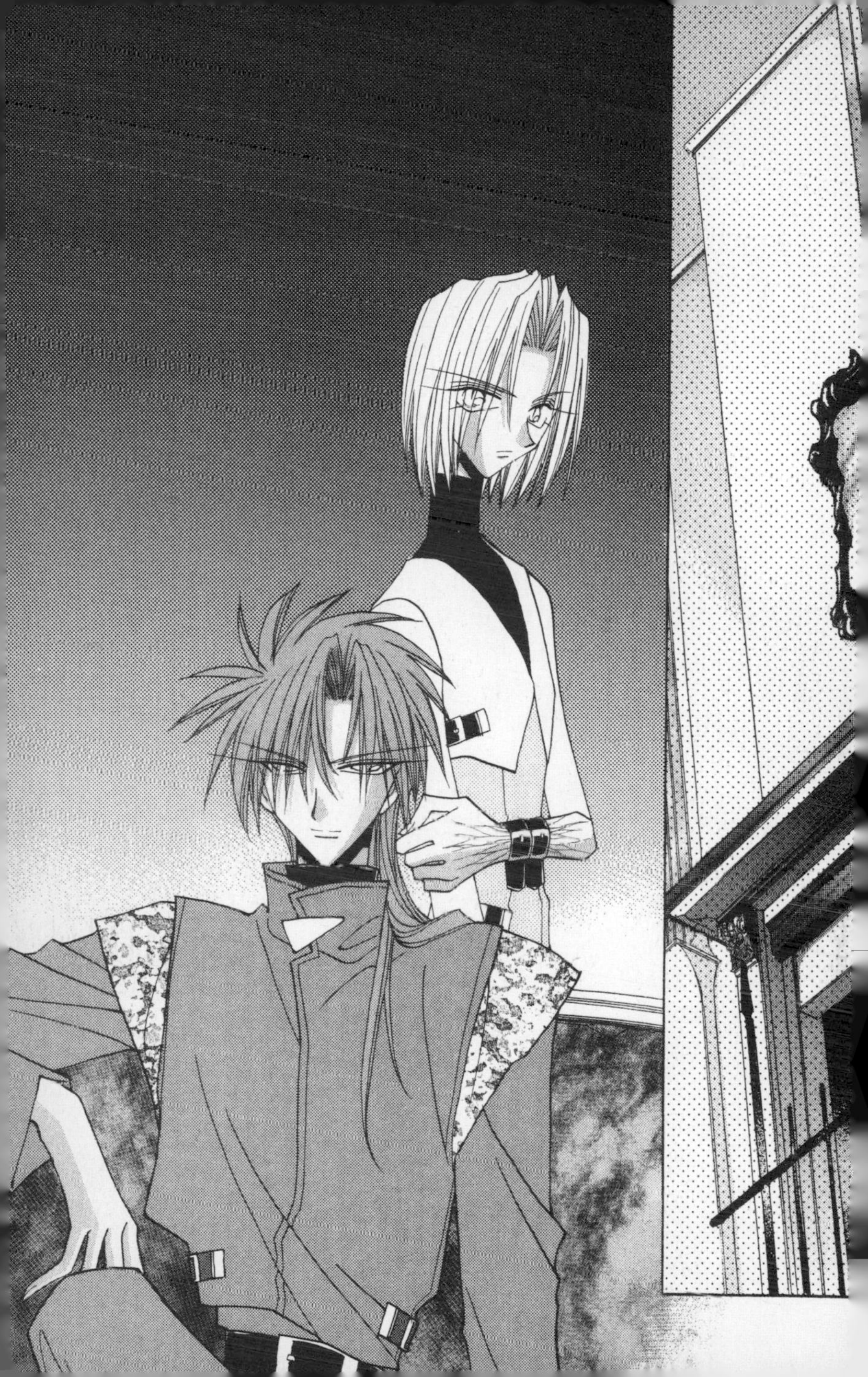

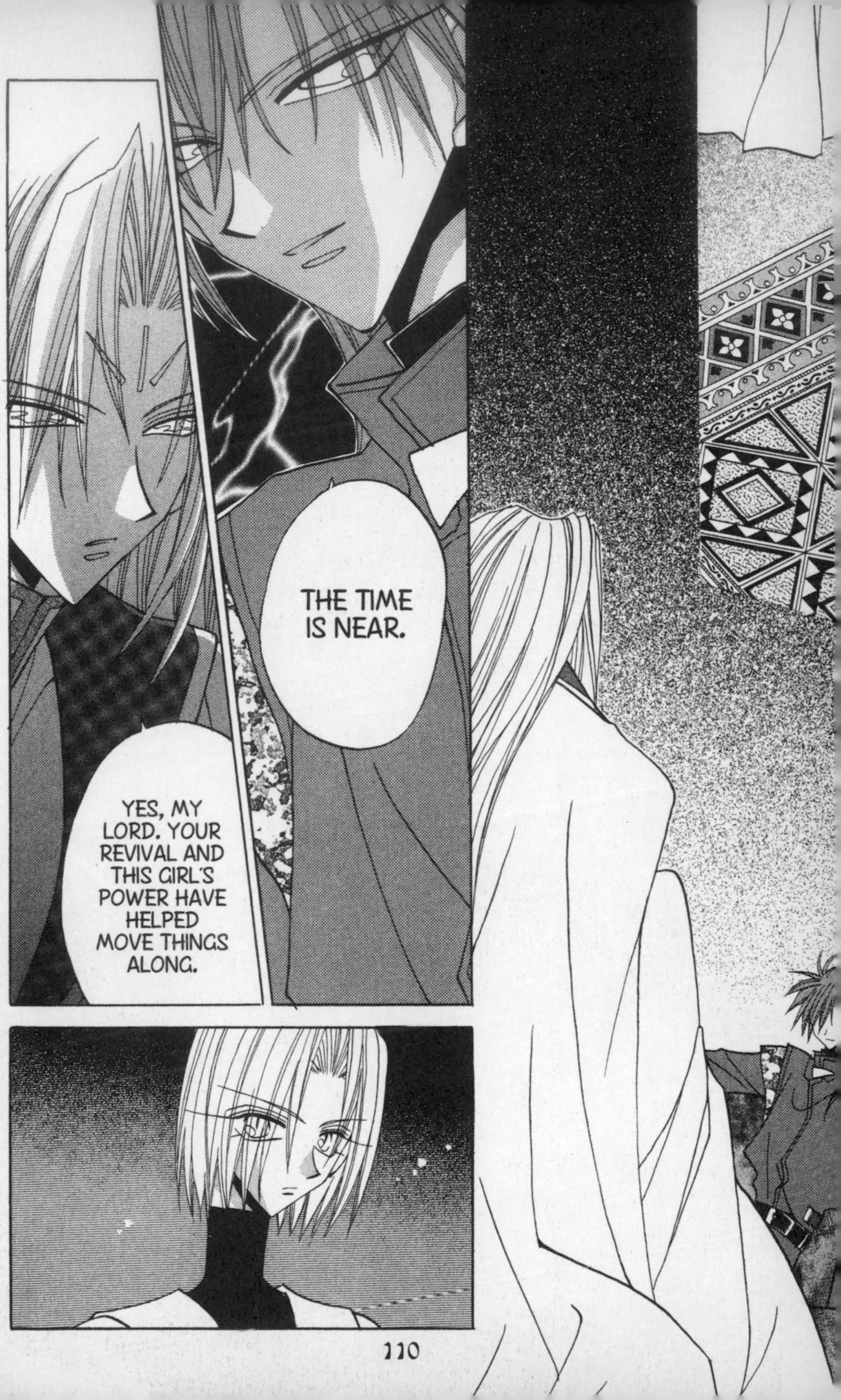
THE TIME IS NEAR.
YES, MY LORD. YOUR REVIVAL AND THIS GIRL'S POWER HAVE HELPED MOVE THINGS ALONG.

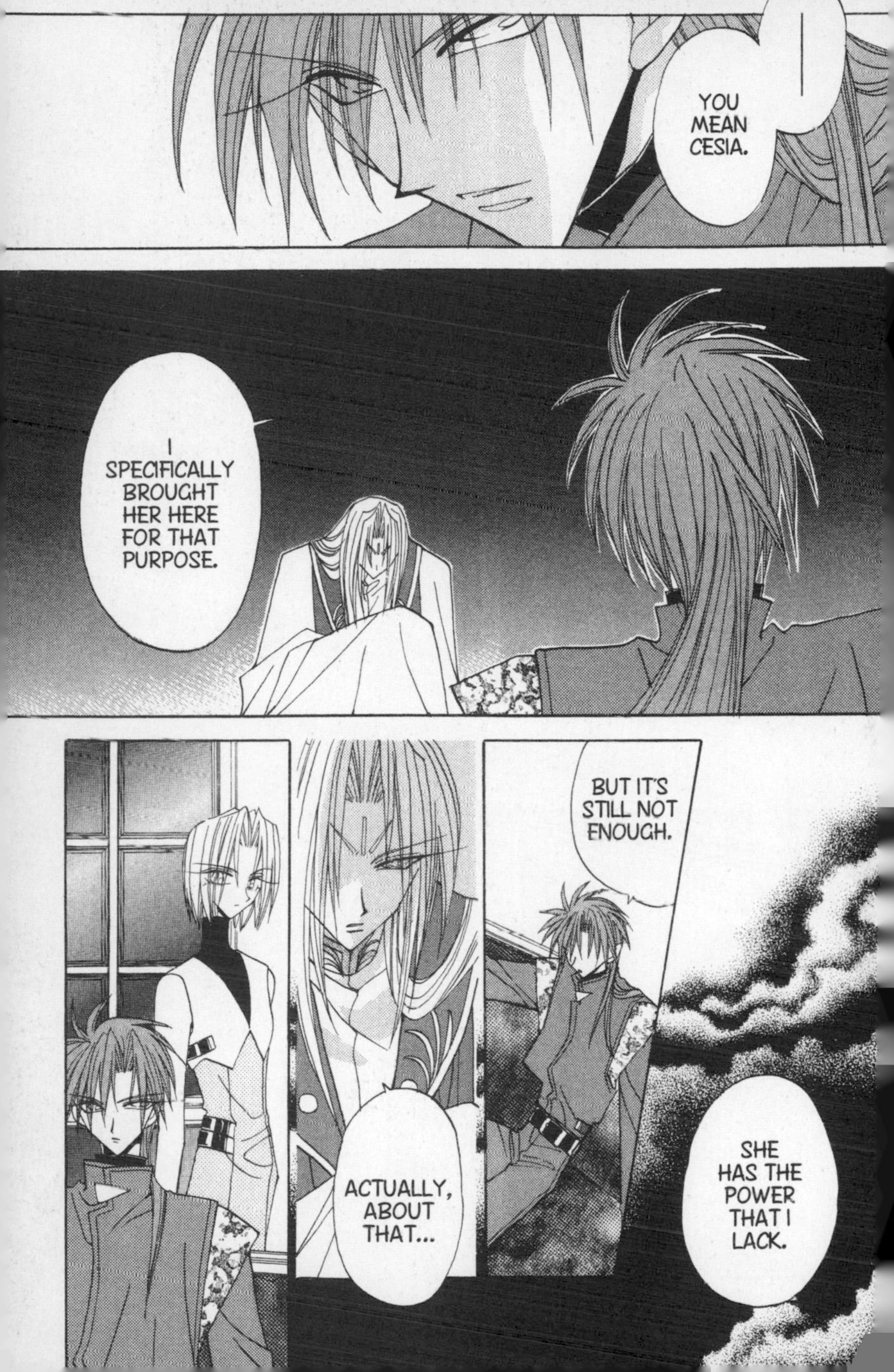
—
YOU MEAN CESIA.
I SPECIFICALLY BROUGHT HER HERE FOR THAT PURPOSE.
SHE HAS THE POWER THAT I LACK.
BUT IT'S STILL NOT ENOUGH.
ACTUALLY, ABOUT THAT...

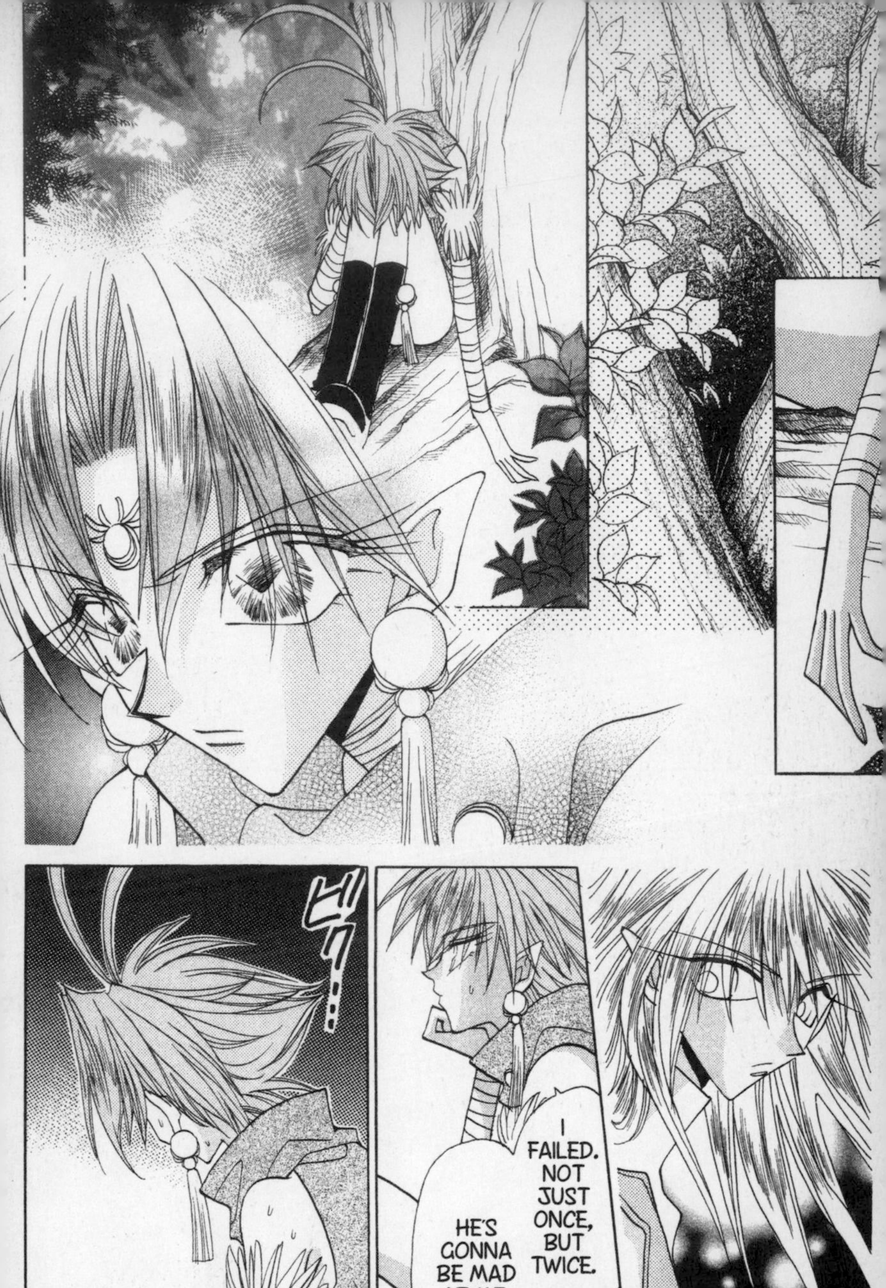
I FAILED. NOT JUST ONCE, BUT TWICE.
HE'S GONNA BE MAD AT ME.

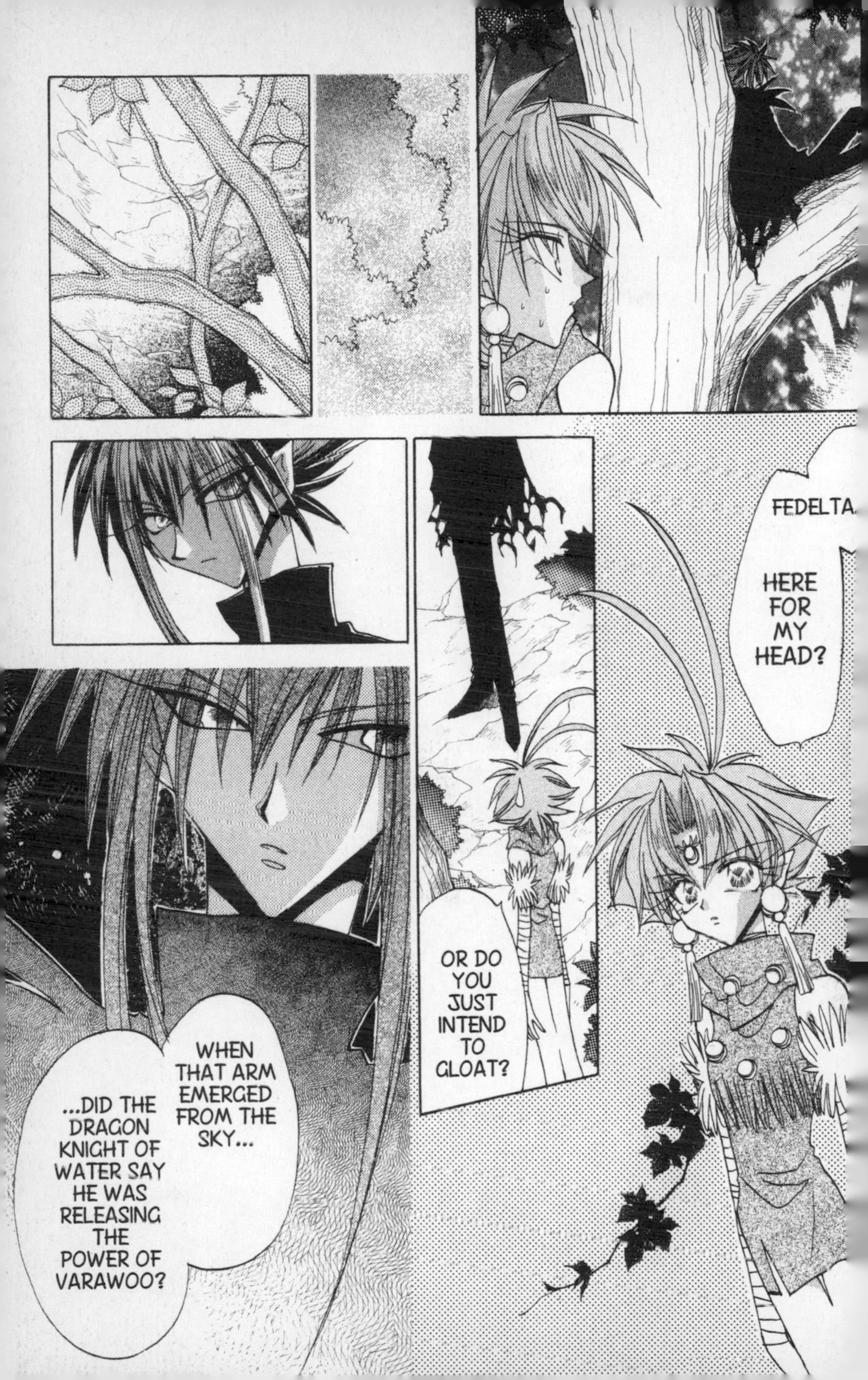
FEDELTA.
HERE FOR MY HEAD?
OR DO YOU JUST INTEND TO GLOAT?
WHEN THAT ARM EMERGED FROM THE SKY...
...DID THE DRAGON KNIGHT OF WATER SAY HE WAS RELEASING THE POWER OF VARAWOO?

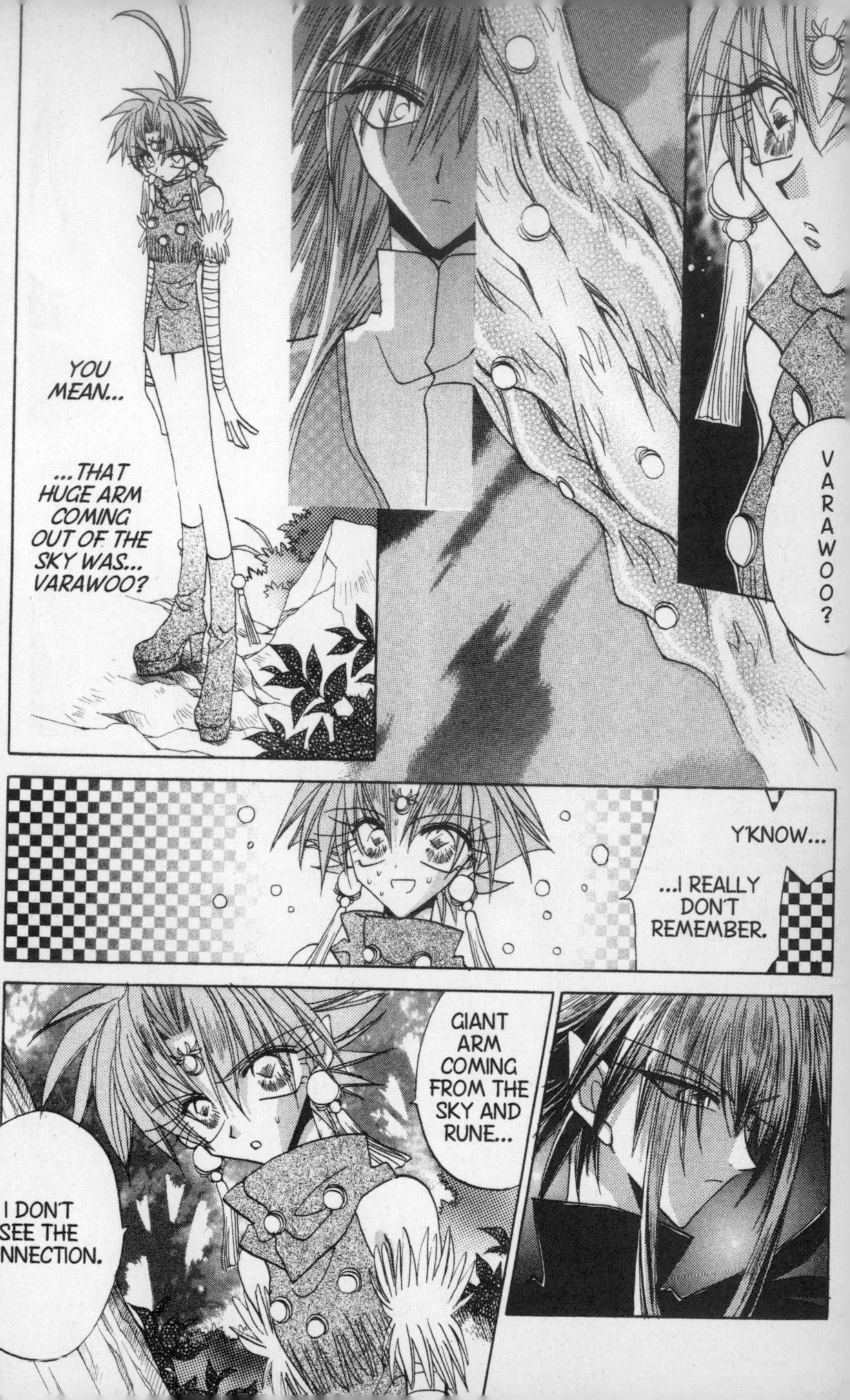
VARAWOO?
YOU MEAN...
...THAT HUGE ARM COMING OUT OF THE SKY WAS... VARAWOO?
Y'KNOW...
...I REALLY DON'T REMEMBER.
GIANT ARM COMING FROM THE SKY AND RUNE...
I DON'T SEE THE ONNECTION.

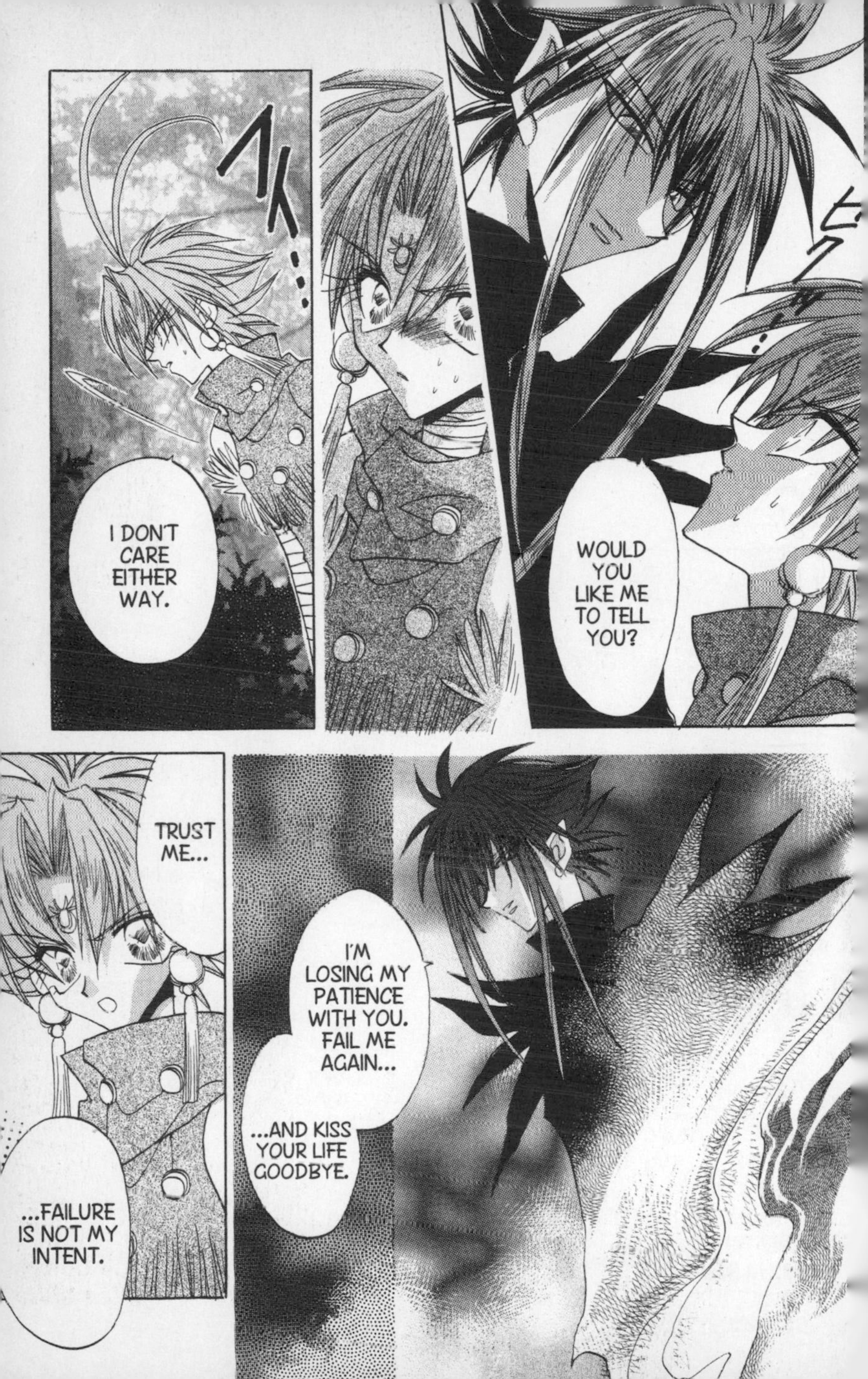
WOULD YOU LIKE ME TO TELL YOU?
I DON'T CARE EITHER WAY.
I'M LOSING MY PATIENCE WITH YOU. FAIL ME AGAIN...
...AND KISS YOUR LIFE GOODBYE.
TRUST ME...
...FAILURE IS NOT MY INTENT.

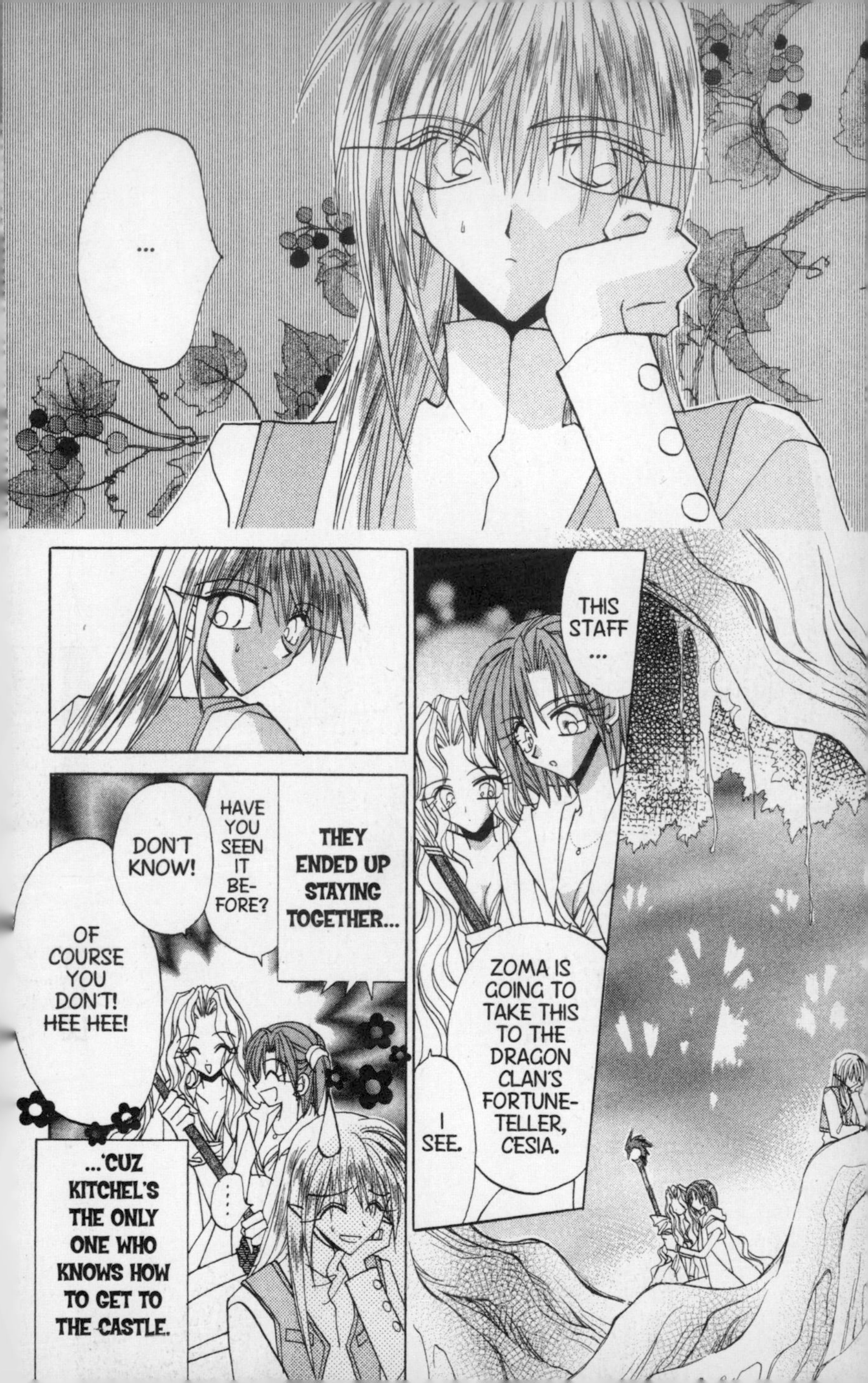
...
THIS STAFF ...
ZOMA IS GOING TO TAKE THIS TO THE DRAGON CLAN'S FORTUNE-TELLER, CESIA.
I SEE.
THEY ENDED UP STAYING TOGETHER...
HAVE YOU SEEN IT BEFORE?
DON'T KNOW!
OF COURSE YOU DON'T! HEE HEE!
....
...'CUZ KITCHEL'S THE ONLY ONE WHO KNOWS HOW TO GET TO THE CASTLE.

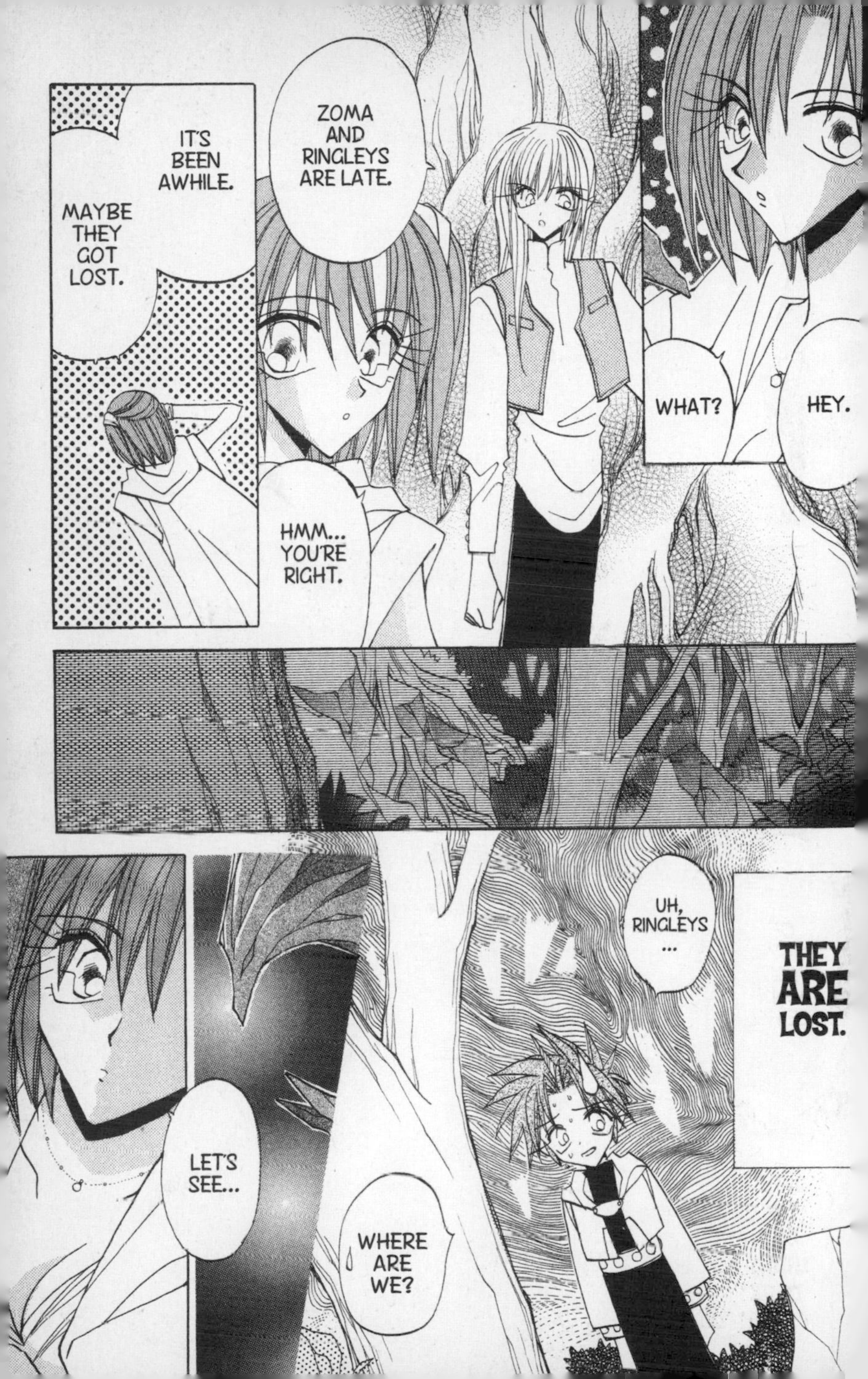
HEY.
WHAT?
ZOMA AND RINGLEYS ARE LATE.
IT'S BEEN AWHILE.
MAYBE THEY GOT LOST.
HMM... YOU'RE RIGHT.
THEY ARE LOST.
UH, RINGLEYS ...
WHERE ARE WE?
LET'S SEE...

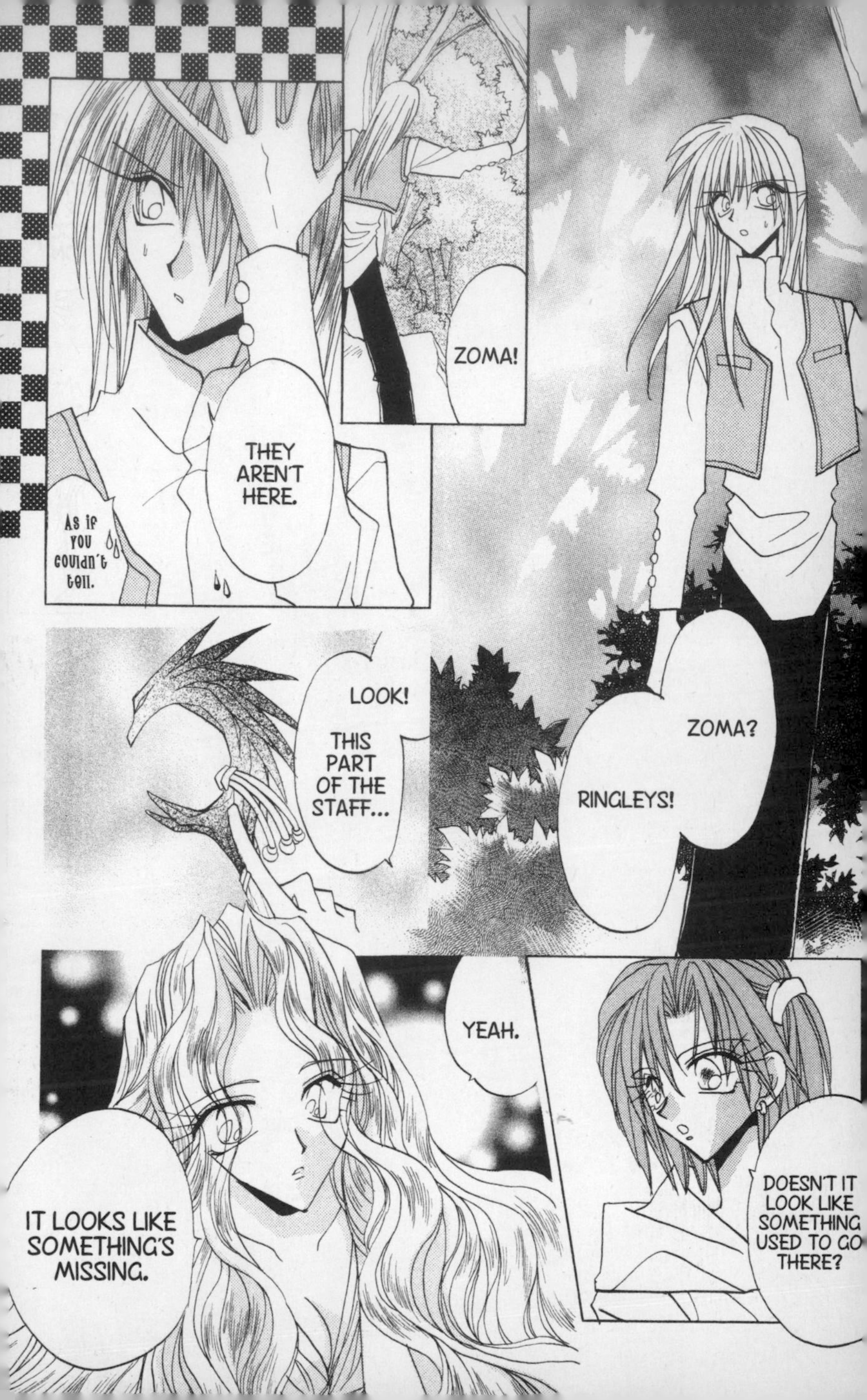
ZOMA?
RINGLEYS!
ZOMA!
THEY AREN'T HERE.
As if you couldn't tell.
LOOK!
THIS PART OF THE STAFF...
DOESN'T IT LOOK LIKE SOMETHING USED TO GO THERE?
YEAH.
IT LOOKS LIKE SOMETHING'S MISSING.

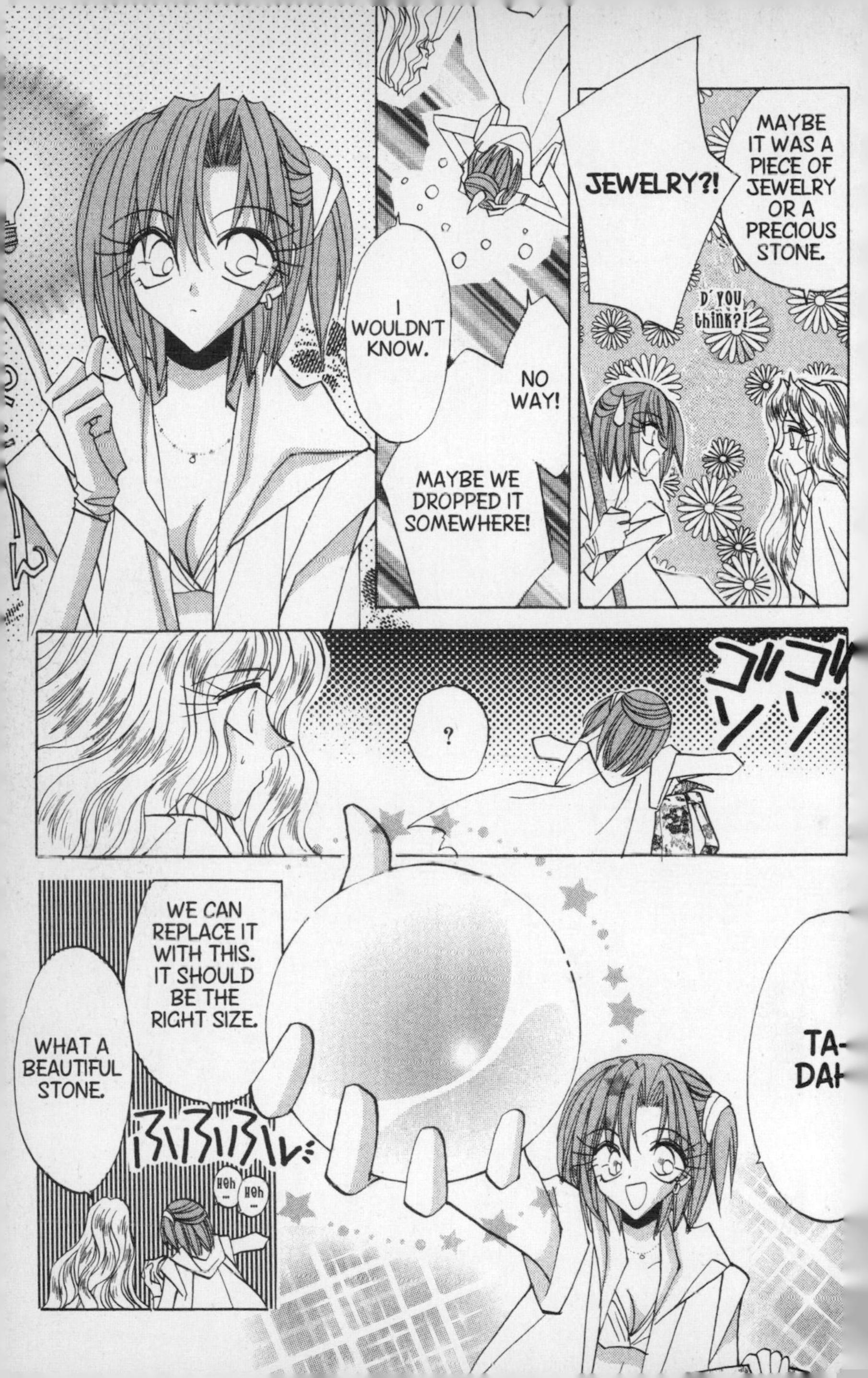
MAYBE IT WAS A PIECE OF JEWELRY OR A PRECIOUS STONE.
D'YOU THINK?!
JEWELRY?!
I WOULDN'T KNOW.
NO WAY!
MAYBE WE DROPPED IT SOMEWHERE!
ゴソゴソ
?
TA-
DA
WE CAN REPLACE IT WITH THIS. IT SHOULD BE THE RIGHT SIZE.
WHAT A BEAUTIFUL STONE.
Heh... Heh...

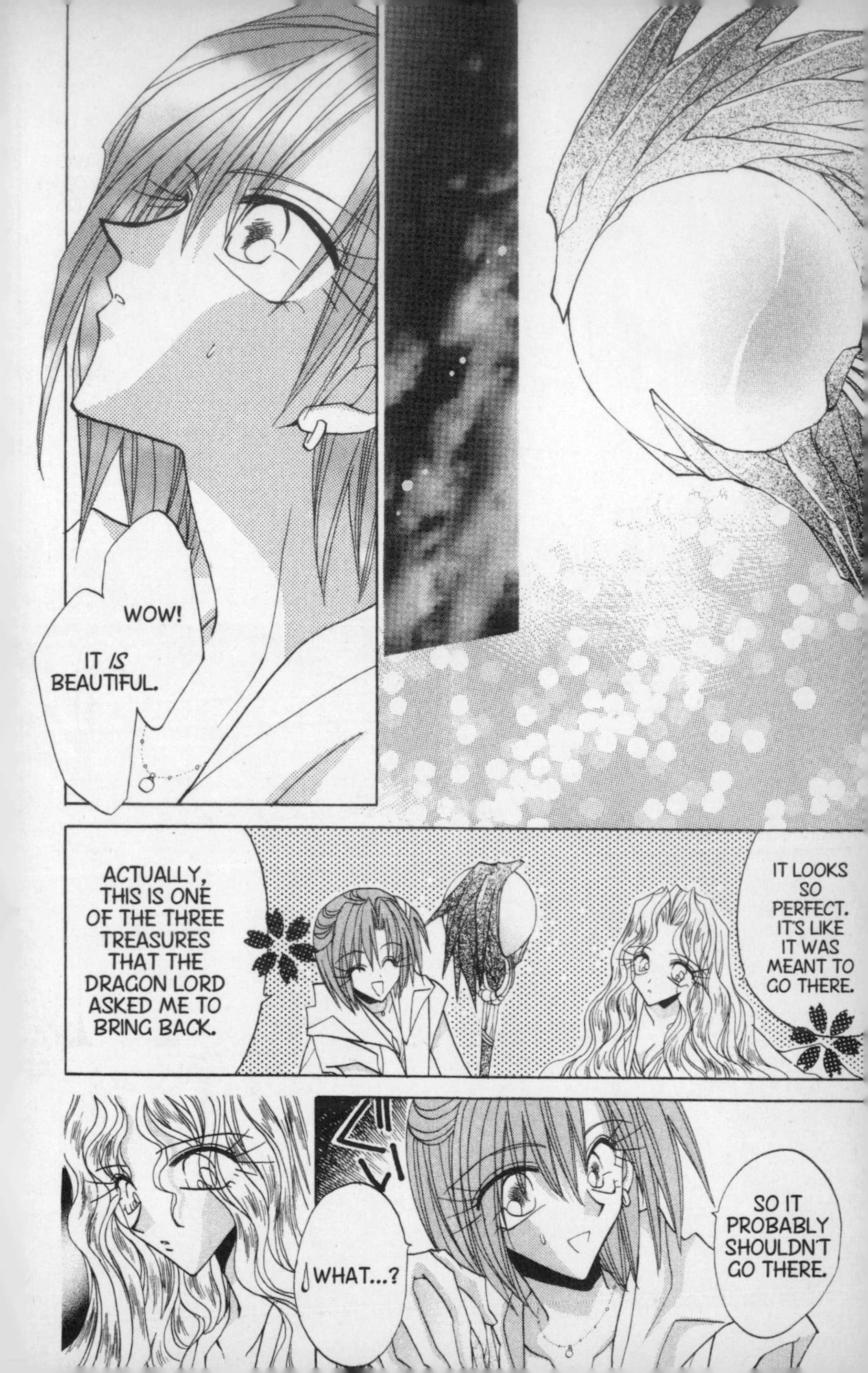
WOW!
IT *IS* BEAUTIFUL.
IT LOOKS SO PERFECT. IT'S LIKE IT WAS MEANT TO GO THERE.
ACTUALLY, THIS IS ONE OF THE THREE TREASURES THAT THE DRAGON LORD ASKED ME TO BRING BACK.
SO IT PROBABLY SHOULDN'T GO THERE.
WHAT...?

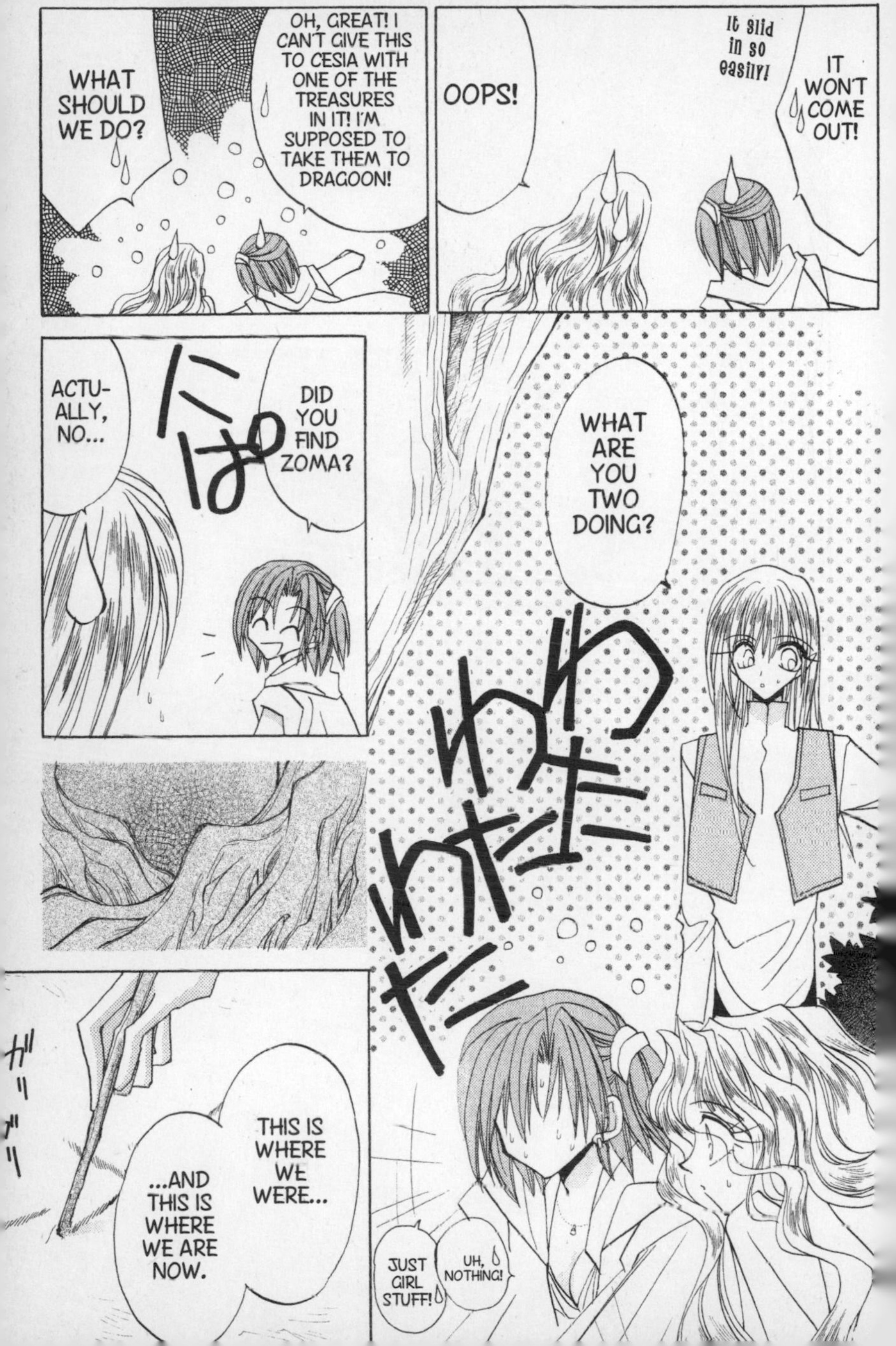

IT WON'T COME OUT!
It slid in so easily!
OOPS!
OH, GREAT! I CAN'T GIVE THIS TO CESIA WITH ONE OF THE TREASURES IN IT! I'M SUPPOSED TO TAKE THEM TO DRAGOON!
WHAT SHOULD WE DO?
WHAT ARE YOU TWO DOING?
UH, NOTHING!
JUST GIRL STUFF!
DID YOU FIND ZOMA?
にぱ
ACTU-ALLY, NO...
THIS IS WHERE WE WERE...
...AND THIS IS WHERE WE ARE NOW.
ガリガリ

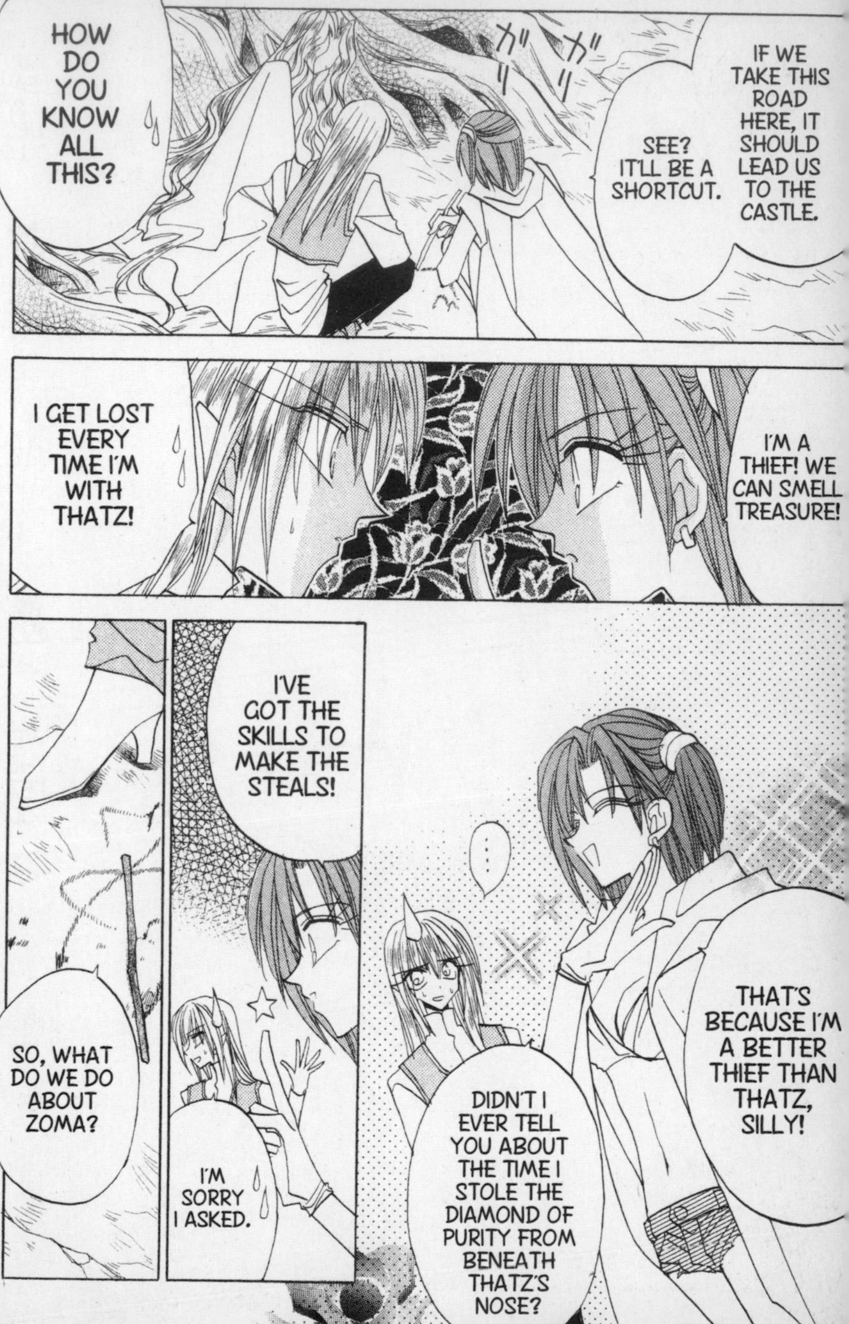
IF WE TAKE THIS ROAD HERE, IT SHOULD LEAD US TO THE CASTLE.
SEE? IT'LL BE A SHORTCUT.
HOW DO YOU KNOW ALL THIS?
I'M A THIEF! WE CAN SMELL TREASURE!
I GET LOST EVERY TIME I'M WITH THATZ!
THAT'S BECAUSE I'M A BETTER THIEF THAN THATZ, SILLY!
...
DIDN'T I EVER TELL YOU ABOUT THE TIME I STOLE THE DIAMOND OF PURITY FROM BENEATH THATZ'S NOSE?
I'VE GOT THE SKILLS TO MAKE THE STEALS!
I'M SORRY I ASKED.
SO, WHAT DO WE DO ABOUT ZOMA?

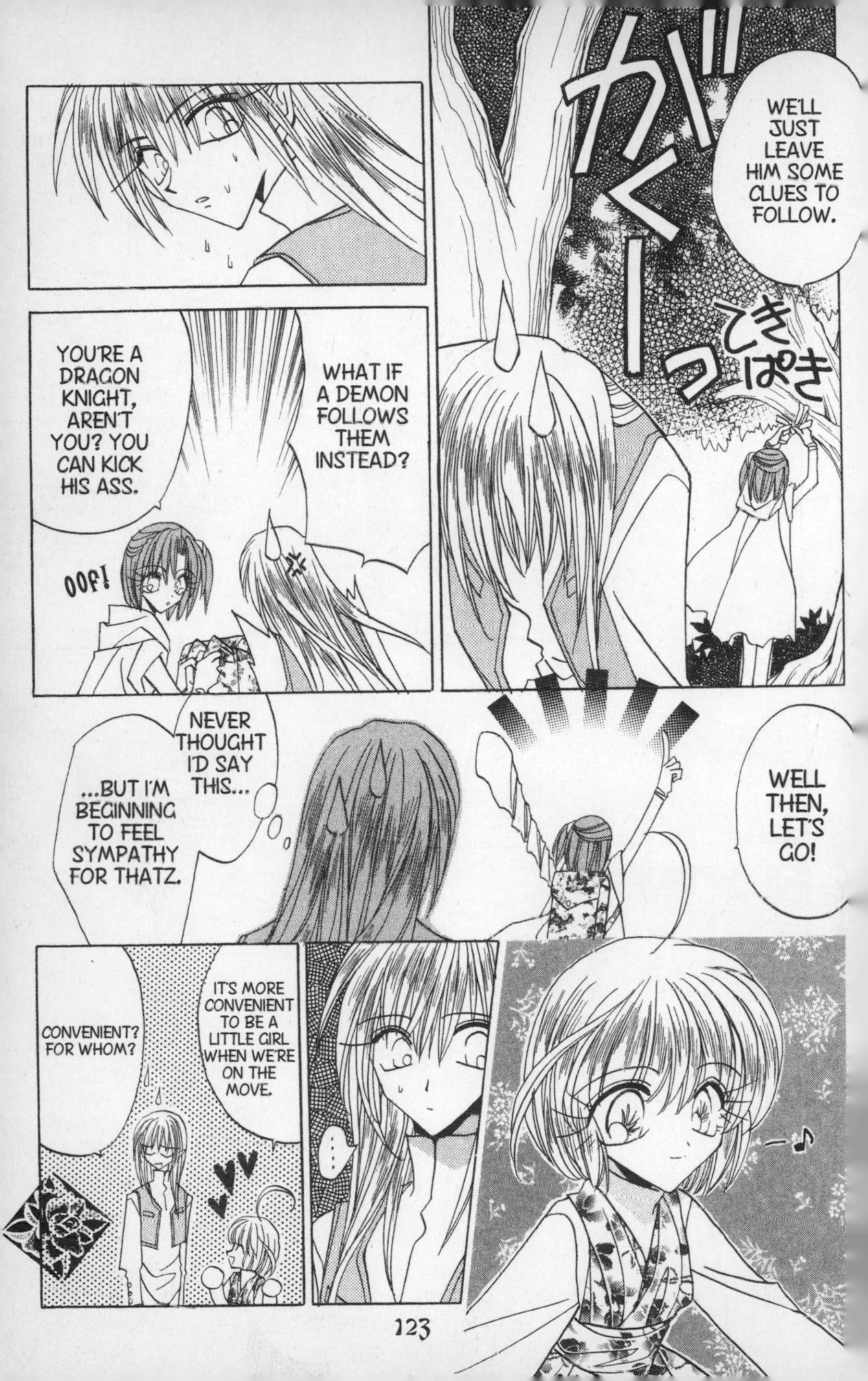

WE'LL JUST LEAVE HIM SOME CLUES TO FOLLOW.
がくーっ
てきぱき
WHAT IF A DEMON FOLLOWS THEM INSTEAD?
YOU'RE A DRAGON KNIGHT, AREN'T YOU? YOU CAN KICK HIS ASS.
OOF!
WELL THEN, LET'S GO!
NEVER THOUGHT I'D SAY THIS...
...BUT I'M BEGINNING TO FEEL SYMPATHY FOR THATZ.
—♪
...
IT'S MORE CONVENIENT TO BE A LITTLE GIRL WHEN WE'RE ON THE MOVE.
CONVENIENT? FOR WHOM?

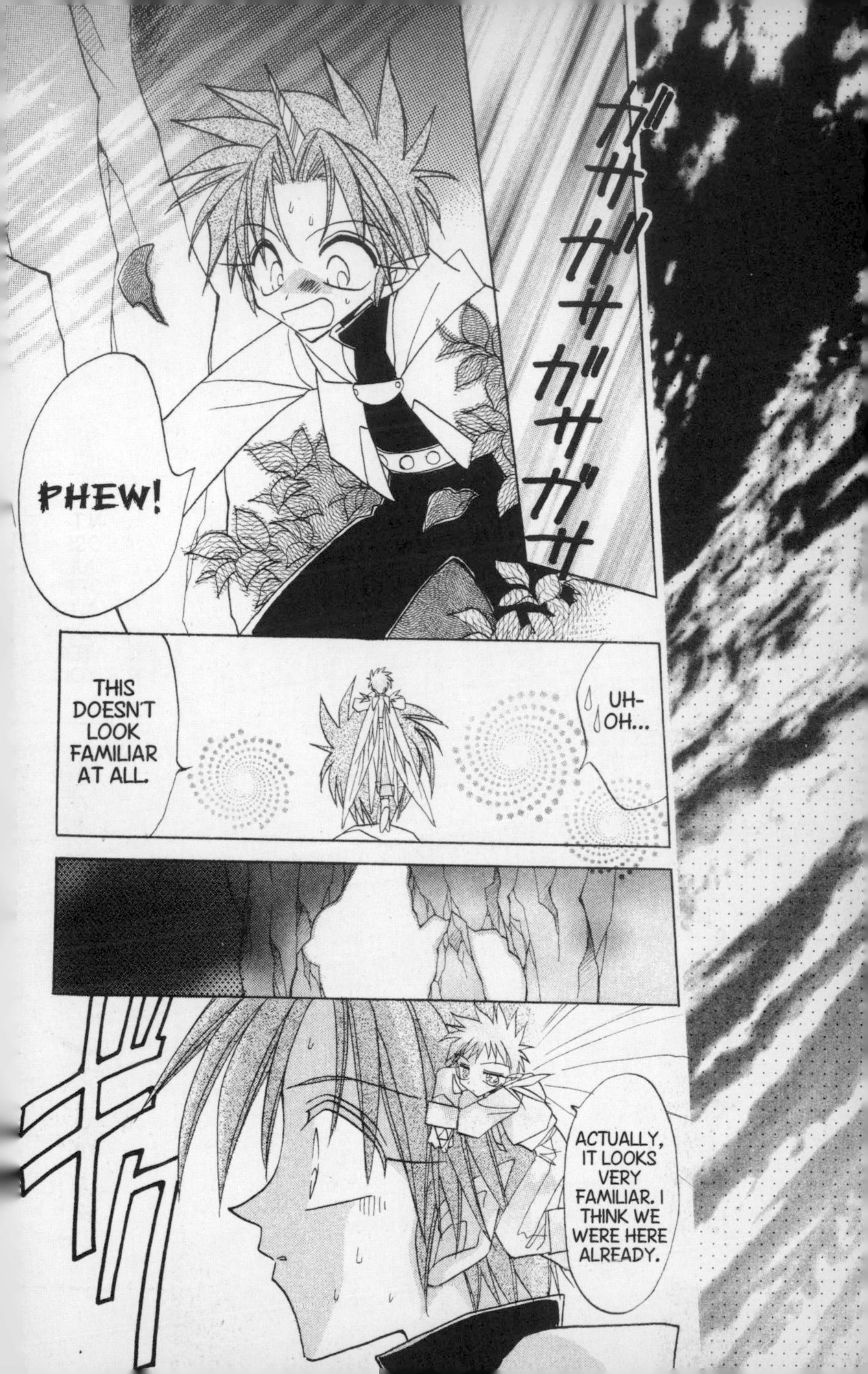
ガサガサガサガサ
PHEW!
UH-OH...
THIS DOESN'T LOOK FAMILIAR AT ALL.
ACTUALLY, IT LOOKS VERY FAMILIAR. I THINK WE WERE HERE ALREADY.

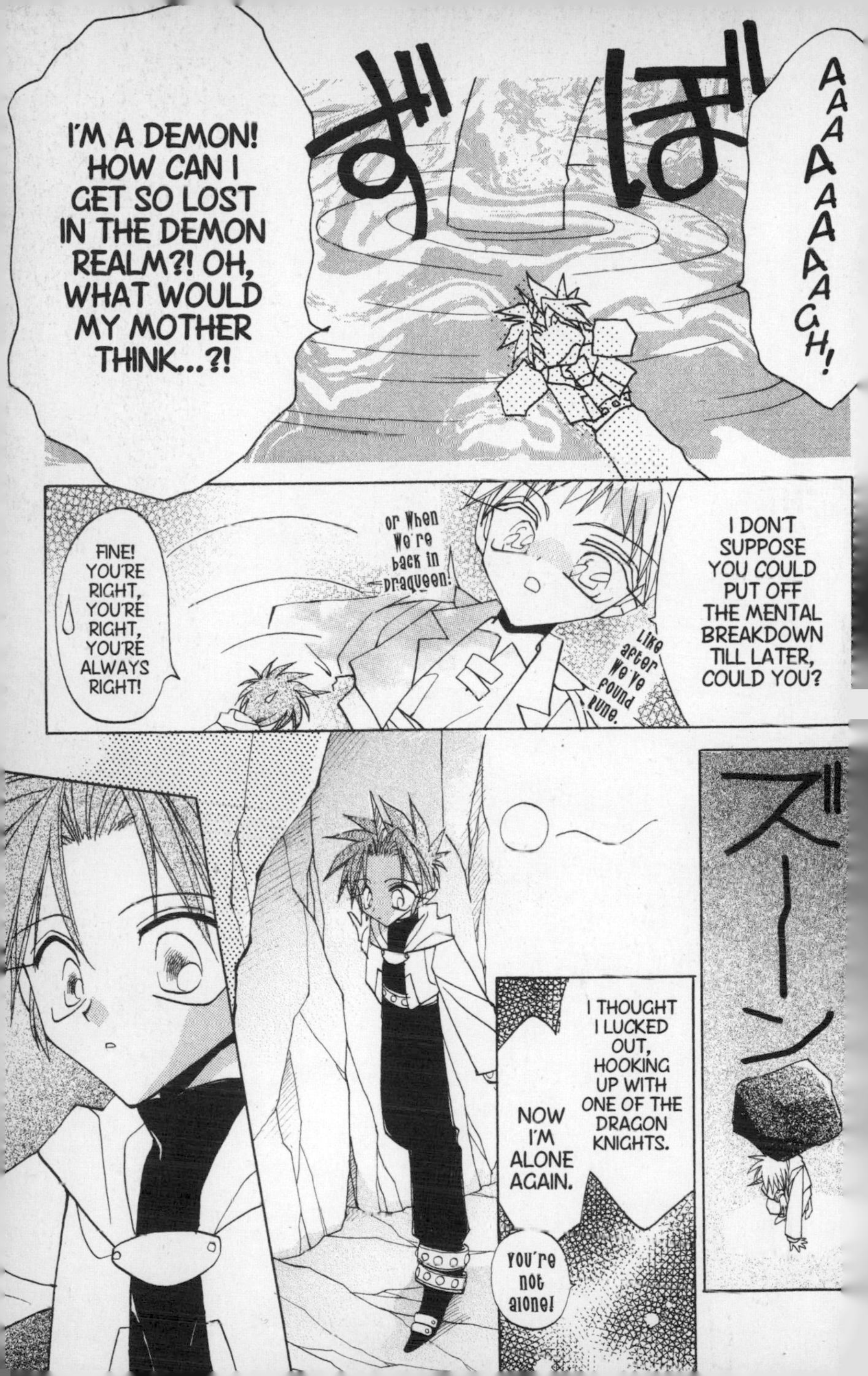
AAAAAAAAAGH!
ずぼ
I'M A DEMON! HOW CAN I GET SO LOST IN THE DEMON REALM?! OH, WHAT WOULD MY MOTHER THINK...?!
I DON'T SUPPOSE YOU COULD PUT OFF THE MENTAL BREAKDOWN TILL LATER, COULD YOU?
Like after we've found Rune.
or when we're back in Draqueen!
FINE! YOU'RE RIGHT, YOU'RE RIGHT, YOU'RE ALWAYS RIGHT!
ズーン
I THOUGHT I LUCKED OUT, HOOKING UP WITH ONE OF THE DRAGON KNIGHTS.
NOW I'M ALONE AGAIN.
You're not alone!

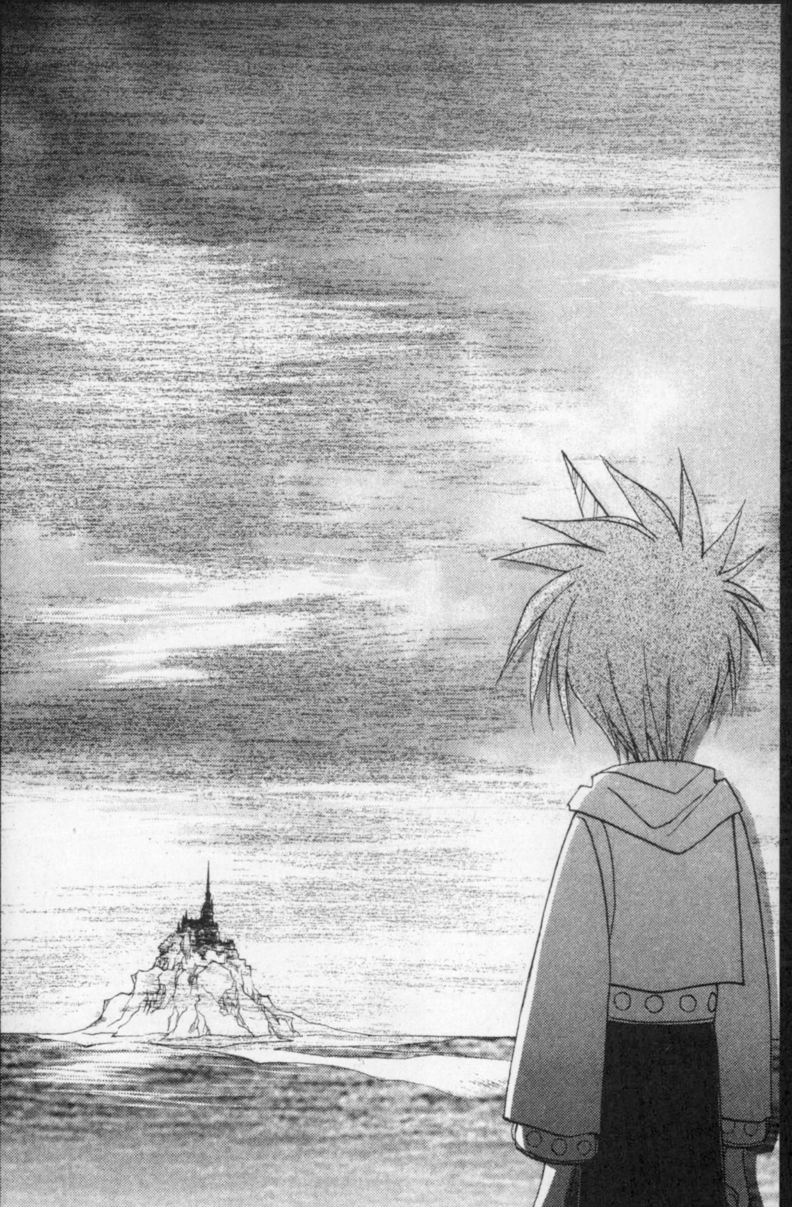

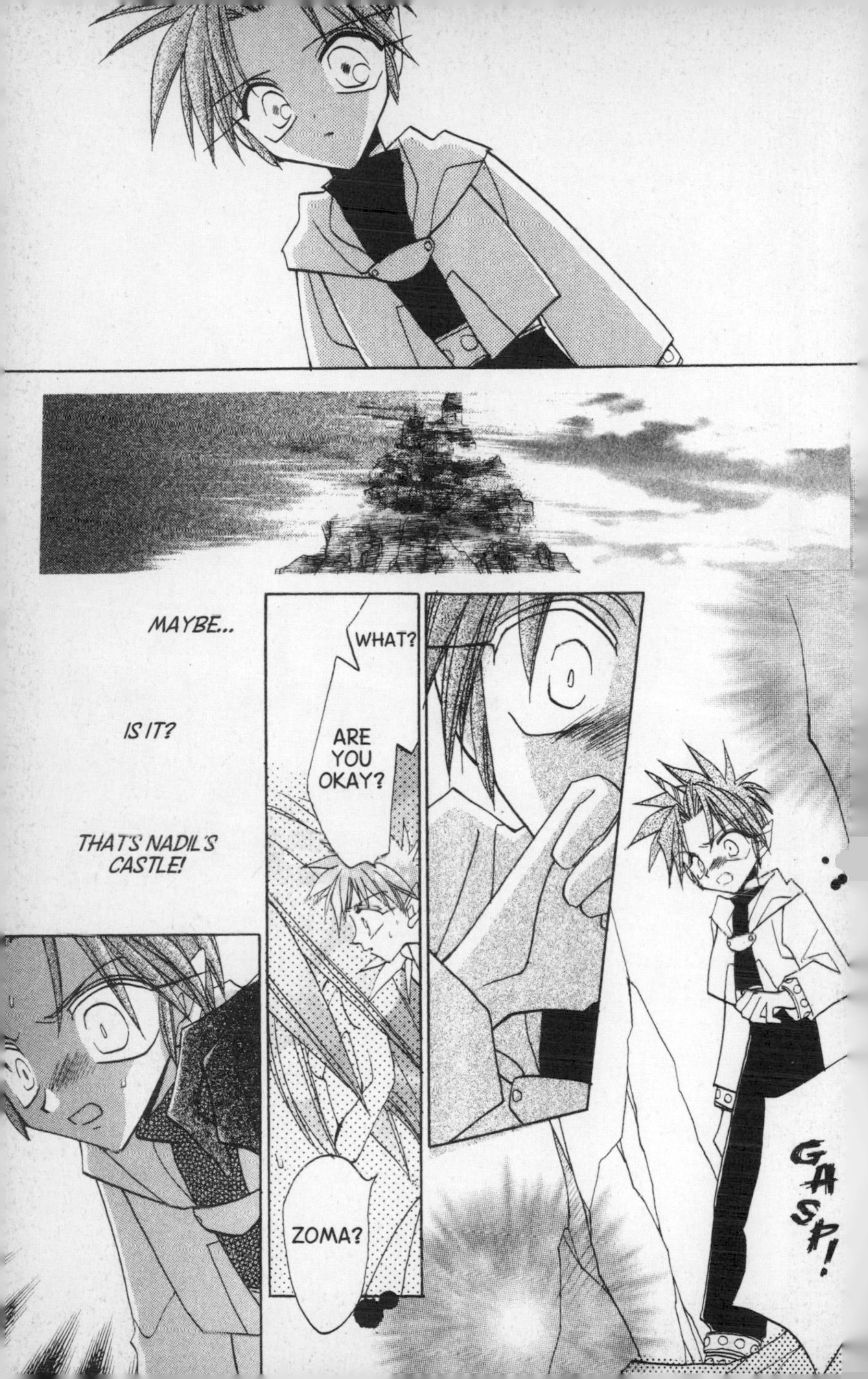
MAYBE...
IS IT?
THAT'S NADIL'S CASTLE!
GASP!
WHAT?
ARE YOU OKAY?
ZOMA?

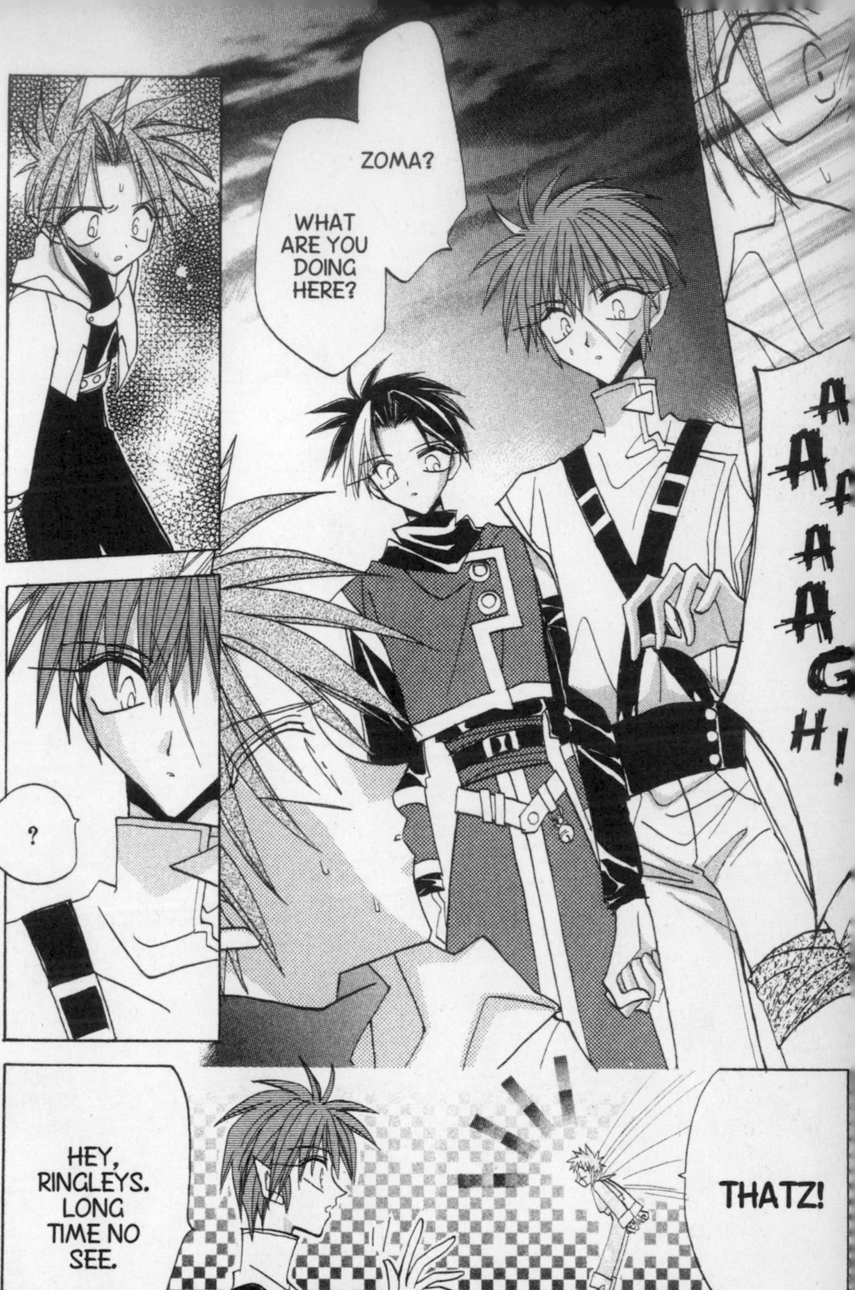
ZOMA?
WHAT ARE YOU DOING HERE?
AAAAAGH!
?
THATZ!
HEY, RINGLEYS. LONG TIME NO SEE.

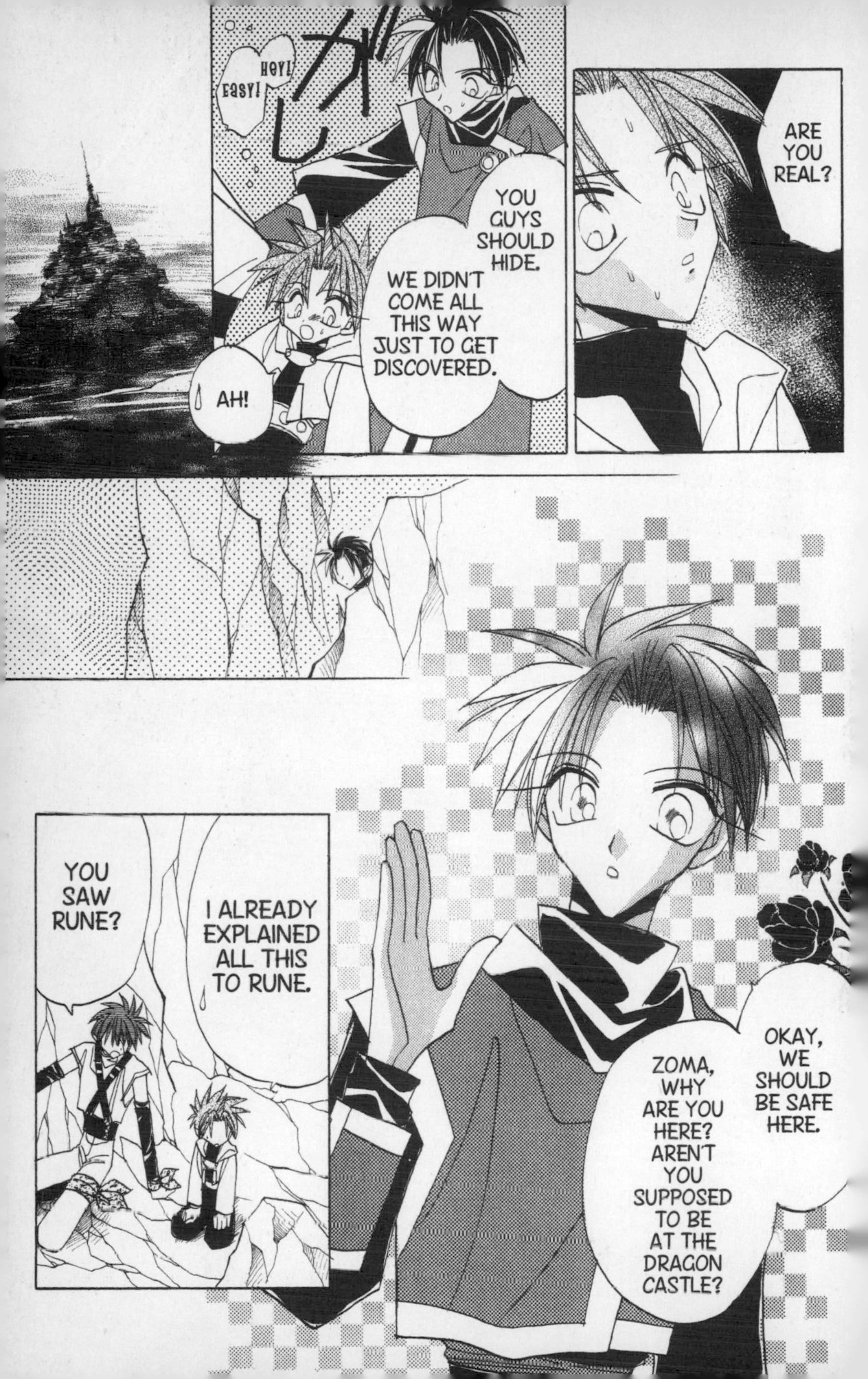
ARE YOU REAL?
HEY! EASY!
YOU GUYS SHOULD HIDE.
WE DIDN'T COME ALL THIS WAY JUST TO GET DISCOVERED.
AH!
OKAY, WE SHOULD BE SAFE HERE.
ZOMA, WHY ARE YOU HERE? AREN'T YOU SUPPOSED TO BE AT THE DRAGON CASTLE?
I ALREADY EXPLAINED ALL THIS TO RUNE.
YOU SAW RUNE?

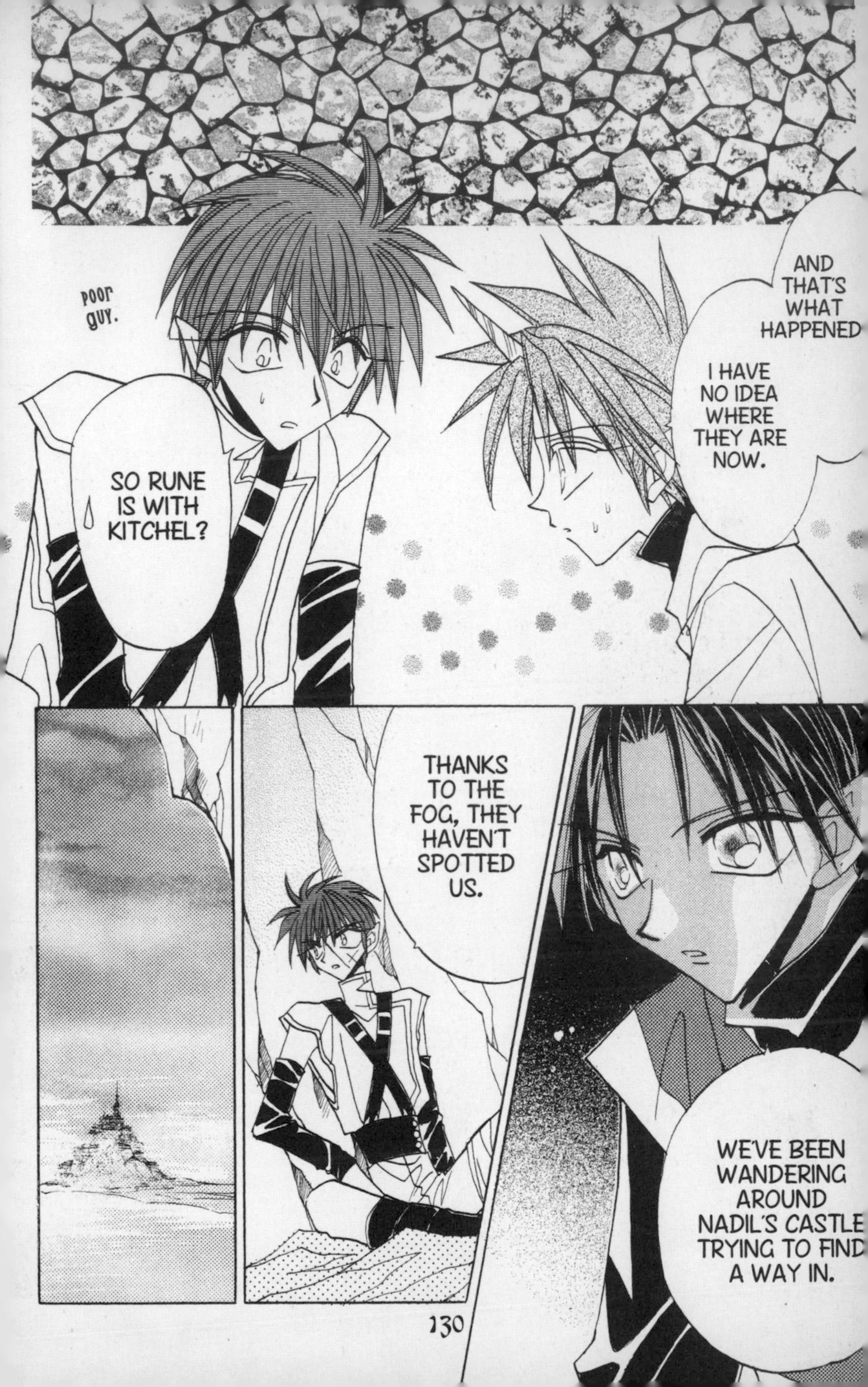
AND THAT'S WHAT HAPPENED
I HAVE NO IDEA WHERE THEY ARE NOW.
SO RUNE IS WITH KITCHEL?
poor guy.
WE'VE BEEN WANDERING AROUND NADIL'S CASTLE TRYING TO FIND A WAY IN.
THANKS TO THE FOG, THEY HAVEN'T SPOTTED US.

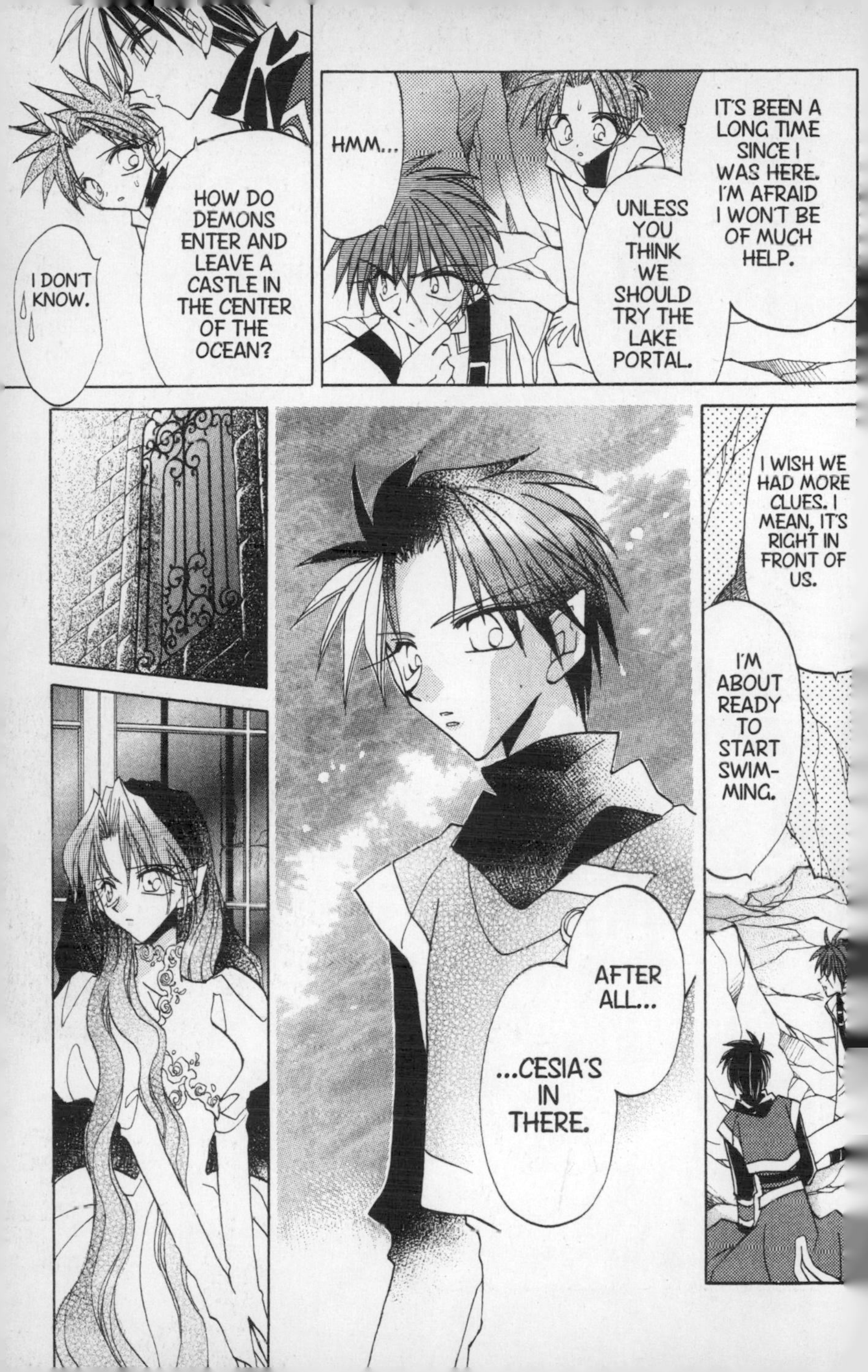
IT'S BEEN A LONG TIME SINCE I WAS HERE. I'M AFRAID I WON'T BE OF MUCH HELP.
HMM...
UNLESS YOU THINK WE SHOULD TRY THE LAKE PORTAL.
HOW DO DEMONS ENTER AND LEAVE A CASTLE IN THE CENTER OF THE OCEAN?
I DON'T KNOW.
I WISH WE HAD MORE CLUES. I MEAN, IT'S RIGHT IN FRONT OF US.
I'M ABOUT READY TO START SWIM-MING.
AFTER ALL...
...CESIA'S IN THERE.

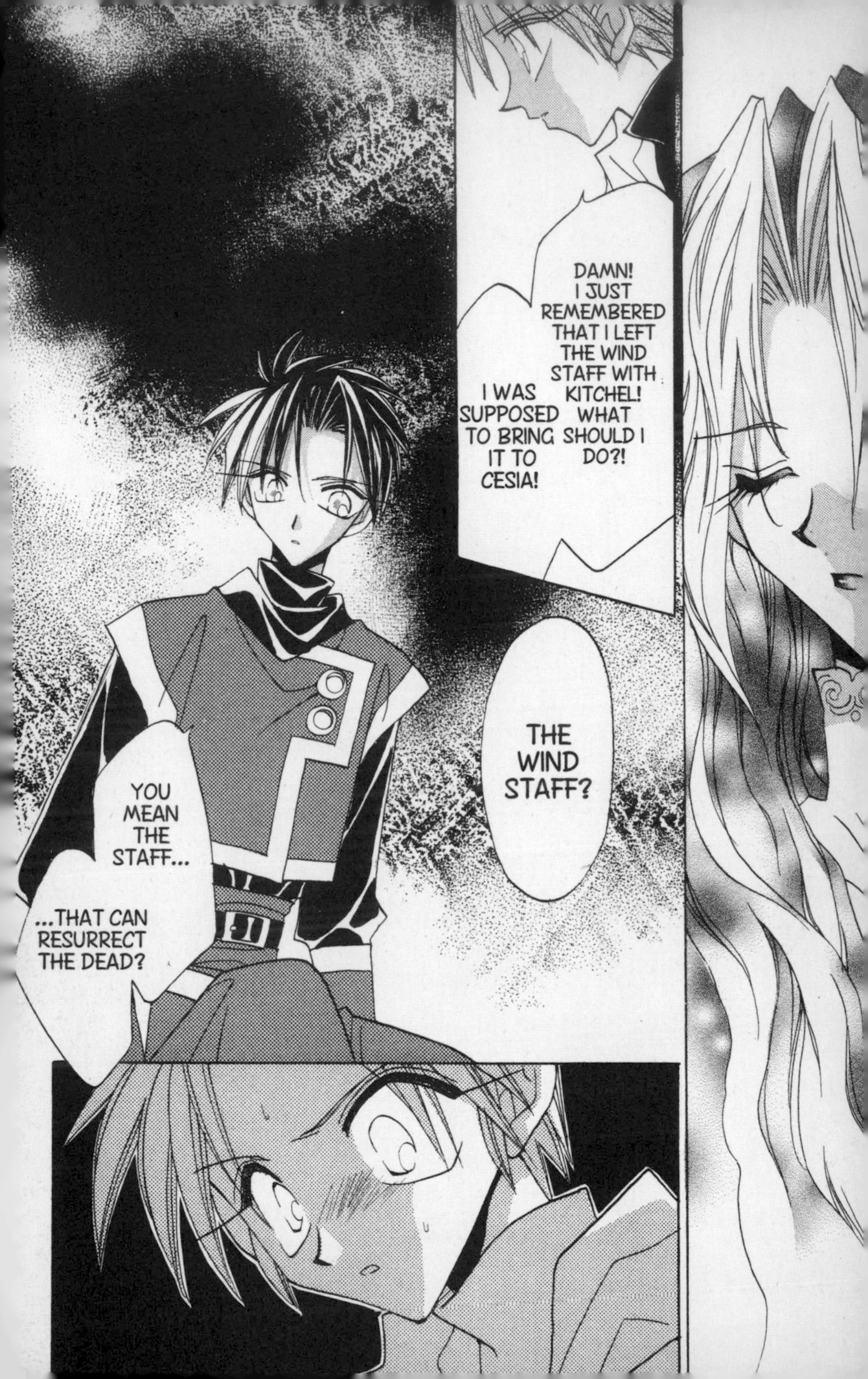
DAMN! I JUST REMEMBERED THAT I LEFT THE WIND STAFF WITH KITCHEL! WHAT SHOULD I DO?!
I WAS SUPPOSED TO BRING IT TO CESIA!
THE WIND STAFF?
YOU MEAN THE STAFF...
...THAT CAN RESURRECT THE DEAD?

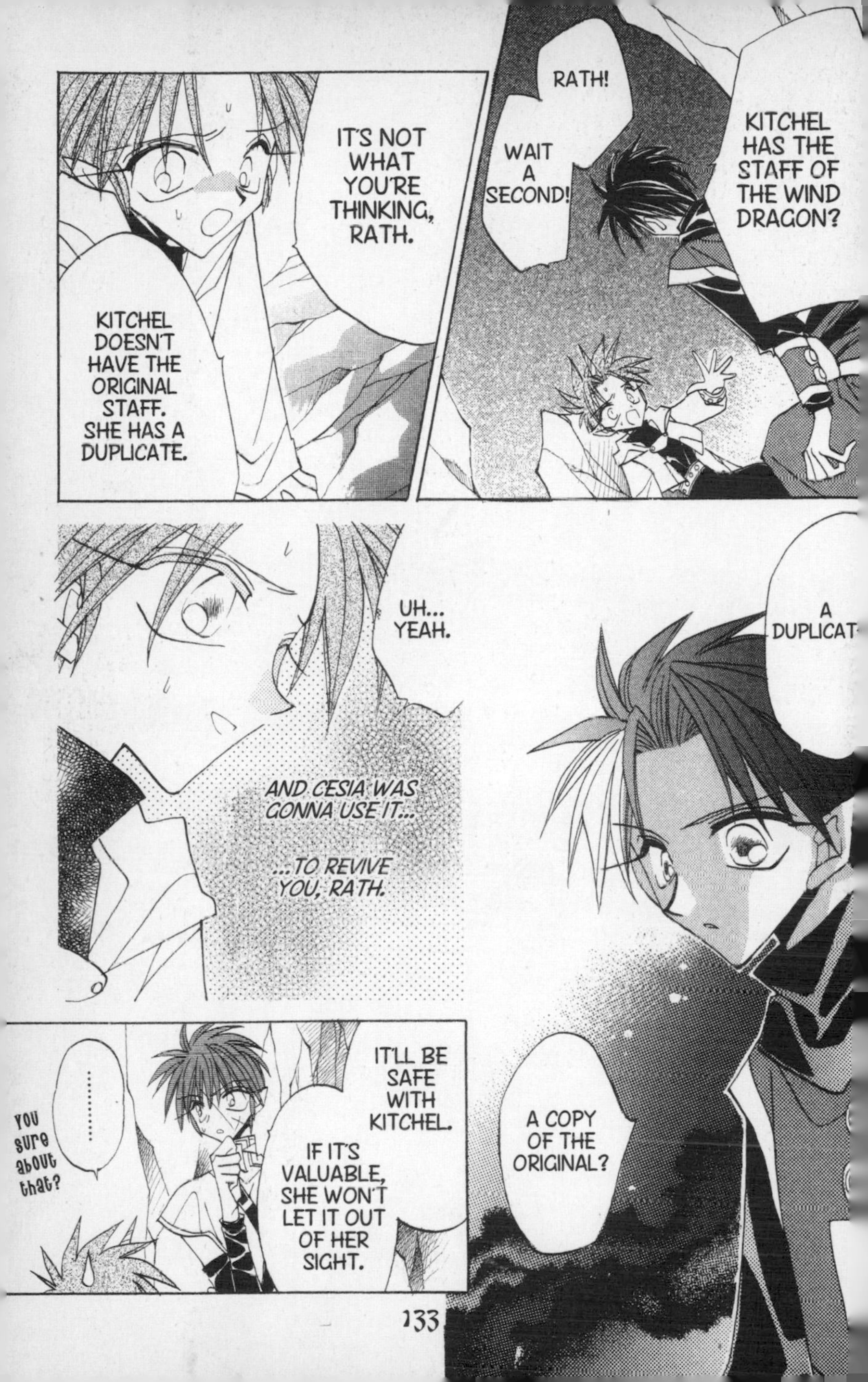
KITCHEL HAS THE STAFF OF THE WIND DRAGON?
RATH!
WAIT A SECOND!
IT'S NOT WHAT YOU'RE THINKING, RATH.
KITCHEL DOESN'T HAVE THE ORIGINAL STAFF. SHE HAS A DUPLICATE.
A DUPLICAT-
A COPY OF THE ORIGINAL?
UH... YEAH.
AND CESIA WAS GONNA USE IT...
...TO REVIVE YOU, RATH.
IT'LL BE SAFE WITH KITCHEL.
IF IT'S VALUABLE, SHE WON'T LET IT OUT OF HER SIGHT.
......
YOU sure about that?

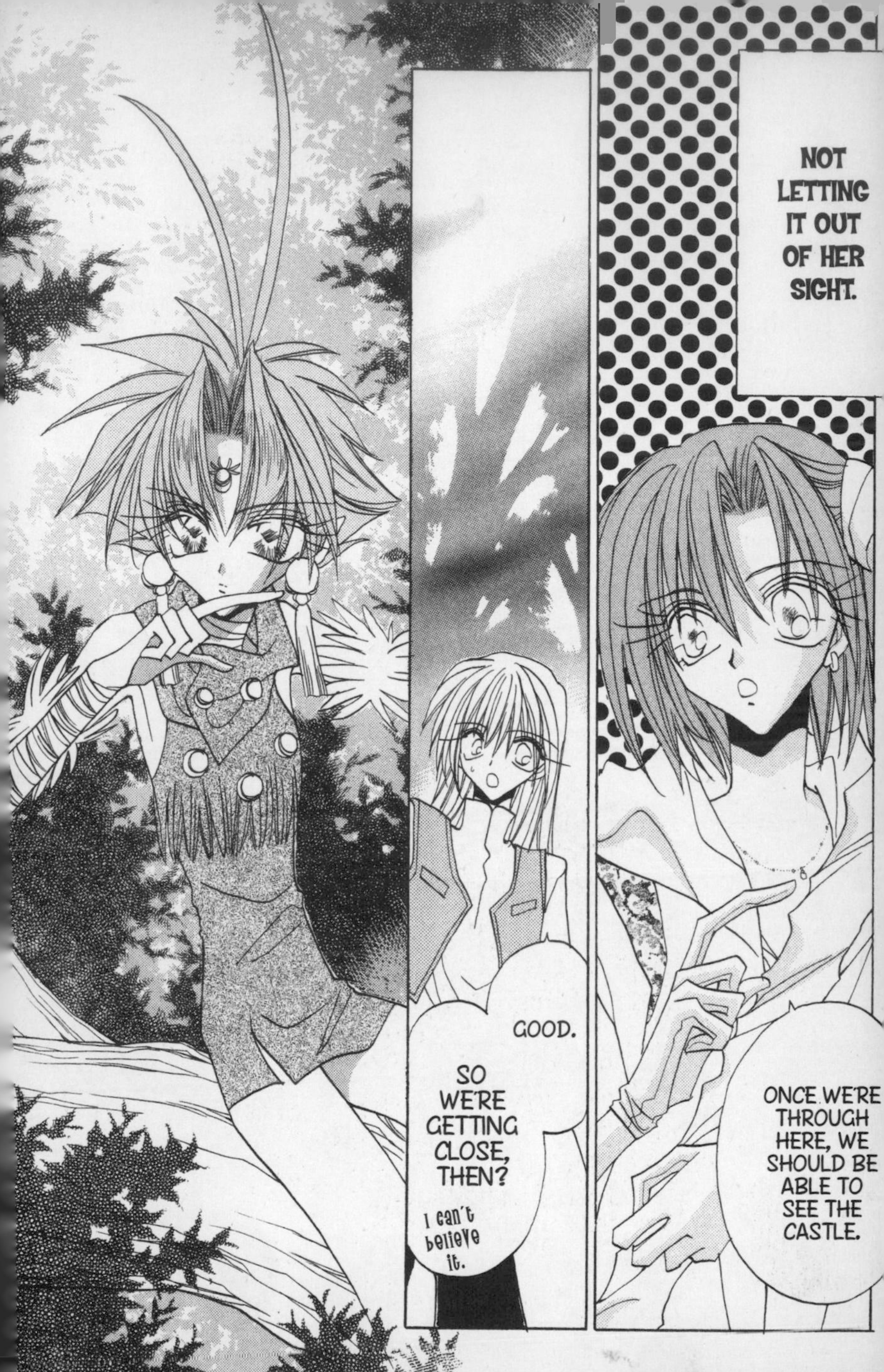
NOT LETTING IT OUT OF HER SIGHT.
ONCE WE'RE THROUGH HERE, WE SHOULD BE ABLE TO SEE THE CASTLE.
GOOD.
SO WE'RE GETTING CLOSE, THEN?
I can't believe it.

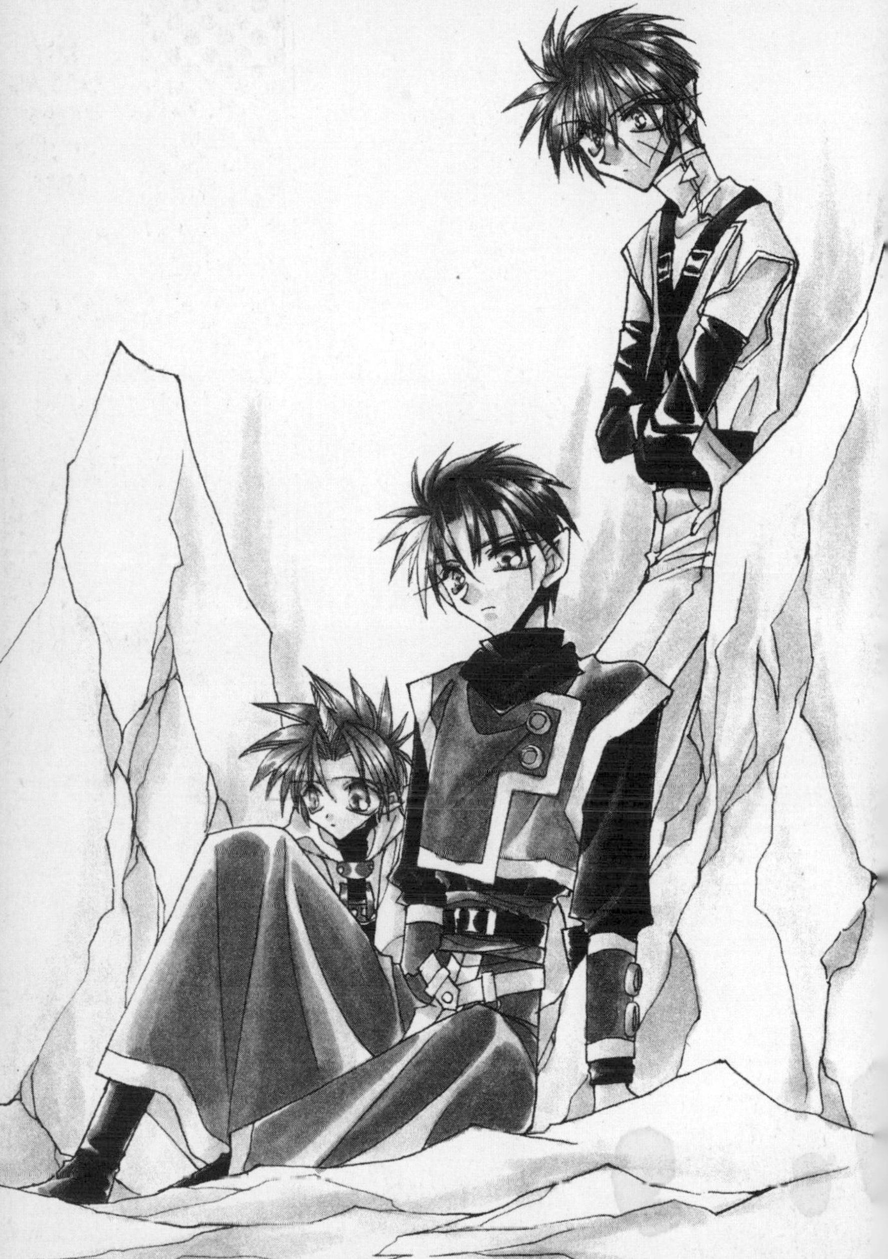

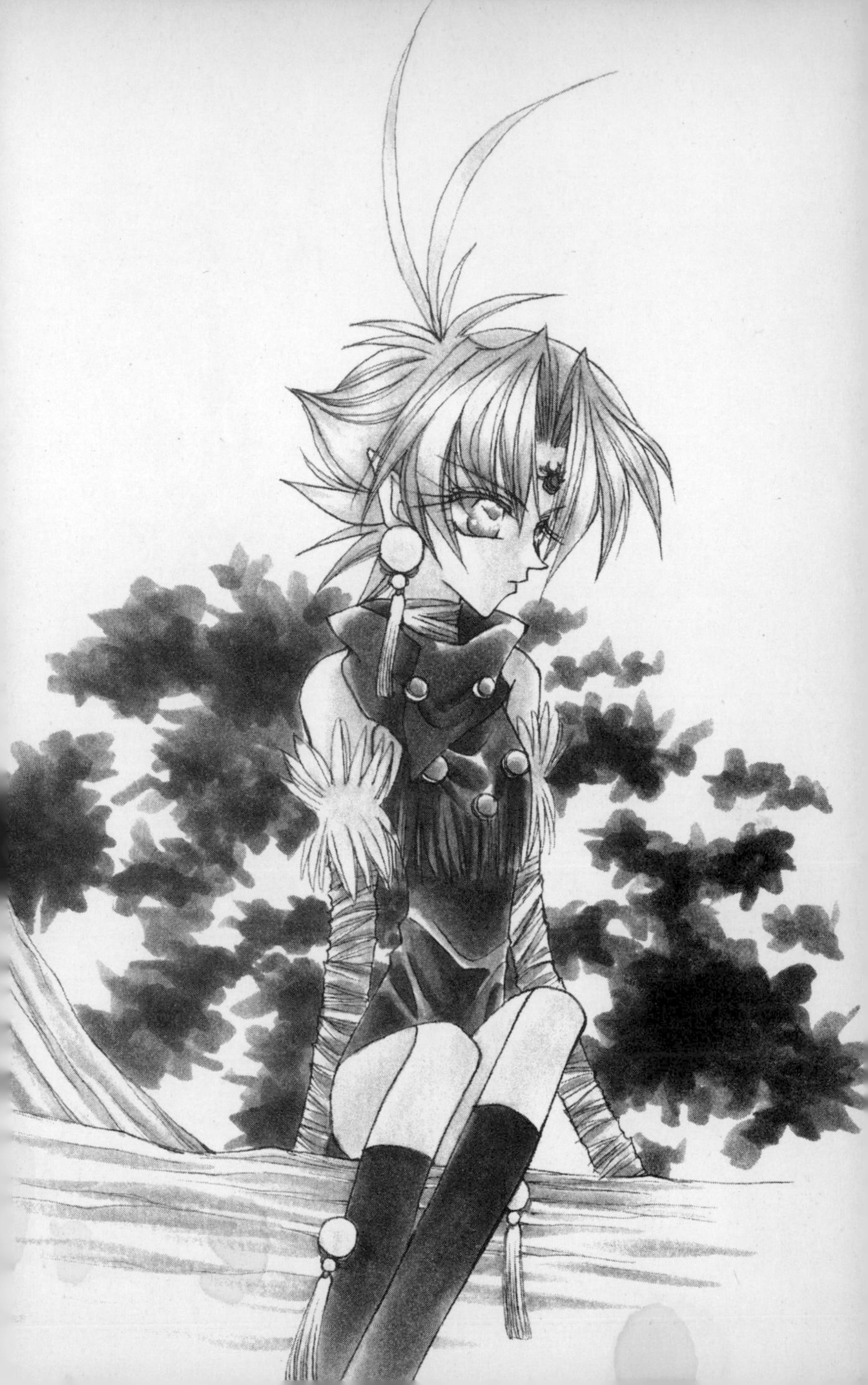

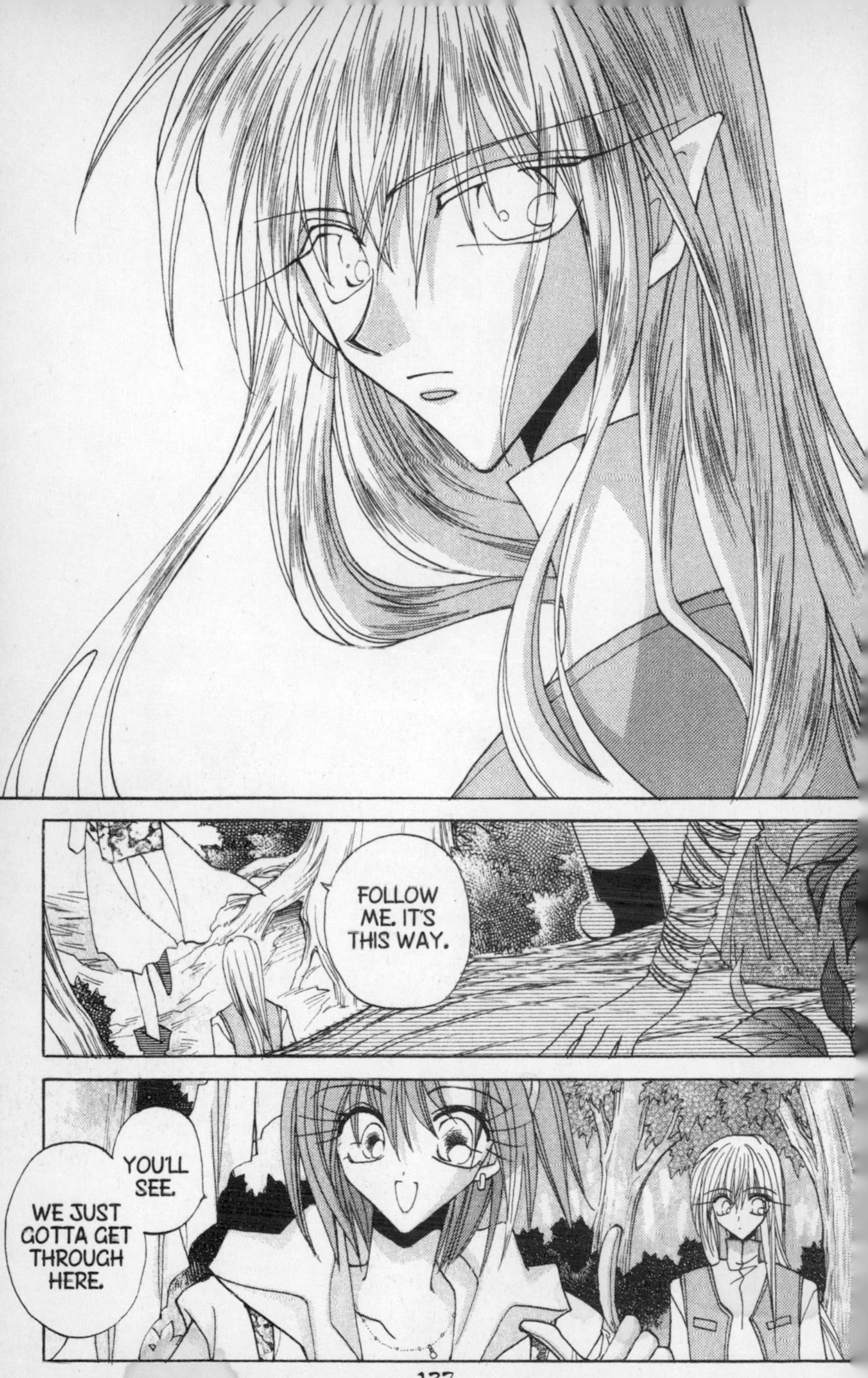
FOLLOW ME. IT'S THIS WAY.
YOU'LL SEE.
WE JUST GOTTA GET THROUGH HERE.

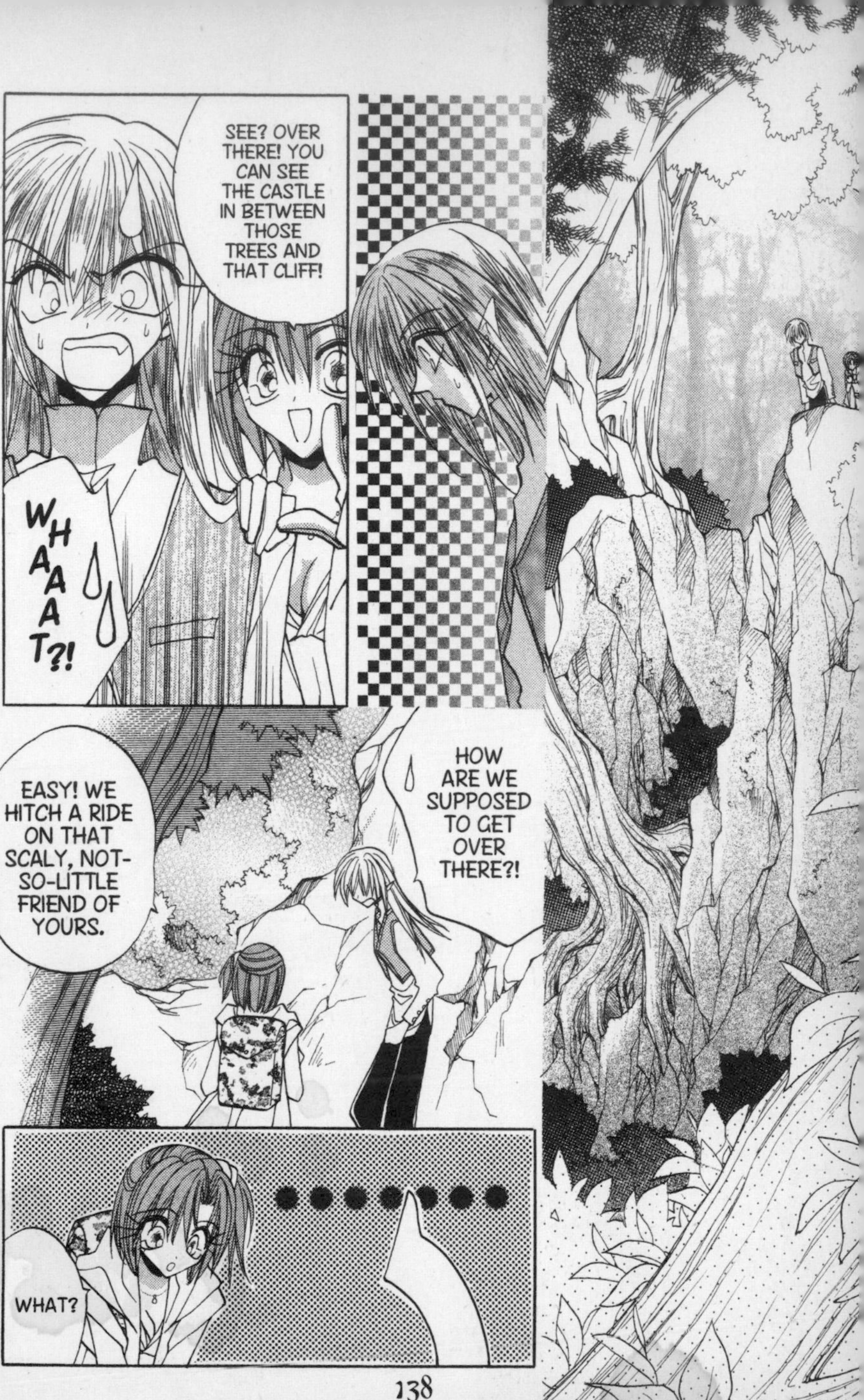

SEE? OVER THERE! YOU CAN SEE THE CASTLE IN BETWEEN THOSE TREES AND THAT CLIFF!
WHAAAT?!
HOW ARE WE SUPPOSED TO GET OVER THERE?!
EASY! WE HITCH A RIDE ON THAT SCALY, NOT-SO-LITTLE FRIEND OF YOURS.
WHAT?

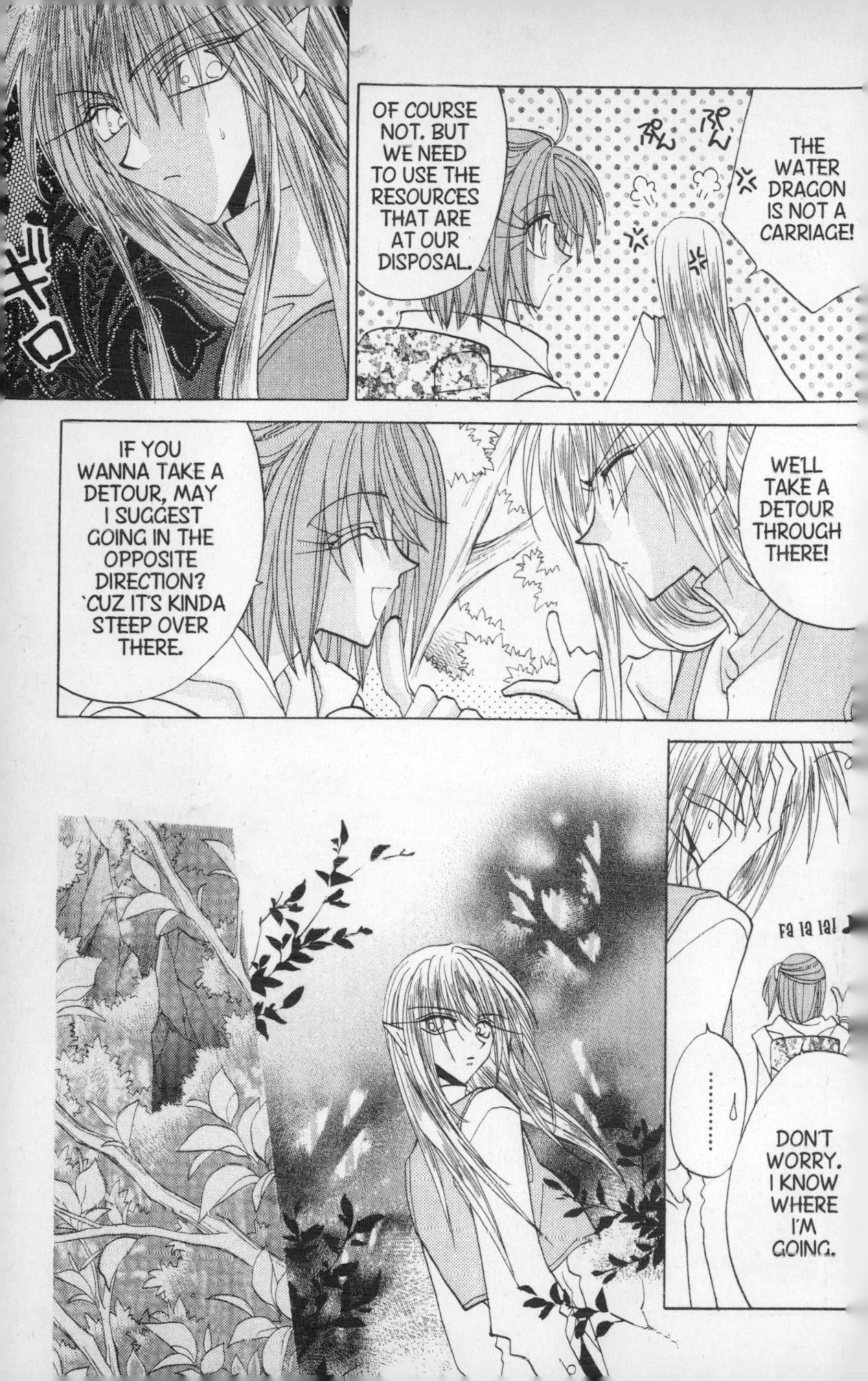
THE WATER DRAGON IS NOT A CARRIAGE!
ぷん ぷん
OF COURSE NOT. BUT WE NEED TO USE THE RESOURCES THAT ARE AT OUR DISPOSAL.
ギロ
WE'LL TAKE A DETOUR THROUGH THERE!
IF YOU WANNA TAKE A DETOUR, MAY I SUGGEST GOING IN THE OPPOSITE DIRECTION? `CUZ IT'S KINDA STEEP OVER THERE.
Fa la la!
DON'T WORRY. I KNOW WHERE I'M GOING.
......

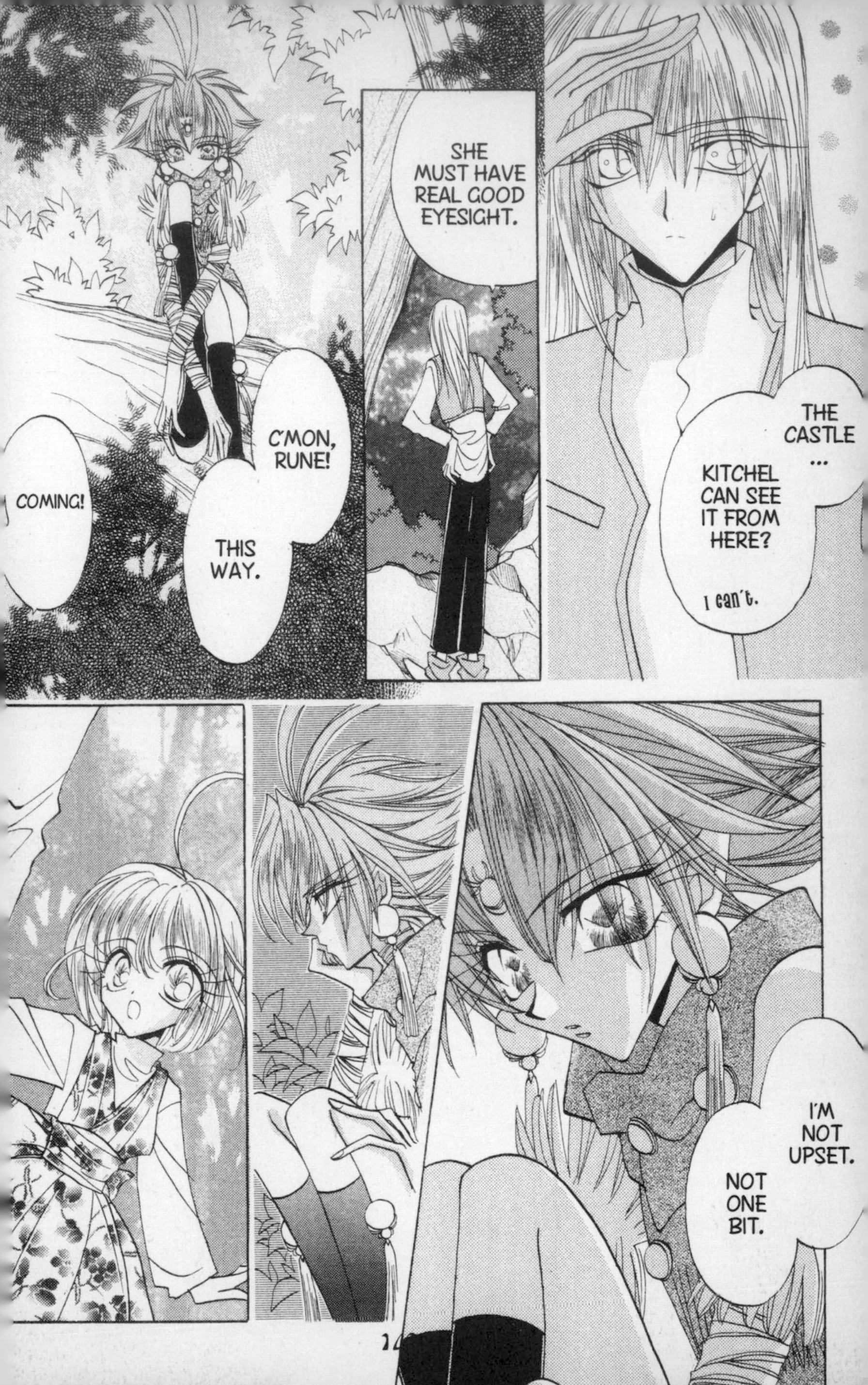
THE CASTLE ...
KITCHEL CAN SEE IT FROM HERE?
I can't.
SHE MUST HAVE REAL GOOD EYESIGHT.
C'MON, RUNE!
THIS WAY.
COMING!
I'M NOT UPSET.
NOT ONE BIT.

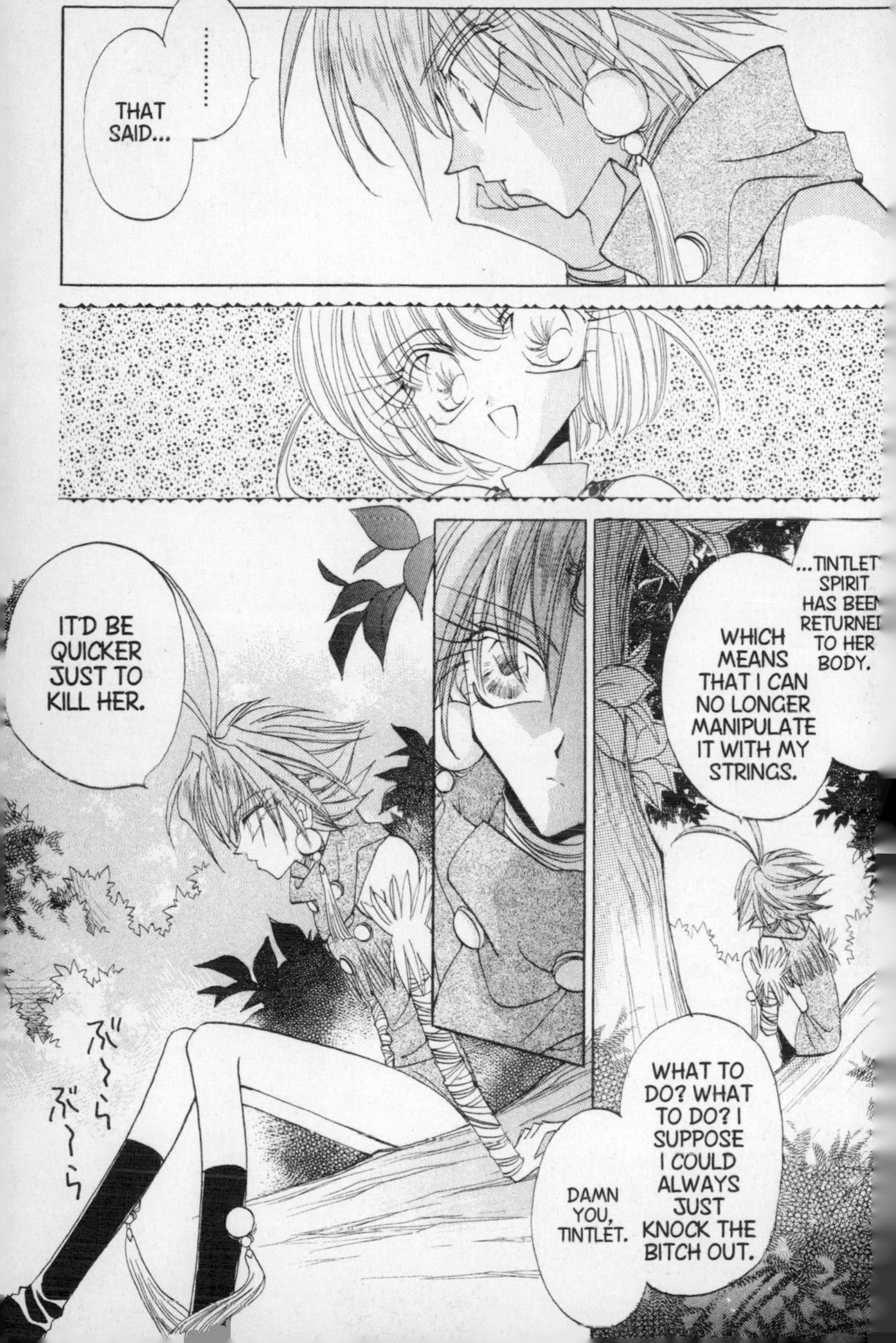

......
THAT SAID...
...TINTLET' SPIRIT HAS BEEN RETURNE TO HER BODY.
WHICH MEANS THAT I CAN NO LONGER MANIPULATE IT WITH MY STRINGS.
IT'D BE QUICKER JUST TO KILL HER.
WHAT TO DO? WHAT TO DO? I SUPPOSE I COULD ALWAYS JUST KNOCK THE BITCH OUT.
DAMN YOU, TINTLET.
ぶ〜ら ぶ〜ら

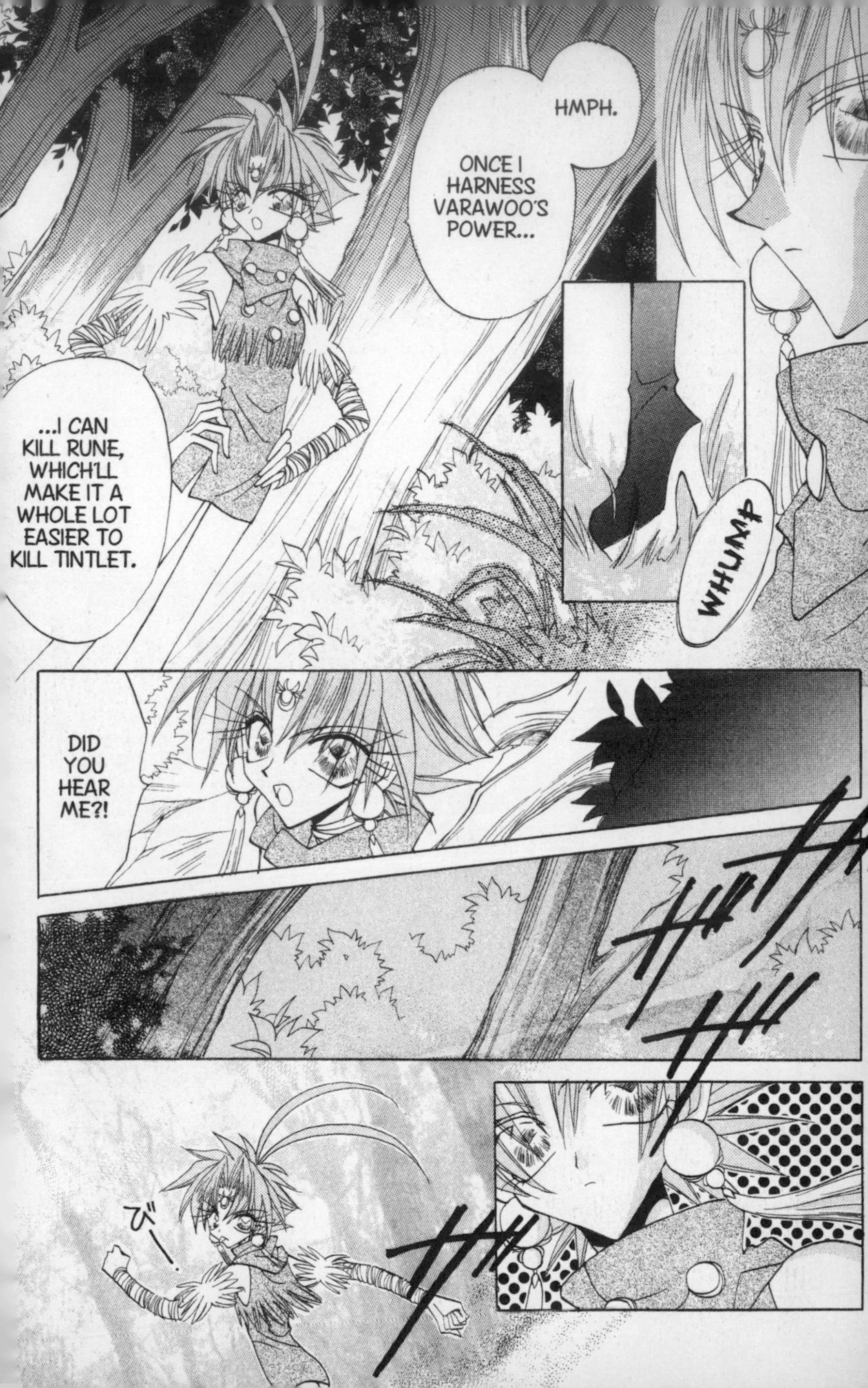
HMPH.
ONCE I HARNESS VARAWOO'S POWER...
...I CAN KILL RUNE, WHICH'LL MAKE IT A WHOLE LOT EASIER TO KILL TINTLET.
WHUMP
DID YOU HEAR ME?!
びー.

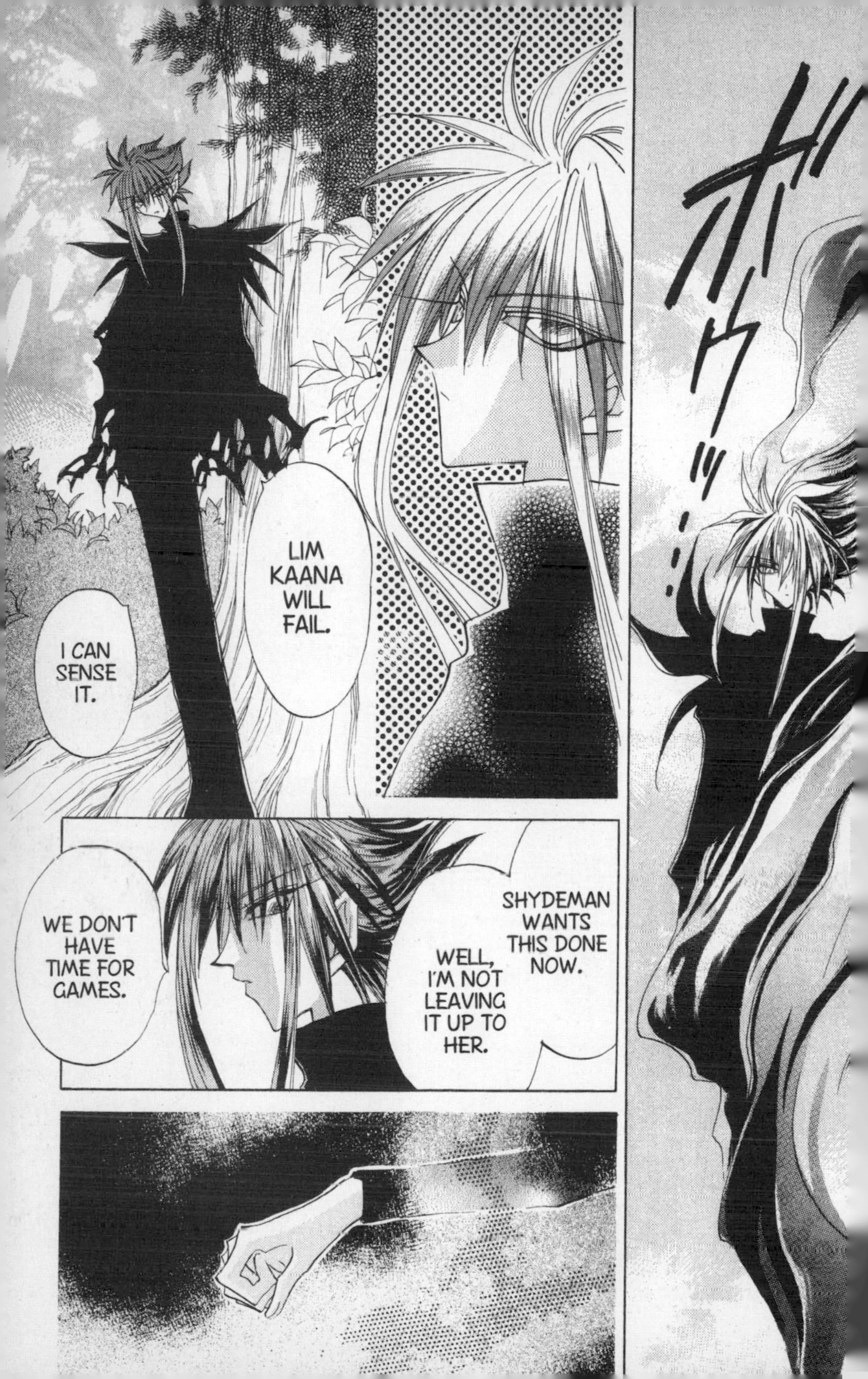
LIM KAANA WILL FAIL.
I CAN SENSE IT.
SHYDEMAN WANTS THIS DONE NOW.
WELL, I'M NOT LEAVING IT UP TO HER.
WE DON'T HAVE TIME FOR GAMES.

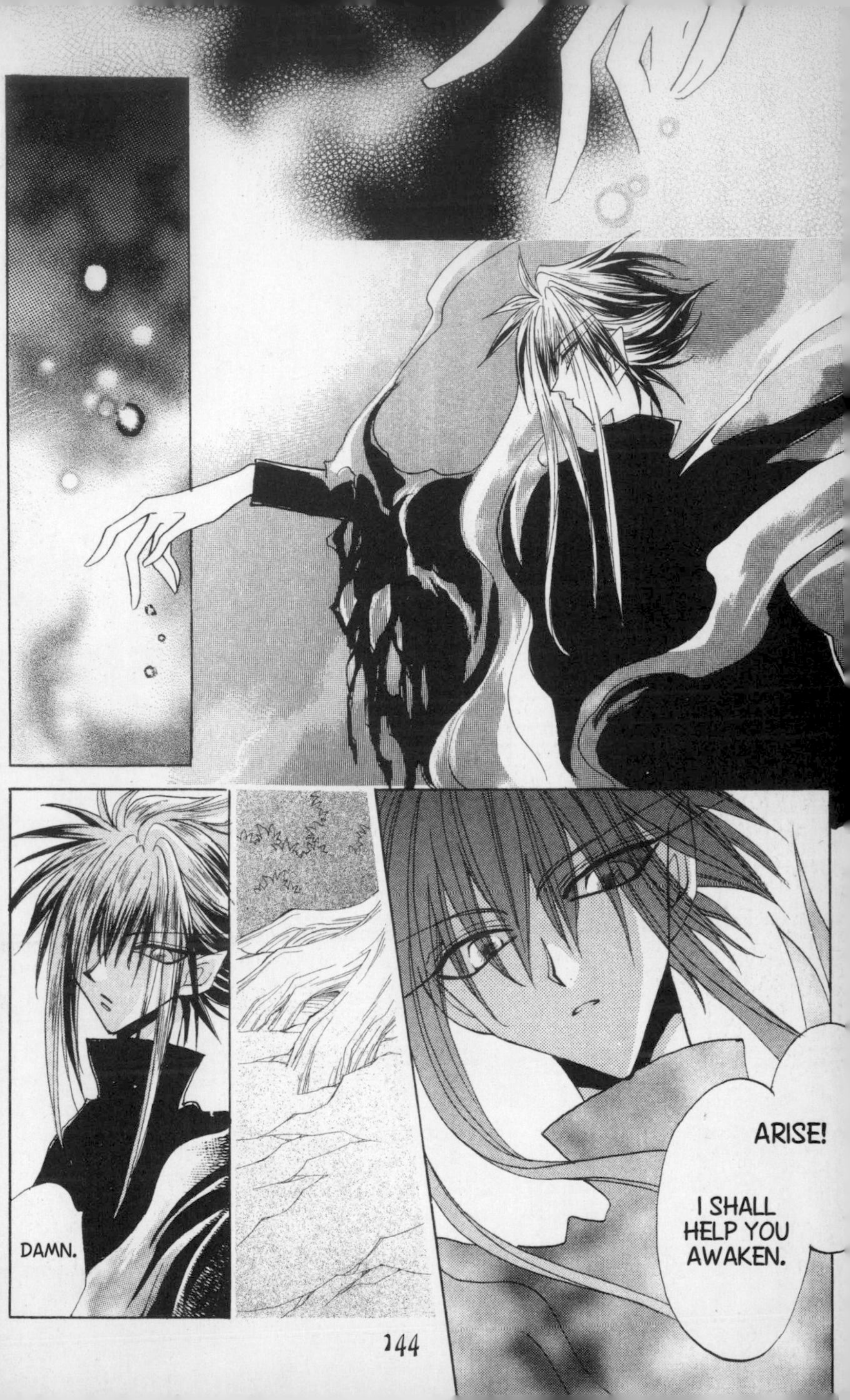
ARISE!
I SHALL HELP YOU AWAKEN.
DAMN.

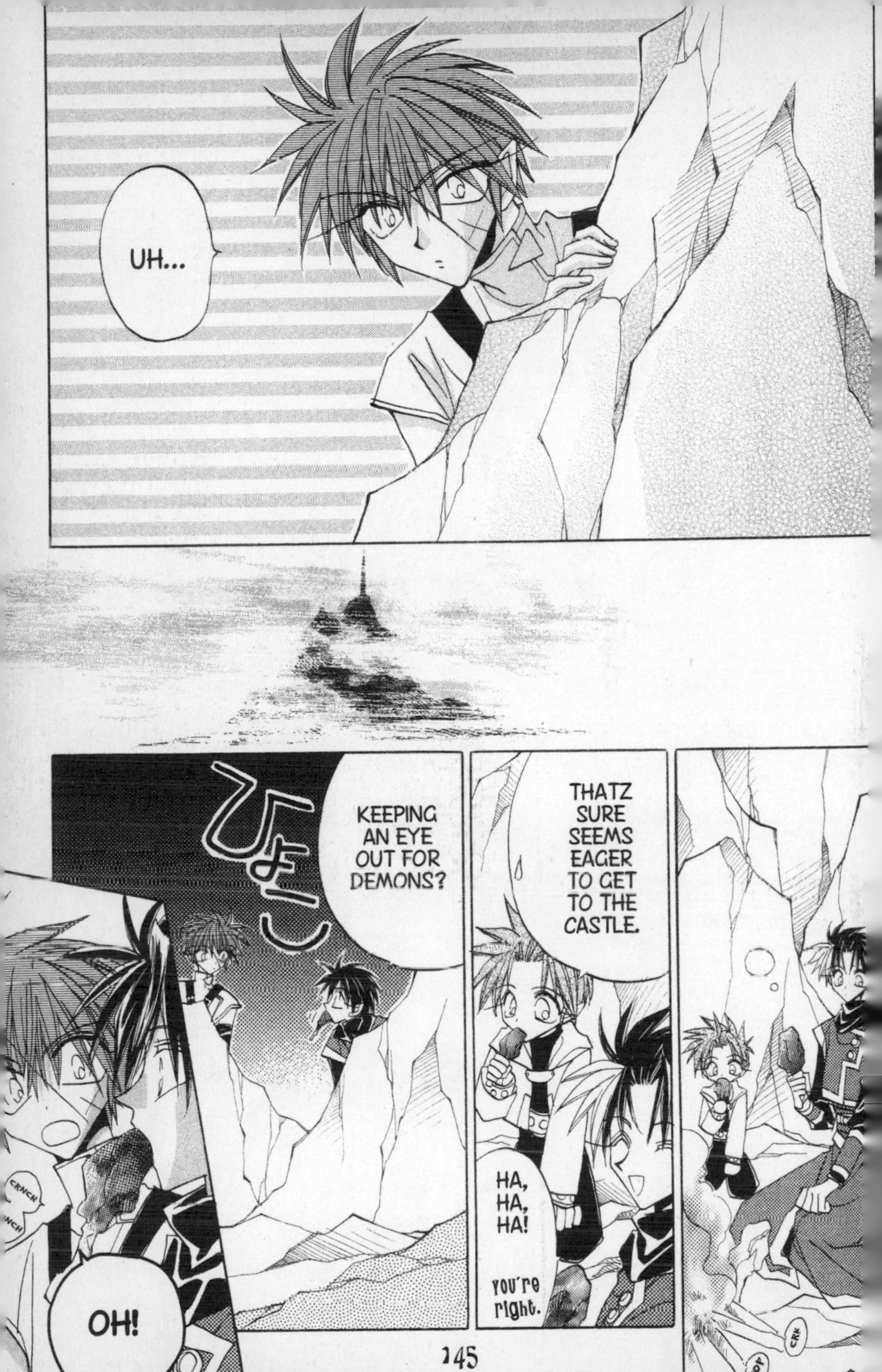
UH...
CRK
THATZ SURE SEEMS EAGER TO GET TO THE CASTLE.
HA, HA, HA!
You're right.
KEEPING AN EYE OUT FOR DEMONS?
ひょこ
CRNCH
OH!

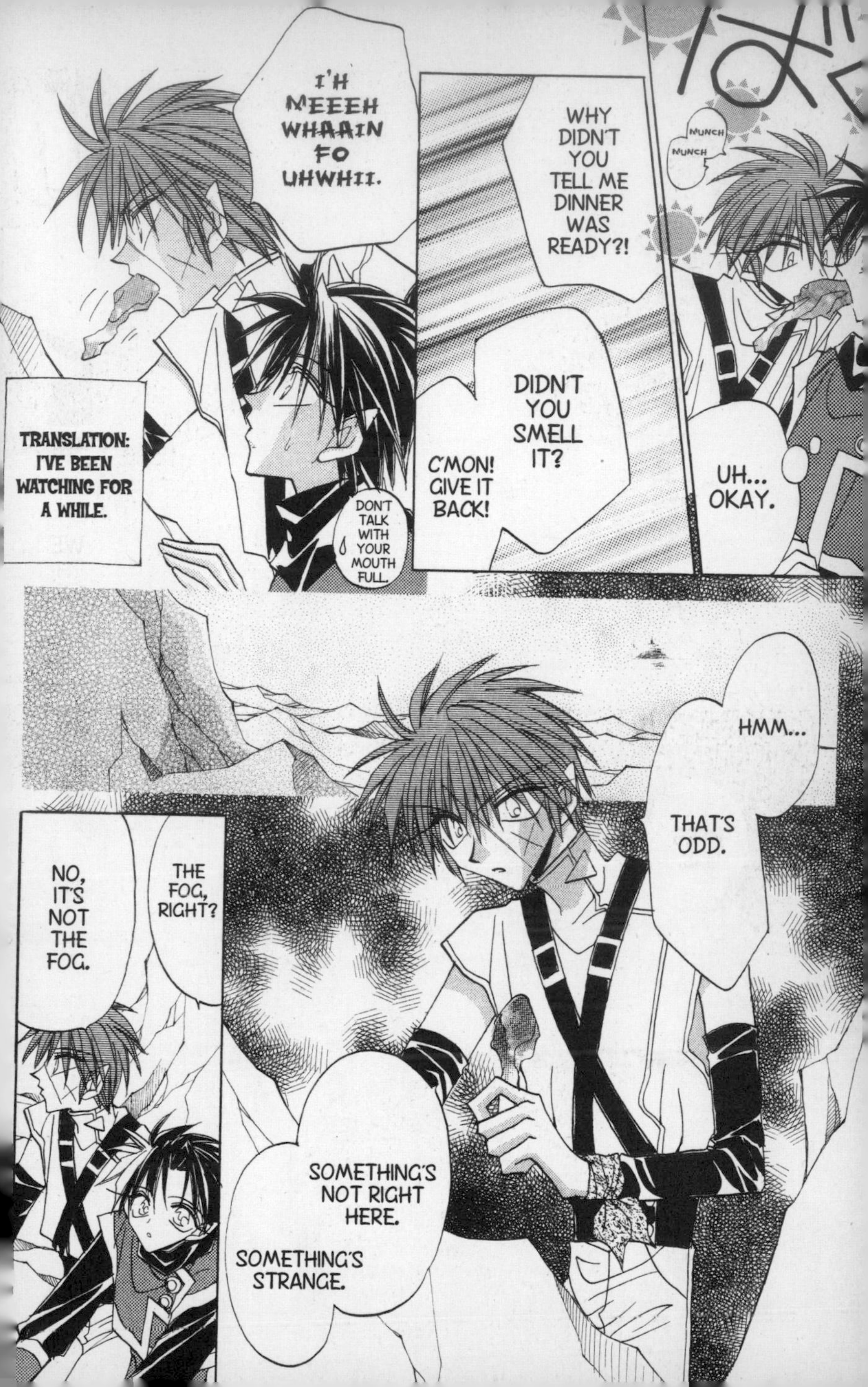
MUNCH
MUNCH
UH... OKAY.
WHY DIDN'T YOU TELL ME DINNER WAS READY?!
DIDN'T YOU SMELL IT?
C'MON! GIVE IT BACK!
I'H MEEEH WHAAIN FO UHWHII.
TRANSLATION: I'VE BEEN WATCHING FOR A WHILE.
DON'T TALK WITH YOUR MOUTH FULL.
HMM...
THAT'S ODD.
THE FOG, RIGHT?
NO, IT'S NOT THE FOG.
SOMETHING'S NOT RIGHT HERE.
SOMETHING'S STRANGE.

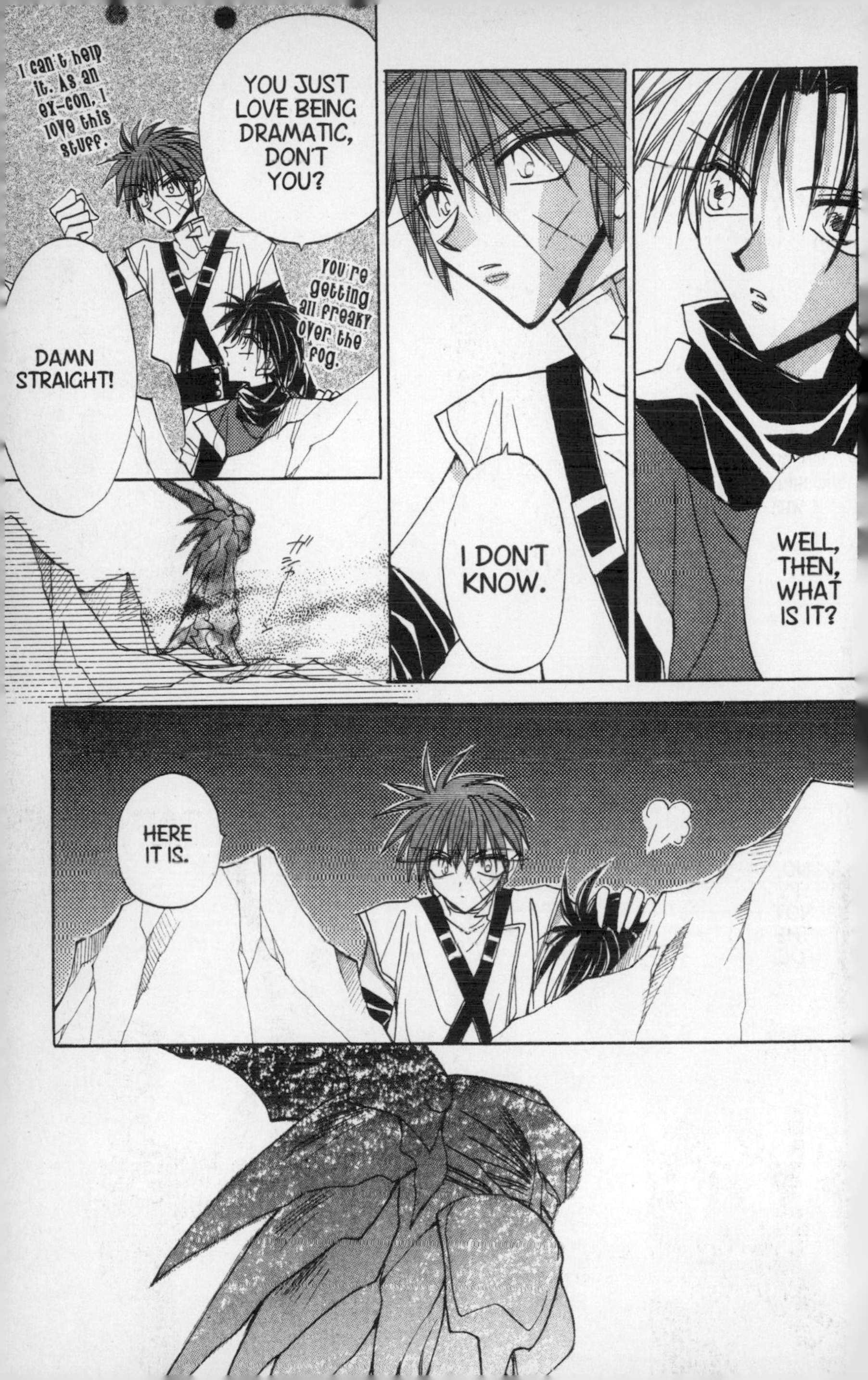
WELL, THEN, WHAT IS IT?
I DON'T KNOW.
YOU JUST LOVE BEING DRAMATIC, DON'T YOU?
You're getting all freaky over the fog.
DAMN STRAIGHT!
I can't help it. As an ex-con, I love this stuff.
HERE IT IS.

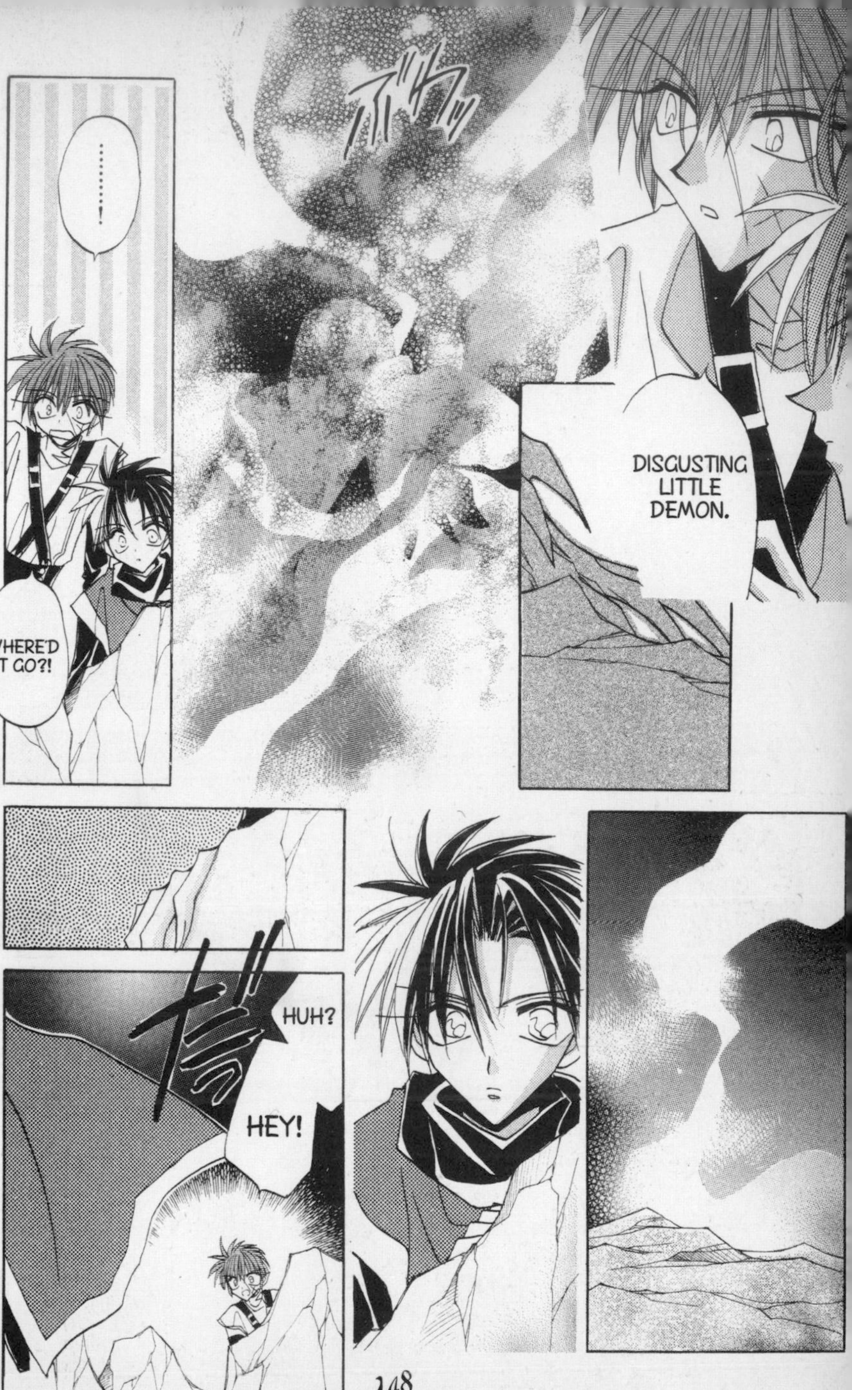
DISGUSTING LITTLE DEMON.
......!
WHERE'D IT GO?!
HUH?
HEY!

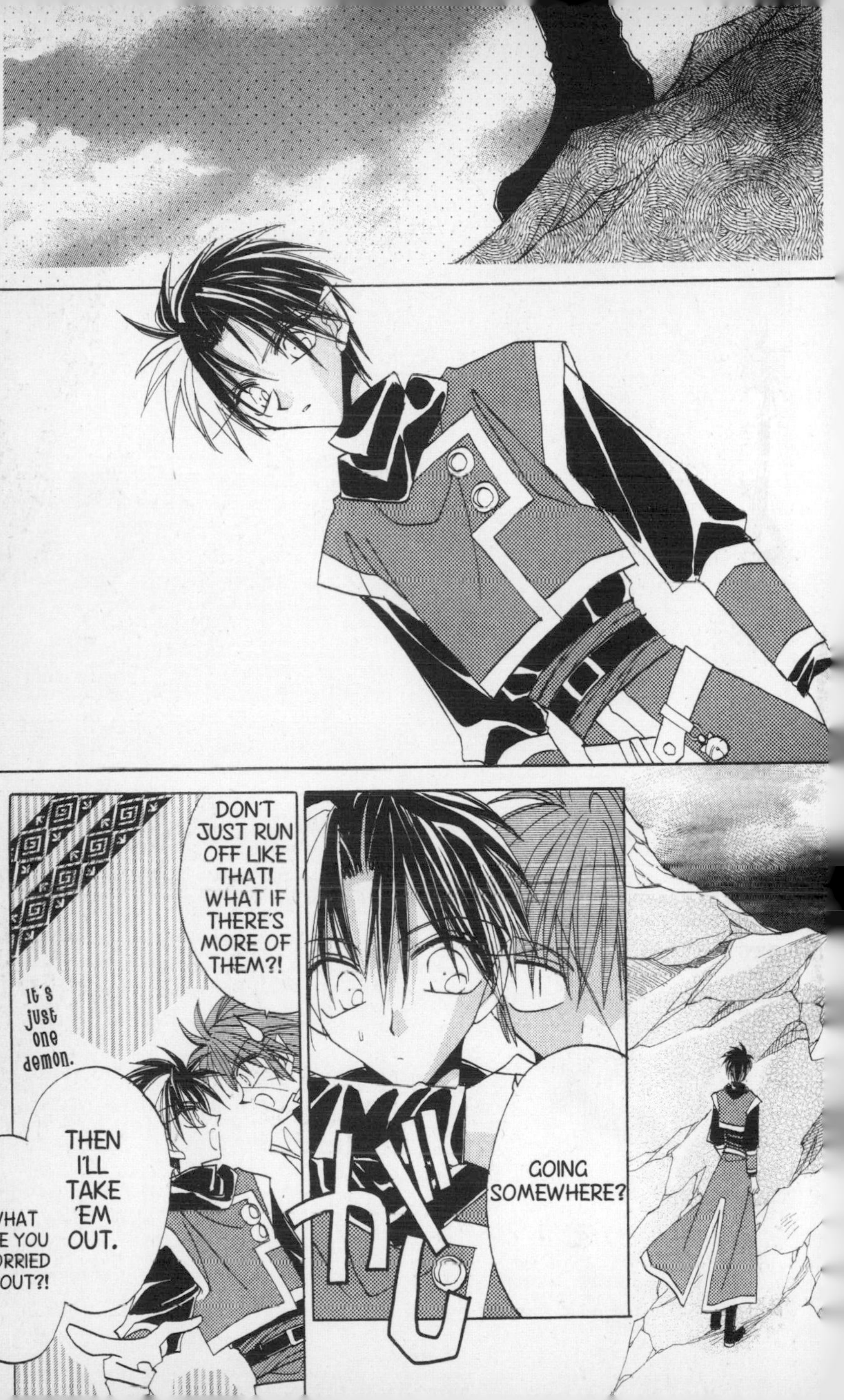
GOING SOMEWHERE?
DON'T JUST RUN OFF LIKE THAT! WHAT IF THERE'S MORE OF THEM?!
It's just one demon.
THEN I'LL TAKE 'EM OUT.
WHAT ARE YOU WORRIED ABOUT?!

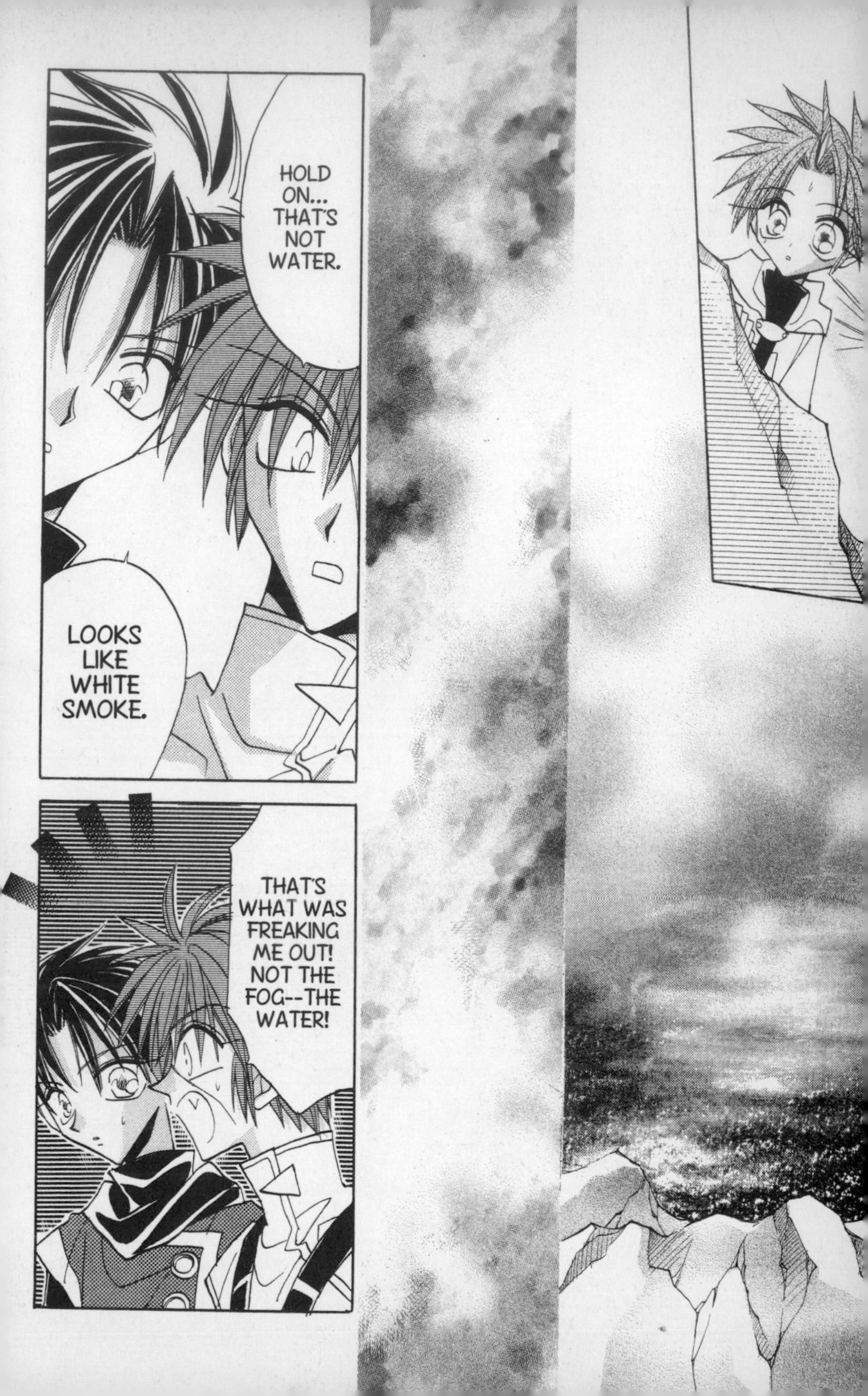
HOLD ON... THAT'S NOT WATER.
LOOKS LIKE WHITE SMOKE.
THAT'S WHAT WAS FREAKING ME OUT! NOT THE FOG--THE WATER!

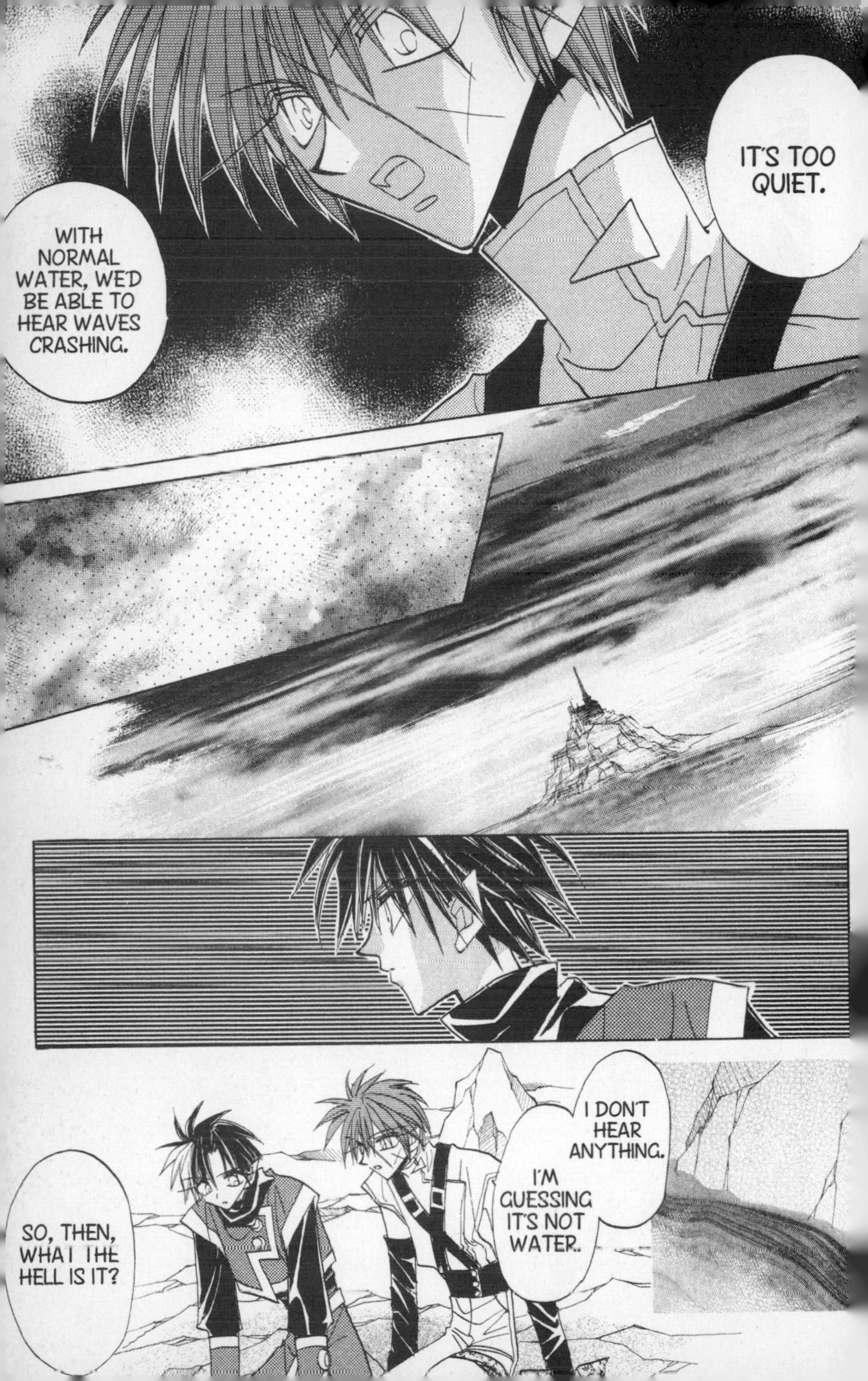
IT'S TOO QUIET.
WITH NORMAL WATER, WE'D BE ABLE TO HEAR WAVES CRASHING.
I DON'T HEAR ANYTHING.
I'M GUESSING IT'S NOT WATER.
SO, THEN, WHAT THE HELL IS IT?

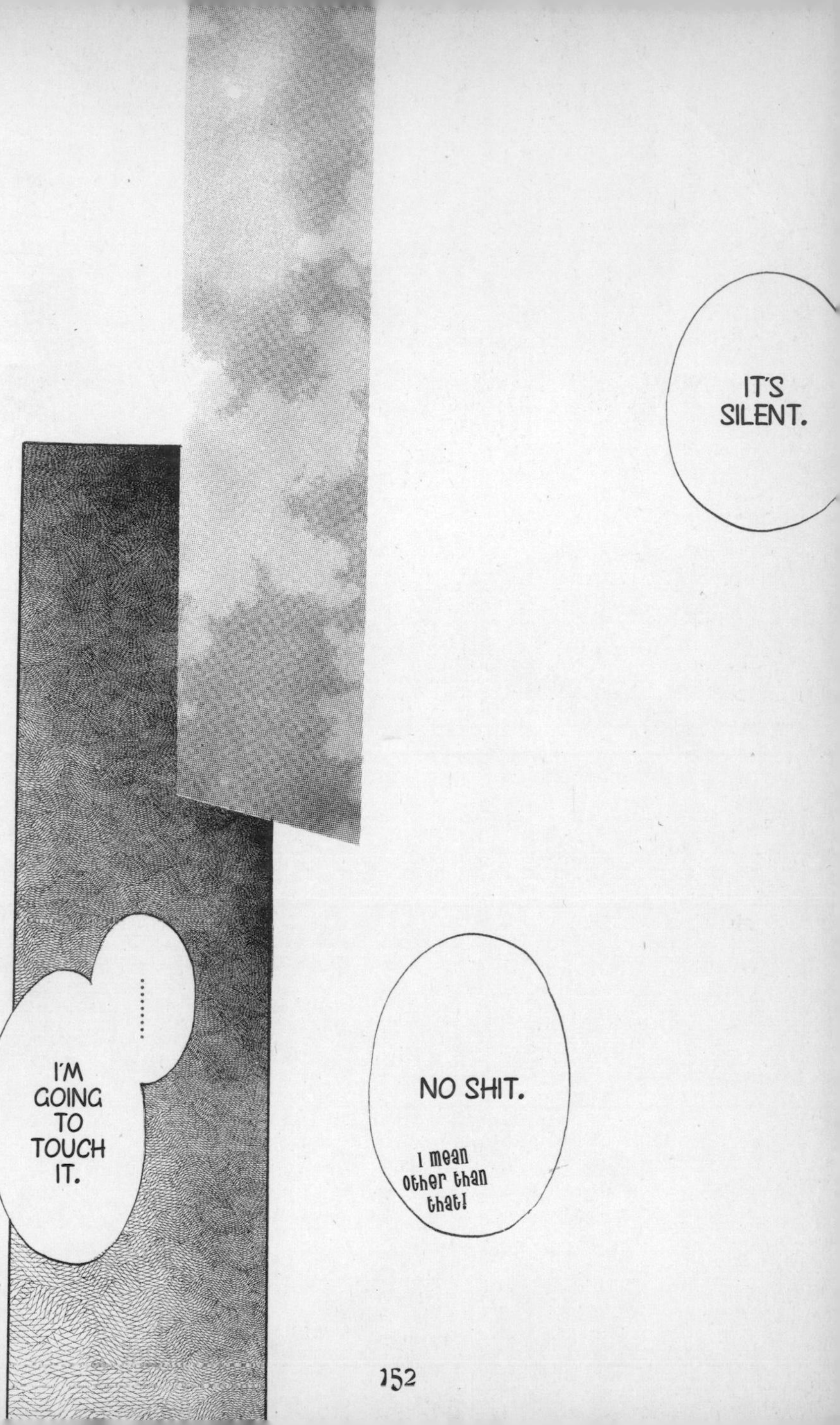
IT'S SILENT.
NO SHIT.
I mean other than that!
....
I'M GOING TO TOUCH IT.

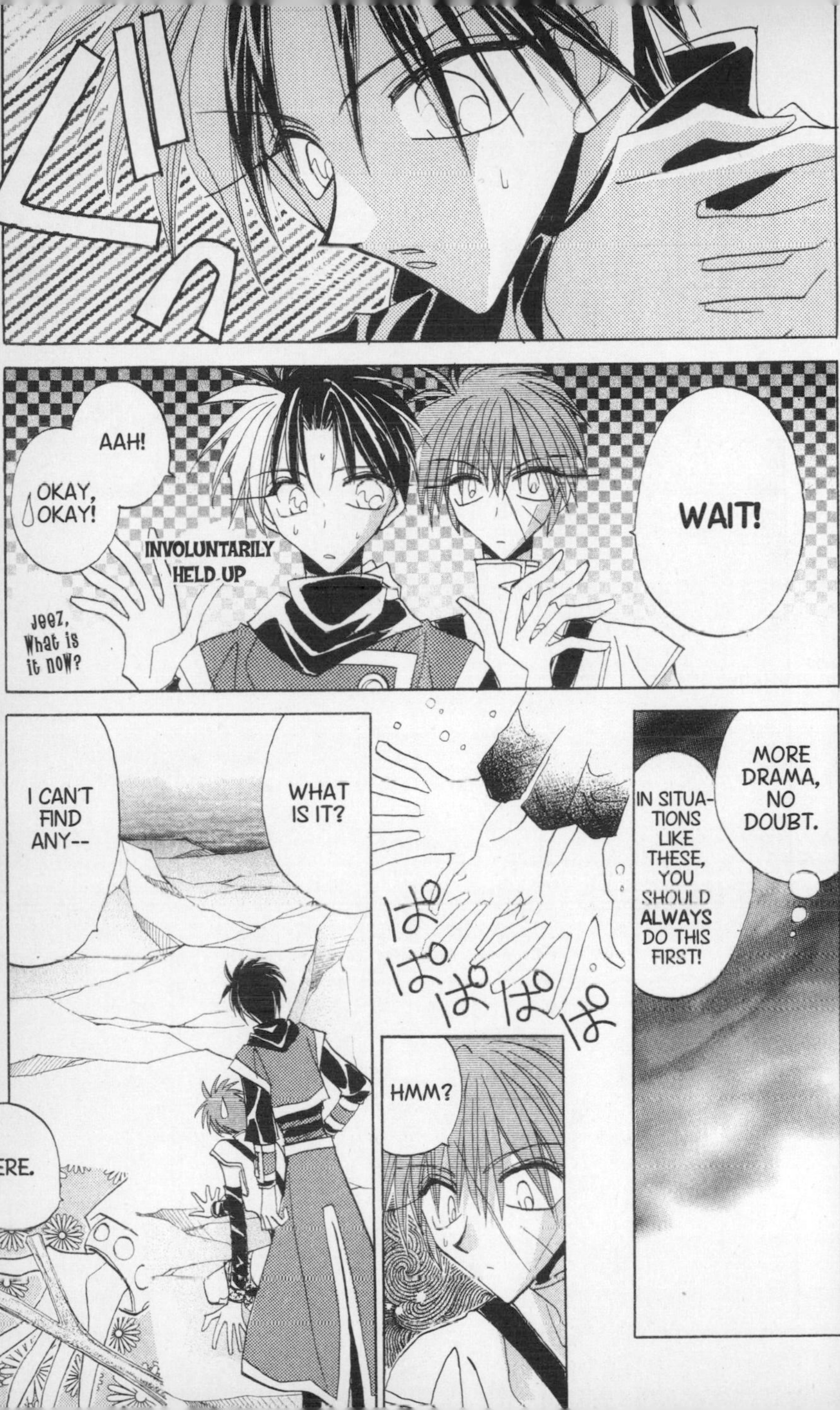
WAIT!
AAH!
OKAY, OKAY!
INVOLUNTARILY HELD UP
Jeez, What is it now?
MORE DRAMA, NO DOUBT.
IN SITUATIONS LIKE THESE, YOU SHOULD ALWAYS DO THIS FIRST!
ぱぱぱぱぱ
HMM?
WHAT IS IT?
I CAN'T FIND ANY--
HERE.

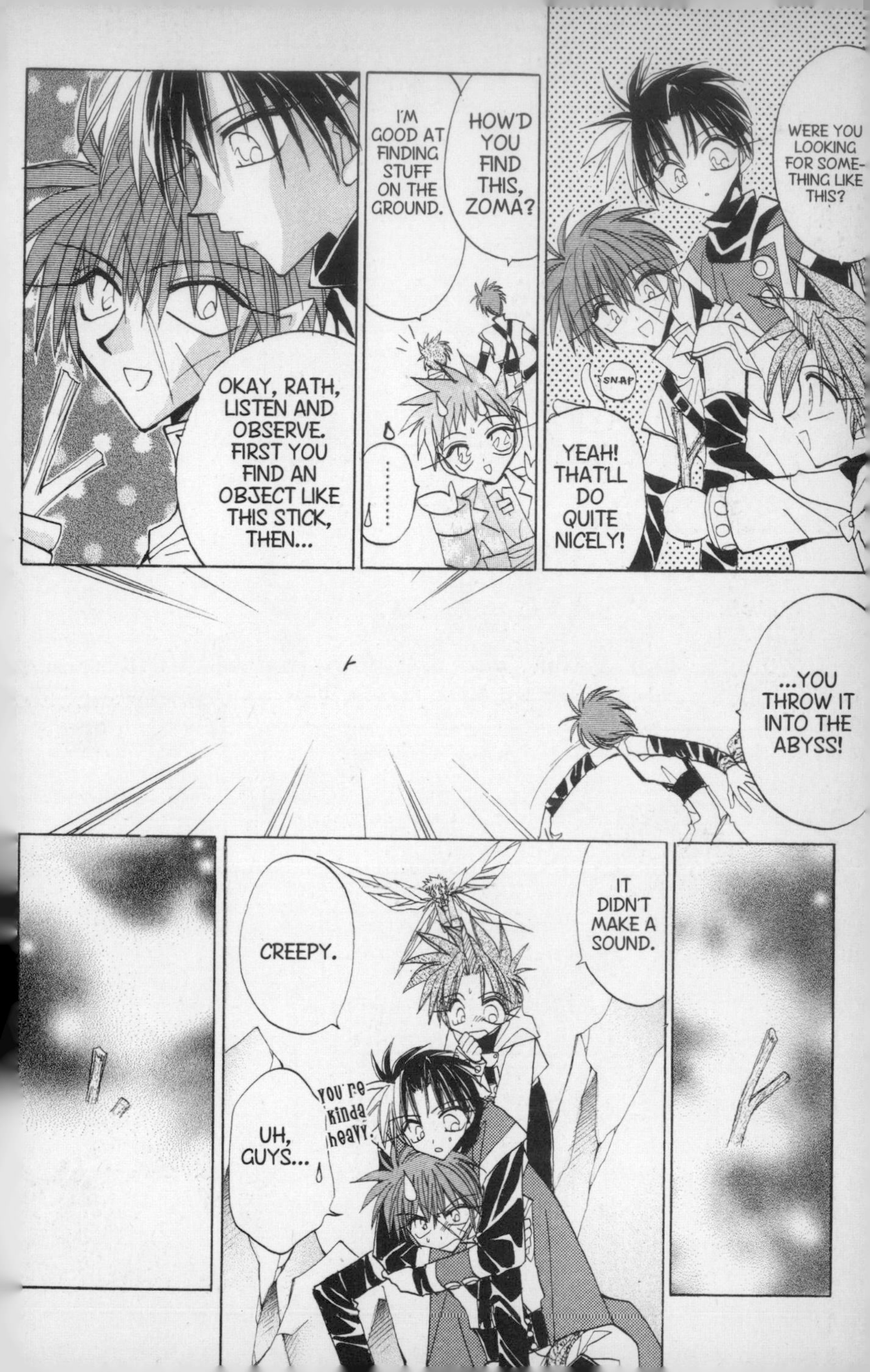
WERE YOU LOOKING FOR SOME-THING LIKE THIS?
SNAP
YEAH! THAT'LL DO QUITE NICELY!
HOW'D YOU FIND THIS, ZOMA?
I'M GOOD AT FINDING STUFF ON THE GROUND.
......
OKAY, RATH, LISTEN AND OBSERVE. FIRST YOU FIND AN OBJECT LIKE THIS STICK, THEN...
...YOU THROW IT INTO THE ABYSS!
IT DIDN'T MAKE A SOUND.
CREEPY.
YOU'RE KINDA HEAVY.
UH, GUYS...

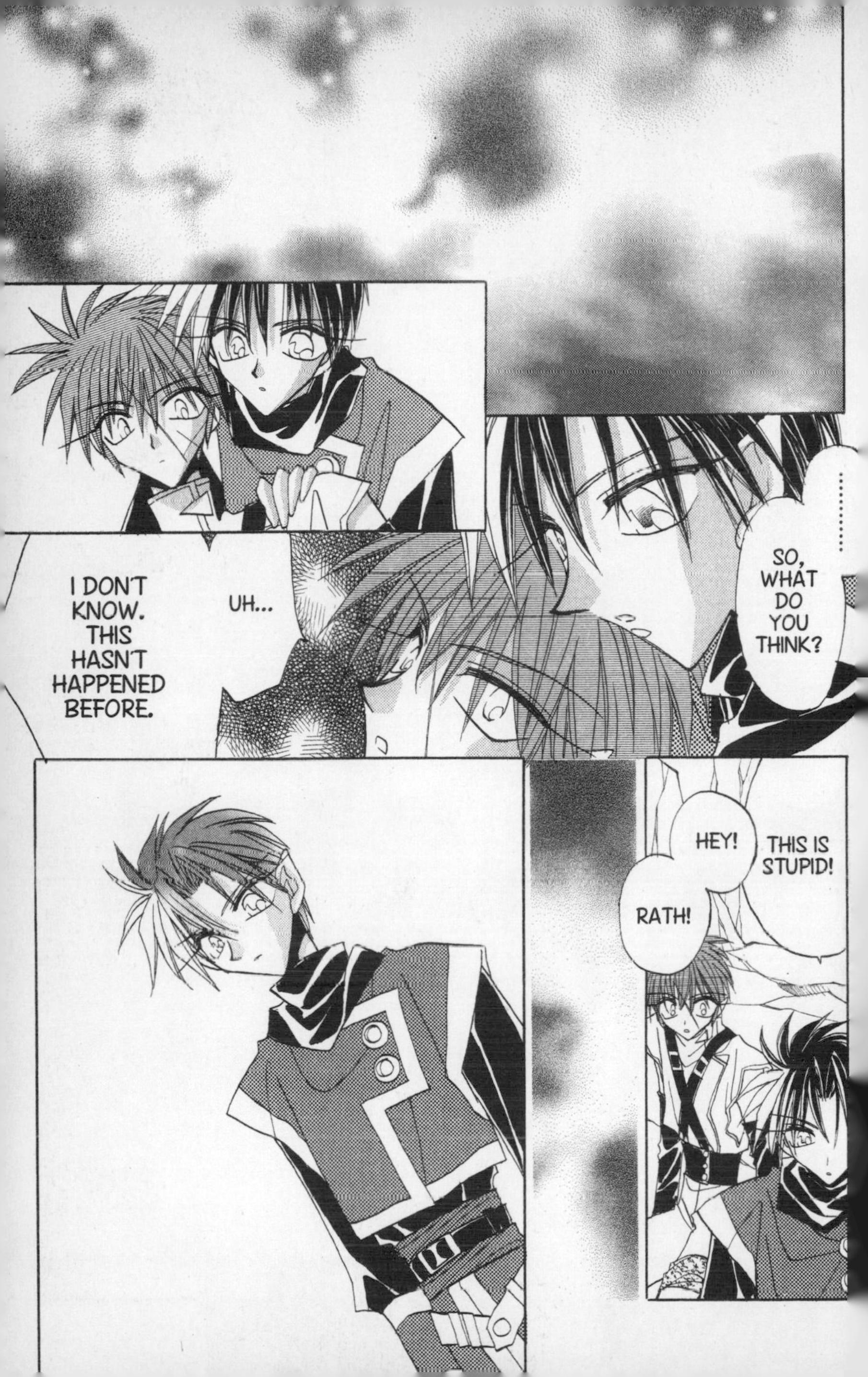
......
SO, WHAT DO YOU THINK?
UH...
I DON'T KNOW. THIS HASN'T HAPPENED BEFORE.
THIS IS STUPID!
HEY!
RATH!

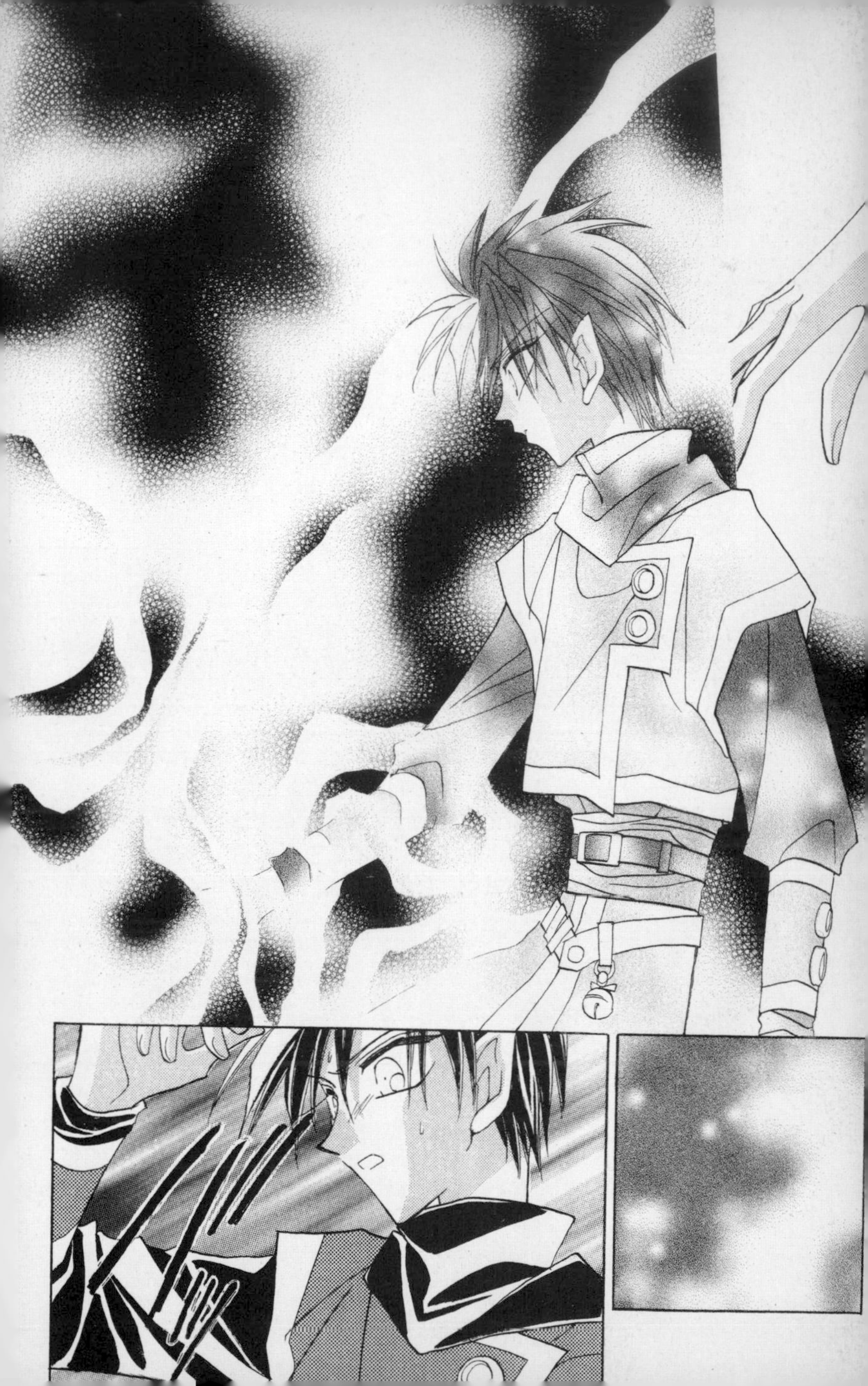

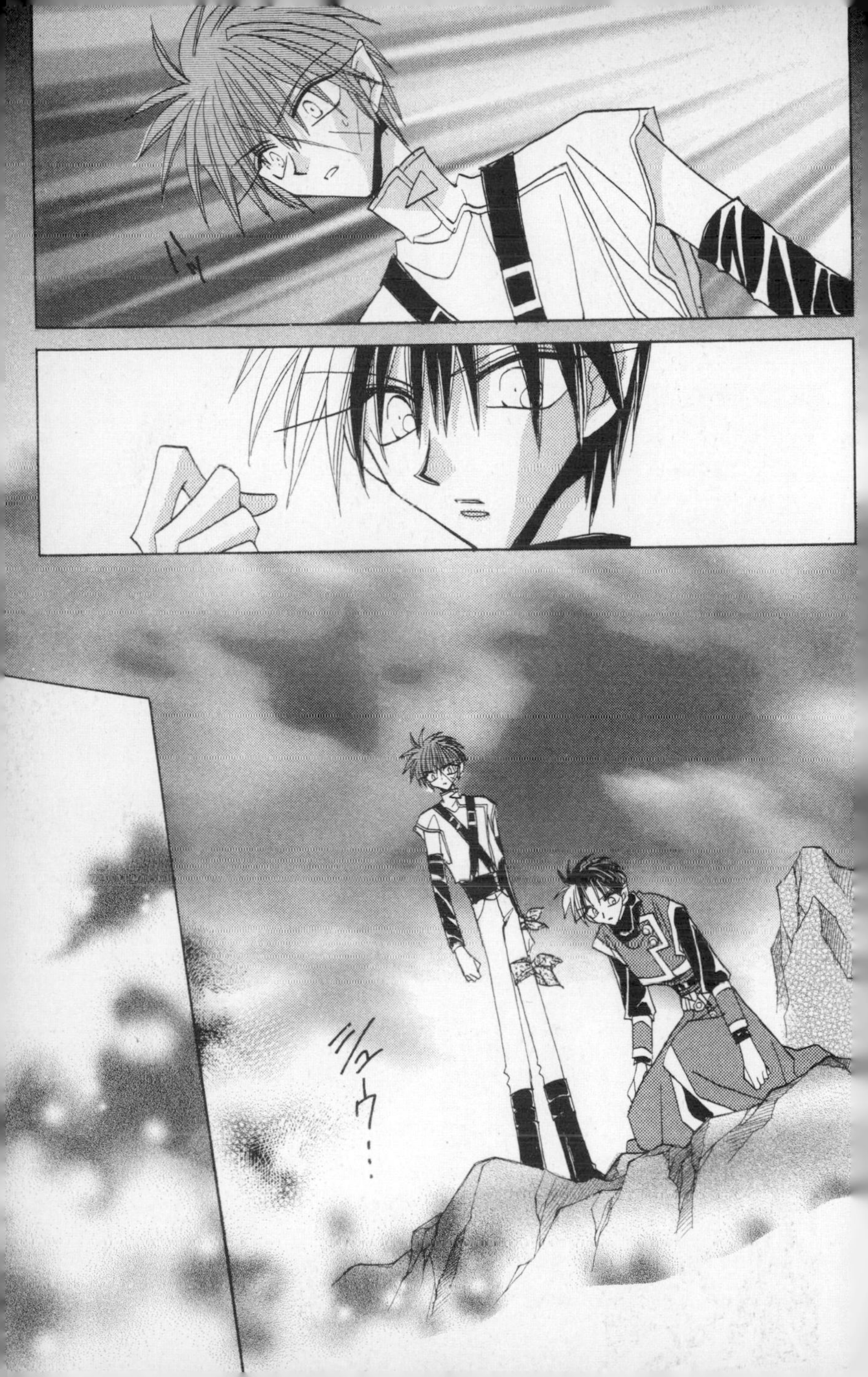
ハッ
シュウ…

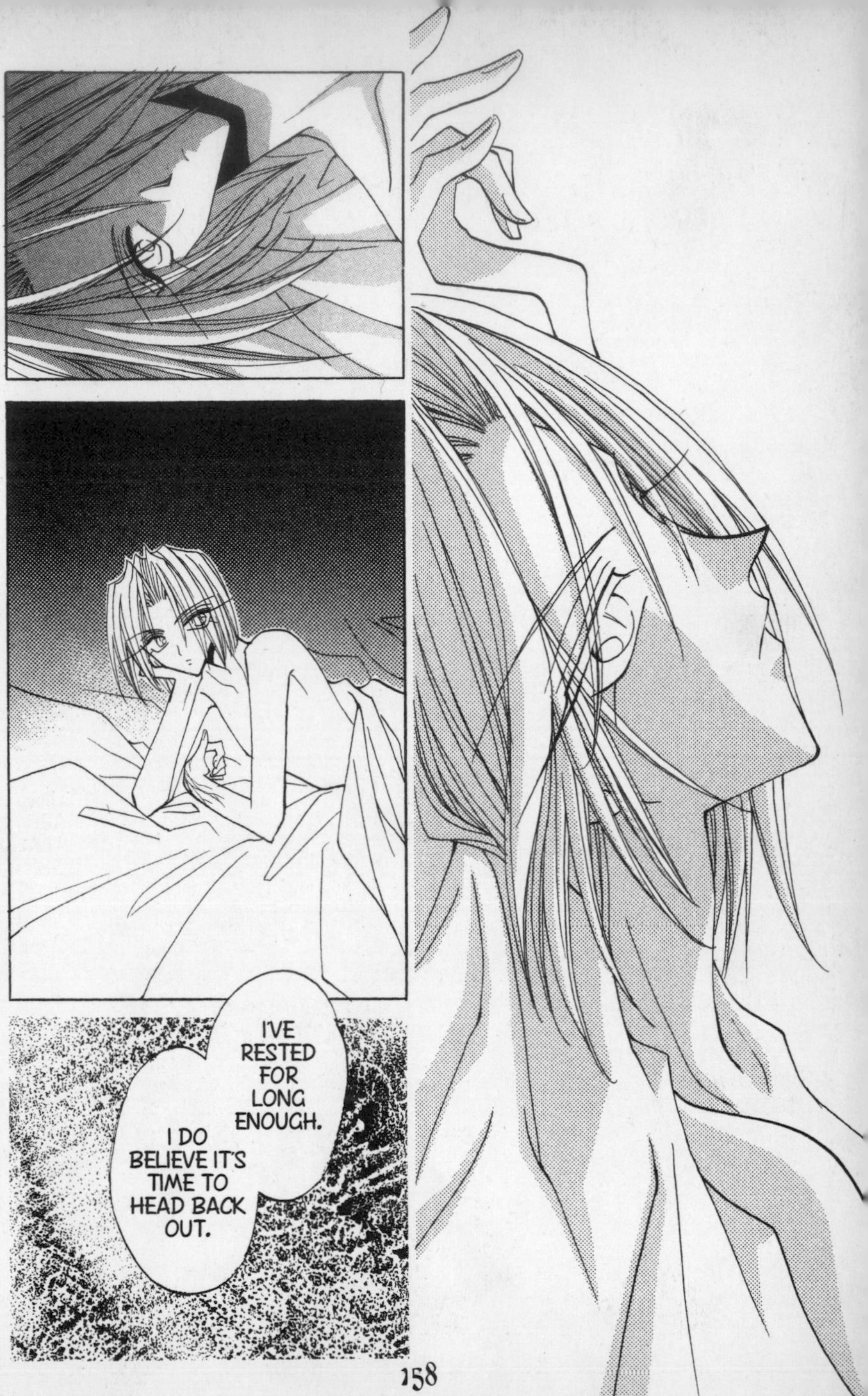
I'VE RESTED FOR LONG ENOUGH.
I DO BELIEVE IT'S TIME TO HEAD BACK OUT.

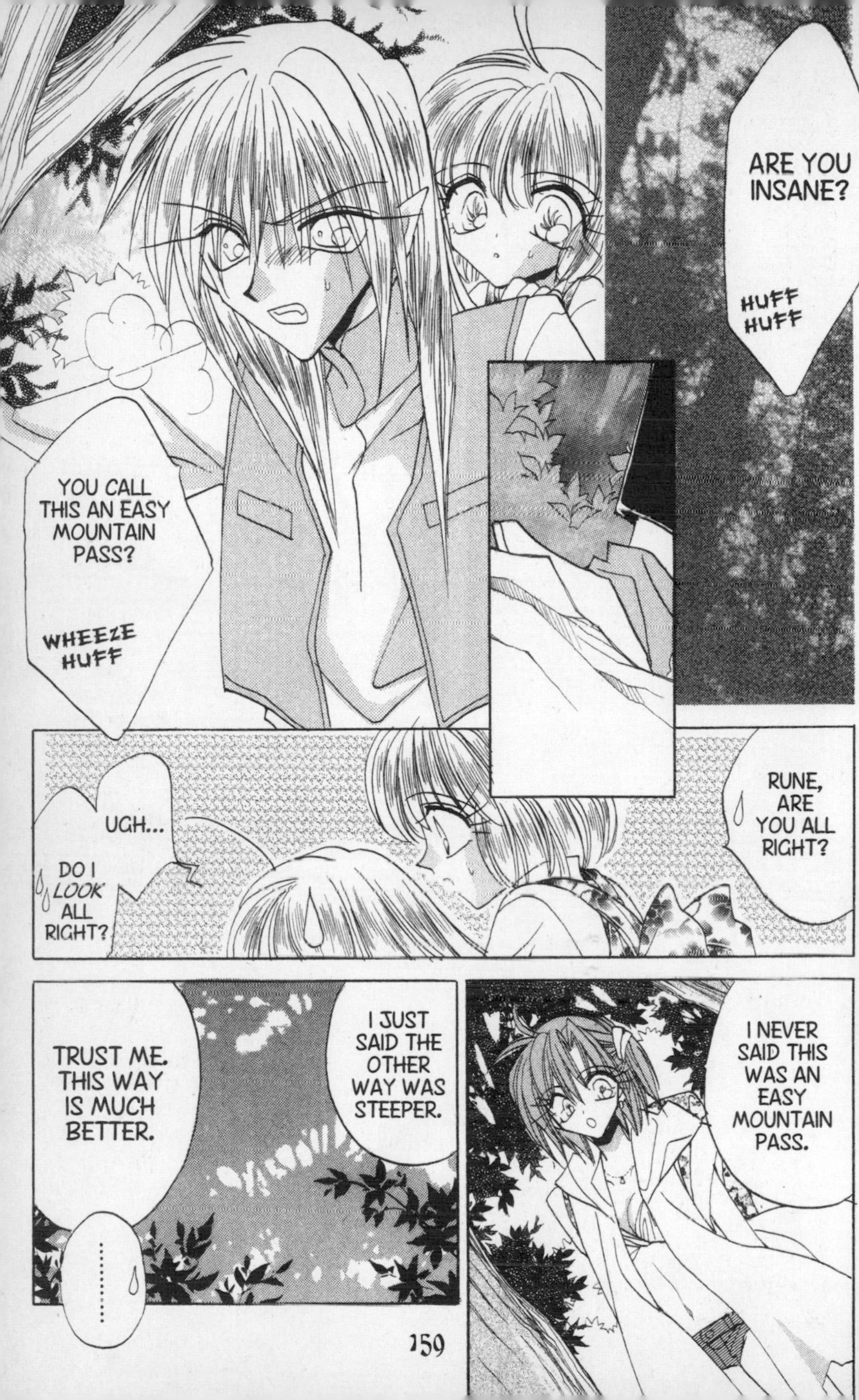

ARE YOU INSANE?
HUFF HUFF
YOU CALL THIS AN EASY MOUNTAIN PASS?
WHEEZE HUFF
RUNE, ARE YOU ALL RIGHT?
UGH...
DO I *LOOK* ALL RIGHT?
I NEVER SAID THIS WAS AN EASY MOUNTAIN PASS.
I JUST SAID THE OTHER WAY WAS STEEPER.
TRUST ME. THIS WAY IS MUCH BETTER.
......

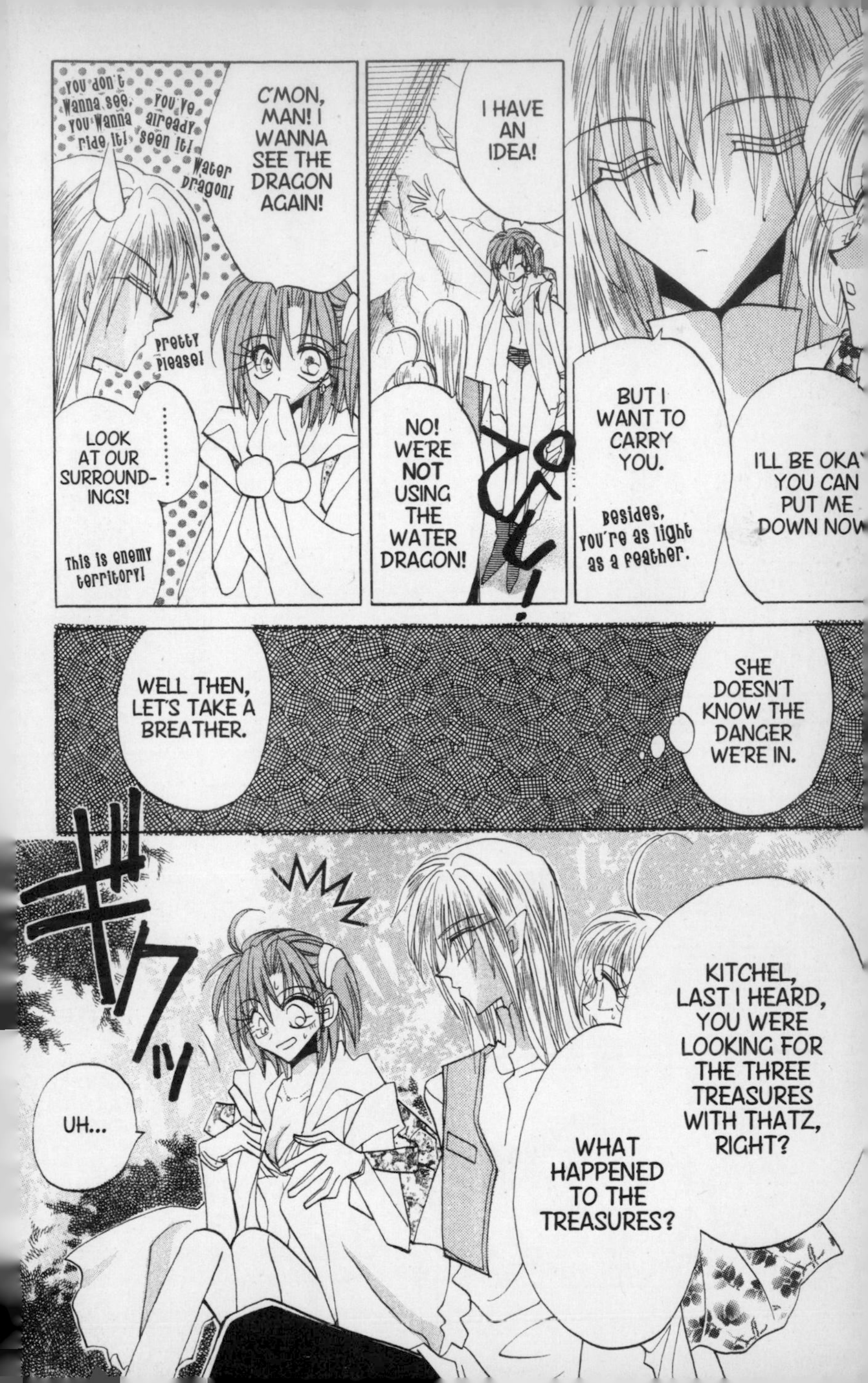
I'LL BE OKA YOU CAN PUT ME DOWN NOW
BUT I WANT TO CARRY YOU.
Besides, you're as light as a feather.
I HAVE AN IDEA!
NO! WE'RE NOT USING THE WATER DRAGON!
C'MON, MAN! I WANNA SEE THE DRAGON AGAIN!
Water Dragon!
You don't wanna see, you wanna ride it!
You've already seen it!
Pretty Please!
......
LOOK AT OUR SURROUND-INGS!
This is enemy territory!
SHE DOESN'T KNOW THE DANGER WE'RE IN.
WELL THEN, LET'S TAKE A BREATHER.
KITCHEL, LAST I HEARD, YOU WERE LOOKING FOR THE THREE TREASURES WITH THATZ, RIGHT?
WHAT HAPPENED TO THE TREASURES?
UH...

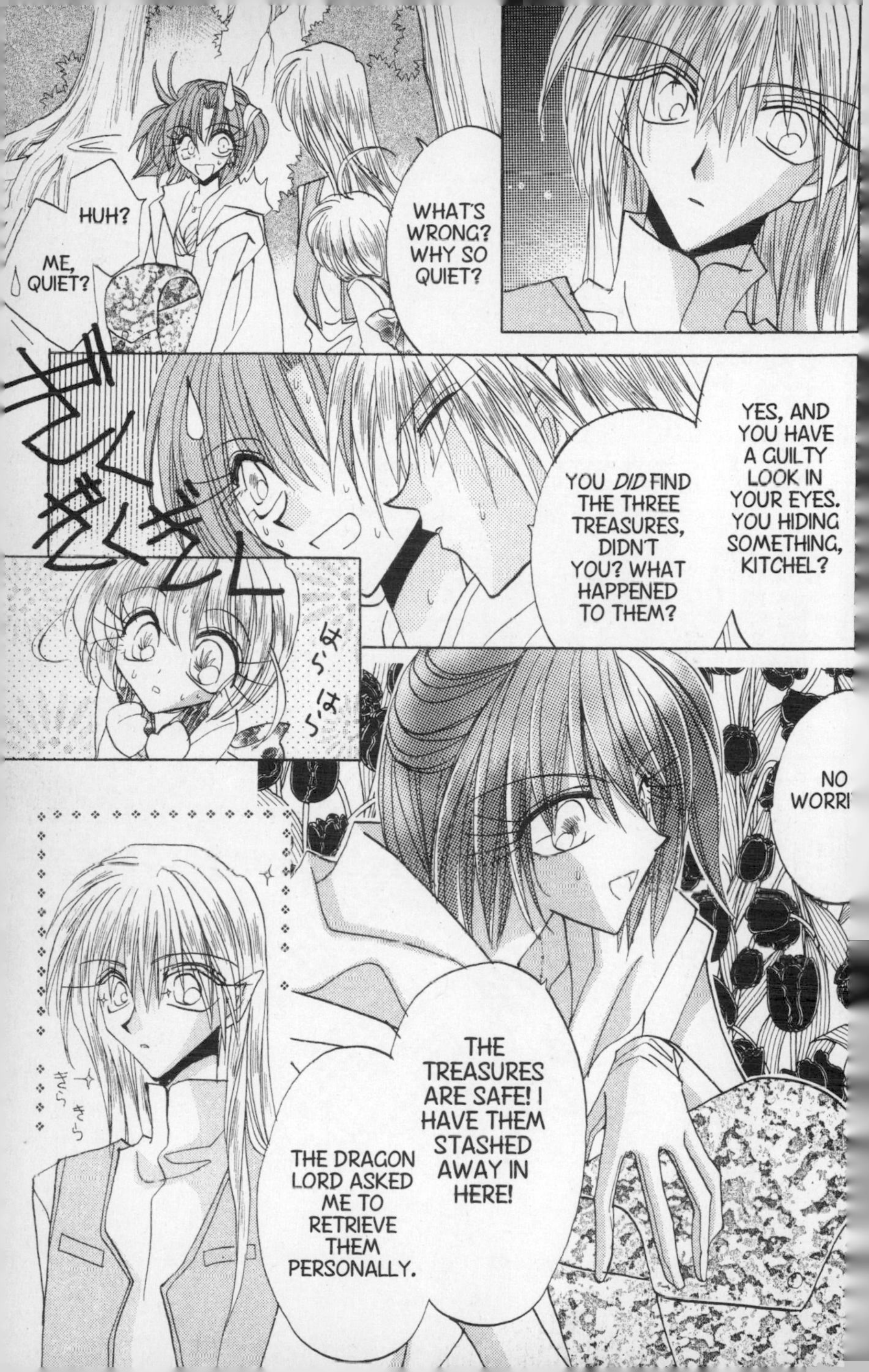
WHAT'S WRONG? WHY SO QUIET?
HUH?
ME, QUIET?
YES, AND YOU HAVE A GUILTY LOOK IN YOUR EYES. YOU HIDING SOMETHING, KITCHEL?
YOU *DID* FIND THE THREE TREASURES, DIDN'T YOU? WHAT HAPPENED TO THEM?
ぎくぎくん
はらはら
NO WORRI
THE TREASURES ARE SAFE! I HAVE THEM STASHED AWAY IN HERE!
THE DRAGON LORD ASKED ME TO RETRIEVE THEM PERSONALLY.
きらきら

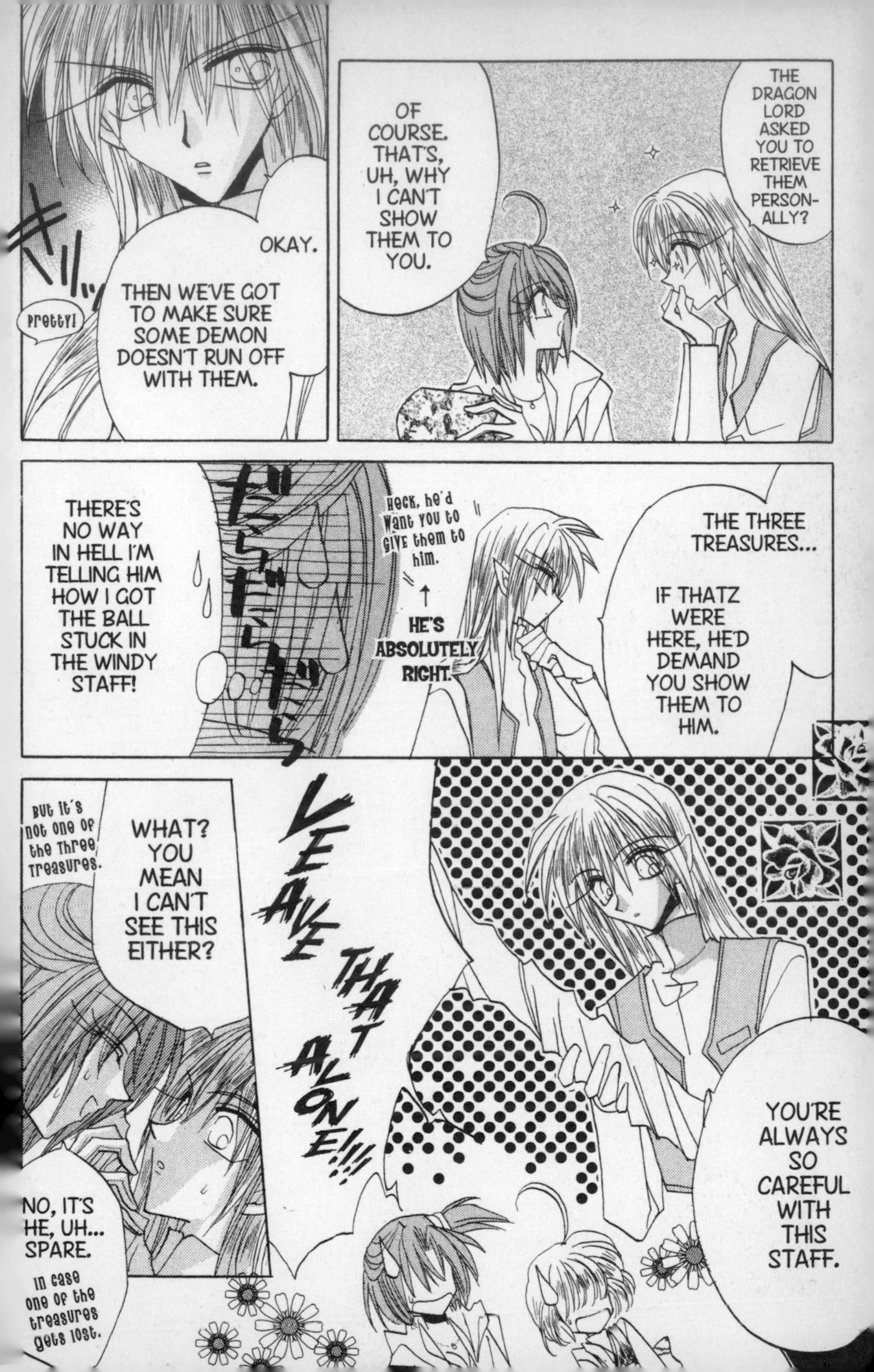
THE DRAGON LORD ASKED YOU TO RETRIEVE THEM PERSON-ALLY?
OF COURSE. THAT'S, UH, WHY I CAN'T SHOW THEM TO YOU.
OKAY.
THEN WE'VE GOT TO MAKE SURE SOME DEMON DOESN'T RUN OFF WITH THEM.
Pretty!
THE THREE TREASURES...
IF THATZ WERE HERE, HE'D DEMAND YOU SHOW THEM TO HIM.
Heck, he'd want you to give them to him.
HE'S ABSOLUTELY RIGHT.
THERE'S NO WAY IN HELL I'M TELLING HIM HOW I GOT THE BALL STUCK IN THE WINDY STAFF!
YOU'RE ALWAYS SO CAREFUL WITH THIS STAFF.
LEAVE THAT ALONE!!!!
WHAT? YOU MEAN I CAN'T SEE THIS EITHER?
But it's not one of the Three Treasures.
NO, IT'S HE, UH... SPARE.
In case one of the treasures gets lost.

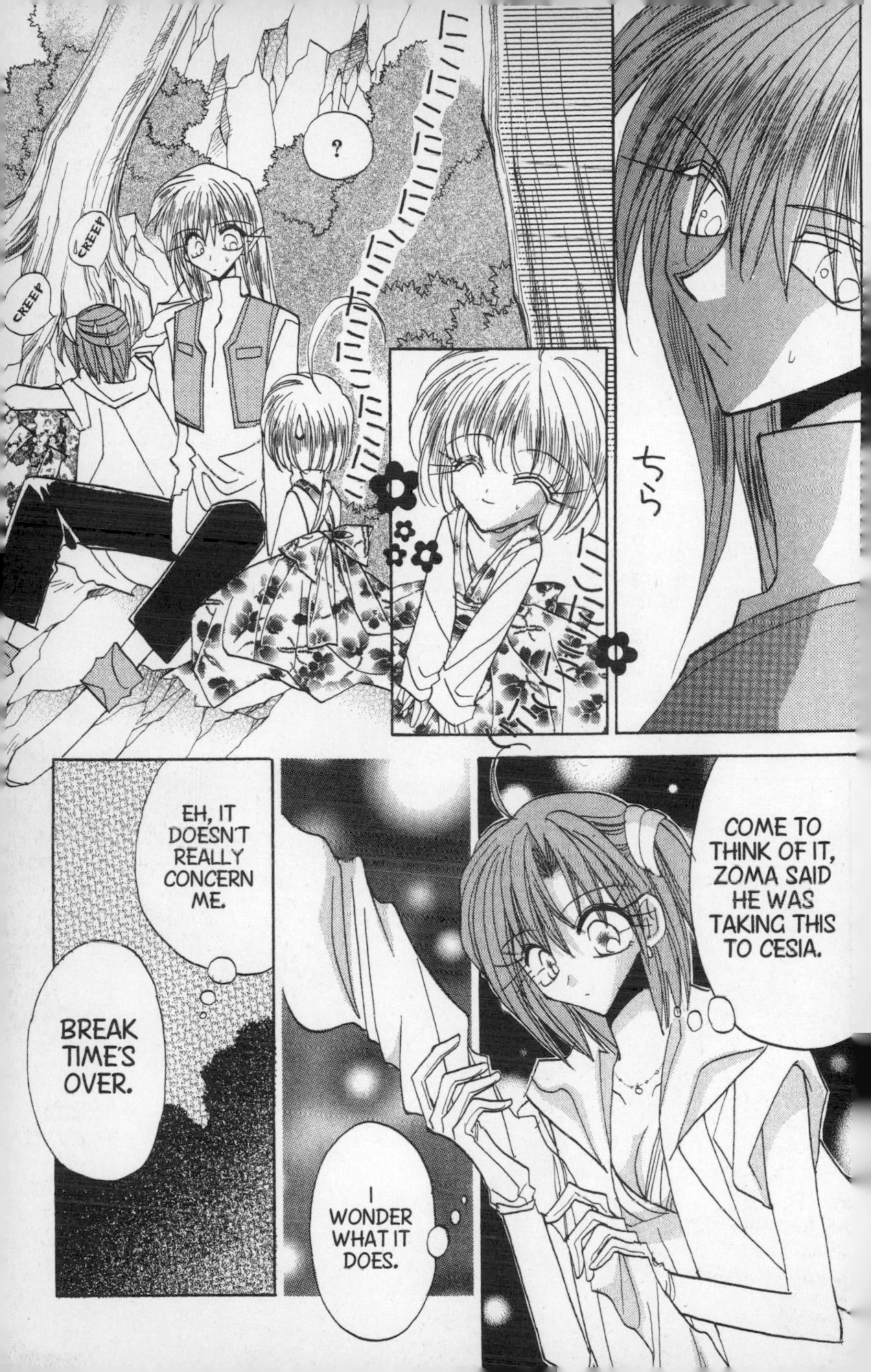
ちら
?
CREEP
CREEP
COME TO THINK OF IT, ZOMA SAID HE WAS TAKING THIS TO CESIA.
I WONDER WHAT IT DOES.
EH, IT DOESN'T REALLY CONCERN ME.
BREAK TIME'S OVER.

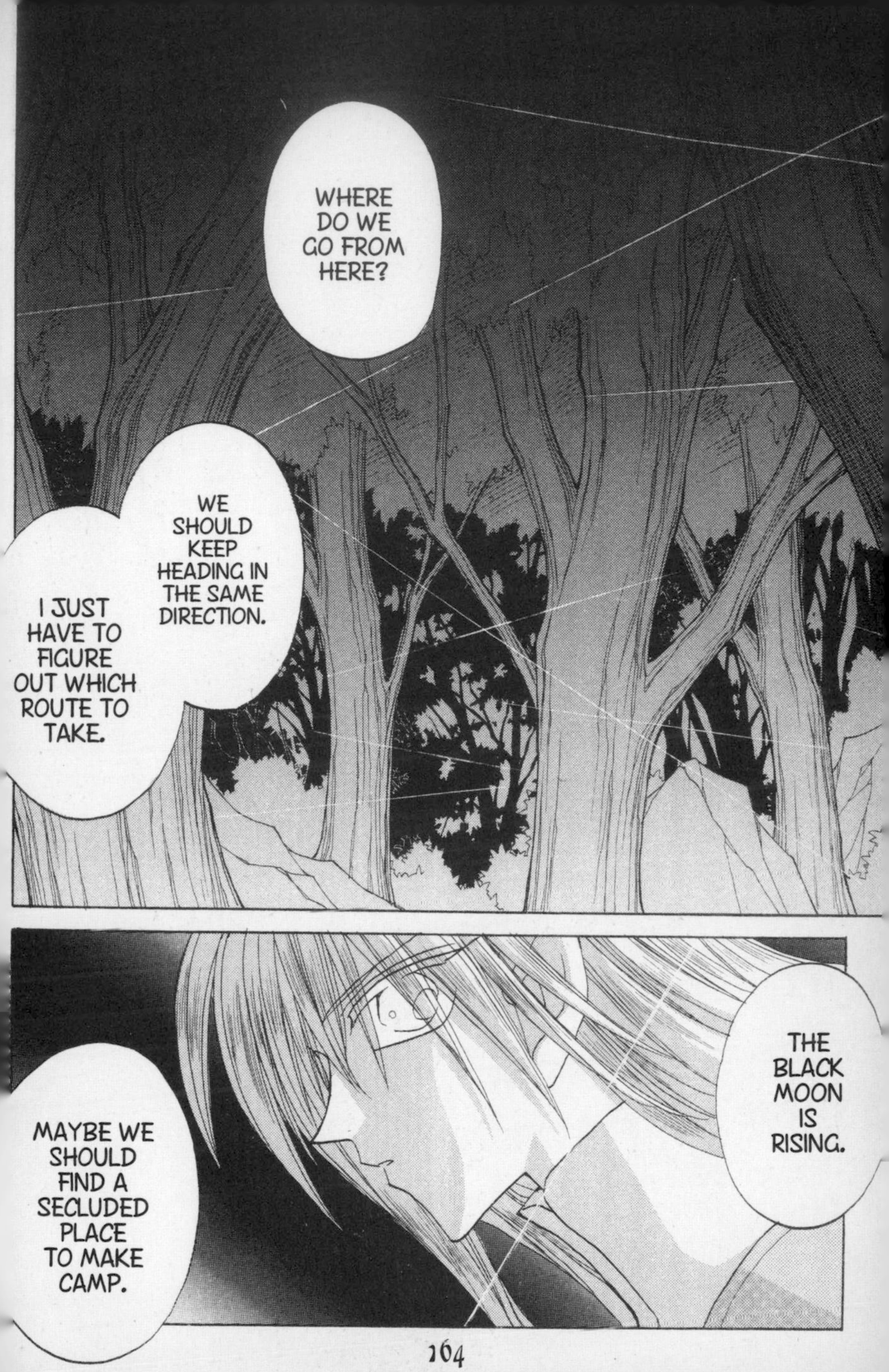
WHERE DO WE GO FROM HERE?
WE SHOULD KEEP HEADING IN THE SAME DIRECTION.
I JUST HAVE TO FIGURE OUT WHICH ROUTE TO TAKE.
THE BLACK MOON IS RISING.
MAYBE WE SHOULD FIND A SECLUDED PLACE TO MAKE CAMP.

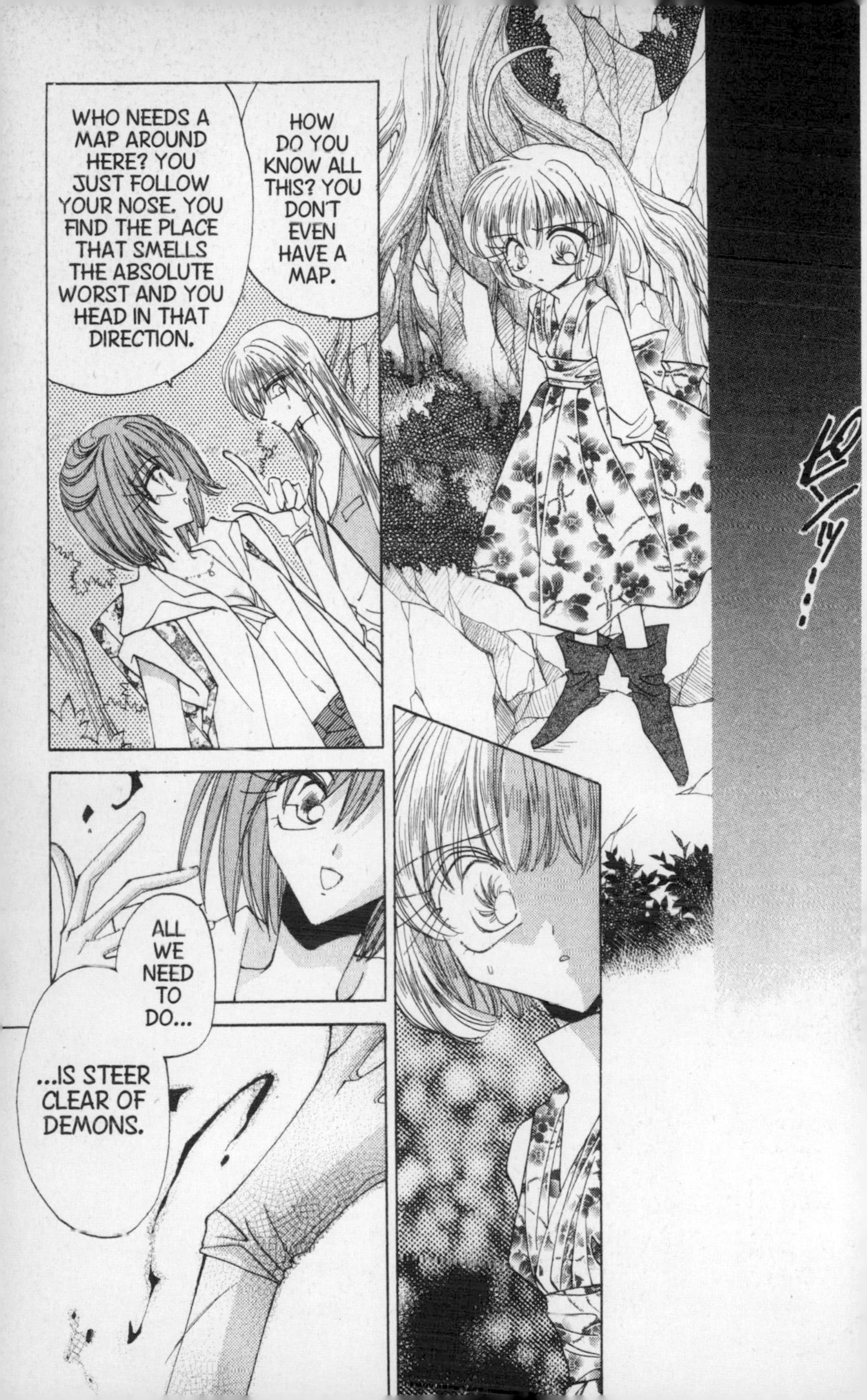
HOW DO YOU KNOW ALL THIS? YOU DON'T EVEN HAVE A MAP.
WHO NEEDS A MAP AROUND HERE? YOU JUST FOLLOW YOUR NOSE. YOU FIND THE PLACE THAT SMELLS THE ABSOLUTE WORST AND YOU HEAD IN THAT DIRECTION.
ALL WE NEED TO DO...
...IS STEER CLEAR OF DEMONS.

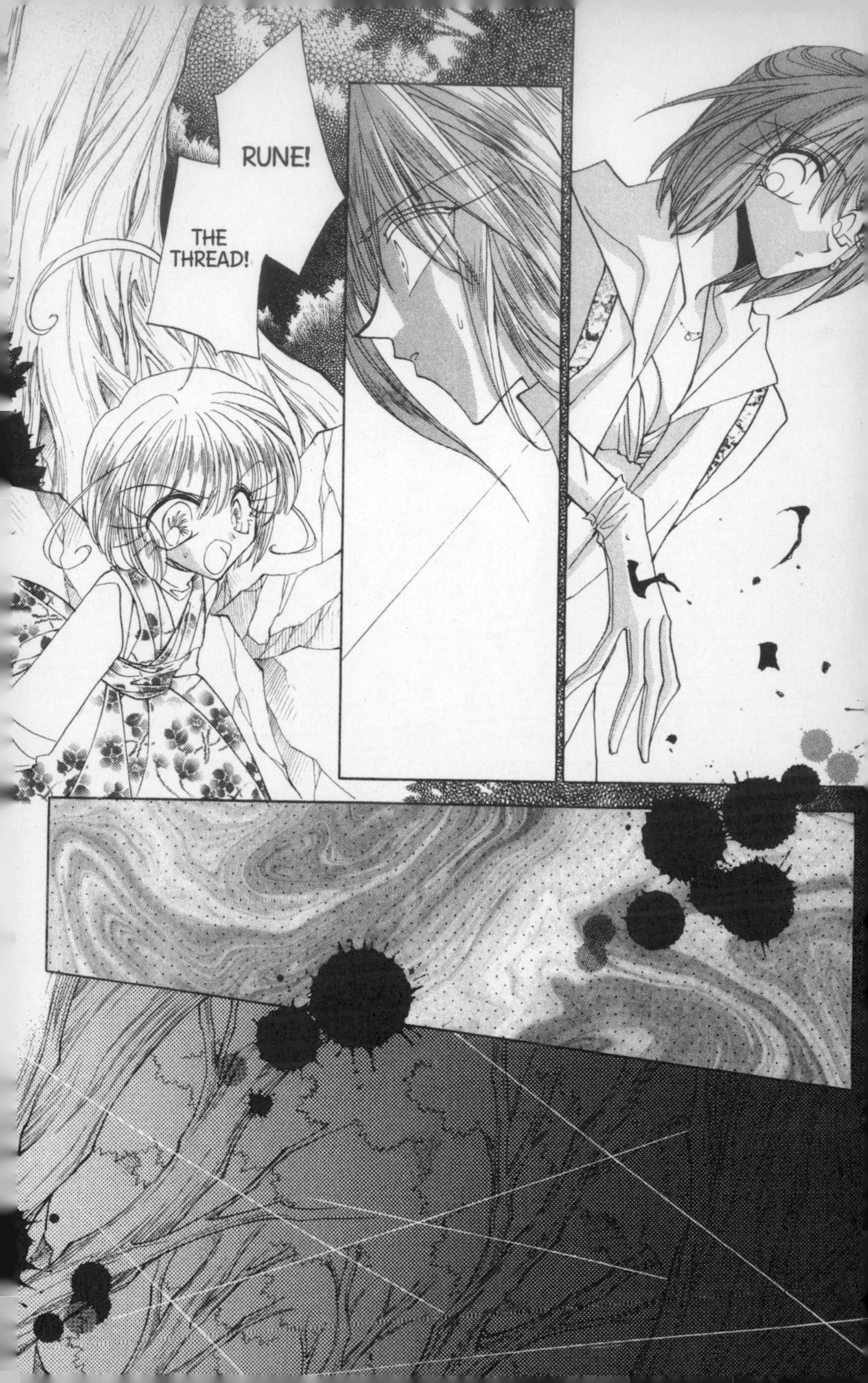
RUNE!
THE THREAD!

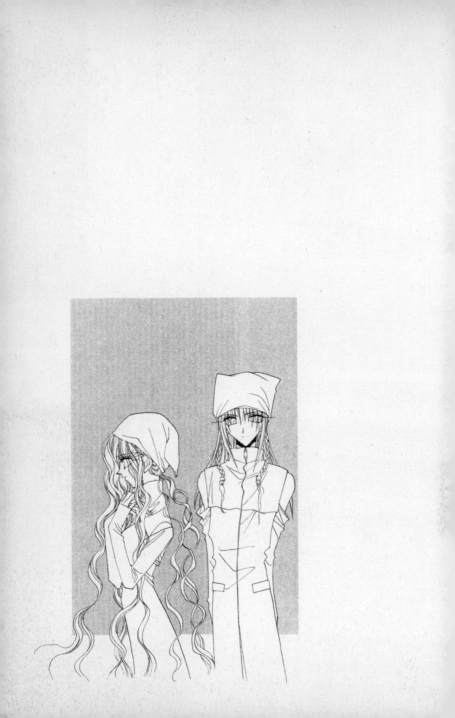

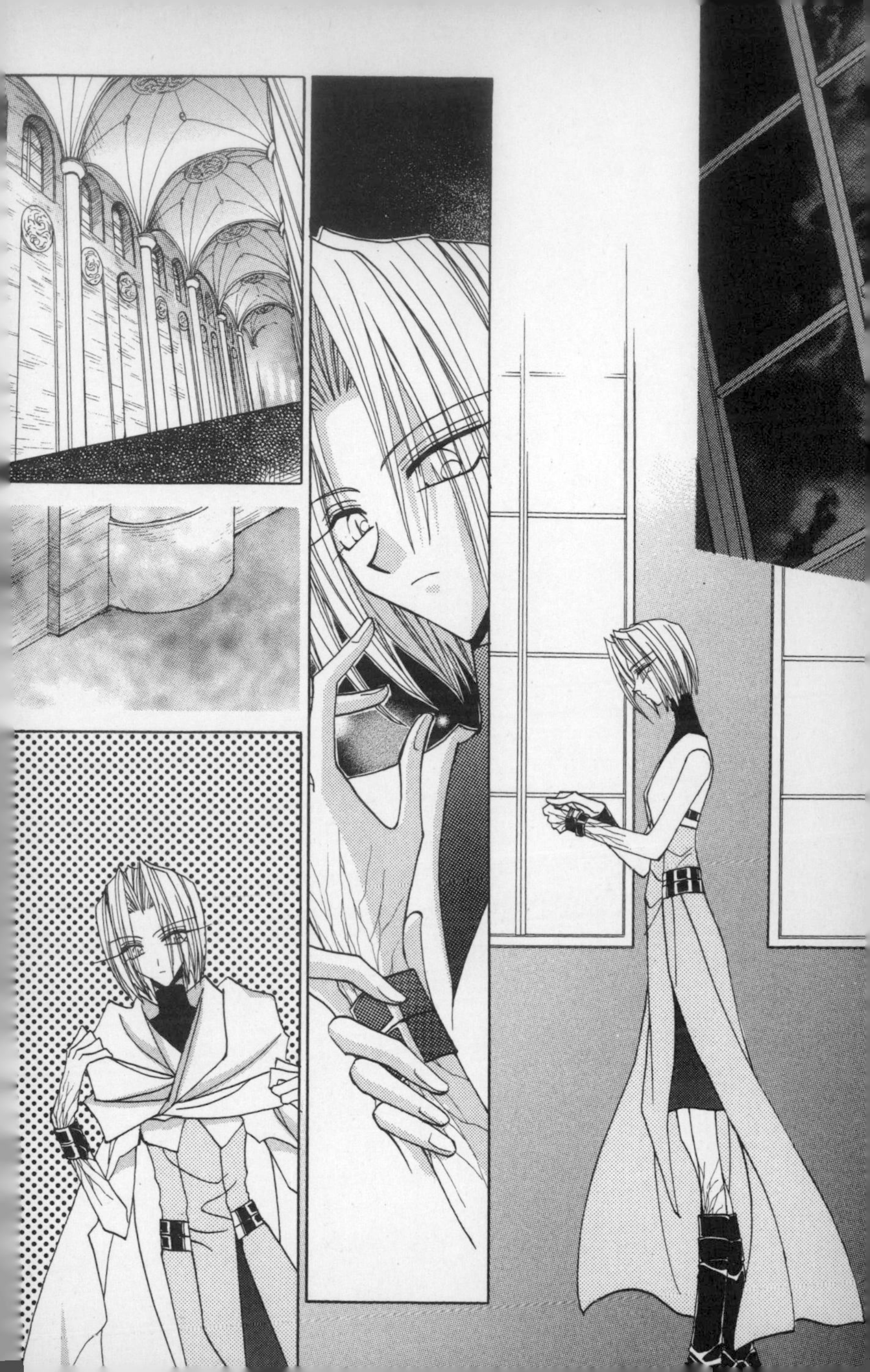

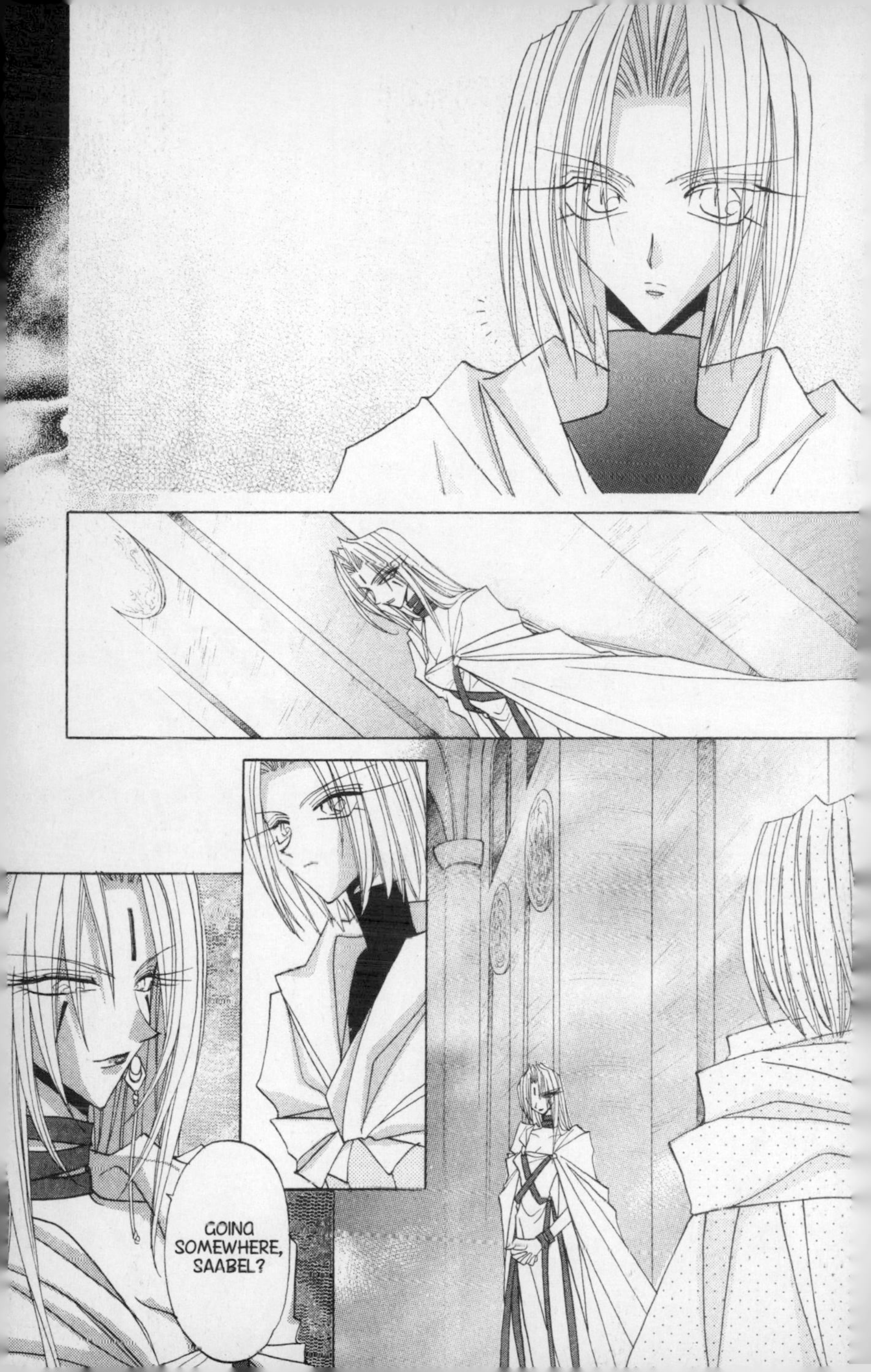
GOING SOMEWHERE, SAABEL?

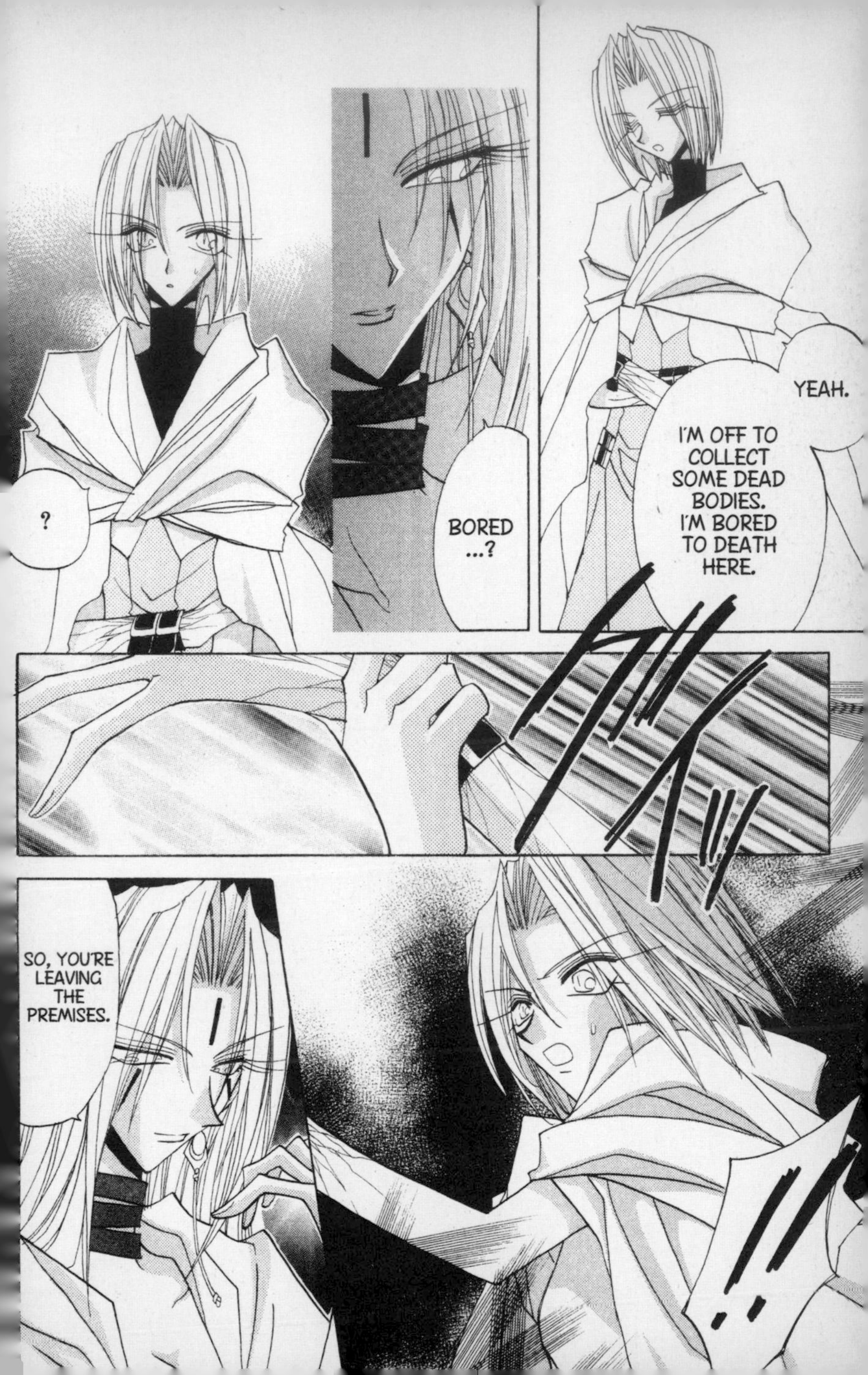
YEAH.
I'M OFF TO COLLECT SOME DEAD BODIES. I'M BORED TO DEATH HERE.
BORED ...?
?
!!
SO, YOU'RE LEAVING THE PREMISES.

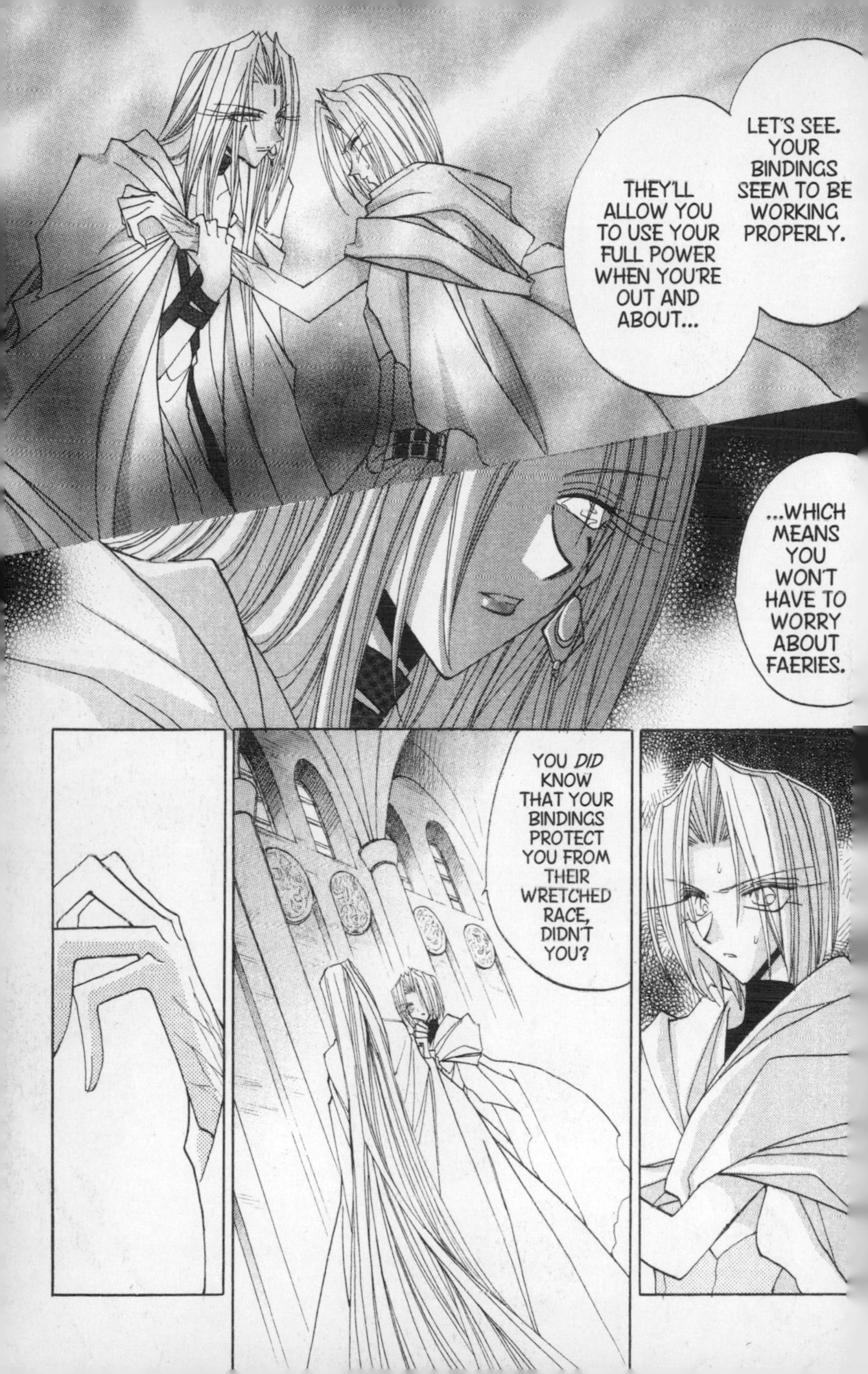
LET'S SEE. YOUR BINDINGS SEEM TO BE WORKING PROPERLY.
THEY'LL ALLOW YOU TO USE YOUR FULL POWER WHEN YOU'RE OUT AND ABOUT...
...WHICH MEANS YOU WON'T HAVE TO WORRY ABOUT FAERIES.
YOU *DID* KNOW THAT YOUR BINDINGS PROTECT YOU FROM THEIR WRETCHED RACE, DIDN'T YOU?

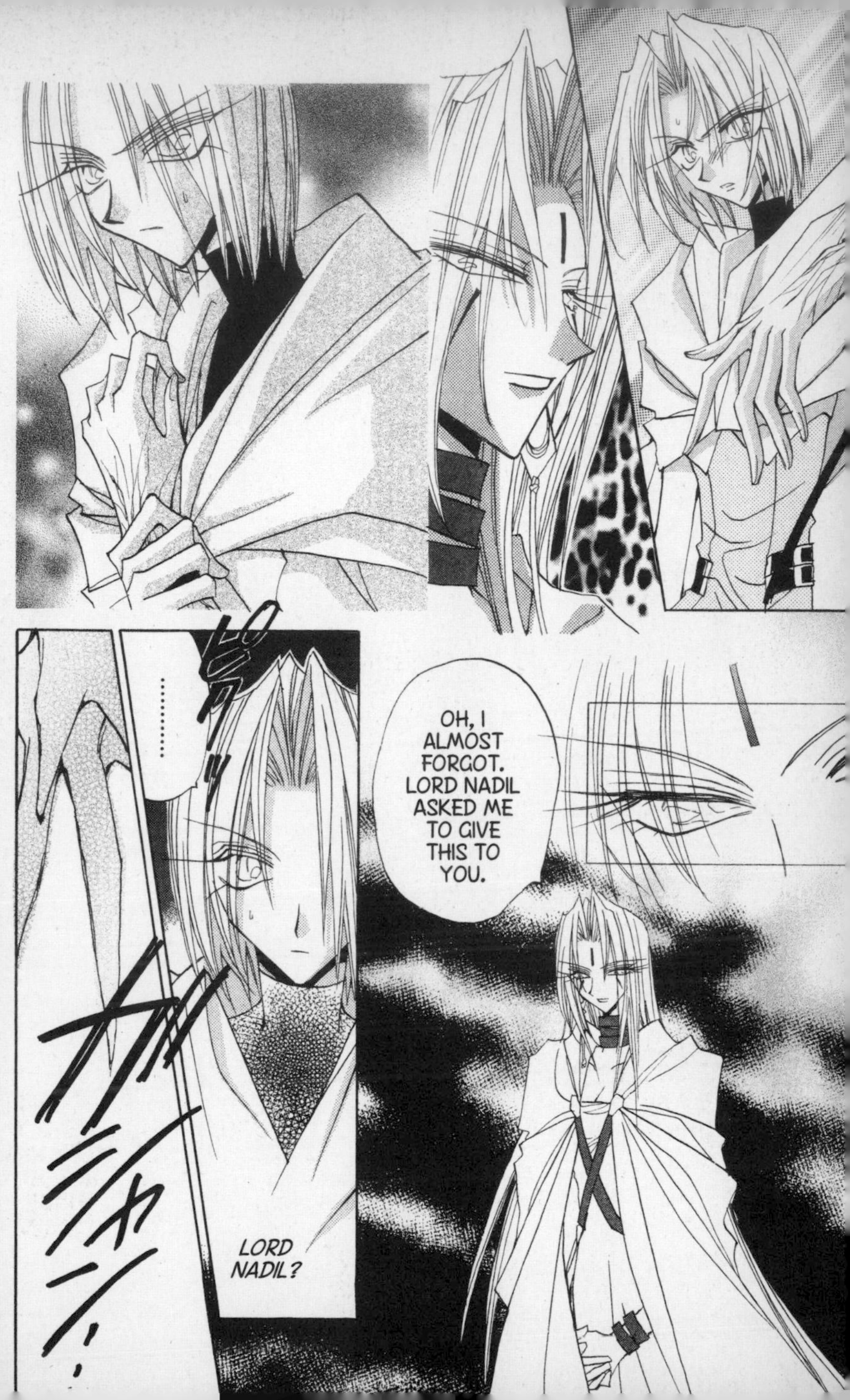
OH, I ALMOST FORGOT. LORD NADIL ASKED ME TO GIVE THIS TO YOU.
......
LORD NADIL?

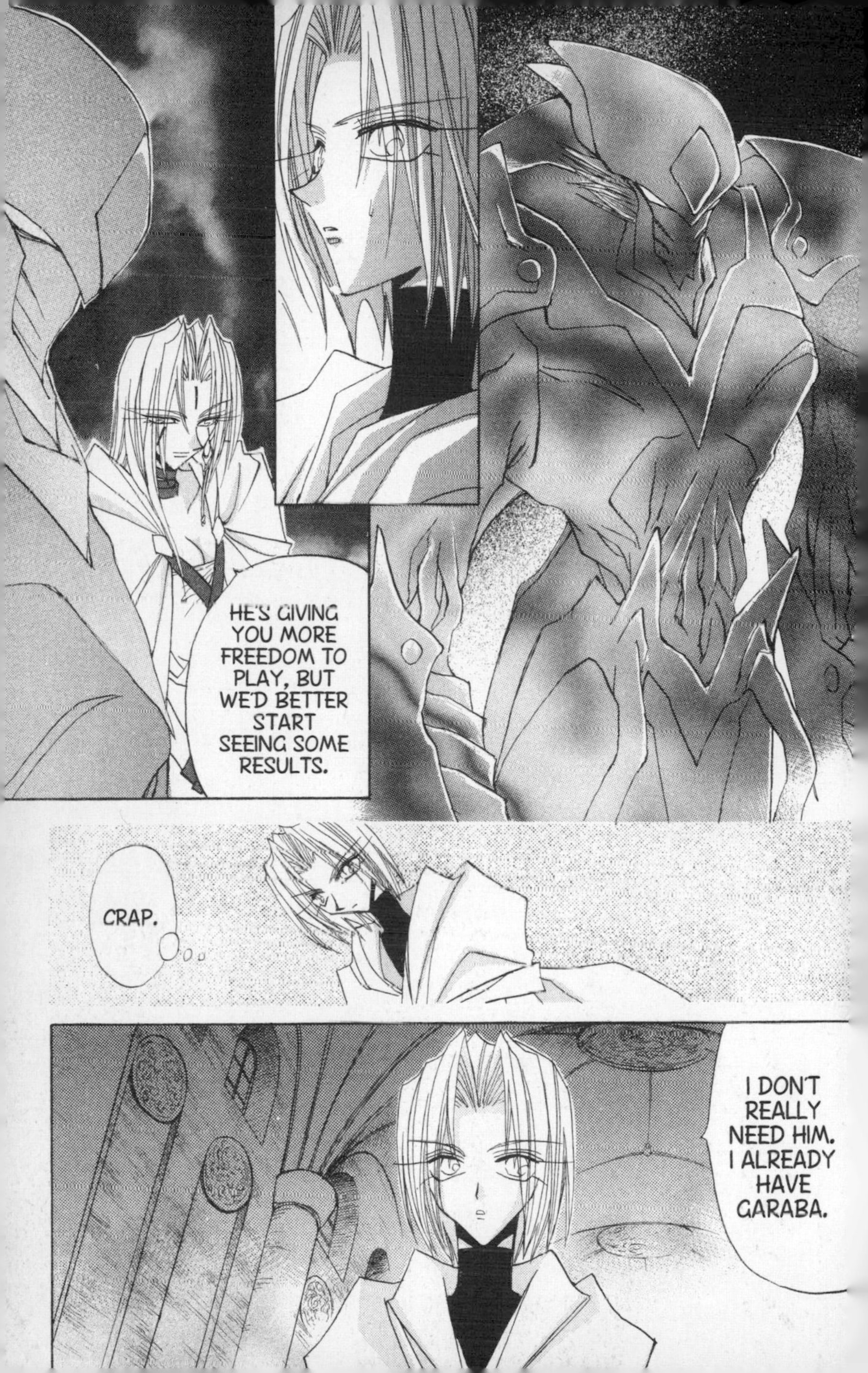
HE'S GIVING YOU MORE FREEDOM TO PLAY, BUT WE'D BETTER START SEEING SOME RESULTS.
CRAP.
I DON'T REALLY NEED HIM. I ALREADY HAVE GARABA.

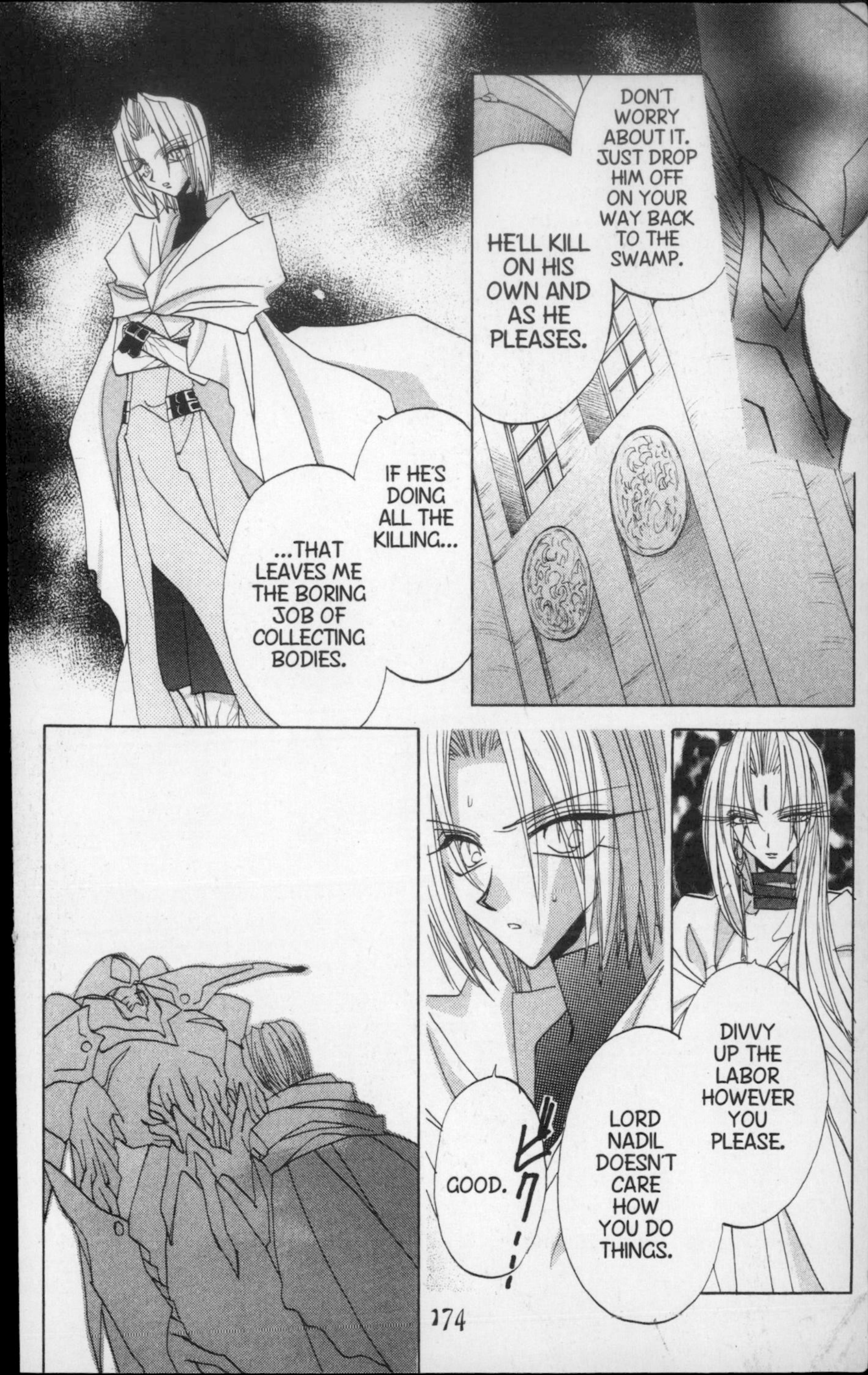
DON'T WORRY ABOUT IT. JUST DROP HIM OFF ON YOUR WAY BACK TO THE SWAMP.
HE'LL KILL ON HIS OWN AND AS HE PLEASES.
IF HE'S DOING ALL THE KILLING...
...THAT LEAVES ME THE BORING JOB OF COLLECTING BODIES.
DIVVY UP THE LABOR HOWEVER YOU PLEASE.
LORD NADIL DOESN'T CARE HOW YOU DO THINGS.
GOOD.

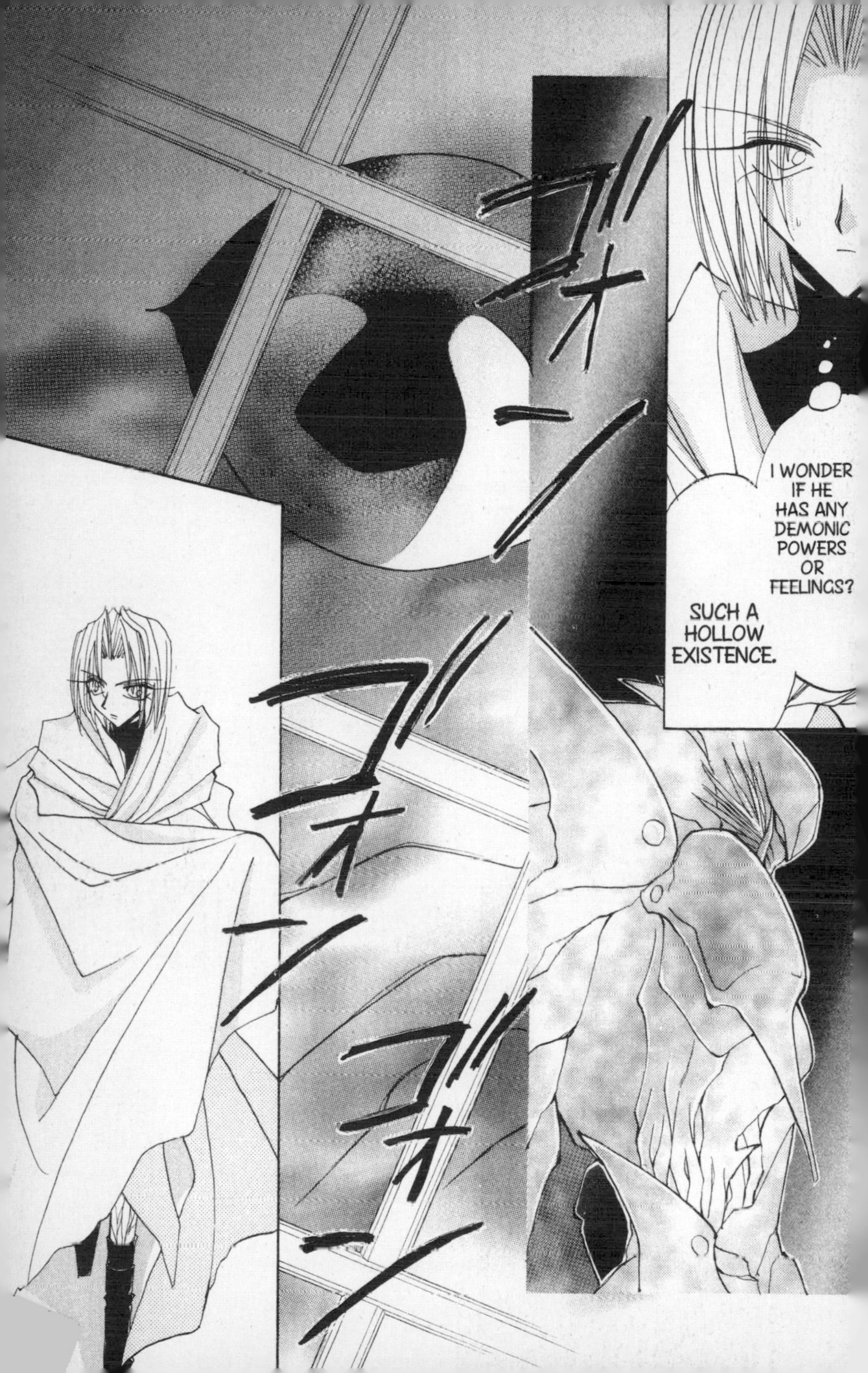
I WONDER IF HE HAS ANY DEMONIC POWERS OR FEELINGS?
SUCH A HOLLOW EXISTENCE.
ゴォーン
ゴォーン
ゴォーン

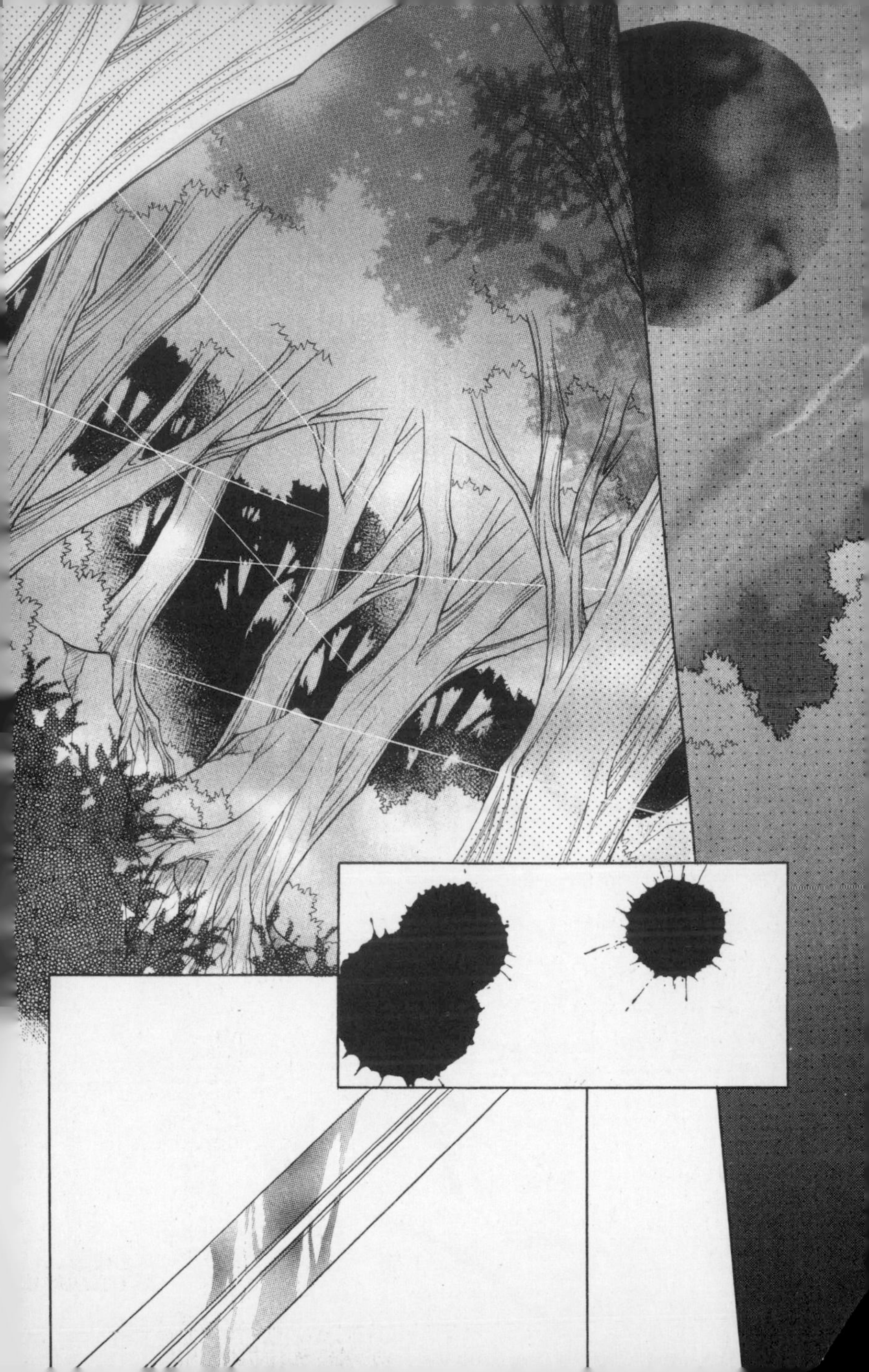

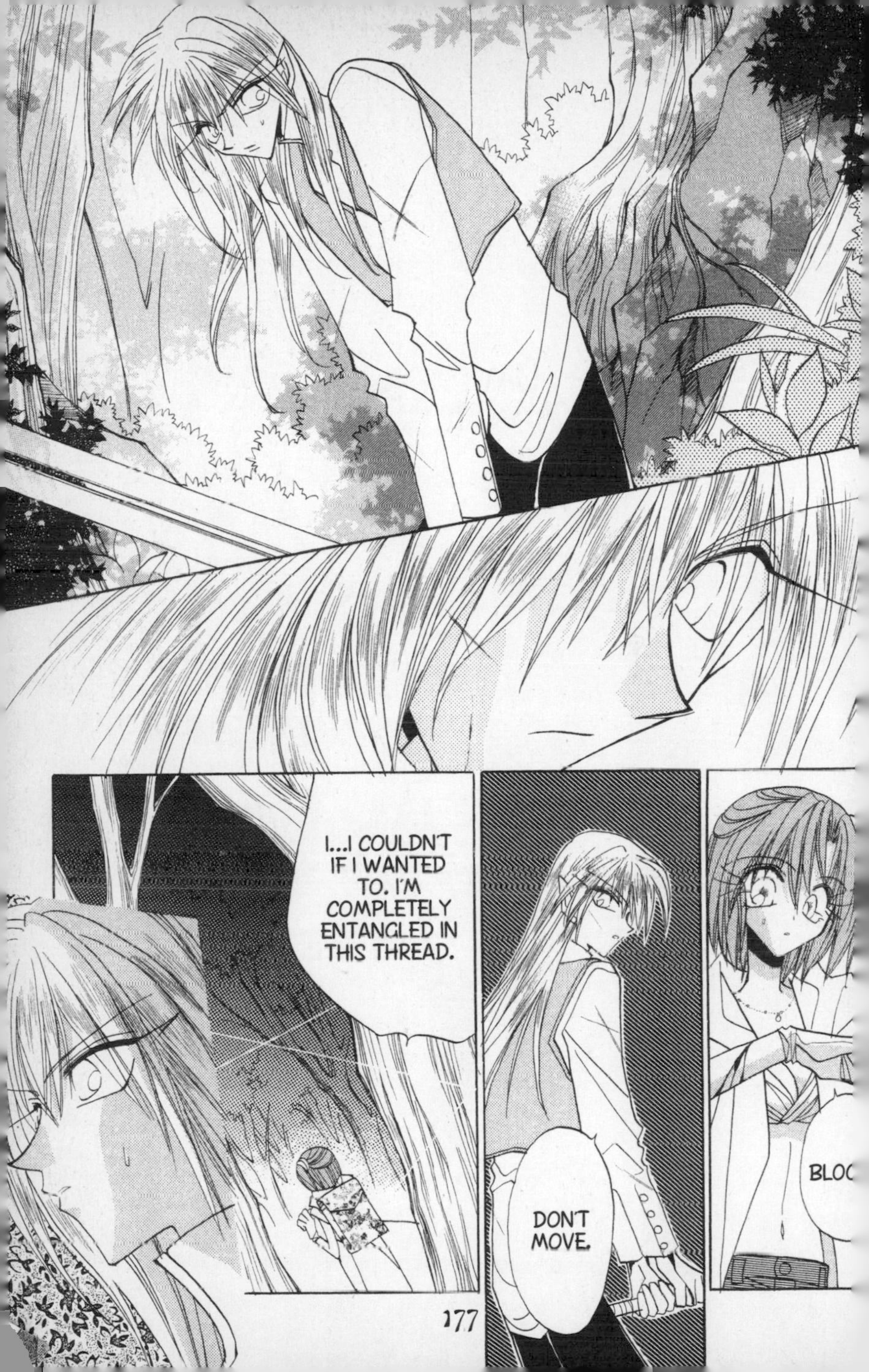
BLOC
DON'T MOVE.
I...I COULDN'T IF I WANTED TO. I'M COMPLETELY ENTANGLED IN THIS THREAD.

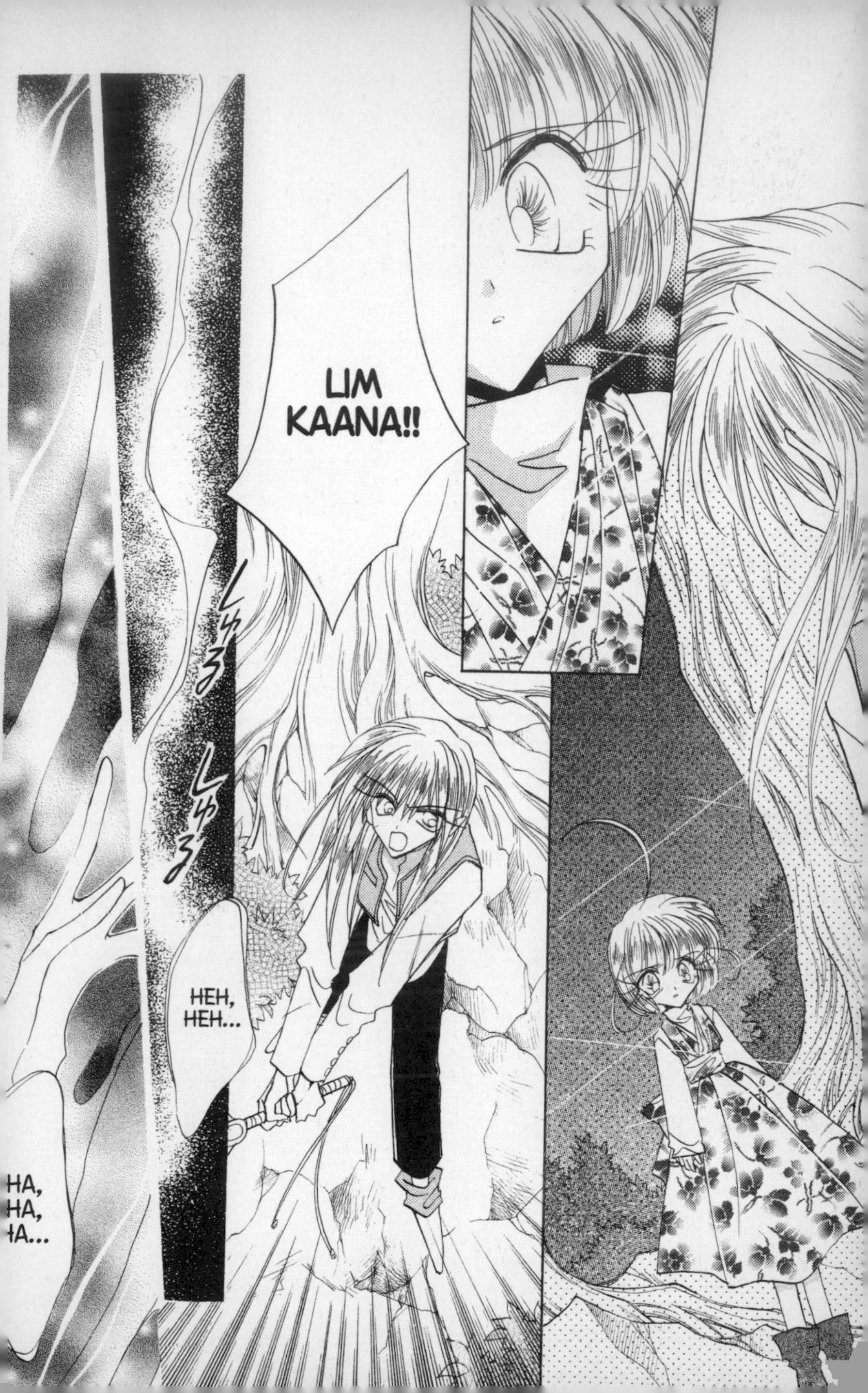
LIM KAANA!!
しゅる しゅる
HEH, HEH...
HA, HA, HA...

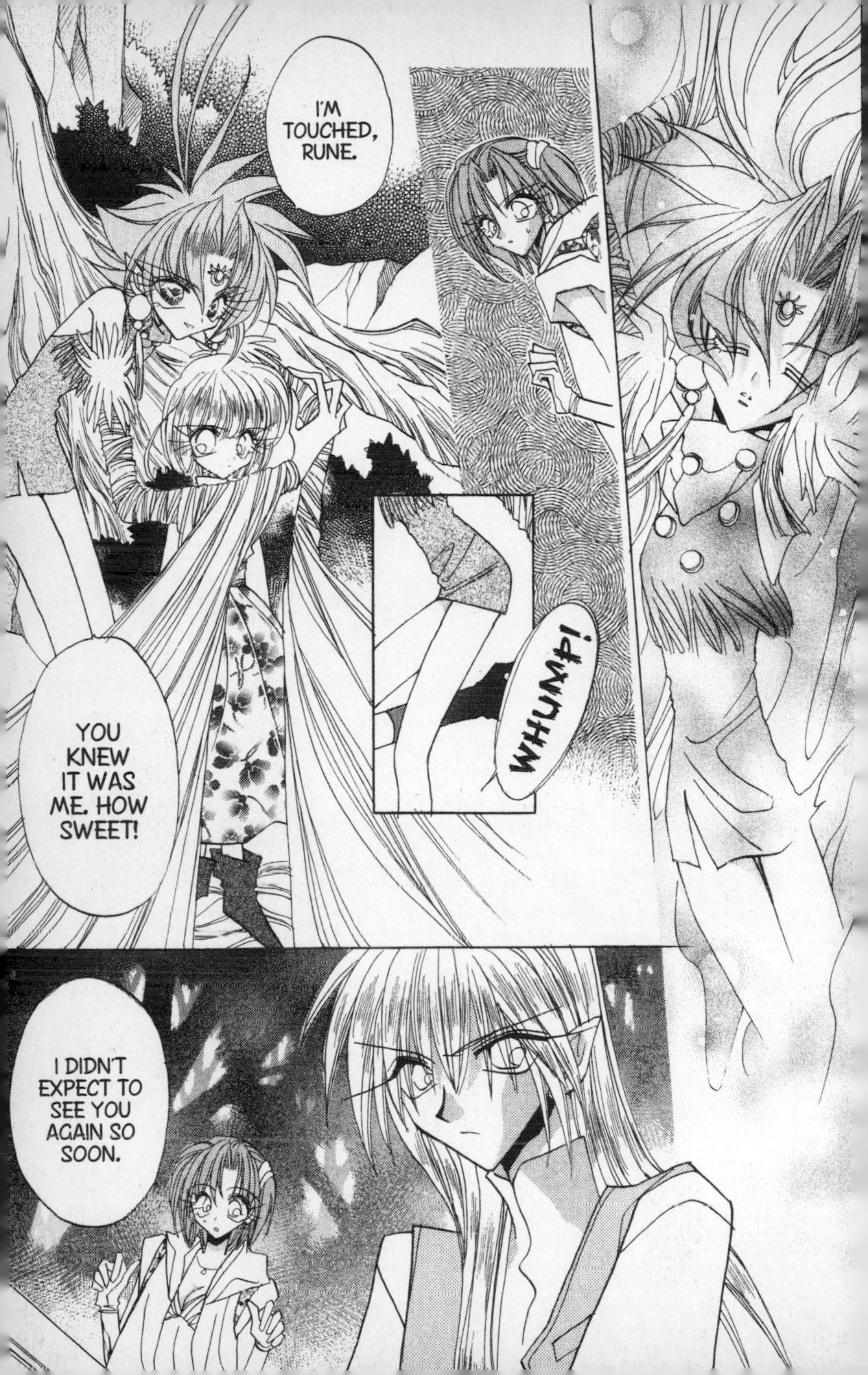
WHUMP!
I'M TOUCHED, RUNE.
YOU KNEW IT WAS ME. HOW SWEET!
I DIDN'T EXPECT TO SEE YOU AGAIN SO SOON.

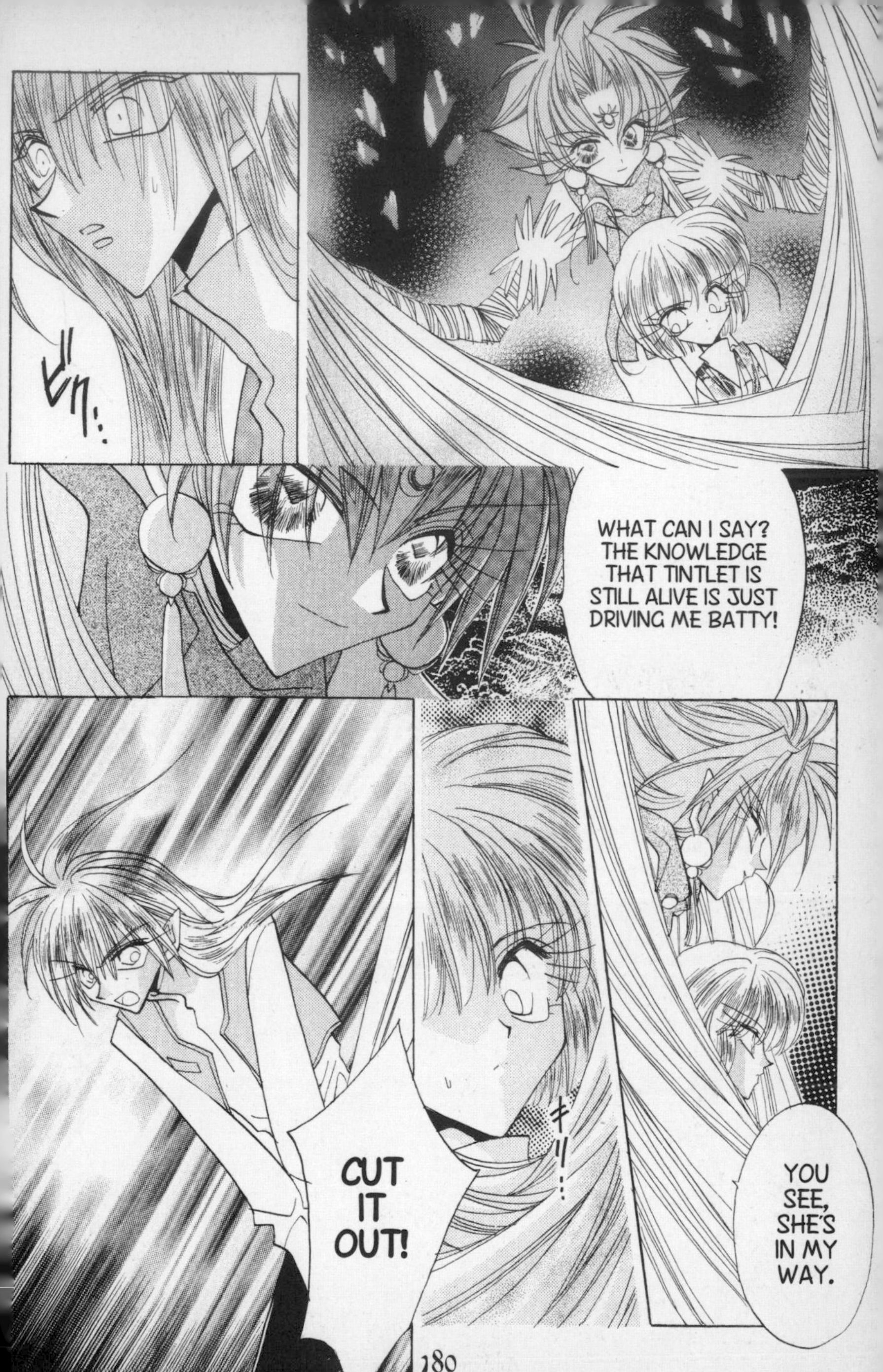
ビク!!
WHAT CAN I SAY? THE KNOWLEDGE THAT TINTLET IS STILL ALIVE IS JUST DRIVING ME BATTY!
YOU SEE, SHE'S IN MY WAY.
キリ!!
CUT IT OUT!

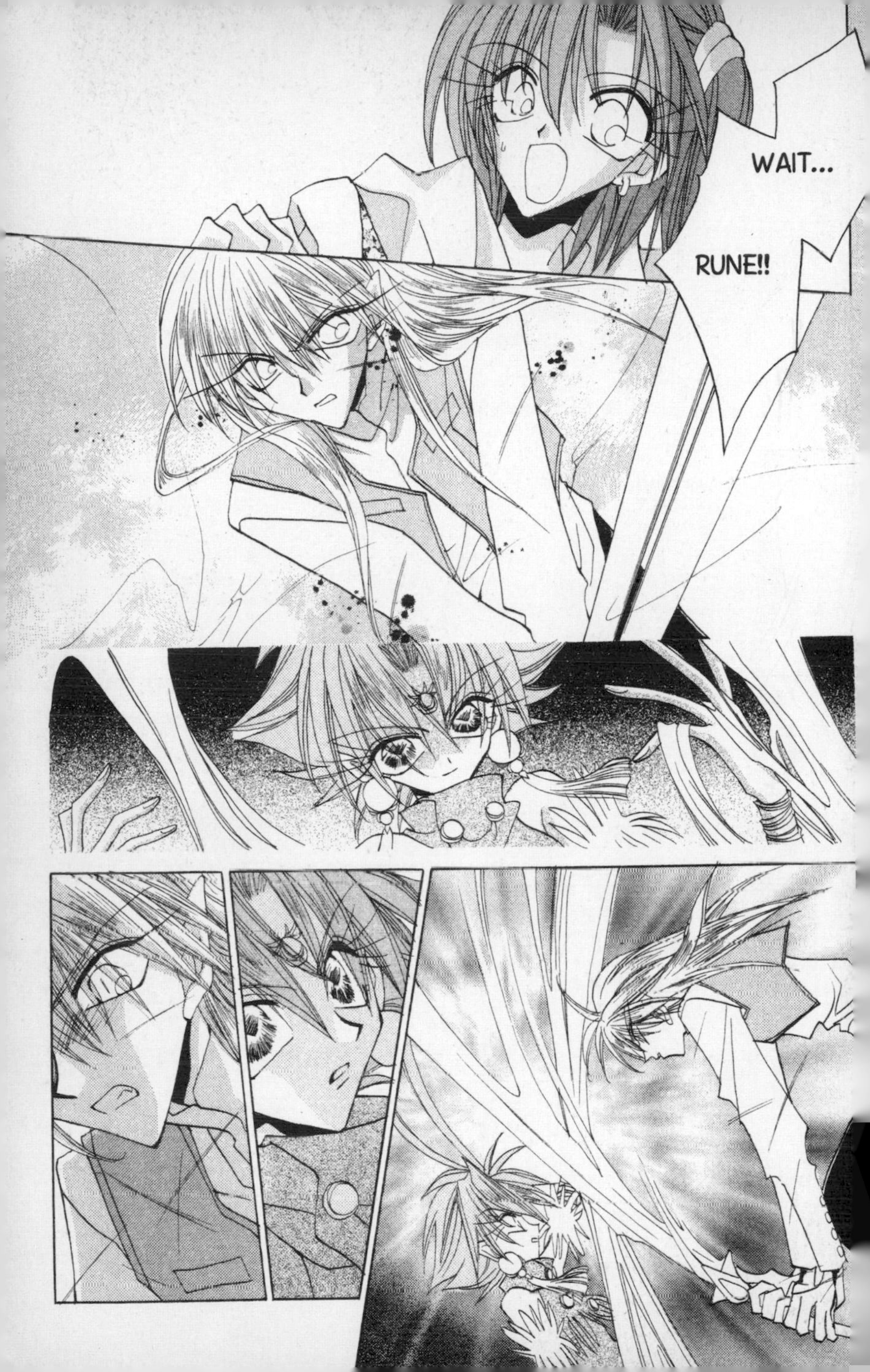
WAIT...
RUNE!!

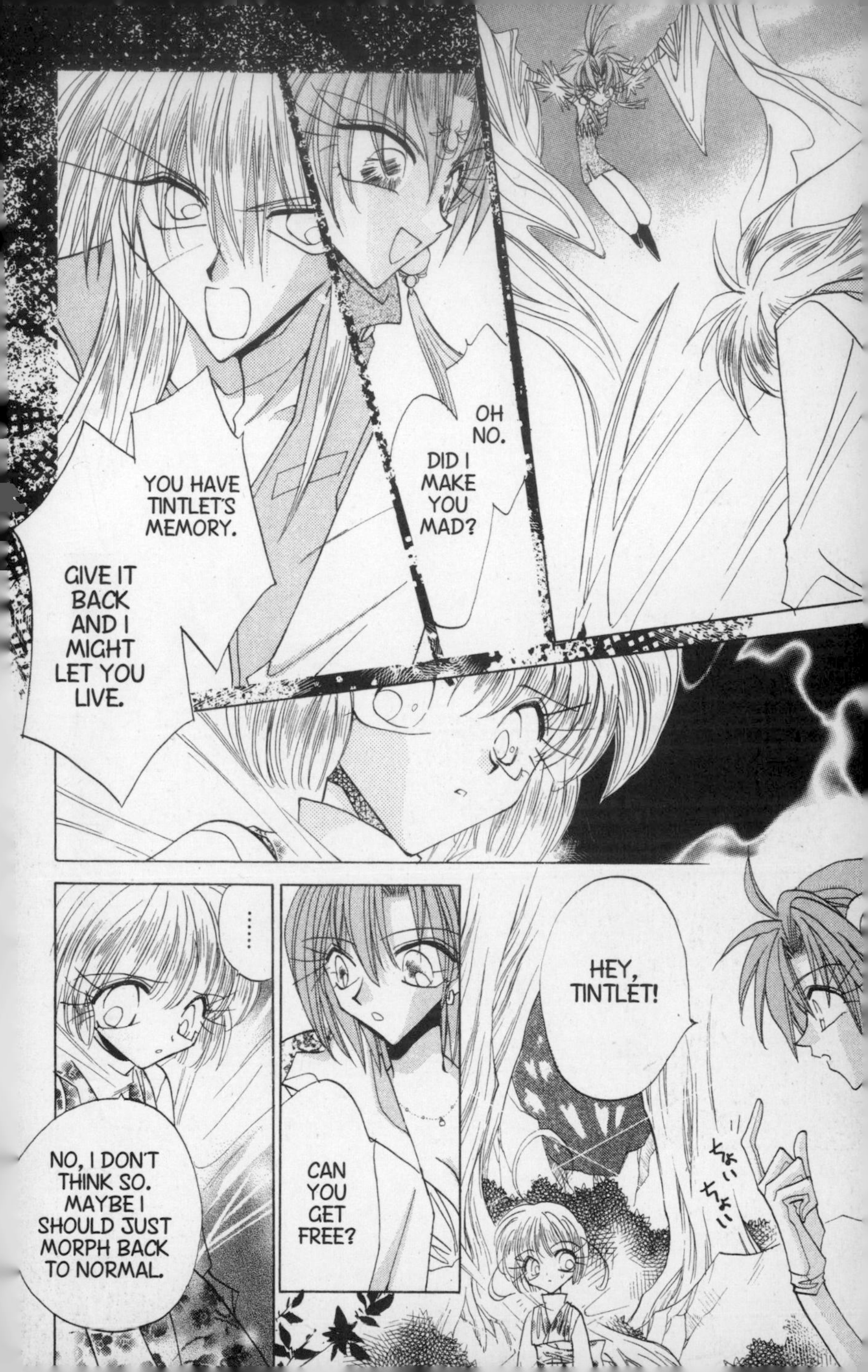
OH NO.
DID I MAKE YOU MAD?
YOU HAVE TINTLET'S MEMORY.
GIVE IT BACK AND I MIGHT LET YOU LIVE.
HEY, TINTLET!
ちょいちょい
CAN YOU GET FREE?
......
NO, I DON'T THINK SO. MAYBE I SHOULD JUST MORPH BACK TO NORMAL.

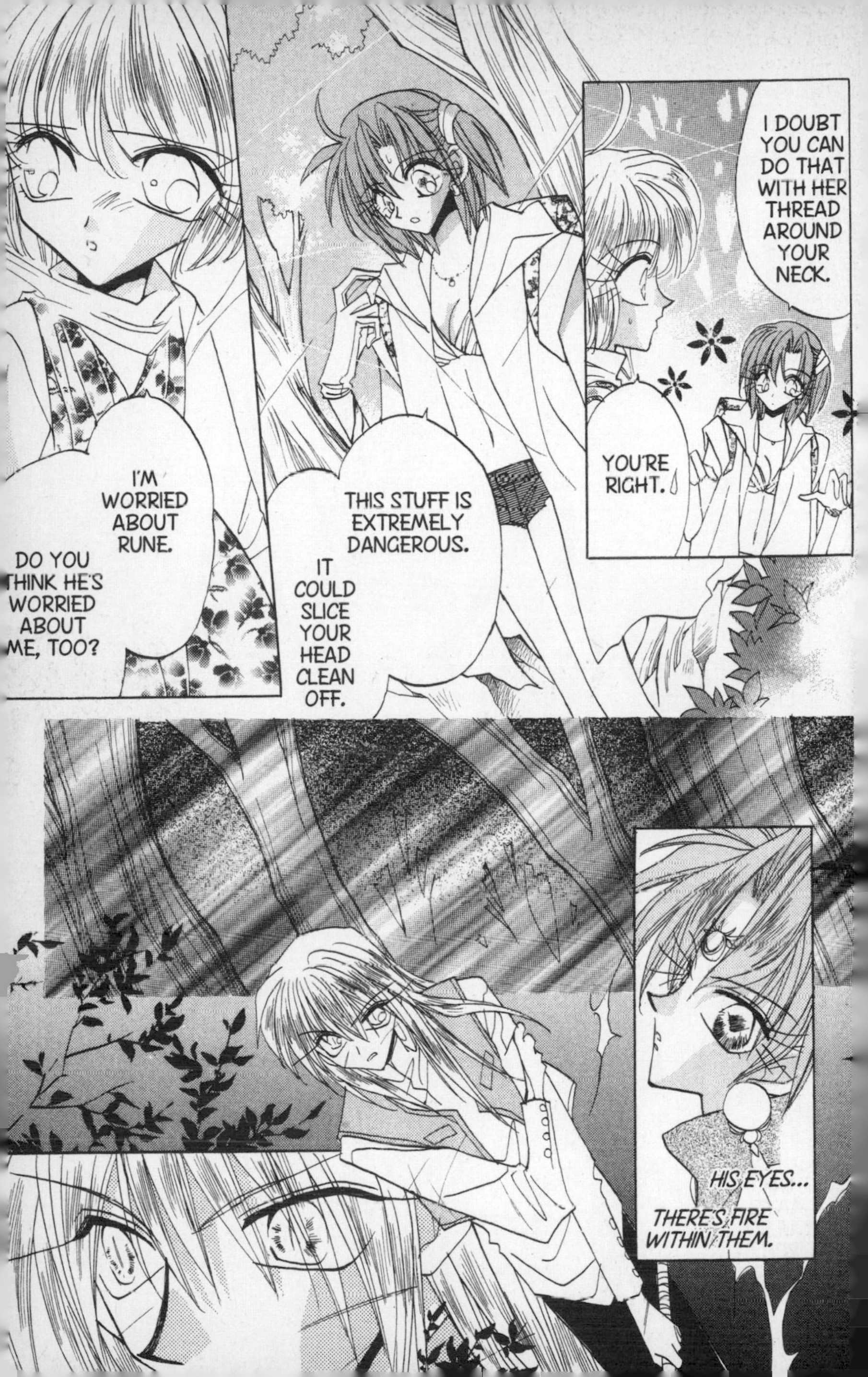
I DOUBT YOU CAN DO THAT WITH HER THREAD AROUND YOUR NECK.
YOU'RE RIGHT.
THIS STUFF IS EXTREMELY DANGEROUS.
IT COULD SLICE YOUR HEAD CLEAN OFF.
I'M WORRIED ABOUT RUNE.
DO YOU THINK HE'S WORRIED ABOUT ME, TOO?
HIS EYES...
THERE'S FIRE WITHIN THEM.

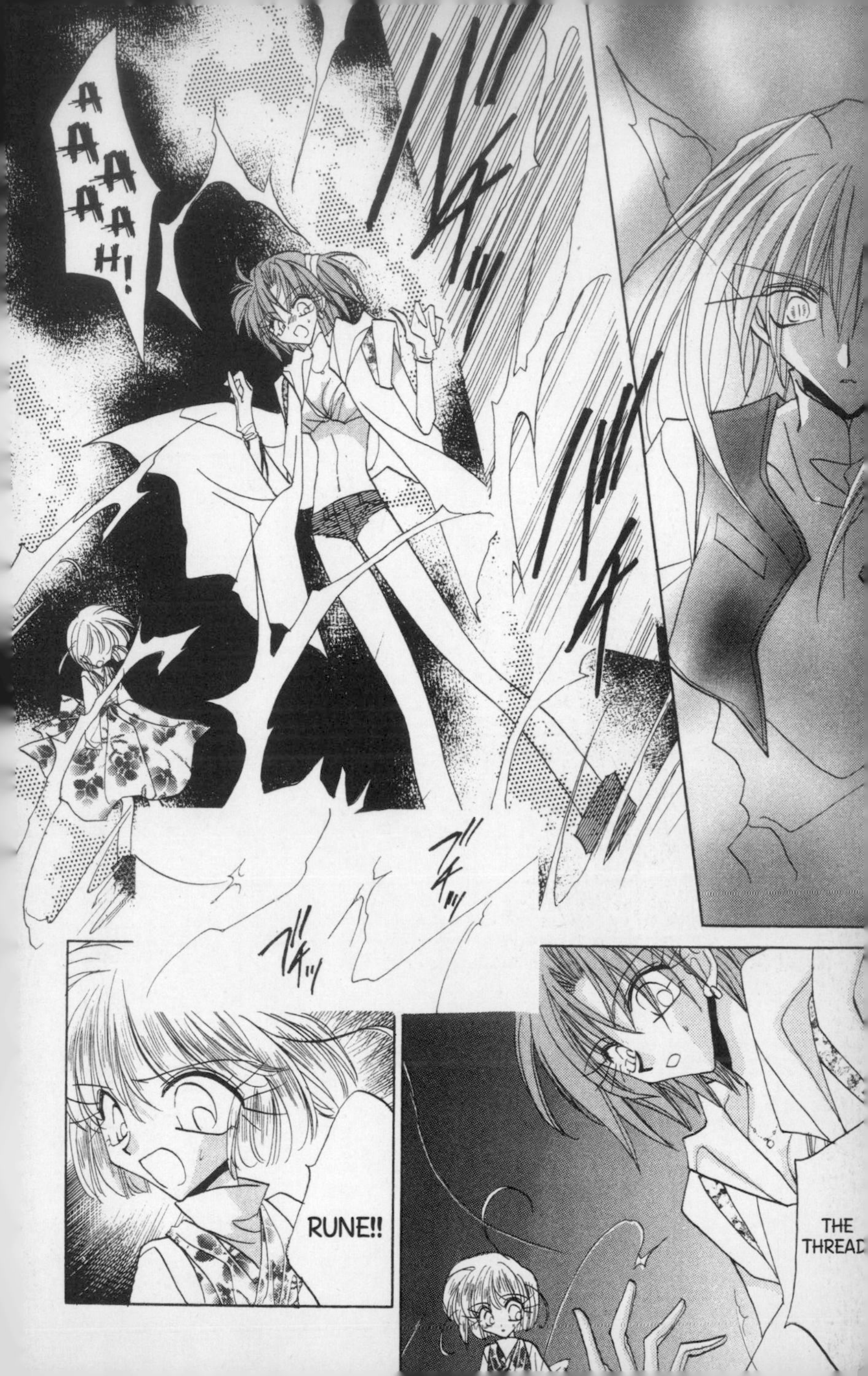
AAAAAAH!
ブチッ
ブチッ
THE THREAD
RUNE!!

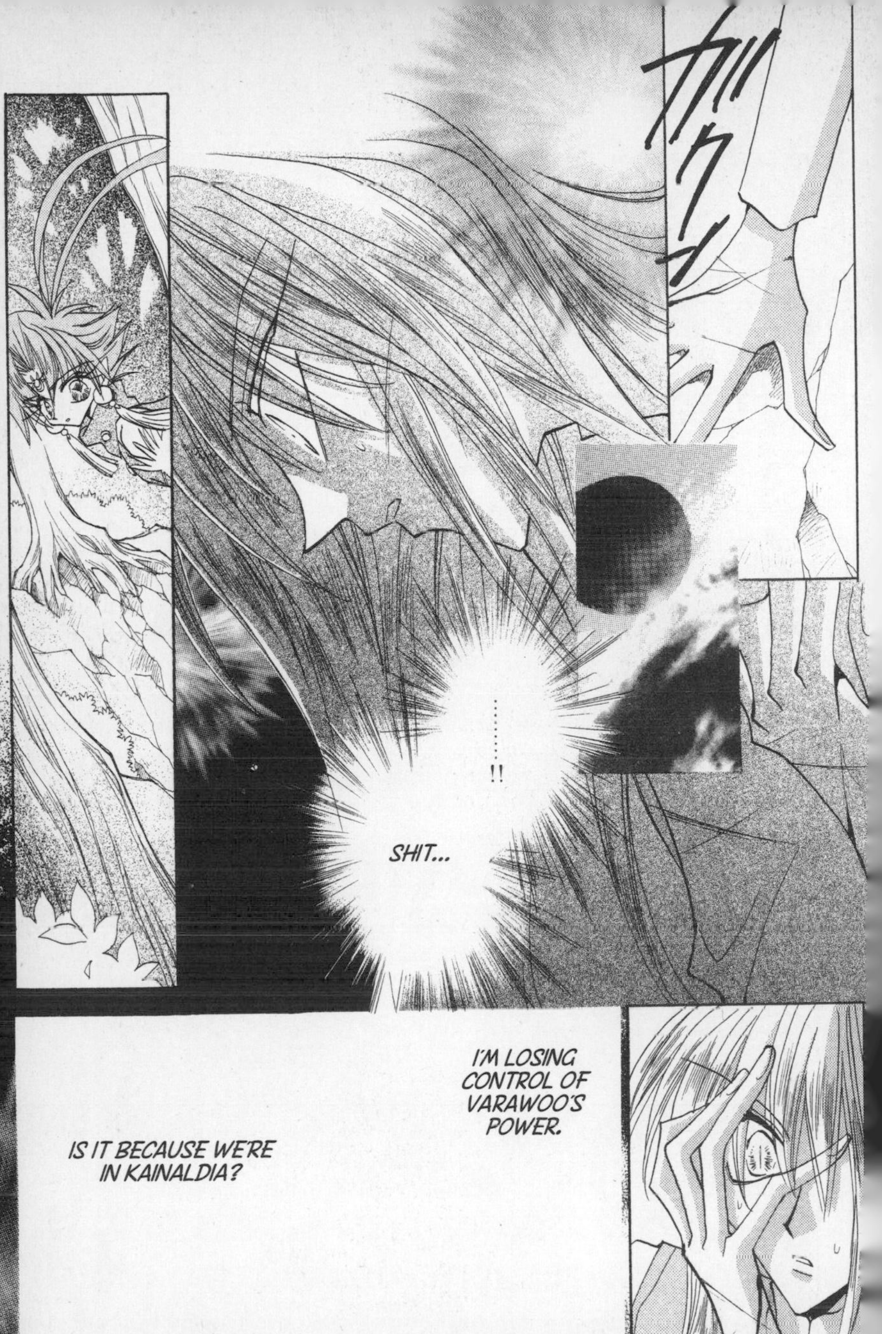
......!!
SHIT...
I'M LOSING CONTROL OF VARAWOO'S POWER.
IS IT BECAUSE WE'RE IN KAINALDIA?

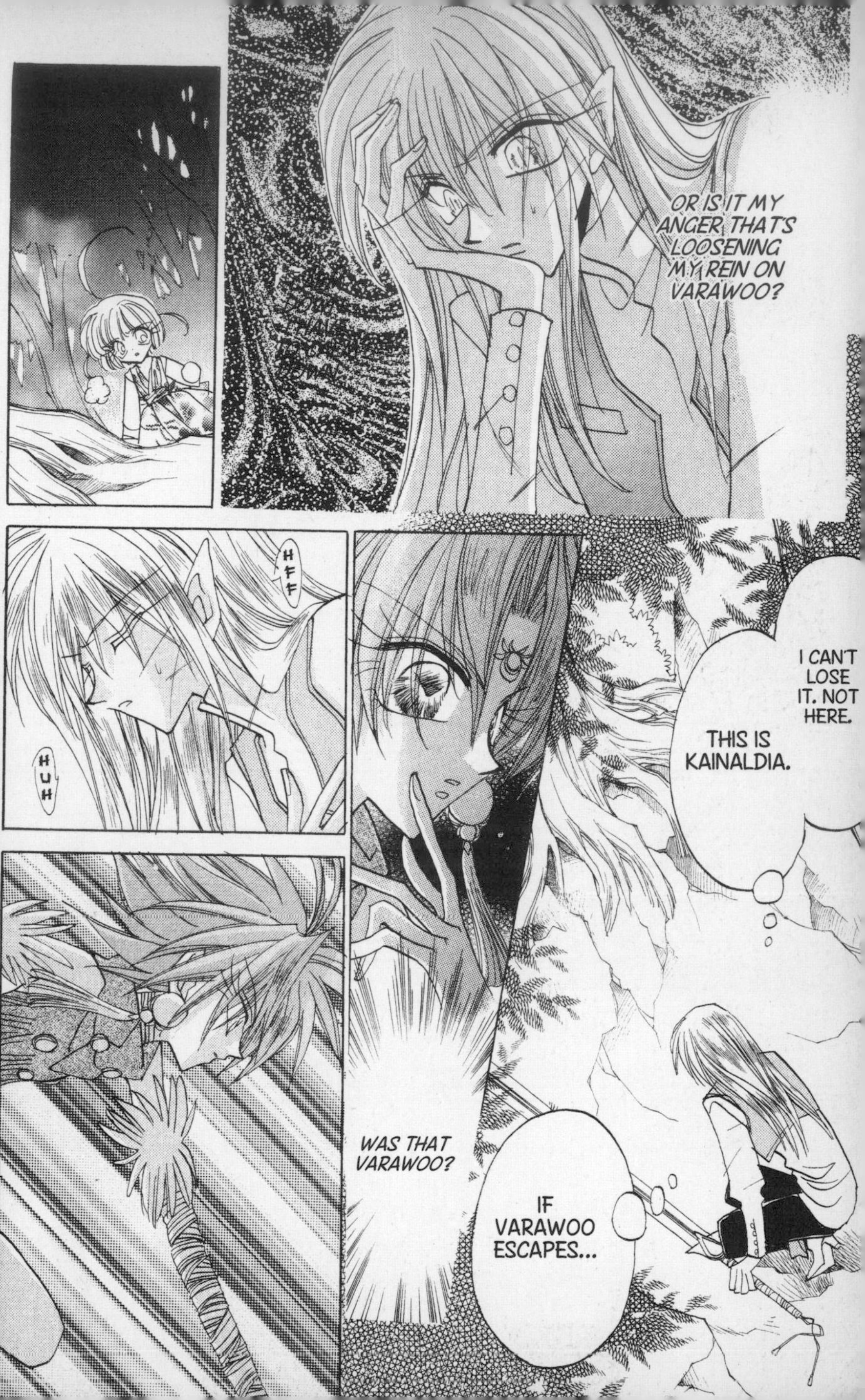
OR IS IT MY ANGER THAT'S LOOSENING MY REIN ON VARAWOO?
I CAN'T LOSE IT. NOT HERE.
THIS IS KAINALDIA.
IF VARAWOO ESCAPES...
WAS THAT VARAWOO?
HFF
HUH

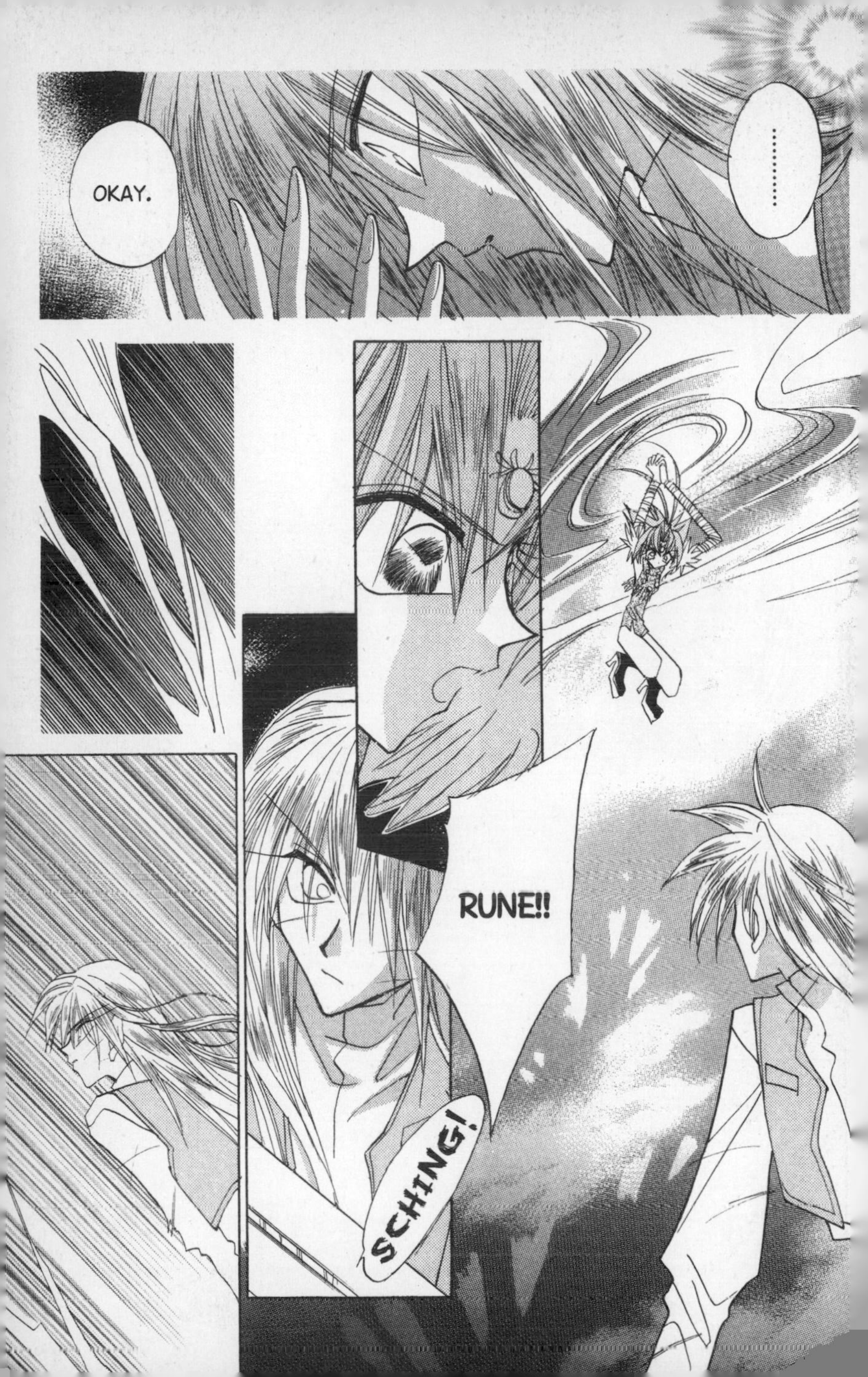
......
OKAY.
RUNE!!
SCHING!

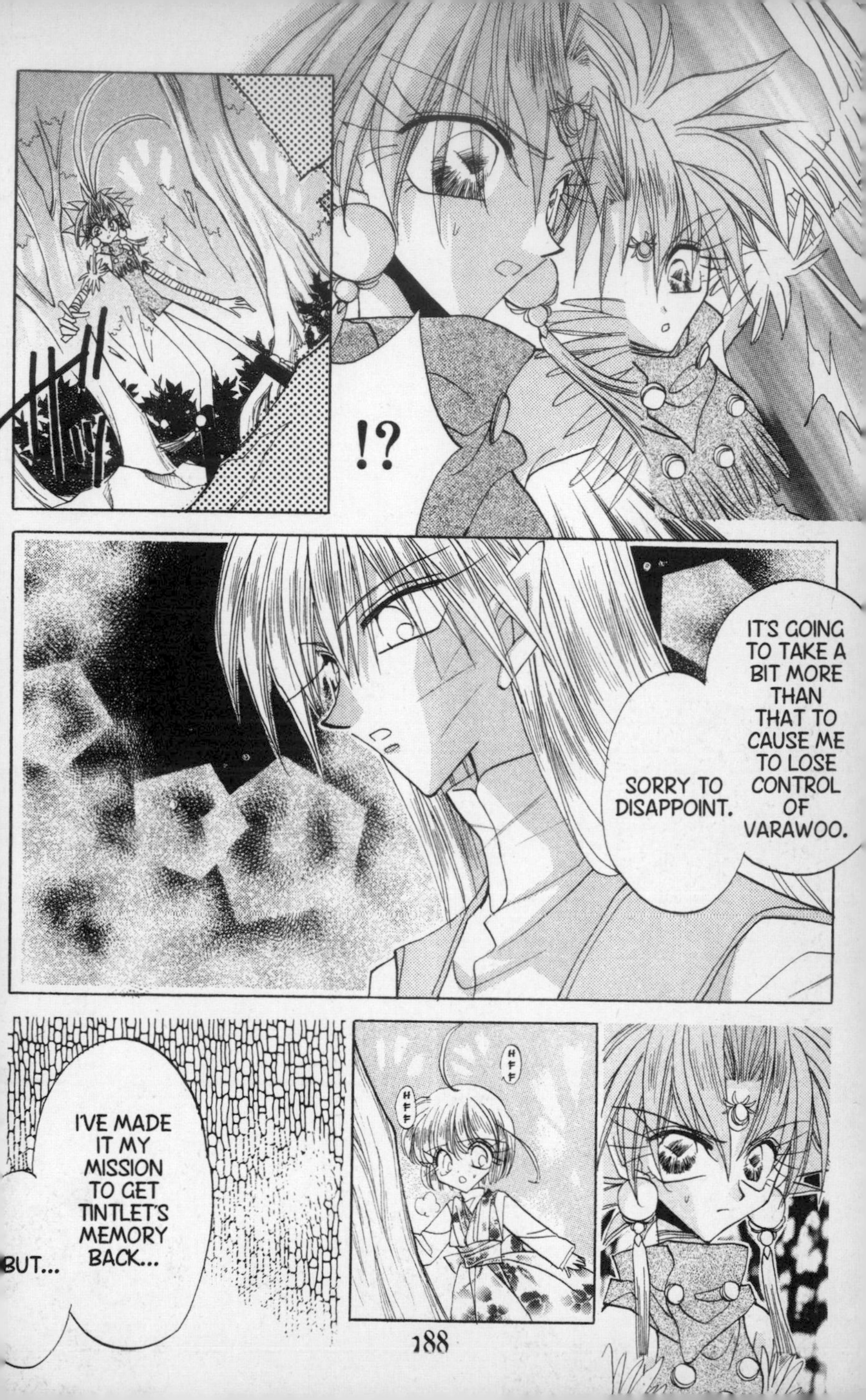
!?
IT'S GOING TO TAKE A BIT MORE THAN THAT TO CAUSE ME TO LOSE CONTROL OF VARAWOO.
SORRY TO DISAPPOINT.
HFF
HFF
I'VE MADE IT MY MISSION TO GET TINTLET'S MEMORY BACK... BUT...

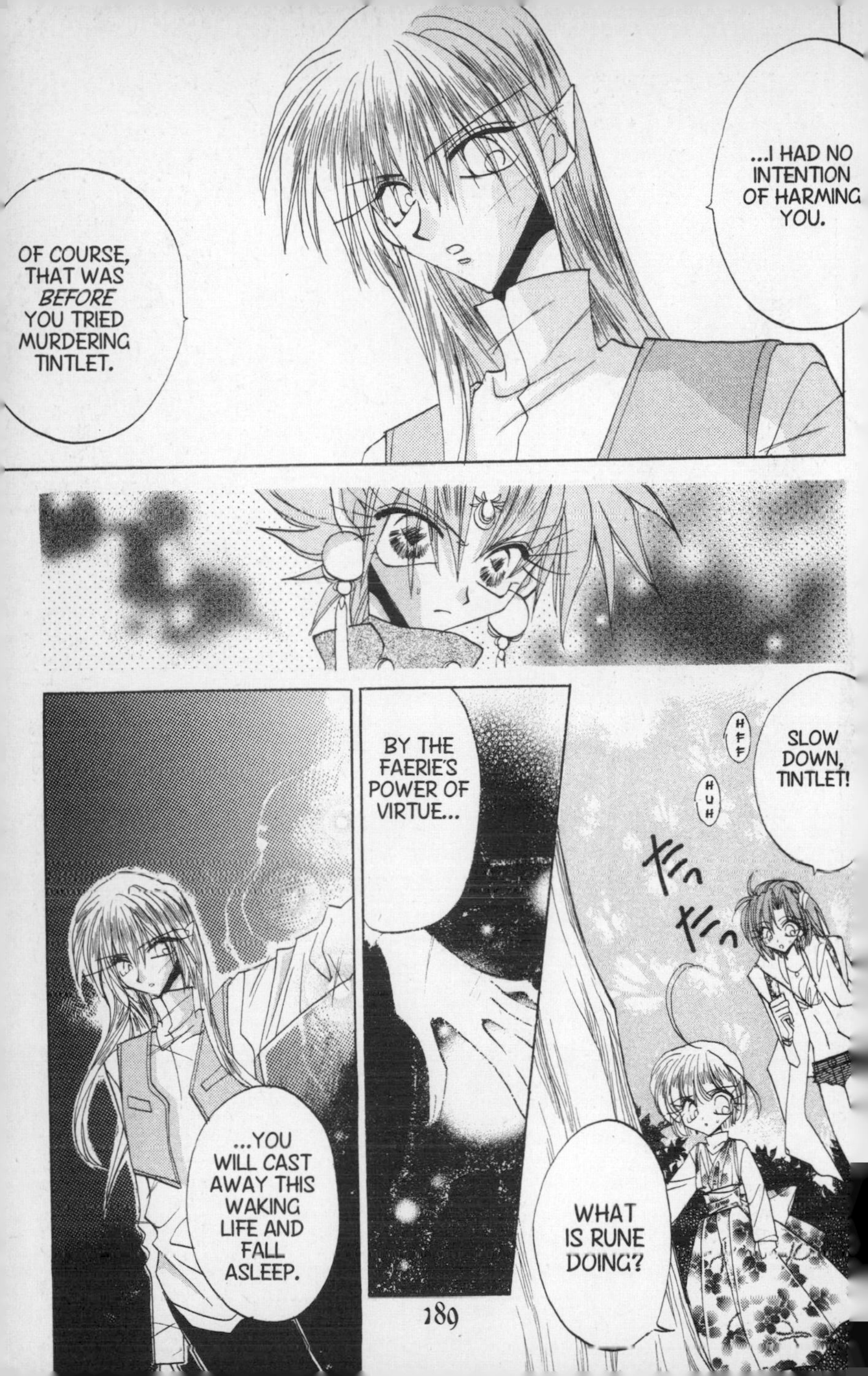
...I HAD NO INTENTION OF HARMING YOU.
OF COURSE, THAT WAS *BEFORE* YOU TRIED MURDERING TINTLET.
SLOW DOWN, TINTLET!
HFF
HUH
だっ
だっ
WHAT IS RUNE DOING?
BY THE FAERIE'S POWER OF VIRTUE...
...YOU WILL CAST AWAY THIS WAKING LIFE AND FALL ASLEEP.

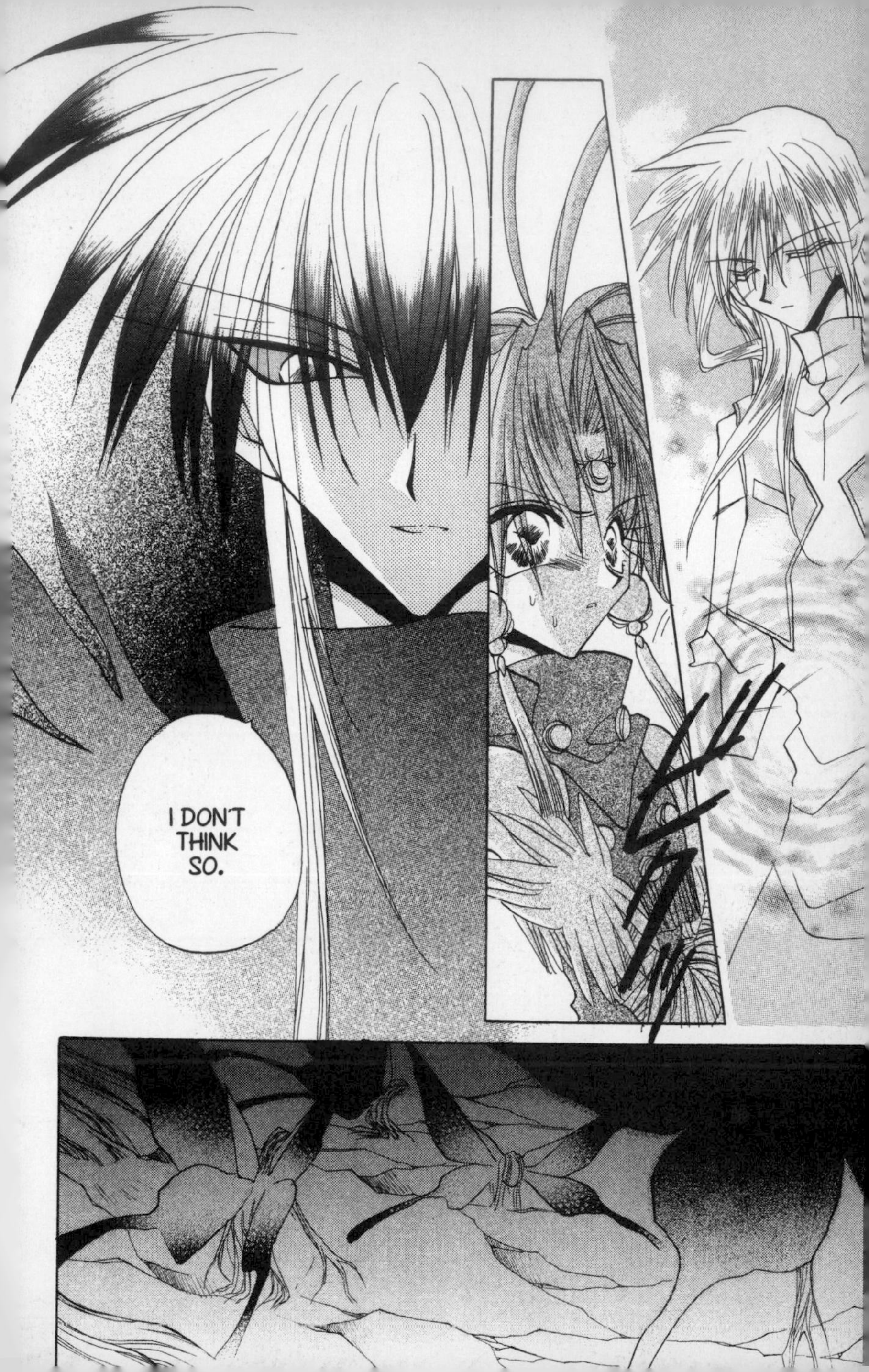
I DON'T THINK SO.

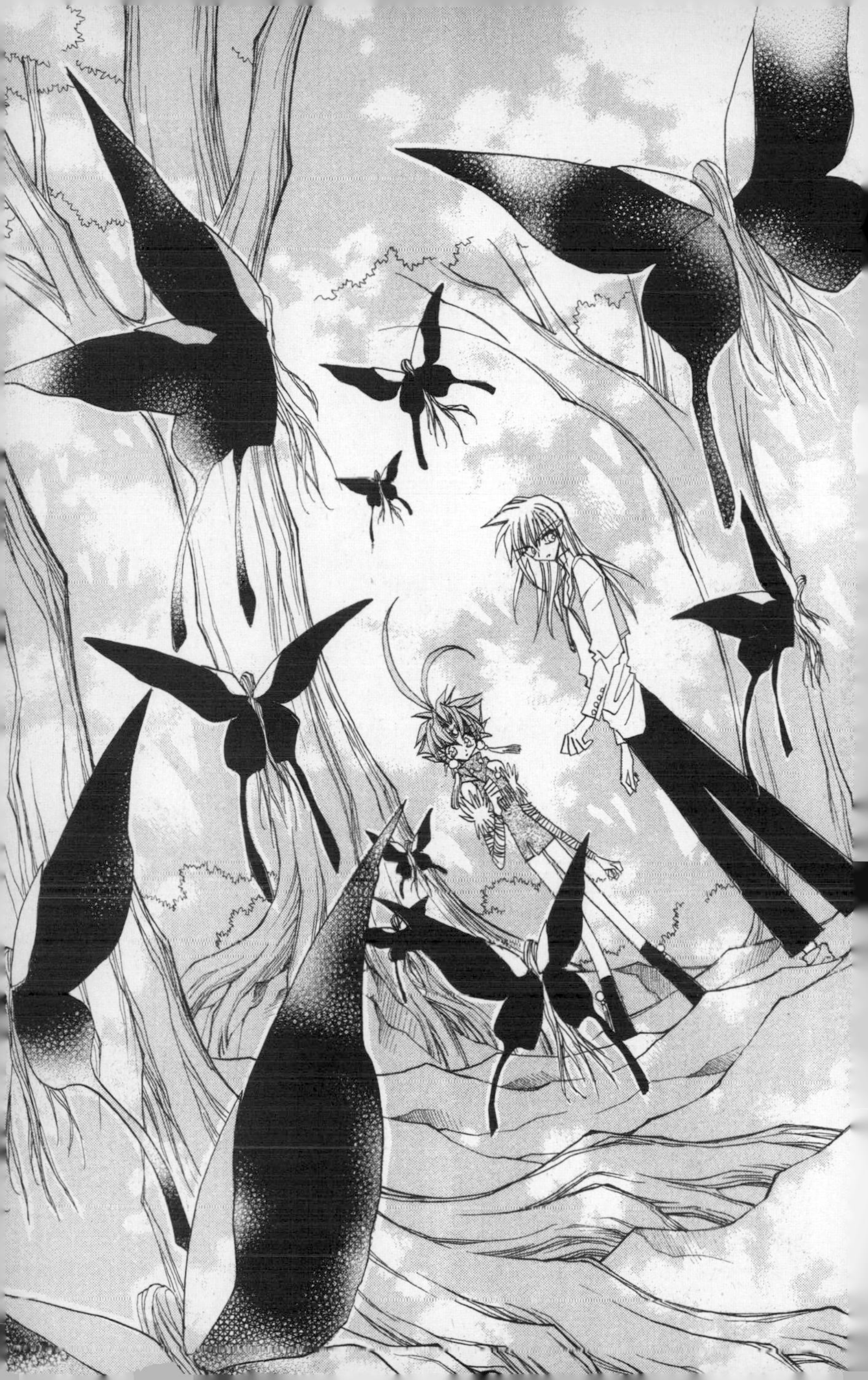

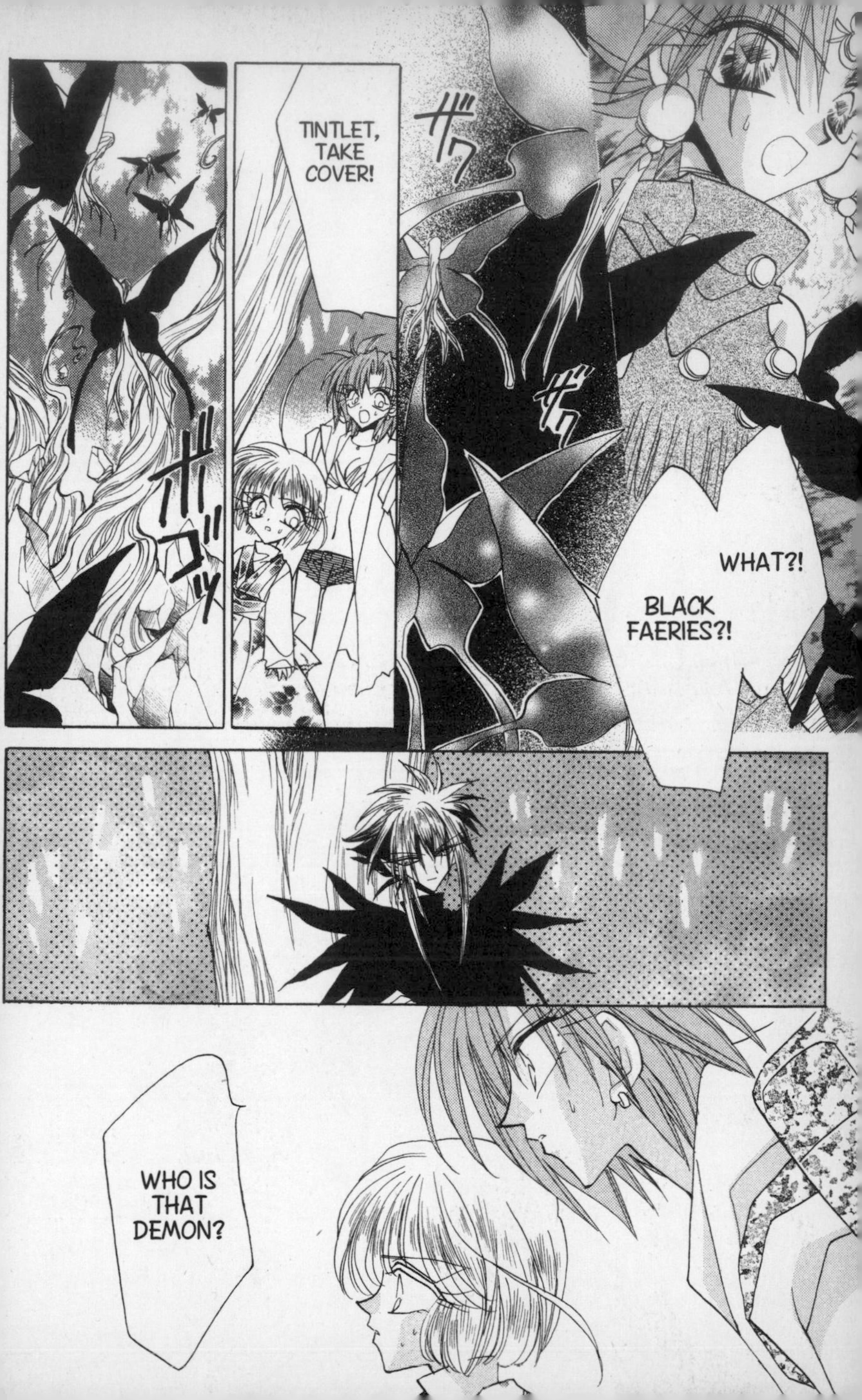
WHAT?!
BLACK FAERIES?!
TINTLET, TAKE COVER!
WHO IS THAT DEMON?

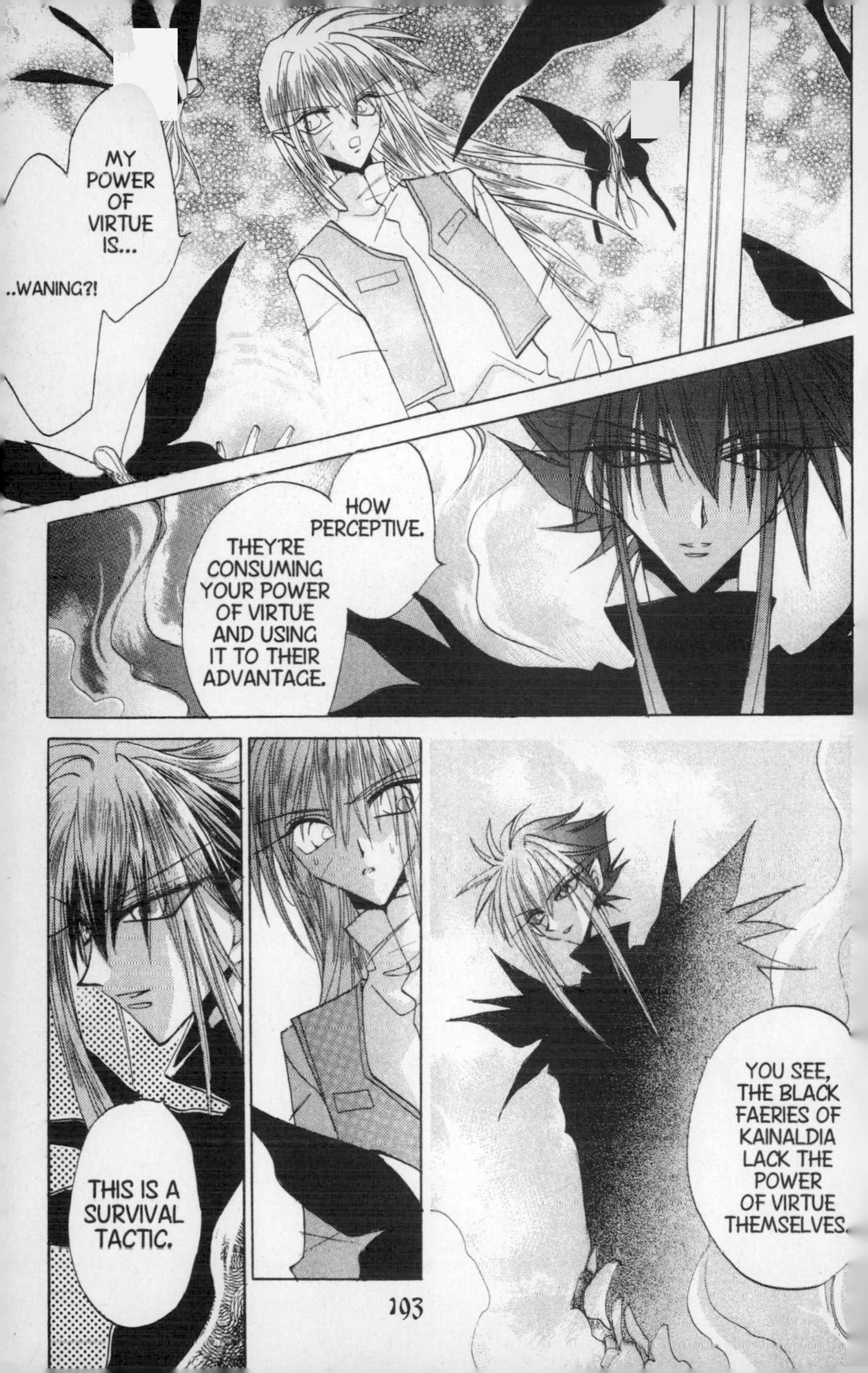
MY POWER OF VIRTUE IS...
..WANING?!
HOW PERCEPTIVE. THEY'RE CONSUMING YOUR POWER OF VIRTUE AND USING IT TO THEIR ADVANTAGE.
YOU SEE, THE BLACK FAERIES OF KAINALDIA LACK THE POWER OF VIRTUE THEMSELVES.
THIS IS A SURVIVAL TACTIC.

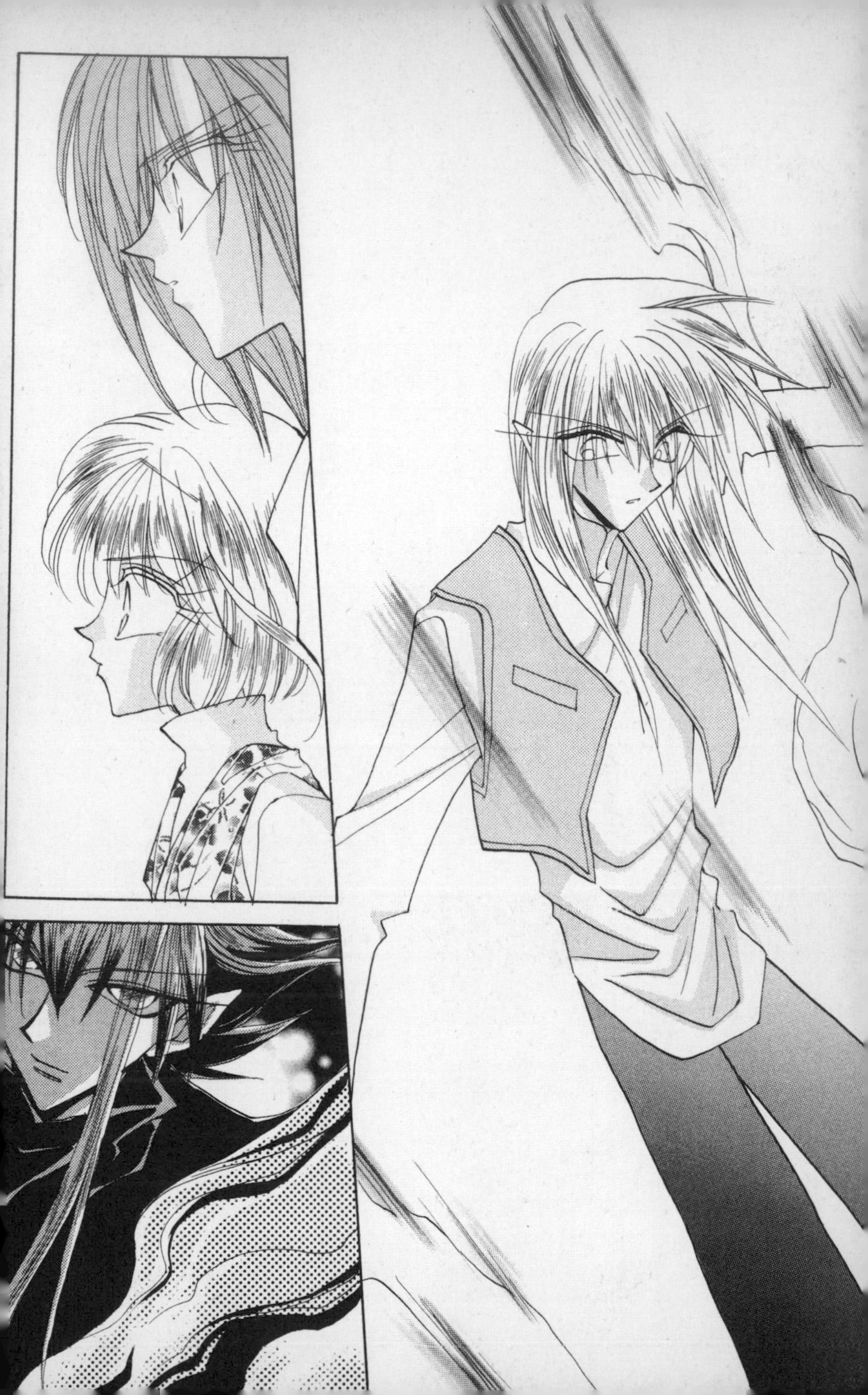

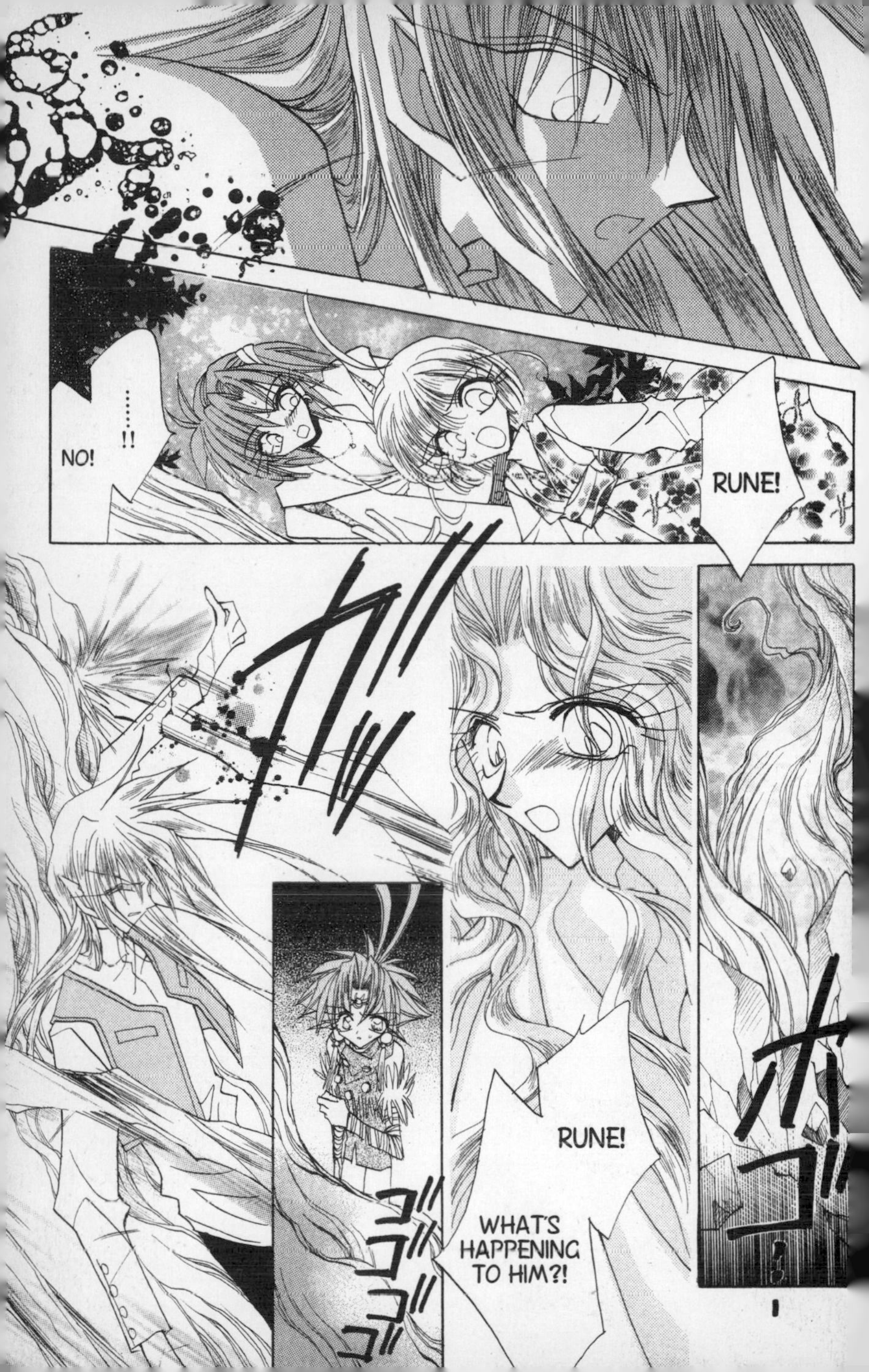
RUNE!
......!!
NO!
RUNE!
WHAT'S HAPPENING TO HIM?!

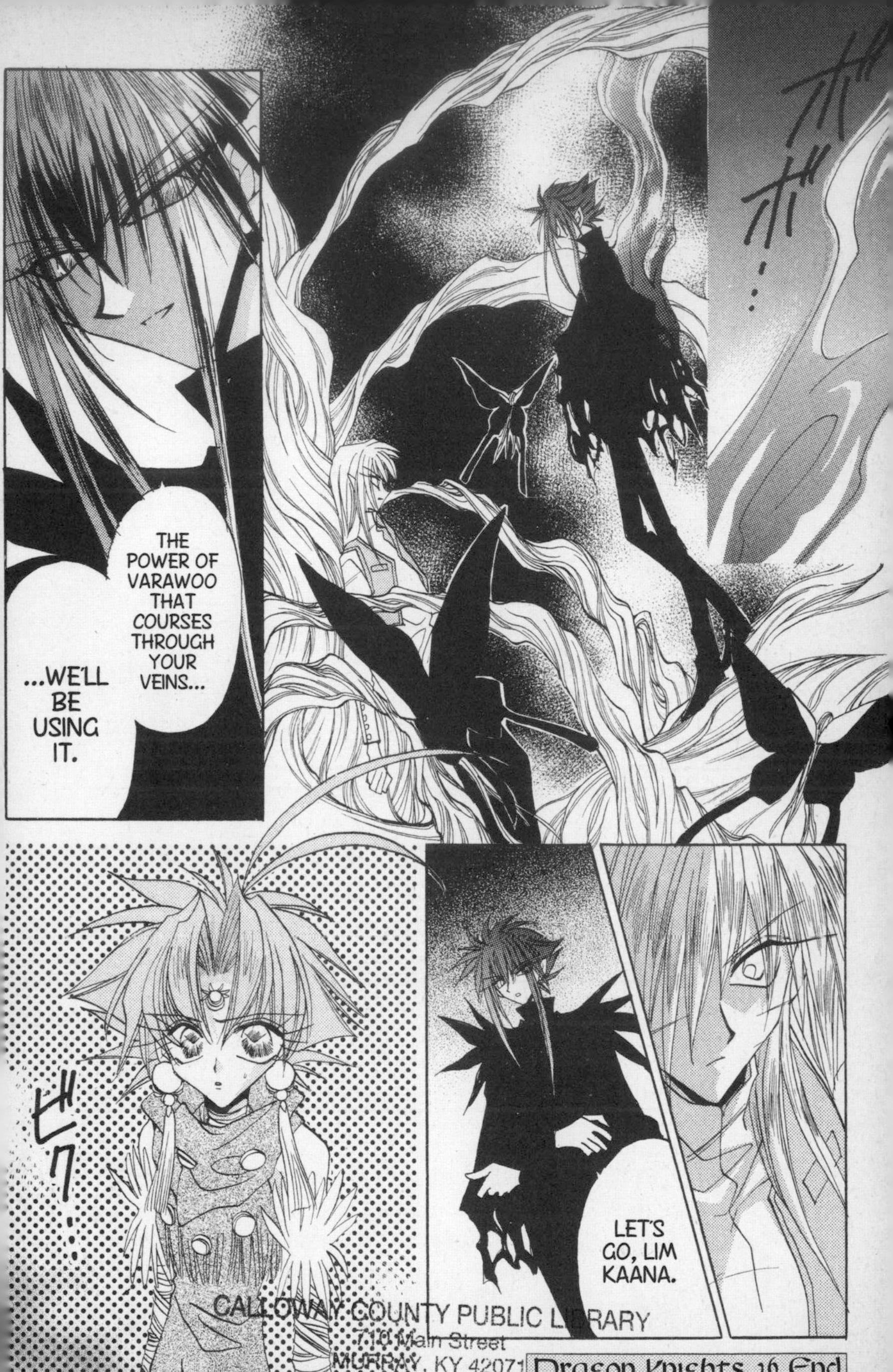
THE POWER OF VARAWOO THAT COURSES THROUGH YOUR VEINS...
...WE'LL BE USING IT.
LET'S GO, LIM KAANA.
ビク…
Dragon Knights 16 End

Dragon Knights

17

In Volume 17:

Captured and imprisoned, things aren't looking good for our Dragon Knight of Water, and while Rune faces the terror of uncertainty, Rath and Thatz have far worse horrors to contend with outside the castle. The mysterious white haze surrounding Nadil's palace is no ordinary fog. It's a sinister trap of human souls making the castle impenetrable to all who oppose Nadil. It's a formidable obstacle, but with the situation looking grim for all three Dragon Knights, hope arrives in two entirely unexpected places. As desperation sets in, an enemy will become a friend, and a former ally will return from the grave...

Mineko Ohkami

"ROSE ANGEL"
DRAGON KNIGHTS
RATH & CESIA

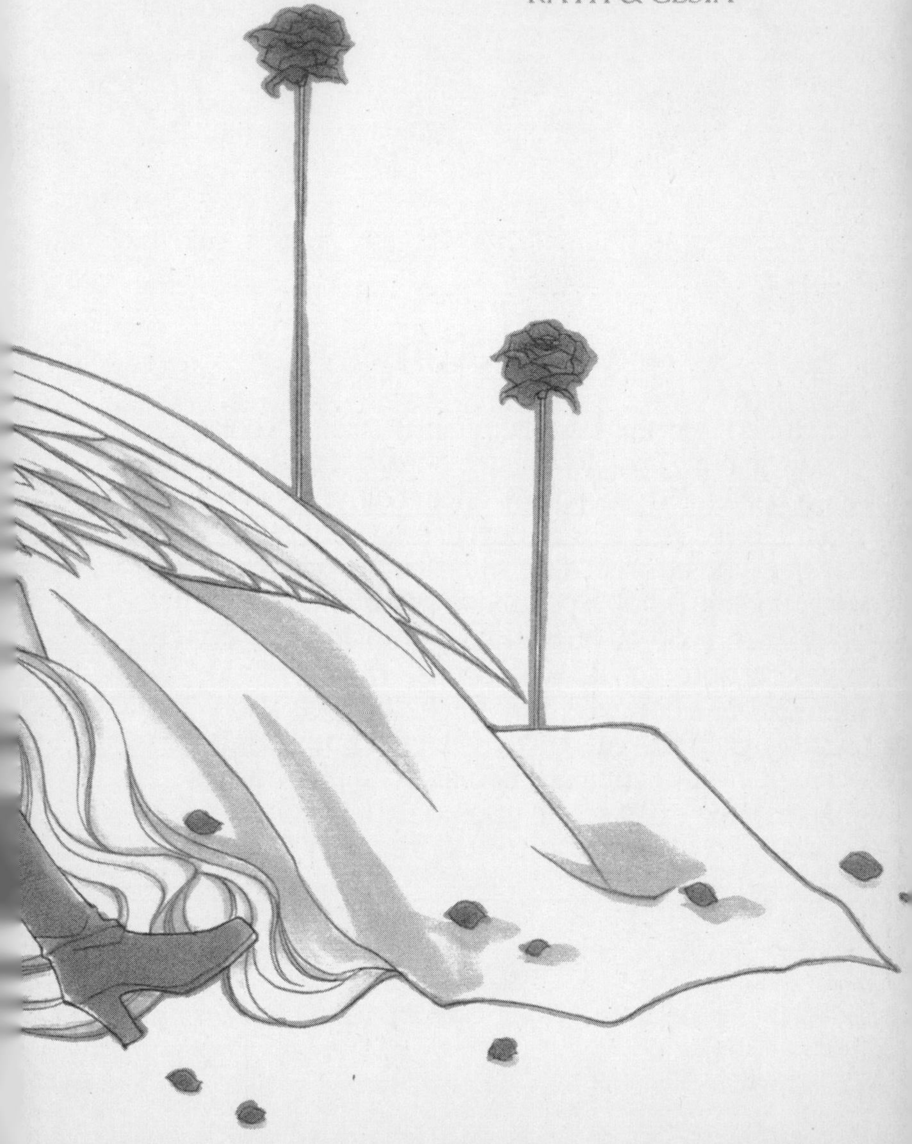

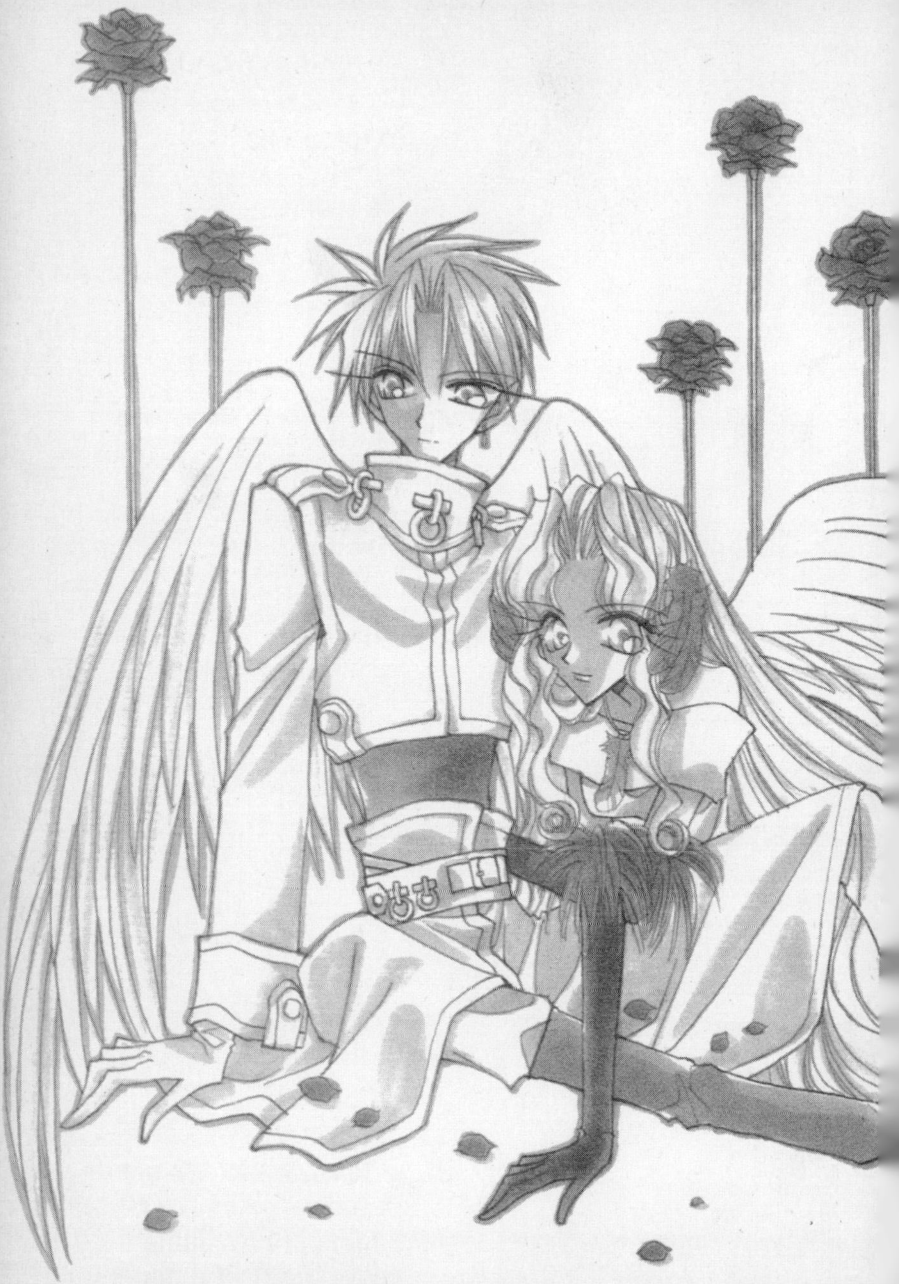

ALSO AVAILABLE FROM TOKYOPOP

PLANET LADDER
PLANETES
PRESIDENT DAD
PRIEST
PRINCESS AI
PSYCHIC ACADEMY
QUEEN'S KNIGHT, THE
RAGNAROK
RAVE MASTER
REALITY CHECK
REBIRTH
REBOUND
REMOTE
RISING STARS OF MANGA
SABER MARIONETTE J
SAILOR MOON
SAINT TAIL
SAIYUKI
SAMURAI DEEPER KYO
SAMURAI GIRL REAL BOUT HIGH SCHOOL
SCRYED
SEIKAI TRILOGY, THE
SGT. FROG
SHAOLIN SISTERS
SHIRAHIME-SYO: SNOW GODDESS TALES
SHUTTERBOX
SKULL MAN, THE
SNOW DROP
SORCERER HUNTERS
STONE
SUIKODEN III
SUKI
THREADS OF TIME
TOKYO BABYLON
TOKYO MEW MEW
TOKYO TRIBES
TRAMPS LIKE US
UNDER THE GLASS MOON
VAMPIRE GAME
VISION OF ESCAFLOWNE, THE
WARRIORS OF TAO
WILD ACT
WISH
WORLD OF HARTZ
X-DAY
ZODIAC P.I.

NOVELS

CLAMP SCHOOL PARANORMAL INVESTIGATORS
SAILOR MOON
SLAYERS

ART BOOKS

ART OF CARDCAPTOR SAKURA
ART OF MAGIC KNIGHT RAYEARTH, THE
PEACH: MIWA UEDA ILLUSTRATIONS

ANIME GUIDES

COWBOY BEBOP
GUNDAM TECHNICAL MANUALS
SAILOR MOON SCOUT GUIDES

TOKYOPOP KIDS

STRAY SHEEP

CINE-MANGA™

ALADDIN
CARDCAPTORS
DUEL MASTERS
FAIRLY ODDPARENTS, THE
FAMILY GUY
FINDING NEMO
G.I. JOE SPY TROOPS
GREATEST STARS OF THE NBA: SHAQUILLE O'NEAL
GREATEST STARS OF THE NBA: TIM DUNCAN
JACKIE CHAN ADVENTURES
JIMMY NEUTRON: BOY GENIUS, THE ADVENTURES OF
KIM POSSIBLE
LILO & STITCH: THE SERIES
LIZZIE MCGUIRE
LIZZIE MCGUIRE MOVIE, THE
MALCOLM IN THE MIDDLE
POWER RANGERS: DINO THUNDER
POWER RANGERS: NINJA STORM
PRINCESS DIARIES 2
RAVE MASTER
SHREK 2
SIMPLE LIFE, THE
SPONGEBOB SQUAREPANTS
SPY KIDS 2
SPY KIDS 3-D: GAME OVER
TEENAGE MUTANT NINJA TURTLES
THAT'S SO RAVEN
TOTALLY SPIES
TRANSFORMERS: ARMADA
TRANSFORMERS: ENERGON

**You want it? We got it!
A full range of TOKYOPOP
products are available now at:
www.TOKYOPOP.com/shop**

07.15.04T

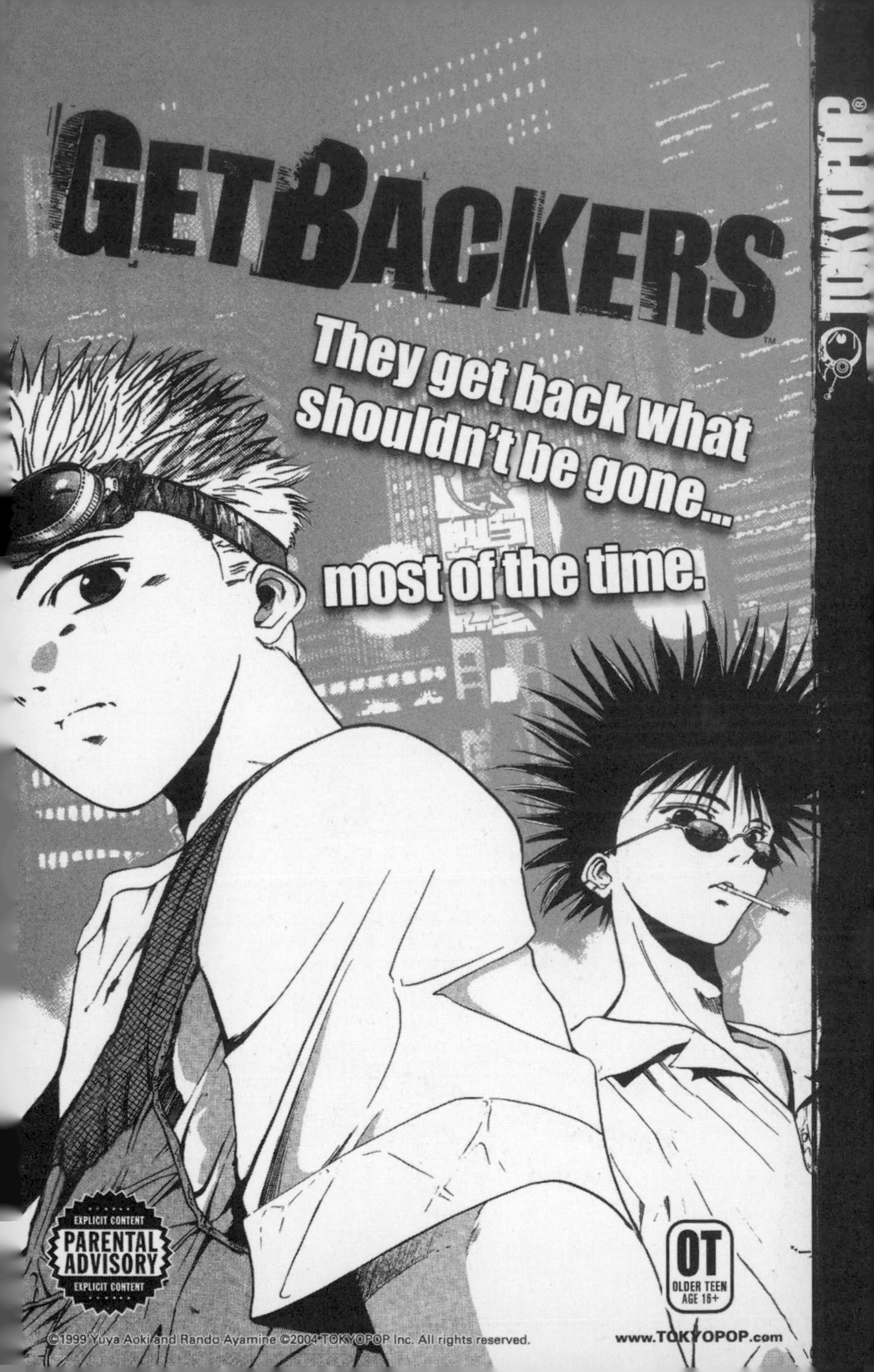
GETBACKERS™
They get back what shouldn't be gone...
most of the time.
TOKYOPOP®
EXPLICIT CONTENT
PARENTAL ADVISORY
EXPLICIT CONTENT
OT
OLDER TEEN
AGE 16+
©1999 Yuya Aoki and Rando Ayamine ©2004 TOKYOPOP Inc. All rights reserved.
www.TOKYOPOP.com

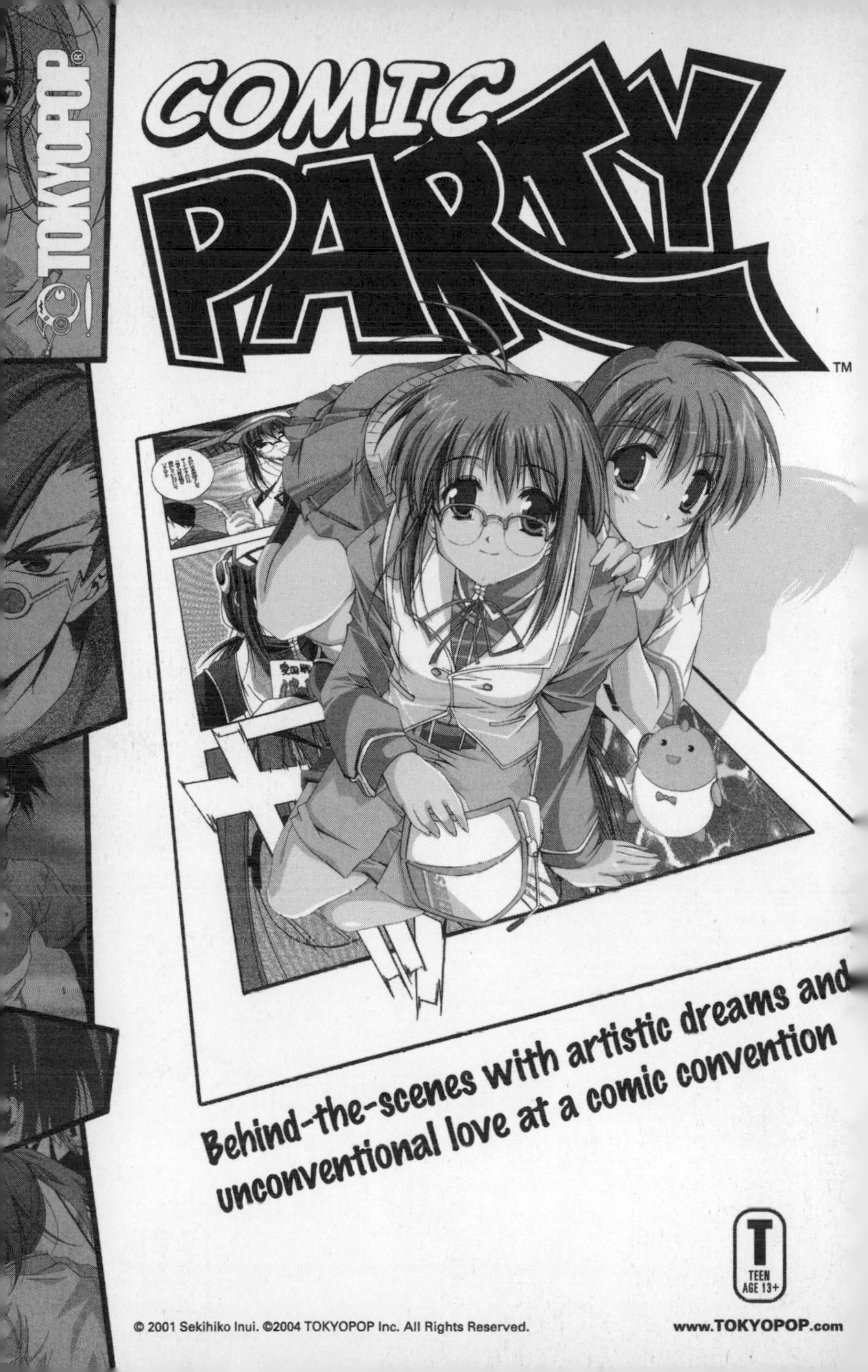
TOKYOPOP
COMIC PARTY™

PITA-TEN™

By Koge-Donbo - Creator of Digicharat

The girl next door is bringing a touch of heaven to the neighborhood.

TEEN
AGE 13+

DRAGON HUNTER

By HONG SEOCK SEO

**SLAYING DRAGONS IS HARD...
MAKING A LIVING
FROM IT IS BRUTAL!**

TEEN
AGE 13+

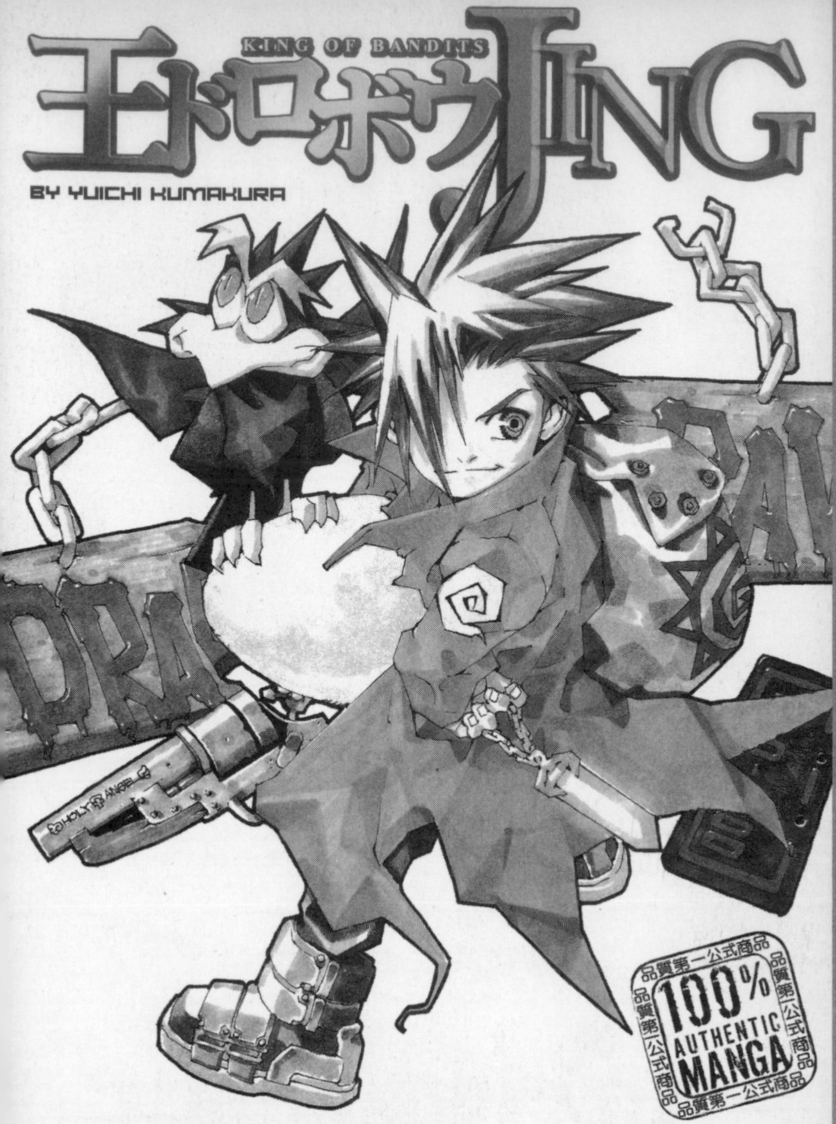
KING OF BANDITS
王ドロボウJING
BY YUICHI KUMAKURA
100% AUTHENTIC MANGA
品質第一公式商品

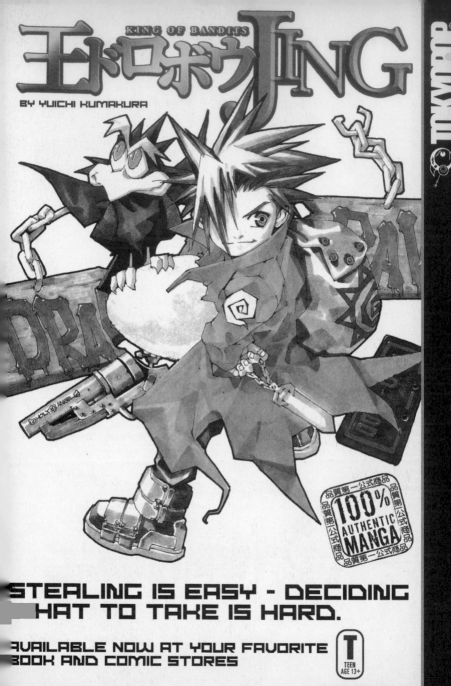

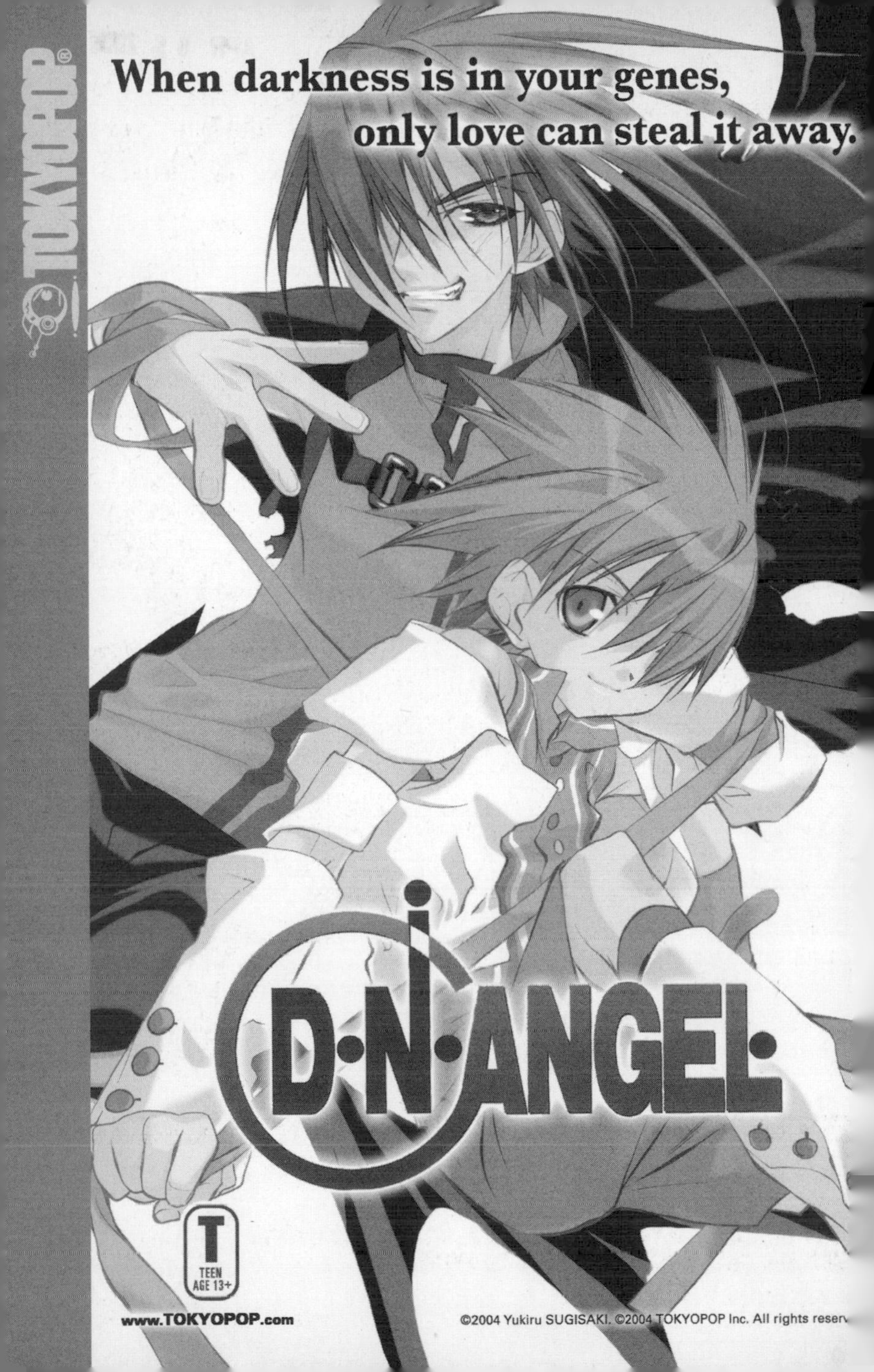
TOKYOPOP
When darkness is in your genes,
only love can steal it away.
D•N•ANGEL
T
TEEN
AGE 13+
www.TOKYOPOP.com
©2004 Yukiru SUGISAKI. ©2004 TOKYOPOP Inc. All rights reserv

STOP!

This is the back of the book.
You wouldn't want to spoil a great ending!

This book is printed "manga-style," in the authentic Japanese right-to-left format. Since none of the artwork has been flipped or altered, readers get to experience the story just as the creator intended. You've been asking for it, so TOKYOPOP® delivered: authentic, hot-off-the-press, and far more fun!

DIRECTIONS

If this is your first time reading manga-style, here's a quick guide to help you understand how it works.

It's easy... just start in the top right panel and follow the numbers. Have fun, and look for more 100% authentic manga from TOKYOPOP®!